Library of
Davidson College

Library of
Davidson College

Recent IEA conference volumes

Béla Balassa and Herbert Giersch (*editors*)
ECONOMIC INCENTIVES

William J. Baumol (*editor*)
PUBLIC AND PRIVATE ENTERPRISE IN A MIXED ECONOMY

Ansley J. Coale (*editor*)
ECONOMIC FACTORS IN POPULATION GROWTH

Béla Csikós-Nagy and Douglas Hague (*editors*)
THE ECONOMICS OF RELATIVE PRICES

Béla Csikós-Nagy and David G. Young (*editors*)
EAST–WEST ECONOMIC RELATIONS IN THE CHANGING GLOBAL ENVIRONMENT

Marcello de Cecco and Jean-Paul Fitoussi (*editors*)
MONETARY THEORY AND ECONOMIC INSTITUTIONS

Léon Dupriez with Douglas Hague (*editors*)
ECONOMIC PROGRESS (Second Edition by Austin Robinson)

Martin S. Feldstein and Robert P. Inman (*editors*)
THE ECONOMICS OF PUBLIC SERVICES

Armin Gutowski, A. A. Arnaúdo and Hans-Eckart Scharrer
FINANCING PROBLEMS OF DEVELOPING COUNTRIES

Karl Jungenfelt and Douglas Hague (*editors*)
STRUCTURAL ADJUSTMENT IN DEVELOPED OPEN ECONOMIES

T. S. Khachaturov and P. B. Goodwin (*editors*)
THE ECONOMICS OF LONG-DISTANCE TRANSPORTATION

Pierre Maillet, Douglas Hague and Chris Rowland (*editors*)
THE ECONOMICS OF CHOICE BETWEEN ENERGY SOURCES

Edmond Malinvaud and Jean-Paul Fitoussi (*editors*)
UNEMPLOYMENT IN WESTERN COUNTRIES

R. C. O. Matthews and G. B. Stafford (*editors*)
THE GRANTS ECONOMY AND COLLECTIVE CONSUMPTION

Franco Modigliani and Richard Hemming (*editors*)
THE DETERMINANTS OF NATIONAL SAVING AND WEALTH

Josef Pajestka and C. H. Feinstein (*editors*)
THE RELEVANCE OF ECONOMIC THEORIES

Mark Perlman (*editor*)
THE ECONOMICS OF HEALTH AND MEDICAL CARE
THE ORGANIZATION AND RETRIEVAL OF ECONOMIC KNOWLEDGE

Austin Robinson, P. R. Brahmananda and L. K. Deshpande (*editors*)
EMPLOYMENT POLICY IN A DEVELOPING COUNTRY (2 *volumes*)

Paul A. Samuelson (*editor*)
INTERNATIONAL ECONOMIC RELATIONS

Christian Schmidt (*editor*)
THE ECONOMICS OF MILITARY EXPENDITURES

Joseph E. Stiglitz and G. Frank Mathewson (*editors*)
NEW DEVELOPMENTS IN THE ANALYSIS OF MARKET STRUCTURE

Richard Stone and William Peterson (*editors*)
ECONOMETRIC CONTRIBUTIONS TO PUBLIC POLICY

Nina G. M. Watts (*editor*)
ECONOMIC RELATIONS BETWEEN EAST AND WEST

ECONOMIC GROWTH AND RESOURCES

Edmond Malinvaud (*editor*)
1 THE MAJOR ISSUES

R. C. O. Matthews (*editor*)
2 TRENDS AND FACTORS

Christopher Bliss and M. Boserup (*editors*)
3 NATURAL RESOURCES

Irma Adelman (*editor*)
4 INTERNATIONAL POLICIES

Shigeto Tsuru (*editor*)
5 PROBLEMS RELATED TO JAPAN

HUMAN RESOURCES, EMPLOYMENT AND DEVELOPMENT

Shigeto Tsuru (editor)
1 THE ISSUES

Paul Streeten and Harry Maier (*editors*)
2 CONCEPTS, MEASUREMENT AND LONG-RUN PERSPECTIVE

Burton Weisbrod and Helen Hughes (*editors*)
3 THE PROBLEM OF DEVELOPED COUNTRIES AND THE INTERNATIONAL ECONOMY

Victor L. Urquidi and Saúl Trejo Reyes (*editors*)
4 LATIN AMERICA

Samir Amin (*editor*)
5 DEVELOPING COUNTRIES

The Economics of Military Expenditures

Military Expenditures, Economic Growth and Fluctuations

Proceedings of a Conference held by the International Economic Association in Paris, France

Edited by

Christian Schmidt

St. Martin's Press New York

© International Economic Association, 1987

All rights reserved. For information, write:
Scholarly & Reference Division,
St. Martin's Press, Inc., 175 Fifth Avenue, New York, NY 10010

First published in the United States of America in 1987

Printed in Hong Kong

ISBN 0-312-00421-4

Library of Congress Cataloging-in-Publication Data
The Economics of military expenditures.
Papers from a meeting of the International
Economic Association held in Paris.
Bibliography: p.
Includes index.
1. Armaments—Economic aspects—Congresses.
I. Schmidt, Christian. II. International Economic
Association.
HC79.D4E27   1987   338.4'7355   86-27886
ISBN 0-312-00421-4

Contents

Acknowledgements	vii
List of Participants	viii
Abbreviations and Acronyms	xi
Introductory Remarks: Victor L. Urquidi	xiii
INTRODUCTION Christian Schmidt	xvii

PART ONE: STATISTICAL TREATMENT OF ARMAMENT AND DISARMAMENT

1 Military Expenditure and the Arms Trade: Problems of the Data *Frank Blackaby and Thomas Ohlson* 3
  Note on the paper by Blackaby and Ohlson *Jacques Fontanel* 25
2 A Note on the International Comparison of Military Expenditures *Jacques Fontanel* 29
  Note on the paper by Fontanel *Frank Blackaby* 44
3 Quantitative and Causal Analysis of Military Expenditures *Louis Pilandon* 47
4 Negotiations to Reduce Military Expenditures – Problems and Possibilities *Hans Christian Cars* 69

PART TWO: MACROECONOMIC ANALYSIS OF THE IMPACT OF MILITARY EXPENDITURE

5 Military Expenditures and Economic Growth: Some Theoretical Remarks *Hendrik de Haan* 87
  Note on the Impact of Military Expenditure on Economic Growth and Performance *David Greenwood* 98
6 The Burden of Defence in Developing Countries *Paul Rivlin* 104
7 Economic Growth, Military Expenditure, the Arms Industry and Arms Transfer in Latin America *Luis Herrera-Lasso* 113

Note on the Impact of Military Expenditure on the
Japanese Economy *Jun Nishikawa* 135
Further Note on the Impact of Military Expenditure on
the Japanese Economy *Isamu Miyasaki* 138

PART THREE: STRATEGIC/ECONOMIC APPROACHES TO ARMAMENTS DYNAMICS

8 Semantic Variations on Richardson's Armaments
Dynamics *Christian Schmidt* 141
Note on the Paper by Schmidt *Michael D. Intriligator* 176
9 Can Arms Races Lead to the Outbreak of
War? *Michael D. Intriligator and Dagobert L. Brito* 180
10 US Foreign Assistance, Israeli Resource Allocation and
the Arms Race in the Middle East: an Analysis of
Three Interdependent Resource Allocation
Processes *Martin C. McGuire* 197
11 Arms Resupply *During* Conflict: a Framework for
Analysis *R. E. Harkavy* 239

PART FOUR: THE ANATOMY OF ARMS INDUSTRIES

12 Efficiency, Industry and Alternative Weapons
Procurement Policies *Keith Hartley* 283
Note on the Paper by Hartley *Edwin Deutsch* 301
13 Re-evaluating Economic and Technological Variables to
Explain Global Arms Production and Sales
Edward A. Kolodziej 304
14 Civil versus Military R & D Expenditures and Industrial
Productivity *Edwin Deutsch and Wolfgang Schöpp* 336
15 Arms Production in Third World Countries, Effects on
Industrialisation *Herbert Wulf* 357

Name Index 385

Subject Index 388

Acknowledgements

This conference owed much to the assistance of the Government of France, both of individuals and ministries. The organisers would like to thank the Prime Minister, the Ministry of the Economy and Finance, the General Planning Authority, the Ministry of Industry and Research, the Ministry of Defence, the Ministry of Education, the National Centre for Scientific Research, the University Paris IX–Dauphine where the sessions were held and the LESOD (Laboratorie d'Economie et de Sociologie des Organisations de Défense headed by Christian Schmidt).

The International Economic Association gratefully acknowledges the continued assistance of UNESCO in support of its activities.

Programme committee

Christian Schmidt (Chairman)
Edwin Deutsch
David Greenwood
Michael E. Intriligator
Edward A. Kolodziej
Robert Neild
Victor L. Urquidi

List of Participants

Mr Frank Blackaby, Director, Stockholm International Peace Research Institute, Sweden

Professor Kenneth E. Boulding, University of Colorado at Boulder, Institute of Behavioral Science, USA

Professor Dagobert L. Brito, Department of Economics, Tulane University, New Orleans, USA

Dr Hans Christian Cars, Försvarsdepartementet, Fack, Stockholm, Sweden

Dr Edwin Deutsch, Institut für Ökonometrie, Vienna, Austria

Mr Hervé Douard, CASCI, Paris, France

Dr Gérard Duchene, Université de Paris I, France

Dr Pierre Dussauge, CASCI, Paris, France

Professor José Antonio Encinas, Department of Political Science, Kansas State University, USA

Professor Luc Fauvel, Secretary General, International Economic Association, Paris, France

Professor Jacques Fontanel, Université des Sciences Sociales de Grenoble – UER – Faculté des Sciences Economiques, Grenoble, France

Professor Giancarlo Graziola, Universitá Cattolica di Sacro Cuore Instituto di Scienze Economiche, Milan, Italy

Professor Henri Guitton, Member of the Institute, Paris, France

Dr David Greenwood, Director, Centre for Defence Studies, Aberdeen, Great Britain

Professor H. de Haan, Rijksuniversiteit Faculteit der Economische Wetenschappen, Gröningen, Netherlands

List of Participants

Professor R. E. Harkavy, Department of Political Science, Pennsylvania State University, USA

Dr Keith Hartley, University of York, Department of Economics and Related Studies, Great Britain

Professor Luis Herrera-Lasso, Centro de Estudios Economicos y Sociales del Tercer Mundo AC, Mexico

Professor Michael D. Intriligator, University of California, Center for International and Strategic Affairs, Los Angeles, USA

Professor Edward A. Kolodziej, University of Illinois at Urbana–Champaign, Department of Political Science, Illinois, USA

Professor Jacques Lesourne, Coservatoire National des Arts & Métiers, Chaire d'Economie et Statistiques Industrielles, Paris, France

Professor Emile Levy, Université de Paris IX – Dauphine, Paris, France

Professor Martin McGuire, University of Maryland, Department of Economics, USA

Professor Edmond Malinvaud, Directeur Général Institut National de la Statistique & des Etudes Economiques, Paris, France

Mr Isamu Miyasaki, Special Adviser, Economic Planning Agency Japanese Government, Japan

Professor Robert Neild, Economic Faculty Board, Cambridge, Great Britain

Dr Jun Nishikawa, Special Fellow, UNITAR, New York, USA

Mr Thomas Ohlson, Stockholm International Peace Research Institute, Sweden

Miss Sophie Pansieri, CASCI, Paris, France

Dr C. Passadeos, Université d'Amiens, France

Professor Louis Pilandon, Université de Clermont II, France

Dr Paul Rivlin, International Institute for Strategic Studies, London, Great Britain

Dr Michael Rudnianski, Université de Paris VII, CASCI, Paris, France

Professor Christian Schmidt, Directeur, CASCI, Paris, France

Dip. Ing. W. Schöpp, Institut für Ökonometrie, Vienna, Austria

Professor Ron Smith, Department of Economics, Birkbeck College, London University, Great Britain

Professor Adam Szeworski, University of Warsaw, Poland

Professor Victor L. Urquidi, President IEA, President, El Colegio de Mexico, Mexico

Professor Herbert Wulf, Institut für Friedensforschung und Sicherheitspolitik, Hamburg, W. Germany

Observers:

Dr Peter Lengyel, Division for International Development of Social Sciences, UNESCO, Paris, France

Mr Jean-Alphonse Bernard, Chargé de Mission, Ministère des Finances, Paris, France

Abbreviations and Acronyms

ACDA	US Arms Control and Disarmament Agency (see also USACDA)
CASCI	Centre d'Analyse Scientifique des Conflicts Internationaux
CIA	Central Intelligence Agency (of USA)
CITEFA	Instituto de Investigaciones Cientisicas y Tecnicas de las Fuerzas Armadas
CMEA	Council for Mutual Economic Assistance
DPPP	Domestic Purchasing Power Parity
ECU	European Currency Unit
FR	Federal Republic
GDP	Gross Domestic Product
GNP	Gross National Product
HMSO	Her Majesty's Stationary Office
ICP	International Comparison Project
IFS	'International Financial Statistics'
IFSH	Institut für Friedensforschung und Sicherheitspolitik, Hamburg
IISS	International Institute for Strategic Studies
IMF	International Monetary Fund
ISIC	International Standard Industrial Classification
LDC	Less-developed countries
MB	Military balance
NAMMA	NATO MRCA Management Agency
MRCA	Multi-role Combat Aircraft (Tornado)
NATO	North Atlantic Treaty Organisation
OECD	Organisation for Economic Co-operation and Development
OEEC	Organisation for European Economic Cooperation
OPEC	Organisation of Petroleum Exporting Countries
PPP	Purchasing Power Parity

PRC	People's Republic of China
R & D	Research and Development
SDR	Special Drawing Rights
SIPRI	Stockholm International Peace Research Institute
SSRC	Social Science Research Council
UNITAR	United Nations Institute for Training and Research
USACDA	*see* ACDA
USSR	Union of Soviet Socialist Republics
VTOL	Vertical Take-off and Landing
WMEAT	World Military Expenditures and Arms Transfers
WTO	Warsaw Treaty Organisation

Introductory Remarks

by Professor Victor L. Urquidi
President of the International Economic Association

On the significance of our present round table conference, I would like first to say that it was Christian Schmidt who drew our attention to the fact that the International Economic Association had never dealt with the subject matter of this conference and that, although a number of institutions, in Sweden, the United Kingdom, France, the United States, and other parts of the world, were concerned with compiling data and analysing the implications of defence expenditures, and trade in arms, especially from the point of view of security, political, and strategic considerations, even of human survival, there had been less work on the purely economic aspects. The United Nations, of course, through various committees and special conferences has held discusssions and issued reports on disarmament, and the disarmament/development issue has been discussed in many quarters and is found in many reports on the global situation and prospects. It was also found that research on methodology and economic analysis was being conducted by economists in universities and special research institutions in various parts, on the economic impact of defence expenditures, the arms industry, international transfer and trade in arms, disarmament, and arms limitation.

Now, how do defence expenditures affect economic growth and short term fluctuations? Can inflation be attributed partly to such expenditures, and to what extent? Do defence expenditures constitute an important factor in reducing unemployment, and in stimulating the economy in the industrially advanced countries? What is the trade-off and the interaction between defence expenditures and economic development in the developing countries? How in effect do such expenditures affect the main economic policy variables in both the developed and the developing countries?

It is easy, I think, to imagine the various consequences and interactions, but, surprisingly, little work has been done, partly because of the inadequacy of the data, despite heroic efforts at gathering such data by certain research groups. From the point of view of development of the developing countries, and of the need to transfer resources from developed to developing countries, to which so many reports have drawn attention, it is unfortunately not quite clear, in my mind, how real and financial resources withdrawn or diverted from military expenditures can be specifically applied to development.

We always learned, I think, in some of the earlier textbooks, that factories that produce machine-guns can be converted to producing bicycles. And one can assume that industrial facilities for the production of tanks can be transformed into facilities for the production of new and better tractors, and so on. But what about the high-powered missiles that we hear so much about in these days? What about the installations that produce nuclear weapons?

What is the spin-off from defence R & D to civilian industrial innovation, especially for the benefit of the developing countries? What are the conversion processes in terms of manpower, budgets and decision-making? How can bilateral and multilateral sources of development cooperation be strengthened as a result of, let us say, disarmament?

Here, of course, one can see the inseparability of the economic, political, strategic and technological considerations.

It is not the purpose of this meeting to delve into and to cover all such aspects. Its aims are more modest: to generate more knowledge about the economic aspects, the data requirements, the methodological possibilities, and to suggest means of furthering such work in the coming years. It might be tempting to get side-tracked into purely topical discussions such as: what goes on in the Middle East, West Asia, Southwest Africa, the South Atlantic, Central America and the Caribbean, or, for that matter, what goes on in the talks on arms limitation to be held soon in Geneva, or in the disarmament discussions at the United Nations. And I am sure that references will come up if only because some of these events generate, as we were discussing informally last night, all sorts of speculations as to their economic consequences, let alone the political and strategic consequences.

But that is not our task, and I am sure that these topical matters will probably be discussed more during lunch and dinner, than here at our meeting table. Let us hope we can stick to our subject matter

Introductory Remarks

in the short time available. We are not going to invent the wheel, but at least to learn more on how and why it turns, and where it may lead to.

I understand, if my counting is correct, that we are about forty participants, not all here at the moment, of some thirteen different nationalities. In other International Economic Association meetings of this nature we have had as many as twenty to twenty-two nationalities represented. On this occasion there were unfortunately some last-minute regrets from participants from certain countries, and also, the limited number of nationalities represented here reflects possibly the fact that especially among the developing countries, not much work has been done on our subject matter, or at least it is not known internationally. And the same perhaps can be said of economists in the centrally-planned economies. In any event this is a start. I do not know whether to say START with capital letters, or just say a small start.

In addition, I wanted to make a few remarks on the content of the meeting, I think it goes back to the question partly of disaggregation and the identification of what exactly are military expenditures, in different contexts. For example, we used to hear a lot about the impact of defence expenditures on imports of strategic materials; this has not been mentioned here. In other words, if a large industrial country goes into a large defence expansion, does it increase its imports of the so-called strategic materials? And how does that affect other parts of the world? It may lead to quite a development, say, of mining or something else. Today one asks oneself the question: What is happening to strategic reserves of oil, in the face of either a possible future scarcity of oil, or increases in prices and so on. That is more the sort of specific aspect that I think needs to be discussed much more fully, because there are all these structural changes taking place in the world economy, with regard, for example, to oil and gas.

Then there is the question of exports. A country increases its military expenditures not just to keep its weapons in reserve but actually to export, and this has a balance of payments consequence for the country that has increased its defence expenditures. For example, I was interested to note that Greece has developed an arms industry for export, because it is pretty close, I suppose, to one of the conflict areas, where they can gain a few hundred million dollars, or more, a year. We know that Brazil is exporting a billion dollars worth a year of military equipment, to various parts of the world. I think all of these specific cases should be investigated much more, in order to find out what are the relationships between the aggregates and the specific kinds of expenditures.

Another thing I believe one should remember in the case especially of developing countries, is the corruption of the military. We have heard of cases where military officers are involved in industrial enterprises and in the military industry. Now, what happens to the income, if you can call it that, that the military get from these transactions in weapons and so on? Well, a lot of it is probably converted into capital flight. It weakens the balance of payments. Then some of it just goes into ordinary consumption, real estate, housing, etc. I think there is a qualitative distinction in that you do not get the same degree of corruption among business people, or among other kinds of expenditure for investment or consumption in some of the developing countries. And of course, it does not happen only in the developing countries. So I think that the more we can get down to a typification of conditions under which military expenditures take place in different kinds of economies and levels of economies, the closer we are going to get to understanding the significance of these changes in the short run or in the long run.

Introduction
Christian Schmidt
Chairman of the Conference

Today over 5 per cent of world GNP goes directly on military spending. International transfers on average grew twice as fast as total world trade between 1974 and 1982. Another point is that whereas it used to be only the most advanced industrialised countries that could produce armaments, they are also being produced nowadays by such different developing countries as Brazil, India, South Korea and, of course, Israel.[1] The sheer scale of this process, and the fact that it coincides with a general downturn in growth rates and with international imbalances have naturally prompted economists to look with concern into its effects on contemporary economic growth and fluctuations.

It is worth noting at the outset that with a few well known exceptions, including the now relatively older studies of E. Benoit, K. Boulding, G. Kennedy and S. Melman,[2] together with more recent contributions from J. Gansler and W. Leontief,[3] economic analysis of military and armaments spending is still a little explored field.[4] For example, one need only compare the number of articles published on these matters in the economic journals with the number dealing with the economics of health or education in the same journals. There are several factors explaining though not excusing the discrepancy. There are difficulties in obtaining access to the information and the unreliability of the data available for military spending are a curb on empirical research. At the same time, the main currents in macroeconomic analysis combine to label such spending 'unproductive', thereby reducing the interest of theoretical investigation of the subject. But the most important factor is that the majority of the studies in this area have been carried out by political scientists and have therefore remained unknown to many professional economists.

The reasons just quoted to explain this situation are no longer wholly valid. Accordingly, the IEA has organised a meeting on the subject for the first time. Several leading agencies, including SIPRI[5] and ACDA[6] gather information and publish regular data, so that for military spending and to a lesser extent, sales of military equipment, we nowadays have statistical series over long enough periods to begin to be meaningful. Furthermore, recent developments in the theory of government economics and especially work on the theory of bureaucracy find an ideal field of application in defence.[7] Lastly, certain contributions from political scientists on the subject, notably including research by B. Russet[8] and work by E. Kolodziej[9] make extensive use of the 'tools' of economic analysis.

Nevertheless, defence economics is still very much at the embryonic stage. It is more like a research programme (a group of varied research programmes has been initiated) than a particular field in economic science. Accordingly, the first merit of the set of contributions brought together here is to allow us to draw out the contours of that programme from a joint 'survey' highlighting the present limits of our knowledge of the subject. It also enables us to identify and to rank the main gaps, which can be classified as falling into one of three categories.

1 *Lack of quantitative data, the problematical character of evaluation procedures for military expenditures, and difficulties about international comparisons*

F. Blackaby and Ch. Ohlson present a comprehensive view of the statistical difficulties one encounters in attempting a quantitative evaluation of the military sector. These points are taken further in J. Fontanel's paper on the difficult question of the international comparison of military budgets. J. Fontanel reviews several alternative methods in detail, showing that they often lead to extremely different results. These issues also come up in H. C. Cars' paper, which looks into the conditions that ought to be satisfied in designing a relevant conceptual framework with which to enter into negotiations on reducing military expenditures at world level. The full range of statistical problems deplored by those authors come up again in connection with L. Pilandon's findings from his attempt to investigate a set of econometric correlations between defence budgets and a battery of national macroeconomic indications for a large number of countries in different world regions.

Introduction

2 Unsuitability of traditional categories in macroeconomic analysis and the need for a theoretical renewal

H. de Haan shows clearly, with some very simple models, that no significant theoretical result relating to the effect of military spending on the state of the economy can be shown within the framework of conventional macroeconomic analysis on neoclassical or Keynesian lines. From this he concludes that the economic effect of a lower military budget ultimately depends only on individual, empirical factors peculiar to the country economy concerned. This ties in with D. Greenwood's somewhat provocative remark that the conclusions of a macroeconomic study of military spending depend mainly on the political predispositions of its author. Meanwhile K. Hartley's contribution makes the point that analysis in terms of Pareto effectiveness is out of place in estimating the performance of the arms industry in a European context and comes down more in favour of resorting to 'public choice' theory.

Looking at the comparative effects of civilian and military R & D outlays on industrial productivity in six countries (Canada, United States, France, Germany, the Netherlands and Japan), by means of a conventional production model, E. Deutsch and W. Schöpp emphasise the inherent limitations of the CES type of production function which they use especially because of scale effects.

3 Difficulties in interpreting information yielded by the military/economic model and the ambiguity of the results

Modelling the international dynamics of military outlays is not new. C. Schmidt presents a critical overview of several recent extensions to Richardson's well known model. He shows that Richardson only contributed a broad syntax, from which different models of interpretation can be drawn. He offers a classification and then goes on to assess how much still remains to be done before operational tools can become available in this subject. Starting from the same general conceptual framework, M. Intriligator and D. Brito, pursuing their work on relations between the arms race and nuclear war, suggest enriching the Richardson dynamics with a potential nuclear war component and an economic resource allocation component. In this way they sketch out a chain of models whose linkages remain to be specified. Economic instruments of a more conventional kind are used for applied studies, like the one M. McGuire describes on relations between US aid, the trend in the military budget and the arms race in the Middle East. This highlights the constraints imposed on a model like this by the information available about these subjects.

But the interest of this volume does not lie solely in its critical stock-taking. Beyond the challenge to certain preconceptions, such as the existence of a general and universal phenomenon of an international arms race, a number of positive comments can be drawn. They will be grouped here around three central ideas: diversity of the economic effect of military outlays according to the country or groups of countries concerned; variety of possible patterns for economic policy towards arms, complexity of interactions between military/strategic factors and the technological/economic factors in the dynamics of arms.

(i) DIVERSITY OF THE EFFECT OF MILITARY OUTLAYS ACCORDING TO COUNTRY OR COUNTRY GROUP

One of the striking facts of the last ten years has been the growing proportion of the developing countries in total world military outlays, from just under 8 per cent in 1972 to an estimate of nearly 16 per cent today.[10] Not only is it impossible to compare the impact of military outlays on developing economies with their effects on industrialised countries, but perhaps even more important, the situation has to be analysed very differently according to whether one is considering, among the developing countries, those which import most of their arms or those which already have an armaments industry of their own. These considerations have prompted the organisers to devote particular attention to the developing countries.

Thus P. Rivlin attempts to derive a trend for the economic cost of defence in the developing countries, emphasising the particular case of Israel for which the most extensive information is publicly available. Meanwhile H. Wulf suggests a preliminary classification of the different developing countries with their own arms industries on the basis of a combination of criteria borrowed from macroeconomic analysis of resources and the industrial economy, which reveals the extreme variety of these new arms producers. That conclusion is to some extent confirmed by studies of a specific regional zone, as shown by, for example, that of Herrera-Lasso, who highlights the relative heterogeneity of the Latin American countries, both as regards development of a local military equipment industry and in

Introduction

amounts spent on defence, which, with the structure of arms imports, affect their respective internal and external financial situations.

Comparing these different standpoints, one might be tempted to imagine that defence economics provides an ideal field in which to rehabilitate and deepen institutional economic analysis, since it is so clear that the impossibility of drawing any general principles has to be related to the diversity of the institutional and socioeconomic contexts under consideration.

(ii) VARIETY OF POSSIBLE ARMS POLICY PATTERNS

Certain studies, like K. Hartley's, suggest in comparisons between the respective performances of the arms industries in Western Europe and the United States, the differences in the aims being pursued and the corresponding consequences for methods of evaluation. Wulf's contribution confirms this hypothesis for the developing countries, because it clearly emphasises the contrast between an 'outward-looking' industrial strategy as exemplified, for example, by Brazil's military equipment production and export policy, as against India's 'inward-looking' policy geared mainly to its own needs. Adopting one or other stance affects the way production is organised and directly impacts upon funding structures.[11]

Taking these points further, one is prompted to consider that military spending policies in general, and selection of an arms industry in particular, are issues lending themselves to analysis of alternatives in terms of collective well-being, subject to specifying beforehand the function of defence understood as a collective good.

(iii) COMPLEXITY OF INTERACTIONS BETWEEN MILITARY/
STRATEGIC FACTORS AND THE TECHNOLOGICAL/
ECONOMIC FACTORS IN THE DYNAMICS OF ARMS

The contributions from Ch. Schmidt and, to an even greater extent, M. Intriligator and D. Brito, show how in formalising the arms dynamic, economic and also military variables must be taken into account. R. Harkavy's report emphasises the special and crucial problem of this interlinkage between military requirements and economic constraints in the delicate issue of military procurement in the course of a conflict. His analysis, based on a wealth of historical material, clearly shows how this relationship presents itself according to the particular nature of the conflict concerned and the various phases through which it proceeds. This issue comes up again in the paper by E. Kolodziej who, relying on examples chosen both from the western industrialised countries like France, and from developing countries like Brazil, argues for the decisiveness of industrial and technological considerations over the geopolitical conditions most often advanced, especially by political scientists. His arguments have to be compared against some findings of L. Pilandon, who shows how on the contrary, the ranking of military effort worldwide still seems to depend on geopolitical factors.

These analyses seem to urge cogently that exploring the conditions in which the defence economy functions demands very close interdisciplinary co-operation. They also suggest certain conceptual frameworks, such as hierarchical systems theory and dynamic games theory.[12]

In conclusion, this first meeting of the IEA on the economic impact of arms spending has provided an opportunity for critical comparison of assessments, and for more rigorous analysis. But it has to be regarded as a preliminary phase, opening up on to several avenues for research in so crucial yet still poorly explored a subject.[13]

The set of contributions delivered and discussed is presented in the following order: in *Part One*, those concerning statistical data and quantitative processing for arms and disarmament: in *Part Two*, those dealing with macroeconomic analysis of military outlays from a theoretical and empirical standpoint, especially for developing countries. *Part Three* consists of those on strategic/economic models proposed to describe the dynamics of arms and investigations into the relationships between military and economic factors. *Part Four*, the last, deals with the special characteristics and features of arms industries.

NOTES AND REFERENCES

1. Wulf, H., 'Developing countries', in Ball, N. and Leittenberg, M. *The Structure of the Defense Industry, an International Survey* (New York: St. Martin's Press, 1983) and Neuman, S. (ed), *Defense Planning in Less-Industrialized States* (Lexington Books, 1984).
2. Benoit, E., *Defense and Economic Growth in Developing Countries* (Lexington Books, 1973); Boulding, K., *Conflict and Defense, A General Theory* (Harper & Row 1963); G. Kennedy *Defense Economics* (New York: St. Martin's Press, 1975) (new edition revised and corrected, 1983); Melman, S., *The Defense Economy: Co-regional Industries and Civilian Needs* (New York: Praeger, 1980) and *The Permanent War Economy* (Simon & Schuster, 1974).

3. Gansler, J., *The Defense Industry* (MIT Press, 1980); Leontief, W. and Duchin, F., *Military Spending – Facts, Figures, Worldwide Implications and Future Outlook* (OUP, 1983).
4. For a recent overview of this question see Ch. Schmidt, 'Dépenses Militaires et analyse économique', preface/study in *Conséquences économiques et sociales de la course aux armements* (Paris: UN Economica, 1983).
5. The Stockholm International Peace Research Institute (SIPRI) publishes a yearly estimate of worldwide military spending and arms sales.
6. The Arms Control and Disarmament Agency regularly publishes reports on the military budgets of different countries and international arms traffic.
7. For what is now already an older application, see Allison, G., *Essence of Decision Explaining the Cuban Missile Crisis* (Little Brown, 1971).
8. Russet, B., *What Price Vigilance? The Garden of National Defense* (York University Press), and 'Defense and National Well-being – Vigilance and Ignorance', *American Political Science Review*, Dec. 1982.
9. Kolodziej, E., 'France and the Arms Trade', *International Affairs*, Jan. 1980.
10. *Economic and Social Consequences of Military Expenditures and Arms Sales*, UN report.
11. This question has been studied by Ch. Schmidt in 'Industries d' armement et endettement dans le Tierce Monde' (Arms industries and Third World indebtedness, cases of Argentina, Brazil, South Korea and Israel), paper to the Clermont-Ferrand colloque 24–26 May 1984, Revue Défense Nationale, Oct. 1984.
12. On this point see M. Rudnianski and Ch. Schmidt 'Course aux armements et risque de guerre nucléaire, une approche formalisée', roneo (Paris: Fondation des Etudes de Défense Nationale, 1984).
13. The International Defense Economic Association (IDEA) was moreover established in the wake of that IEA meeting to pursue this work.

Part One
Statistical Treatment of Armament and Disarmament

Part One

1 Military Expenditure and the Arms Trade: Problems of the Data

Frank Blackaby and Thomas Ohlson
STOCKHOLM INTERNATIONAL PEACE
RESEARCH INSTITUTE

I INTRODUCTION

The theme of this paper is straightforward. The 'world war industry', to use Professor Boulding's useful term, or the world military sector, to use a more formal description, is a very large economic sector. It is true that the main reason for studying it is not economic – it is because within this sector there are powerful forces exacerbating the arms race and increasing the dangers of war. However, the economic characteristics of this sector are not insignificant. This sector consists of the sum total of the resources devoted, not necessarily to defence – the common use of the term 'Ministry of Defence' is often a euphemism – but to preparations for the use of force against other states, and sometimes against dissident elements within the country itself.[1]

The main theme of this paper is that our knowledge – and particularly our statistical knowledge – of this sector is massively deficient. Political scientists in general (with the exception of the adherents to the school of quantitative political science) may not be too disturbed by the absence of an adequate set of numbers. Economists are not in this happy position: they need a statistical framework within which to operate. It follows that the main efforts of economists who wish to study this sector should at this stage be concentrated on improving our knowledge of the data. At SIPRI we speak with some feeling on this question. We have spent a lot of time constructing, as best we can, a picture of the structure of world trade in major weapons. We also have a databank on military expenditure, and on weapons production. We therefore know what we do not know: that is we know how inadequate the figures are, how thin their coverage is and how big the margins of error are in many figures. We are constantly being exasperated by armchair theorists who conduct statistical exercises on some of our figures, without paying any attention to the obvious margins of error. They then complain bitterly when next year's revisions make their correlation coefficients insignificant.

This kind of situation is, of course, not uncommon in economics. In many countries there are a few overworked statisticians doing their best to construct figures for the national accounts, with an army of econometricians waiting to play fancy statistical games with the numbers. There is a disequilibrium between those who want to play with the figures, and those who are prepared to engage in the much less glamorous job of trying to provide a reasonable statistical structure. The main need in the military sector is simply to build up a better picture of what is going on.

Contrast our knowledge of the world military sector with, for example, our knowledge of the world oil producing and consuming sector. We know with a great deal of precision who produces oil, and who consumes it; we know the pattern of trade; we know the diversity of products. In the military sector, there are virtually no military products for which we could produce a world production table – still less a world production and trade matrix. Over a very large area of the world, our knowledge of military expenditure is fragmentary, with large margins of error. To take just one example at this stage, it might be thought that we would at least know with some degree of accuracy the numbers in the world's armed forces. However, the variations in the publicly published estimates of even these elementary figures are very large as shown for two selected areas in Figure 1.1.

II THE ARMS TRADE

For any other category of trade, apart from the trade in weapons, the analysis, of course, begins with the trade accounts. The analysis of the trade in weapons cannot begin there. With a very limited number of honourable exceptions, the published national and international trade statistics tell us nothing about the trade in weapons. First of all, the international trade classification systems are not sufficiently spe-

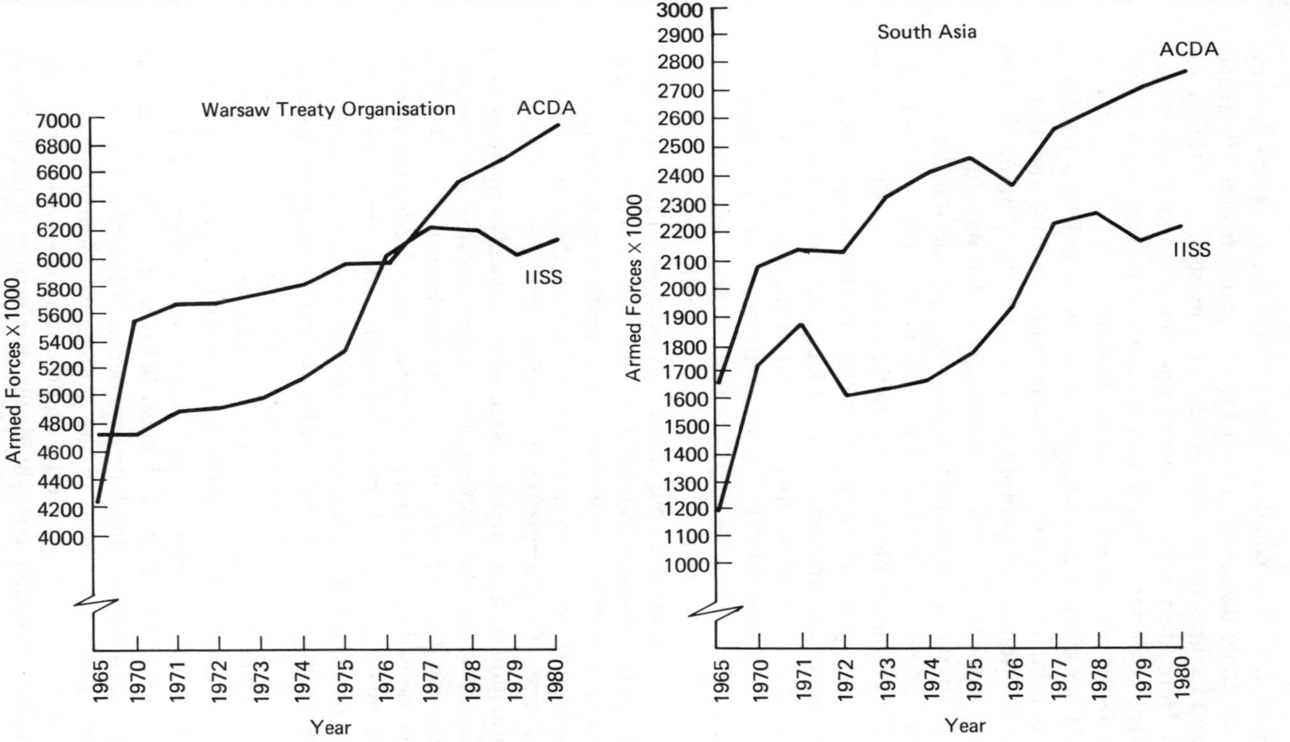

FIGURE 1.1 *Comparison of estimates of numbers in the armed forces by ACDA and IISS.*
SOURCES Prepared by M. Lumsden from: ACDA, *World Military Expenditures and Arms Transfers (WMEAT) 1969–78* (Washington: US Government Printing Office, 1980) and IISS, *The Military Balance 1981–82* (London: IISS, 1981)

cific. Secondly, most countries do not follow these systems anyway. The arms trade figures are either hidden among figures for civilian semimanufactures or finished goods, or – most often – totally excluded. Here, then, we have a very important sector of world trade – important both for political and economic analysis – where our knowledge of what is going on is inadequate.

SIPRI has tried to do something in this field: indeed it has had a continuing interest in the arms trade from the time the Institute began. It attempts to provide a picture of the pattern of arms transfers in the world, and of the changes in that pattern.

In the absence of arms trade figures in the trade statistics, it is a laborious process to build up a picture of the world's arms trade. First, there is the problem of defining the scope of the subject. Arms transfers include a wide variety of military hardware, support equipment, services and know-how. SIPRI has concentrated on the trade in major conventional weapons, i.e. on military aircraft, warships, missiles and armoured vehicles, including heavy artillery. Licences obtained for the assembly or production of major weapons are also included: production under licence is essentially a more ambitious alternative to direct arms purchases. The method SIPRI has to use – of identifying individual transactions – has made it necessary to limit the data collection to major weapons. It would simply not be possible, without an enormous research staff, to trace the pattern of trade in small arms, for example, by this method.

Information on arms transfer agreements normally originates from four basic sources: the supplying firms, the supplying governments, the receiving governments, and various intelligence networks. This information is then published in official national documents, in technical, commercial and military publications and journals, in monographs and annual reference works, and in newspapers. The process of constructing a register of transfers of major weapons therefore begins with a massive literature search through these sources; the total number of sources regularly searched for data is at present about 200. This procedure requires a lot of knowledge of the particular weapon which is reported as being sold or transferred. It is not always an easy matter to distinguish between insubstantial rumour and hard information; the long experience of the past decade has, however, given some clue to the sources which in general have proved to be reliable. As a rule, reports from one single source are not considered reliable enough; ideally, a minimum of five independent sources is required for a reliable report on each item.

This, then, provides a register of the trade in major weapons. The information is stored in a computer databank. It would no longer be possible to process the mass of information without computer assistance: the total number of recorded transactions is some 10 000 for the post-Second World War period. The data which is stored on the computer include among other things, for each transaction: buyer, seller, weapon designation, weapon category, date of order, date of final delivery, status of the weapon (new, second-hand or refurbished), buyer and seller organisation (for example government, air force, army, navy), number ordered, terms of the deal (cash, credit, gift, aid, loan, grant, licence production, offset, etc.), total unit sales price if available, and delivery years and numbers.

This register – together with the arms production register – serves an important purpose in itself: it provides a detailed survey of the qualitative and quantitative flow of major weapons. It is (so far as we know) the only register of its kind in the world. The IISS list of major identified arms agreement is much less comprehensive. The next problem is to turn these transactions into more workable numbers.

1   THE VALUATION OF THE ARMS TRADE

Different objectives, or different questions, will require different valuation systems. If, for instance, one was concerned with the financial burden on the recipients, then the valuation would be according to the cash paid by the recipient, and weapons supplied free under military aid would not feature. The objective of the SIPRI system is to answer questions about the inflation-corrected rates of growth in transfers of major weapons, in total and by area; and to provide valid comparisons of the size of the trade, both by recipient and supplying countries. The figures must reflect changes in the quantity and quality of the weapons transferred. They are based on actual deliveries in the year, not on orders received.

SIPRI constructed a list of comparable prices in 1968 US dollars, based on such actual prices as were known at that time and on such criteria as weight, speed, and the role of the weapon. (1968 was chosen because that was the year in which the data collection began.) Each weapon obtains three separate values – new, second-hand and refurbished. Missiles, however, are only valued as new. Licensed production is valued in the same way as the arms trade. For example, an F-15 fighter built under US licence in Japan in 1982 has the same value as a US-built F-15 delivered to Japan in say, 1980.

The original price list, based on constant 1968 dollars, was then adjusted first to 1973 price levels and then to 1975 price levels. The method used to obtain the factor needed was to construct a weighted index, using three countries – the USA, the UK and France – as the major Western arms exporting countries, and the wholesale finished goods and industrial product price indices for the same countries.

The monetary values chosen do not, therefore, correspond to the actual prices paid, which vary considerably depending on different pricing methods, the length of production runs, and the terms involved in individual transactions. The actual sale price also depends on the coverage of the deal. For instance, a deal may or may not include spare parts, training, support equipment, compensation and offset arrangements for local industry and so on. Moreover, to use only actual sales prices – assuming that the information were available for all deals, which it certainly is not – military aid, gifts, grants and loans would be excluded, and the total flow of arms would therefore not be measured.

The pricing of weapons developed after 1968 is based on information from various producers on the so-called ex-factory unit cost or 'fly-away' unit cost for Western weapons. These costs are then deflated by the indices already described to remove the effects of general inflation. For weapons for which all price information is lacking, a comparison is made with a known weapon of the same type, with the same characteristics. This is the method used for valuing Soviet transfers of major weapons. The final check of the reliability of this performance comparison is made by a military panel.

The comparison between supplying countries, therefore, requires an elaborate exercise of establishing comparability between the weapons systems of different countries. Obviously there have to be a number of rough and ready decisions in the pricing process. However, it does enable us to provide some kind of picture of the pattern of the trade in major weapons, measured in constant 1975 US dollars. The individual 'prices' are less essential to this valuation system than two other main considerations, namely, that the method of pricing is applied consistently and that more sophisticated weapons are always given a higher value than less sophisticated ones. The figures, however, do not measure the payments made by the recipient countries, or received by the supplying countries.

The SIPRI values can be calculated and retrieved from the computer system in any possible combination, ranging from, say, the value of the F-16 fighters supplied by the USA to Israel in 1981, to the aggregated total value of global arms exports during the last five years. We can, for example, measure the total flow of arms over time, the export/import shares or values of any given combination of suppliers or recipients in any year or years, or the total value of all F-16 deliveries compared with the corresponding value for MiG-23s or F-4 Phantoms. Only a selection of this available data can be presented in the *SIPRI Yearbook*.[2]

What could be done to improve this admittedly imperfect and inadequate picture of world arms transfers? There are two things we would like to do, if we had the resources. First, and most important, we would like to overhaul and refine the valuation system. Secondly, we would like to widen our coverage by including additional weapon categories and support equipment (primarily in the field of military electronics).

2   SOME COMPARISONS

The only other quantitative estimates of the trade in arms which exist, to our knowledge, are those of the US Arms Control and Disarmament Agency (ACDA). ACDA and SIPRI differ significantly in pricing and presentation, and the definitions of arms transfers – i.e. the items covered by the data – are also different.

ACDA uses a broader and potentially more useful definition of arms transfers than SIPRI. The section on sources and methods in their yearly publication states:

> Among the items included are tactical guided missiles and rockets, military aircraft, naval vessels, armored and nonarmored military vehicles, military communications and electronic equipment, artillery, infantry weapons, small arms ammunition and other ordnance, parachutes, and uniforms. Also included are transfers of equipment for defence industries.[3]

However, the ACDA figures are not based on an independent data base on arms transfers. ACDA describes their sources in the following way:

> The statistics published here are estimates of the value of goods actually delivered during the reference year, in contrast to the value of programs, agreements, contracts, or orders which may

result in future transfer of goods or to the actual payments made for such deliveries . . . Figures for the US are extracted from official trade statistics on military transfers compiled by the US Departments of State and Defence . . . For data on foreign countries, ACDA used official US Government sources, and the data have been rounded. The difficulties in collecting information on the full scope of Soviet deliveries and in placing a value on them require that the Soviet figure be regarded as an approximation . . . Soviet arms transfer and foreign trade data are taken from sources which present them directly in dollars; hence particular caution should be used in comparing these statistics for arms transfers and foreign trade with other Soviet data.[4]

The figures ACDA publishes therefore come from elsewhere in the US Government machine, and the procedure by which official US Government sources obtain data on the arms transactions of other suppliers is not clear. The sources are presumably intelligence sources. It is not possible, therefore, to check the figures against primary data.

It is not clear what pricing method ACDA uses. It seems, however, that ACDA constructs, or obtains from elsewhere, some index of prices derived from estimates of production costs and military use value.[5] In a CIA publication, the pricing method for measuring the value of Soviet arms transfers is explained as follows:

> The estimates of the volume and the value of Soviet arms flows represented in this paper were developed for the most part on detailed identification and listing of Soviet arms deliveries. The physical items so identified and listed were given a monetary value through the use of estimated prices – Soviet export prices in one comparison and estimated US costs in the other.[6]

The figures presented by ACDA are currently of three kinds. First, aggregated monetary values are given, on a year-by-year basis, for individual countries' imports and exports. The second table shows monetary values for the exports of ten major suppliers to all importing countries over a five-year period (in earlier issues the period was ten years). Thirdly, ACDA reports aggregate numbers (5-year period) of major weapons in thirteen broadly defined subcategories of major weapon systems from six supplier countries to World and Third World regions.

Obviously, from aggregate value tables of this kind, the amount of detailed information which can be obtained is limited. A databank based on a compilation of individual transactions can take out the figures – and indeed the individual transactions – for any pair of countries and for any weapon. Thus it is possible currently to provide from the SIPRI databank an itemised list of transfers of major weapons to Argentina. ACDA tables do not give details of transactions between any individual pair of countries. Such data (according to a 1976 report) is regarded as sensitive and therefore classified.[7]

How far would a student of the two sets of figures – the ACDA series and the SIPRI series – come to the same conclusion about the pattern of the world arms trade? The answer varies according to the question asked. The two sources, for example, give roughly similar figures for the rate of growth in the volume of Third World countries' imports of major weapons between 1970 and 1979. SIPRI shows an average growth-rate over this period, for this particular arms flow, of 12.7 per cent a year; the ACDA figure for the same flow is 11.2 per cent a year. In the period 1975-9, the two sources give a closely similar picture of the recipient area pattern in the Third World (Table 1.1).

However, for the same period – and for the same arms flow – the ACDA and SIPRI pictures of the pattern of supply differ significantly. SIPRI has the United States as a much bigger supplier of arms than the Soviet Union; for ACDA, it is the other way round. The difference probably arises from the different valuation systems used for Soviet weapon transfers – although without more access to ACDA data this proposition cannot be verified. ACDA also has larger shares for West Germany and 'others'. Coverage may be the explanation here. The ACDA figures for West Germany and for 'others' may consist predominantly of military equipment other than 'major weapons', and so be excluded from the SIPRI figures (Table 1.2).

III MILITARY EXPENDITURE

Perhaps the most useful thing to do is to set out some of the problems which SIPRI has encountered over the past thirteen years in its attempt to produce a reasonably comprehensive set of figures on military expenditure in the various countries of the world. The main problem is straightforward. There are some 150 countries in the

TABLE 1.1: *Arms imports by Third World regions, 1975–9 (per cent)*

	ACDA	SIPRI
Middle East	48.0	44.8
Africa	24.9	23.0
Far East (East Asia)	13.9	15.4
Latin America	8.0	10.3
South Asia	5.2	6.5
	100.0	100.00

SOURCES   ACDA, *World Military Expenditures and Arms Transfers* (WMEAT) 1970–79, (Washington: US Government Printing Office, 1980) table 2, pp. 85–8 SIPRI, *World Armaments and Disarmament – SIPRI Yearbook*, 1982 (London: Taylor & Francis, 1982) table 6A1, pp. 190–91. (ACDA figures based on 1978 dollars; SIPRI figures on 1975 dollars.)

TABLE 1.2: *Arms exports to Third World countries, 1975–9 (per cent)*

	ACDA	SIPRI
USSR	37.6	30.0
USA	30.5	41.6
France	7.6	10.3
UK	4.7	6.1
FR Germany	4.2	1.5
Italy	2.9	3.8
Others	12.5	6.7
	100.0	100.0

SOURCES   ACDA, *World Military Expenditures and Arms Transfers* (WMEAT) 1970–79 (Washington: US Government Printing Office, 1980) table 3, p. 127. *SIPRI, World Armaments and Disarmament – SIPRI Yearbook*, 1982 (London: Taylor & Francis, 1982) table 6A2, pp. 192–3. (ACDA figures based on current dollars; SIPRI figures on 1975 dollars.)

world. Out of these, we have only about 25 countries where we would rate the statistical series for military expenditure as 'good'. 'Good' in that sense means that we know the coverage of the figures, and changes in the coverage; that we feel reasonably confident that items are not omitted; and that we believe the year-to-year movements in the published figures properly represent the changes in military expenditure which have taken place. This does not mean that the military expenditure figures for the rest of the world are wholly useless. Certain 'order of magnitude' statements can be made. On the other hand, even for the 25 countries for which we have good figures in aggregate, there may well be questions about the validity of a functional classification. Major items may be deliberately hidden. The comments which follow are first about NATO countries; second, about Third World countries; and thirdly about the Soviet Union and China.

Students of the various sources which give figures of military expenditure will tend to come to the conclusion that NATO figures are highly reliable. Virtually all sources reporting on world military expenditure use the 'standardised' NATO set of figures. They do this with a great sense of relief, since at least in this group of countries an organisation has apparently gone through the process of producing figures to the same definition, with comparable coverage. The whole purpose of this operation, of course, is to assist in any judgement of 'burden-sharing'; hence the comparability exercise.

However, we do not know very much about what the NATO statisticians do to the figures. We do know that for a number of countries they differ widely from the national figures – but we do not have 'tables of reconciliation' which show for the individual countries the various subtractions and additions which account for these differences. Table 1.3 shows that in 1981 the NATO figures for France and Germany exceed the national figures by some 24 per cent; for Italy the excess was 31 per cent. We cannot be statistically happy when a standardised set of military expenditure figures differs from the national set by as much as 25–30 per cent and when we do not know in detail the reasons for the difference. It has been suggested, for example, that NATO includes in its estimates of Italian military expenditure some items which in other countries would be classified as internal rather than external security. Nor can we be wholly happy about the functional classification which these countries provide. We know that from time to time countries wish to conceal, either from a potential enemy, or more commonly from their own citizens, some particular area of military expenditure. For example, in the six years up to 1981 the British Government spent some £1 billion on developing a new warhead for its Polaris missiles. The student of British military statistics would not have been able to discover this fact. The only reason we know it now is that the new Conservative government found the revelation of the figure was a useful way of discomforting the Labour Party. It is just by chance that we know about this concealed item: both in Britain and in other countries, there are in all probabilities other such items of which we are unaware. Again, in

TABLE 1.3: *Comparison of estimates of military expenditure on NATO definitions, with estimates on national definitions*

Local currency in mn

	Year[a]	National	NATO	NATO as percentage of national
Belgium	1981	121 760	124 055	102
Canada	1981	5 695	6 150	108
France	1981	104 440	129 365	124
W Germany	1981	42 090	52 298	124
Greece	1981	71 250	96 975	136
Italy	1981	7 500[b]	9 850[b]	131
Luxembourg	1981	1 230	1 727	140
Netherlands	1981	11 397	11 279	99
Norway	1980	7 210	8 242	114
Portugal	1981	49 000	51 744	106
Turkey	1981	298[b]	313[b]	105
UK	1981	11 901	12 418	104
USA	1981	152[b]	168[b]	111

[a] National figures adjusted to calendar year where necessary.
[b] Billion.

Britain, the initial expenditure on developing the atomic bomb was concealed in the Civil Contingencies Fund under the subhead of 'Public Buildings in Great Britain'.

In general, our knowledge of Third World military expenditure is threadbare. We know this, both from our own revisions of the past figures, and from examination of divergences between our figures and those of the IISS and ACDA. Many countries do not distinguish between internal and external security in their budgets. There are a number of countries which do not have the practice of annual budgets for their expenditure; and many of those which do, often have a number of supplementary budgets during the year, particularly when the rate of inflation is rapid. Further, the figures for actual expenditure may, of course, be very different from the budgeted figures. There are always problems with the figures for those countries which receive military aid from many of the major powers. It is often difficult to establish whether it is included in the country's own budgeted expenditure (with a corresponding credit entry somewhere else) or whether it is excluded.

The fact of the matter is that the military expenditure of most of these countries is a research project of a significant size on its own. Further, even if the resources were there to undertake all these research projects, they would not be easy to do. It would be difficult – though not impossible – for somebody living outside the country; on the other hand, it might well be hazardous for somebody inside the country. For many of these countries, the best thing might be to find out as much as possible about some of the physical quantities – the size of the armed forces, the production of the weapons within the country, and imports or transfers of weapons from outside the country – and to build up an expenditure estimate from pricing these quantities. At least an exercise of this kind would provide a rough check on the numbers given in the budget. For many purposes an attempt to build up an expenditure estimate of this kind from the disaggregated main components, measured initially in physical terms, might be a more useful approach than the pursuit of budget numbers.

The only statements which can be made about the military expenditure of Third World countries are 'orders of magnitude' statements. It would be most unwise to try to validate any hypothesis by using the year-to-year movements of these numbers. It follows that most exercises which attempt to quantify any 'action–reaction' process in pairs of Third World countries, using military expenditure figures, are invalid. Thus we do know that there has been a massive increase since 1973 in the military expenditure of Middle East OPEC countries – we can check this from arms trade figures. We do not know with any precision the year-to-year movements in Saudi Arabia or Iran.

Thirdly, there is the vexed problem of the appropriate figures for the Soviet Union, for other Warsaw Pact countries, and for China. Here the main issue of interest to economists is the famous case of the CIA's dollar estimates of Soviet military expenditure. Since there is virtually no information to be gleaned from the Soviet Union itself, on its military expenditure – they issue just one figure in roubles, which has stayed virtually the same for a number of years now – the CIA make a vast inventory of estimates of production of a huge array of military items, including of course figures for the numbers in the armed forces; and all these items are priced at what it would cost to replicate them in the United States. This process of calculation has produced the 'expenditure gap'. The protagonists of US rearmament have made very effective use of the proposition that the Soviet Union has been outspending the United States in recent years by something of the order of 40–50 per cent.

As it stands, on its own, this is well known to be an illegitimate method of international comparison. Whenever one country's output is valued at another country's prices, the value of that output gets exaggerated. This is because any country adjusts its pattern of production to use more of the factors which are plentiful, and therefore cheap, and less of factors which are scarce, and therefore expensive. It is clear that valuing Soviet military output at US prices produces just this kind of distortion. For example, with an enormous conscript army which is paid very little, the Soviet armed forces can be profligate with the numbers of men they use. The United States uses about 75 000 men to man its strategic nuclear deterrent; the Defence Intelligence Agency calculates that the Soviet Union has approximately five times that number of men, assigned to roughly the same number of missiles, submarines, and bombers. Large numbers of Soviet troops work on construction projects or are assigned to railways or work on military farms to produce food for army mess-halls. When dollar cost of Soviet military expenditure is computed, these men are valued at the high wages paid to US servicemen.

The same problem arises of course with estimates of China's military expenditure. China has some four million men in their armed forces. They are predominantly conscripts: conscription is three years for the army, four years for the air force, and five years in the navy. If each of these members of the Chinese armed forces is valued at $16 000, which is the average pay of the members of the US armed forces, that provides a figure of $65 billion for the Chinese armed forces alone.

The proper procedure for comparing the output (or expenditure) between two countries A and B, is to value country's A output at country's B prices, and also to value country's B output at country's A prices, and then take some average of the two.

The CIA do now make some effort at a rouble comparison of Soviet and US military expenditure. However, they say that a large part of US equipment is beyond Soviet technology and cannot therefore be given an actual rouble price. As a consequence, to quote Professor Holzmann,

> the very dimension of the arms race in which America has the greatest advantage – advanced technology – and which makes most of the difference between military superiority and inferiority is enormously undervalued.[8]

This is not the only example of misuse of military expenditure calculations. Another example arises from the upward revision, by the US military intelligence services, of their calculation of the share of military expenditure in the Soviet gross national product. Up to 1975, the figure was 6–8 per cent of the GNP. One of the assumptions of this calculation was that the military procurement sector was much more efficient than the civil sector, and that consequently the price or cost of military equipment in the Soviet Union, in relation to the price of civil engineering goods, was relatively low. Since 1976, the US intelligence agencies have changed this assumption, and have decided that the rouble prices of Soviet military *matériel* were more than twice as high as they had previously assumed. They now say that Soviet military expenditure is 11–12 per cent of the GNP or even more. This does not in any way imply any upward revision of their estimate of the Soviet military effort; it was the same bundle of defence goods but with higher prices put on them. The change came from a new assumption, that the military procurement sector was not as highly productive as was previously assumed.

This change clearly implies that the Soviet Union is economically weaker, not stronger, than was previously thought. On these new figures the same military effort is more resource-consuming, and more costly, than the earlier estimates suggested. Consequently the burden on the Soviet economy of supporting this large military force is greater than was previously thought. Yet many commentators have used the figures as if they implied that the Soviet threat was much greater than was previously assumed. The most extreme example is perhaps that of Lt.-Gen. Daniel O. Graham (ret.) former director of the Defence Intelligence Agency who produced an even larger figure for the share of Soviet military spending in GNP, 20 per cent, and wrote:

> The Soviets are spending 20 per cent of their GNP on their armed forces and civil defense; Adolf Hitler's Germany was spending somewhat less – 15 per cent of GNP – for armaments just prior to the outbreak of World War II. Can the United States continue to deter the growing military threat with a grudging 5.4 per cent outlay on defense?[9]

The quotation shows this curious inability to comprehend that if country A using $5\frac{1}{2}$ per cent of its GNP is able to match the military effort of country B, which needs 20 per cent of its GNP for the same purpose, it is country A which is in the far better position.

Where were America's economists when methods of international comparison were being used in the military sector which were obviously technically inadequate? We have seen little comment from economists on this matter – with the honourable exception of Professor Holzmann. It is a good example of the way in which economists have neglected to pay attention to military sector questions.

1 PRICE COMPARISONS

It would not be very helpful to publish time series of figures of military expenditure uncorrected for inflation. However, the problem of the best method of correcting military expenditure figures for inflation raises a number of very interesting questions.

SIPRI uses consumer price indices for correcting the military expenditure figures. This is because we are doubtful about the value of using military expenditure figures as measures of relative military strength. The purpose is rather to estimate the civil opportunities which are foregone; for this purpose, the consumer price index is the right one to use. In any case, there is the compelling argument that for a large number of countries other price indices do not exist.

However, there are some purposes for which a military sector price index would be useful: and it is surprising how few countries appear to have attempted to construct a price index of this kind. There are two conceptual questions of great interest. One is the measurement of the rate of 'product improvement' in the military sector. The other is the measurement of the productivity of the average member of the armed forces.

It is a commonplace that the rate of product improvement in military hardware far exceeds the rate of product improvement in the civil sector. One way of establishing this proposition is to express military research and development expenditure as a percentage of the value of total military hardware output; and then compare this percentage with the same figure for the civil sector – that is, total research and development in the manufacturing sector, compared with the total value of manufacturing output (Table 1.4). By this measure of research intensity, the average military product is some twenty times as research-intensive as the average civil product. Another way of looking at the same phenomenon is to compare the

TABLE 1.4 *Research and development input per unit of output: civil and military sectors compared*

Country	Year	Military R&D expenditure as percentage of value of production of military equipment	R&D expenditure as percentage of value of manufacturing output
FR Germany	1975–6	32	1.9
UK	1975–6	34	1.3
USA	FY 1975	43	2.3
Japan	1975	5	1.2

SOURCES Research and development figures for the manufacturing sector are taken from *International Statistical Yearbook 1975* (Paris: OECD, March 1979). Values of gross output of the manufacturing sector are taken from *Statistical Yearbook 1978* (New York: United Nations, 1978).

Military R & D:
FR Germany *Die Wehrstruktur in der Bundesrepublik Deutschland* (Bonn: the Wehrstruktur-Kommission together with the Government of FR Germany, 1972/73).
UK *Research and Development Expenditure and Employment* (London: HMSO, 1976). Military R & D for the UK is intra-plus extra-mural gross expenditure on natural science R & D for defence.
USA 'US defence budget for fiscal year 1981', *International Defence Business*, January/February 1980.
Japan *Defence of Japan 1978* (Defense Agency, July 1978).

Military production:
FR Germany As above.
UK *Defence in the 1980s, Statement on the Defence Estimates 1980* (London: HMSO, April 1980). Production is acquisition of equipment only, plus net exports.
USA As above.
Japan As above.

Arms exports and imports:
FR Germany, USA and Japan *World Military Expenditures and Arms Transfers 1968–77* (Washington, DC, ACDA, Oct. 1979).
UK As above.

rate of increase in the costs of different types of military hardware with the general rise in prices in various countries, and to take any rise in military costs over the general price rise as representing product improvement. In Table 1.5 the comparison is made with the consumer price index. Alternatively, an output price index of the civil sector of the engineering industry could have been used. The calculation suggests an average rate of 'product improvement' varying

TABLE 1.5 Measures of 'product improvement' in the military sector[a]

Product	Cost and date	Product	Cost and date	Annual average change in cost (%)	Annual average change in consumer prices (%)	Annual rate of 'product improvement'[a] (%)
F-104 G Starfighter	DM 5.0 m 1965	Tornado MRCA	DM 40.3 m 1980	15	4	10.5
Canberra medium bomber	US $0.6 m[b] 1951	Buccaneer bomber	US $2.0 m[b] 1962	—	—	12
Hunter fighter	US $0.8 m[b] 1954	Jaguar fighter-bomber	US $4.0 m[b] 1972	—	—	9
M-47 tank	DM 0.5 m 1956	Leopard-2 tank	DM 3.8 m 1980	9	3	6
Morecambe bay frigate	£0.500 m 1949	Ariadne frigate	£7.403 m 1973	12	4	8
Defender destroyer	£2.280 m 1952	Sheffield destroyer	£26.438 m 1975	11	5	6

[a] The rate of 'product improvement' – or, more precisely, the extent to which the rate of product improvement in the military sector exceeds that in the civil sector – is roughly indicated by the extent to which the cost of military products rises faster than the cost of consumer products.
[b] At 1973 constant prices. Costs are SIPRI estimates of what it would have cost in 1973 to build the aircraft in the USA.

SOURCES *Anti-militarismus Information*, vol. 3, 1980; Kaldor, M., 'Defence Cuts and the Defence Industry', *Military Spending and Arms Cuts* (London: Croom-Helm, 1977).

between 6 and 12 per cent a year. It would be important, in any calculation of a price index for the military sector, to ensure that the product improvement in the military sector is counted as a volume and not as a price increase. This probably means that for the military hardware sector, the price index should probably be some weighted average of output prices for civil aircraft, cars, trucks, and civil electronic goods.

There is no problem in calculating the average increase in pay of the average member of the armed forces. There is, however, a problem in deciding whether or not to offset the increase in pay by any assumed increase in productivity. Countries differ in the assumptions they make about the productivity trend in their civil services. Some, like Britain, assume a nil productivity increase. Some, like France, assume the average productivity increase in the rest of the economy. The second of these assumptions seems a slightly less anti-bureaucratic assumption than the first. It is tempting to measure the increase in productivity of the average members of the armed forces, by an index showing an increase in the total quantum of lethal power available to the armed forces, divided by the increase in that number. The output of a soldier, it can be argued, is his kill-potential. Such a calculation would of course produce an astronomical increase in productivity.

There is thus no single unambiguous figure for measuring the volume increase of military expenditure: it depends on the price index used. It seems rather doubtful whether NATO defence ministers were fully appraised of these complications when they collectively set a 3 per cent volume target for the military expenditure trends in their various countries. It seems never to have been made clear what price index should be used to calculate this number. We therefore now have a welter of confusing claims. Defence ministers in NATO countries use their own national figures rather than the NATO standardised figures if this enable them to make a better case; they choose the base year which suits them best, and do not in general disclose the price index which they are using. When the NATO standardised figures are used, with consumer price indices as the deflator (which probably exaggerates the rise in the volume of real military output), we find that in NATO's Europe as a whole, the rise in military expenditure since the announcement of the 3 per cent target has been rather lower than it was in the previous four years, with only a 1 per cent volume rise on the provisional figures for 1981 (Table 1.6).

TABLE 1.6 *NATO countries: estimated volume increases in military expenditure*

Country	Per cent increases			
	'Pre-target': from 1972–4 average to 1976–8 average	*'Post-target':* from 1976–8 average to 1981	*Latest year:* from 1980 to 1981 (estimated)	*Size of military spending in relation to (USA = 100)*[a]
United States	−2.0	3.0	5.9	*100*
Canada	3.9	0.4	1.9	*3*
All NATO Europe	2.3	2.1	1.0	*74*
of which				
FR Germany	1.0	1.7	1.7	*20*
France	3.8	3.0	2.0	*18*
UK	0.3	2.3	−3.6	*16*
Italy	−0.4	4.1	0.5	*6*
Netherlands	3.4	1.3	0.6	*4*
Belgium	5.1	2.3	−0.3	*3*
Turkey	16.0	−1.4	21.1	*2*
Greece	14.4	−2.5	4.1	*2*
Denmark	3.2	1.3	0.8	*1*
Norway	4.1	2.4	1.0	*1*
Portugal	−13.5	2.5	2.4	*1*
Luxembourg	5.8	7.0	4.5	neg

Source   SIPRI *World Armaments and Disarmament – SIPRI Yearbook 1982* (London: Taylor & Francis, 1982). Appendix 5B, table 5B.2, p. 110
[a] Based on 1980 military spending figures, at 1979 prices and exchange rates.

IV STATISTICAL PICTURE OF THE WORLD WAR INDUSTRY

The main theme of this paper has been the inadequacy of our statistical picture of what is going on in the world's military sector. The main need is to improve the statistical data, and there is plenty of scope for economists and statisticians who wish to work in this field to do something to this end.

There is a great deal of scope for work on improving military expenditure estimates. We have a list of some sixty countries, each one of which could probably do with about nine months' work by someone familiar with the language of that country, looking not only at budget and expenditure figures, but also at the possibility of constructing estimates from the physical numbers of those in the armed forces, supplemented by weapons procurement estimates. It ought to be possible with a good deal of humdrum labour, to begin producing time series for world production of particular items of military hardware, by country of production. The next step would be to extend these tables to become estimates of production and trade, so that the production tables are supplemented by a trade matrix. There should first be tables with physical units of output; then prices could be added to turn them into constant price production and trade tables. Once reasonable series exist for production and trade of different types of weapons, there would be no great difficulty in constructing estimates of world stock by country, assuming a certain average life.

Tables of this kind would serve a rather different purpose from the estimates of military power whose main object is to indicate how various countries would stand in relation to each other if war broke out between them. World tables of production and trade would indicate, in a less confrontational way, the trends in weapons production. For instance, we could compare Third World production as a share of the total, and compare world growth rates in the output of various types of weapons, to see the direction which the world arms race is taking.

There is another large area of investigation in the numbers in the armed forces. The collection of these numbers has probably been quite casual up to now; an improvement does depend on researchers in various countries – or researchers familiar with the language of various countries – working to a common definition in their investigation.

So perhaps one might envisage a collective research project which would result in the publication of an annual statistical compendium of the world military sector – analogous to the annual statistical compendiums which exist of the world energy sector, or of the world agricultural sector. Obviously it would initially be much less complete that either of these: but it would at least put in one volume a collection of the statistical series which we have. And if we can get more research effort into the improvement of the statistical base, the coverage and the degree of accuracy could be improved year by year.

It should probably be possible to do more than we are now doing to exploit the interconnections between expenditure, production and trade. It ought to be possible eventually to develop more synergy between these various estimates of numbers in the military sector: for example to reconcile figures for production and trade in weapons with figures for expenditure on military hardware. Military expenditure is, after all, primarily the sum of the pay of the armed forces, purchases of hardware, and the repair and maintenance of existing capital stock. It should be possible to use the various series as checks on each other, so that eventually the figures for numbers in the armed forces, for weapons production, for trade, and for military expenditure are all compatible. This objective is, of course, a very long way off: as yet we only have a few pieces of the jigsaw which we need to put together. The great need is to work hard at putting in more pieces of the jigsaw, before we write discourses on the proportions and composition of a picture which we can hardly see.

NOTES AND REFERENCES

1. There are, of course, always problems of precise definition: in many countries, the dividing line between the military and the police is vague; and of course in many countries also there are military activities which are not included in the defence budgets.
2. SIPRI, *World Armaments and Disarmament – SIPRI Yearbook*, Annual (London: Taylor and Francis).
3. *World Military Expenditures and Arms Transfers (WMEAT) 1969–78*. US Arms Control and Disarmament Agency. (Washington: US Government Printing Office, 1980) p. 28.
4. Ibid., pp. 28–9.
5. Brzoska, M. et al., *An Assessment of Sources and Statistics of Military Expenditures and Arms Transfer Data* – Study for the UN Expert Commission on Disarmament and Development (Hamburg: IFSH, 1980) p. 50.
6. *Arms Flows to LDCs: US – Soviet Comparisons, 1974–77* (Washington: CIA National Foreign Assessment Center, 1978) p. 1.
7. Lawrence, E. and Sherwin, R., 'Understanding Arms Transfers Through Data Analysis, in Ra'anan, Pfalzgraff and Kemp (eds), *Arms Transfers to the Third World: The Military Buildup in Less Industrial Countries* (Boulder, Colorado: Westview Press, 1978) p. 92.
8. Holzmann, F. D., 'Of Dollars and Rubles', *New York Times*, 26 October 1979.
9. Graham, D. O., 'The Soviet Military Budget Controversy', *Air Force Magazine*, May 1976, p. 33.

Note on the paper by Blackaby and Ohlson by Jacques Fontanel, Centre d'Etúdes de Defense et Securíté Internationale, Grenoble
Information concerning military expenditure raises numerous controversies, not the least of which are the political implications. The Soviet proposition of a 10 per cent reduction in military expenditure by the permanent member states of the Security Council in order to aid the development of Third World countries immediately came up against the need for an internationally accepted concept of military expenditure and the institution of adequate verification procedures. The Soviet Union, however, still opposes the disclosure of detailed information in the name of military defence secrets.

The outstanding paper by Frank Blackaby and Thomas Ohlson reminds us above all of the weakness in our statistical knowledge of military expenditure and the arms trade. It exposes several inadequacies which are worth noting: the diversity of definitions, the secrecy which surrounds national defence and the technical difficulties in comparing the expenditures.

(1) The definition of military expenditure still offers a great margin of uncertainty in the use of the definition made by the various sources of information. Thus the differences which are apparent from the estimates made by NATO, USACDA and SIPRI often arise from their narrow or wide conceptions of military expenditure. Contrary to USACDA, SIPRI includes military aid, civil defence and paramilitary forces in its definition of military expenditure. It is agreed that the gap observed between these two institutions would be reduced if a standardised concept of military expenditure were used. The United Nations' Group of Experts responsible for collecting and publishing military expenditure have presented a very interesting project. Three fundamental principles have been retained:

(a) Information required of States should not be excessive.
(b) The statistics required should be fairly general and should allow a general understanding of the structure of expenditure in each country.
(c) Data should be subject to verification.

The military expenditure matrix proposed compares rows of expenditure classification (operational, purchases and construction, research and development) against columns by mission or programme (strategic forces, land forces, naval forces, air forces, military aid, etc. . . .). The countries who have agreed to complete this matrix do not appear to have encountered unsurmountable problems. It will no doubt be very interesting, after discussions with the different national and international sources of military expenditure information to have a matrix of this type applied in all publications. In this way we would avoid the gaps created by differing definitions. However, it does not follow that the notion of military expenditure can be so clearly expressed. In fact, we consider it useful to define several complementary concepts to take account of, for example, civil defence, 'mothballed' military operations, the real ability to convert civil activities to military activities. In this way a country could be analysed, not by one single indicator but by several clearly defined concepts.

As far as the arms trade is concerned, national and international statistics are often silent. Alternatively, the arms trade figures are hidden in the figures for civilian trade making their analysis very difficult. Finally, the sale of arms is normally accompanied by assorted commercial reports, the ins and outs of which are often less than clear. SIPRI calculates the trade in the most important arms only and its research, based on comparative prices, implies numerous hypotheses concerning deflation and exchange rates which are inevitable but also questionable. It is in this area of information that the Member States must concentrate their effort.

(2) The secrecy which surrounds the military sector makes every procedure of verification very difficult. Seen in the context of a reduction of military expenditure negotiated by the Member States, no country either wishes or can agree to reduce its expenditure by accepting an unlimited external control. However, several solutions could be found, if the States really accepted the idea of reducing their military expenditure, to an equivalent level of national security. Although for countries such as the Netherlands or the USA the gaps between the estimates of the different sources of information are not too large (in the order of 6 to 7 per cent), this is not the case for the majority of the Warsaw Pact countries. For example, the Soviet Union declared 17 200 million roubles military expenditure in 1979 while the CIA and China estimate the expenditure at 60 000 million and 102 000 million roubles respectively. As far as the transfer of arms is concerned, we must admit that numerous

transactions are either unknown or little known. According to SIPRI, and contrary to the USACDA estimates, the United States is the largest supplier of arms in the world, far ahead of the Soviet Union.

(3) International and historical comparisons of military expenditure are confronted with numerous technical difficulties. Specifically, the price of military materials is related to special characteristics which make the determination of an index very difficult: the rapid evolution of military technology, one-off products, product quality improvements not always accurately reflected in the prices, oligopolistic or monopsonistic markets, the absence of market prices, partial imputing of the costs of research and development.... No complete and coherent information exists relative to the evolution of military expenditure in constant currency because, in spite of the SIPRI estimates, the methods of adjustment are not sufficiently precise. Moreover, price systems vary with methods of production and their significance is therefore not directly comparable. As far as international comparisons are concerned, it is not sufficient just to use exchange rates. Purchasing power parity is undoubtedly more accurate, but it is difficult to apply without detailed information on materials, prices, and quantities. Currently, international estimates of military expenditure are very imprecise and the Member States hardly seem to concern themselves with the fact that if information is power then the absence of information is a risk. As for the question of security, this risk certainly helps feed the trade in armaments.

The chapter by Frank Blackaby and Thomas Ohlson underlines the difficulties encountered by SIPRI when trying to present a complete enough picture of military expenditure and the transfer of arms. It shows the hypotheses used and clearly indicates the inadequacies of SIPRI's estimates. However, we must admit that these figures are generally considered the most trustworthy of those currently available. This chapter raises several questions:

(1) First, econometricians are reproached for using the figures published by SIPRI. The modesty of this institute demonstrates the importance which it accords to the quality of the data collection and its wish to protect its readers and users from making hasty interpretations. What then should the econometricians do? Should they wait for data which is both precise and verifiable? If

this is the author's proposition, bearing in mind the gaps of unknownss which affect the majority of economic information, then econometricians will join the ranks of the unemployed. In our opinion, after having made extensive use of the SIPRI data, these figures should be used, even if it has to be with great caution. By preventing the analysts from remaining exclusively in the area of deductive methodology, we could avoid the development of a myriad of theories which are contradictory but at the same time all equally coherent and logical when we take account of inherent assumptions. What do you suggest?
(2) In our opinion we should look closer at the details of military expenditure. Global figures do not always give an indication of the country's military effort. A more precise analysis is required and we consider that the work conducted by The Group of Experts at the UN on Arms Expenditure Reduction should encourage SIPRI to widen as far as possible its statistical information. Could you give as complete a picture as possible of what SIPRI includes in its calculations of military expenditure?
(3) Figures in terms of stocks should certainly be included. Unfortunately, this procedure is, to say the least, delicate. Have you started work in this area?
(4) How do you obtain your statistical information? What are your sources?

This very stimulating chapter seems fairly pessimistic, because it underlines the inadequacies of certain information. In proceeding in this way, the authors emphasise that recognising that the inadequacy exists is in itself knowledge. Putting the problem this way also means preparing to resolve it. Which is a resolutely optimistic attitude.

2 A Note on the International Comparison of Military Expenditures

Jacques Fontanel
CENTRE D'ETUDES DE DEFENSE ET
SECURITE INTERNATIONALE, GRENOBLE

The comparison of military expenditures raises a number of technical, economic and political difficulties.[1] These are due to differing monetary units from one country to another, conceptual differences, secrecy, and the statistical difficulty of treating different kinds of armament on the same footing.

Comparative information about military expenditures is usually expressed in United States dollars, because of the widespread use of conversion ratios derived from exchange rates. SIPRI, NATO and USACDA base their estimates on the average annual exchange rates published by the International Monetary Fund, to eliminate short-term speculative fluctuations. Yet exchange rates have several limitations as a conversion factor in international comparisons which seriously undermine the credibility of the results obtained due to:

(1) The very large domestic sector that is not connected with international trade and is broadly independent of exchange rate trends,
(2) Changes in interest-rate differentials, and sudden capital movements attributable to international speculation,
(3) The fact that some exchange rates are set arbitrarily, mostly by countries with planned economies but also by other countries

that exercise a more or less strict control over foreign exchange,
(4) The poor credibility of official exchange rates to adjust prices in different currencies for purposes of international comparisons, because they do not reflect the currencies' internal purchasing power.

If SDRs are used the results are just as dubious, especially for non-IMF countries, because the arithmetic is still based on exchange rates.

There are other methods of analysis, of which the three most important appear to be the study of indicators, 'building blocks' and purchasing-power parities.

So far as *indicators* are concerned, it is sometimes recommended that military expenditure should be regressed on economic, financial or 'physical' variables (the latter being particularly awkward to select). But even when two groups of indicators are distinguished so as to establish an error range, the method has considerable shortcomings. Its results are dubious because the indicators evolve over time and space for no very clear or foreseeable reason, the sensitivity of the coefficients implies rigorous and accurate information, the explanatory variables must not be subject to manipulation by the public sector or by speculation, etc.

The *'building-block' method* used by the United States to ascertain and compare USSR and US military expenditures is designed to answer the question: what would it cost the United States exactly to duplicate the national security programme defined by the USSR? This comparison often leads to errors, substantially because quantities and prices are not independent of one another. To estimate the Soviet military effort in terms of US prices does not seem very realistic since if the USSR has a strong army based on men the main reason is the low cost of manpower, in contrast to manpower costs in the United States. Other problems such as military secrecy, the difficulty of 'sovietising' hardware, the technological gap and the differences in price formation make the building-block method a very awkward one to use.

The *Purchasing Power Parity method* (PPP) is especially interesting. The idea here is to express all outputs by value using a single pricing system. In principle this is no different from comparing a country's output over several different periods. The first OECD study directed by Gilbert and Kravis included 250 classes of products capable of international comparison, in 20 groups including military expenditures. Unfortunately, these expenditures have since disappeared from studies using the PPP method. This method is recommended by the UN Group of Experts on the Reduction of Military Budgets, relying on recent studies of the economic comparison of the main aggregates in national accounts. USACDA would also like to use this method, but considers that the information currently available would hardly permit this.

The International Comparison Project (ICP) funded by the UN sets out to compare the purchasing power of currencies and real GDP per capita (together with some of its components) in different countries. The outstanding work by the Kravis team has enabled three phases to be completed but there are serious political and financial difficulties with the fourth phase now under way, which seeks to analyse purchasing power parities for 77 countries, since World Bank funding has been lost while China and the USSR are refusing to participate.

For an international comparison, all military production and expenditures have to be valued according to a single pricing system. In fact, whether the comparison is over time or over space, the methodological problems are the same, though international comparisons impose additional requirements. The principle is simple: products are selected as representative for all the countries concerned, their prices in the various countries are ascertained, a weighting is chosen to be representative of the structure of the country, inter-country prices ratios are then calculated (weighted by expenditures) and economic (or military) sectors are aggregated so as to determine purchasing power parities by sector or type of expenditure.

The method is described in several publications[2] and need not be discussed further here. However, three comments should be made:

(1) There are several studies comparable to those undertaken by Kravis. For example, the EUROSTAT project sets out to establish purchasing power parities for the EEC member states, while some similar estimates have been undertaken by the CMEA and the Latin American Free Trade Area.[3] The techniques used are slightly different from those in the Kravis project, but the results are not significantly different.[4]

(2) The currency conversion index should have several properties, of which the most important are probably circularity, additivity and the quality of the weightings chosen. While comparisons of countries two by two enable the perverse effects inherent in the

choice of weightings to be limited, they offer no solution in regard to circularity. Conversely, the multilateral method permits circularity, but makes the choice of the statistical structures more difficult.

(3) The published studies can disseminate findings only after a considerable delay. Phase II of the Kravis project gives findings only for 1973 and Phase III, still awaiting publication, will give details only for 1978. Another point is that the operation is a costly one.

Finally in the military sector, there are several characteristics which make purchasing power parities especially difficult to calculate: the rapidity of technological development, absence of markets for certain military equipment, the awkward problem of unique goods, the fact that there are transfers in kind under assistance programmes, the State's position as monopolist or monopsonist in respect of a particular product etc.

The Group of Experts on the Reduction of Military Budgets considers that the PPP procedure should be retained and that involves not just the solution of formidable technical problems but also, and most of all, political will, and agreement on the methods and products to be selected. Taking account of the findings currently available for 1970 and 1973, we have applied the conversion indices which Kravis obtained for civilian products to the military sector. Two points should be noted:

(1) This method is akin to an opportunity cost analysis. It is of particular interest in connection with the implications of disarmament for development, but it hardly permits precise comparison of expenditures. The findings show the direct cost of military expenditure in respect of consumption, production or investment. So these are interesting indicators, even though they lack the precision required for international negotiations on reducing military expenditure.

(2) In view of the time necessary to calculate and publish purchasing power parities, it seems necessary to consider studying the discrepancies between the new estimates and the USACDA and SIPRI estimates, and also to show the variations from one period to another, from significant comparisons of the methods actually used.

Table 2.1 represents military expenditures (in 1973 dollars) by the ICP sample countries for the year 1970 by, respectively, the SIPRI method (ME1) the GDP PPP conversion index (ME2), by the Gov-

TABLE 2.1 *Principal methods for estimating military expenditures for 1970*

Country	ME1 (SIPRI) $(1973)	ME2 (PPP/GDP) $(1973)	ME3 (PPP/Govt Exp) $(1973)	ME4 (PPP/Public Sector indices) $(1973)	National currency
Kenya	21	37	70	69	126
India	1 949	4 818	10 131	9 950	10 840
Philippines	104	256	543	573	500
Korea	334	739	1 342	1 527	102
Colombia	121	258	406	412	1 885
Malaysia	243	392	440	461	510
Iran	959	1 716	1 569	1 352	54 120
Hungary	567	648	819	1 015	9 848
Italy	3 293	3 395	3 124	3 254	1 562
Japan	2 597	2 369	2 836	2 952	570
UK	7 673	8 149	8 952	8 783	2 444
Netherlands	1 788	1 489	1 354	1 242	3 968
Belgium	1 132	984	982	963	37 388
France	8 835	7 420	7 690	7 710	32 672
German FR	10 108	7 524	6 861	7 533	22 573
USA	89 065	77 854	77 854	77 854	77 854

ernment Expenditures index (ME3) and by the application of public sector salary and commodity indices to the structure of military expenditures (ME4).

Table 2.2 is a comparable study for 1973, adding the growth rate for military expenditures calculated as an index by SIPRI between 1970 and 1973, military expenditures in national currencies published by SIPRI for 1973, together with the military budgets index (base 1970) calculated from information published in the *UN Yearbook*.

Table 2.3 shows, from base year 1970, indices for wholesale prices, consumer prices, the real growth rate, the growth rate per capita, variations in the exchange rate and in GDP purchasing power (DPPP GDP), government expenditures (DPPP Govt Exp), salaries (DPPP Salaries) and commodities (DPPP Commodities). For the international comparison indicators, an increase in the index in fact means a reduction in the international dollar purchasing power of the local currency.

Table 2.4 shows the relationship between the PPP estimates and the SIPRI and USACDA estimates.

Table 2.5 shows the PPP value of the increase in military spending for the 16 sample countries.

Several points must be made:

(i) In all developing countries, military expenditures are constantly under-valued.
(ii) For the developed countries, depending on the PPP method used the broad results are similar or slightly upward, but there are also appreciable structural modifications. This is because while ME3 and ME4 lead generally to an over-estimate of SIPRI military expenditures, the same does not apply to ME2. Depending on the method used, either Germany or the United Kingdom rank first or second among the developed countries after the United States.
(iii) For countries such as India the results are highly divergent (a ratio of 1 to 9 between the smallest and the largest estimate).
(iv) Taking the seven leading developing countries in the tables and the other nine developed countries, the proportion of total expenditure they account for rises, depending on which method is applied, from 5.5 per cent 19.3 per cent.

Other findings could be discussed but it seems worthwhile to go further into the assumptions underlying the PPP calculations.

First, as regards using the purchasing-power parity of GDP, this

TABLE 2.2 *Principal methods for estimating military expenditures (ME) for 1973*

Country	Index Defence Budget UN 73/70	ME (SIPRI 1973) National Currency	Index (SIPRI 73/70)	ME1 (SIPRI) $1973	ME2 (PPP/GDP) $1973	ME3 (PPP/Govt Exp) $1973	ME4 (PPP/Pub Sector Indices) $1973	GDP (PPP)
Kenya	205	262	215	37	77	156	155	4 731
India	138	16 737	143	2 165	6 600	18 000	17 550	227 626
Philippines	186	1 398	280	207	603	1 320	1 685	30 283
Korea	178	181	180	456	1 128	2 000	2 160	30 782
Colombia	189	2 479	131	104	261	393	333	24 892
Malaysia	134	681	133	280	520	582	587	13 351
Iran	222	253 950	470	3 691	7 323	7 470	7 175	56 883
Hungary	125	9 489	96	547	663	968	1 630	29 128
Italy	146	2 392	153	4 107	4 736	4 345	4 750	159 953
Japan	178	924	164	3 395	3 595	3 980	4 095	432 232
UK	139	3 512	144	8 614	10 300	11 480	11 700	210 103
Netherland	141	5 465	138	1 967	1 874	1 820	1 750	56 905
Belgium	136	48 941	131	1 259	1 294	1 320	1 180	45 416
France	132	42 284	132	9 513	9 234	10 100	10 800	245 491
German FR	136	31 908	141	12 027	10 326	9 465	10 900	296 940
USA	95	78 358	101	78 358	78 358	78 358	78 358	1 302 920
Total				126 727	136 892	151 757	154 808	

TABLE 2.3 *Significant indices for the country sample 1973 compared with 1970*

Country	Wholesale price index	Consumer price index	Real growth rate	Growth rate per capita
Kenya	108	108	119	107
India	141	128	105	99
Philippines	159	128	121	111
Korea	132	131	137	130
Colombia	169	153	122	113
Malaysia	113	113	125	116
Iran	124	122	148	136
Hungary	107	108	121	120
Italy	126	123	112	109
Japan	116	124	129	124
UK	125	128	110	109
Netherlands	118	125	115	112
Belgium	116	118	117	116
France	122	120	117	114
German FR	114	119	112	110
USA	123	114	115	112

Country	Exchange rate variation	DPPP GDP	DPPP govt exp.	DPPP salaries	DPPP commodities
Kenya	98	101	93	94	96
India	103	112	87	85	104
Philippines	112	119	114	89	133
Korea	128	117	120	121	112
Colombia	130	130	137	150	85
Malaysia	79	100	101	100	107
Iran	91	110	99	96	111
Hungary	83	94	82	80	87
Italy	93	110	111	113	115
Japan	76	107	115	119	107
UK	98	113	112	119	108
Netherlands	78	109	112	113	108
Belgium	79	102	109	112	107
France	81	103	99	101	95
German FR	73	103	102	111	90
USA	100	100	100	100	100

TABLE 2.4 *Indicators of the difference between estimates by the PPP method and those published by SIPRI and USACDA 1973*

Country	SIPRI			ME4 ME (USACDA)	ME (USACDA)
	ME2	ME3	ME4		
Kenya	208	422	421	400	39
India	305	831	811	960	1 828
Philippines	291	638	814	822	205
Korea	247	439	474	334	647
Colombia	250	378	320	261	127
Malaysia	186	208	210	202	291
Iran	198	202	191	193	720
Hungary	121	177	298	123	1 321
Italy	115	106	116	121	3 934
Japan	106	111	114	104	3 857
UK	119	133	136	117	9 873
Netherlands	95	93	89	79	2 275
Belgium	103	105	94	79	1 485
France	97	106	114	111	9 687
German FR	85	79	91	83	13 079
USA	100	100	100	100	78 358
					130 726

clearly gives a somewhat oversimplified representation of opportunity costs; we should merely point out that military expenditures cost 'a little more' in international dollars than appears from the amount expressed in US dollars by the exchange rate system.

Secondly, government spending PPP is used because military expenditures are government expenditures. They can of course behave differently but since a number of procurement, allowance and salary rules are common to the military sector as well as the public sector, the results probably will not diverge unduly. This is an assumption which would be worth validating.

Lastly, the use of PPP for public spending categories applied to each country's own military spending structure enables us to estimate them still more closely.

However, these are assumptions requiring to be tested. But these results will very probably be better than those derived from exchange rates. With a view to reducing military spending, it would seem highly paradoxical and dangerous only to use the figures currently produced.

TABLE 2.5 *Trend in military expenditures from 1970 to 1973 according to estimates using the PPP method*

	IME2	IME3	IME4
Kenya	208	223	225
India	137	178	176
Philippines	236	243	294
Korea	153	149	141
Colombia	101	97	81
Malaysia	133	132	127
Iran	427	476	530
Hungary	102	118	161
Italy	139	139	146
Japan	152	140	139
UK	126	128	133
Netherlands	125	134	137
Belgium	131	134	122
France	124	131	140
German FR	137	139	145
USA	100	100	100

IME2 = Index for the trend of military expenditures based on GDP purchasing-power parity.
IME3 = Index for the trend of military expenditures based on government spending purchasing-power parity.
IME4 = Index for the trend of military expenditures based on purchasing-power parity for components of government spending.

A study of these findings shows:

(1) That the results are highly sensitive to the assumptions made. Since there can be a discrepancy of nearly 300 per cent according to the purchasing-power parity indices selected, it would be clearly undesirable to initiate a disarmament process without a technically and politically acceptable estimate of such parities in the military sector (which should preferably be defined beforehand, doubtless along the lines of the Group of Experts on the Reduction of Military Budgets).

(2) That these calculations produce substantial changes and reclassifications. Developing countries like India apparently have appreciably higher military expenditures than countries like France and Japan. With a view to creating a Disarmament Fund for Development, or when taking account of the most heavily militarily committed countries in international negotiations, these estimates could have substantial impact.

The purchasing-power parity method is costly, and produces findings only after a considerable delay. This means that it is very difficult to apply to the military sector. For the fundamental reason for wishing to compare countries' military spending can only be the express wish of the Governments to reduce such spending, though the economic analysis is in itself of considerable interest. In this case, the information appears far too late to permit straightforward negotiations. If the purpose of the comparison is to determine the military power of states, we must admit that it is not very appropriate, in view of the magnitude of non-market factors in the power relationships of countries – geographical situation, morale of the population, skills of manpower, natural riches, alliances etc.

In the circumstances it seems highly worthwhile, at least as a first approximation, to establish econometric relationships with which to obtain, over a relatively short period, a satisfactory estimate of military spending. Thus for a set date (e.g. every three years), a complete study could be undertaken in terms of purchasing-power parity for the military sector and estimates should then be made for the missing years, from a number of significant indicators or econometric equations for the military expenditure categories selected. With this in view, the inputs available for the present study are obviously very inadequate, because they are not sufficiently disaggregated and not directly applicable to the military sector. By way of a preliminary overall estimate, we have tried to determine the fundamental explanatory variables. However, since a period of three years (1970 to 1973) has been taken for calculating the indices, an estimate produced directly from the regressions calculated would produce results for 1976. Table 2.6 summarises the main econometric findings.

The regressions obtained are interesting for several reasons:

(1) They display the very limited role of exchange rates in calculating military expenditures in foreign currency (in this case the dollar). The exchange rate is never significant with a 0.05 degree of confidence.
(2) They stress the weakness of the impact of economic growth on military expenditures for the period expressed in international dollars.
(3) They indicate that the military spending index (SIPRI estimate) and the consumer price index (or the wholesale price index) off a statistically correct estimate of the military expenditures index expressed by the PPP method. We could therefore try to estimate

TABLE 2.6 *Principal econometric results*

(1) $IME2 = -0.03.ERV + 161$
     (0.03)

(2) $IME2 = 0.13.ERV - 0.57.CPI + 215.6$
     $(1.4) (2.4)$

(3) $IME2 = -0.68.ERV + 5.38.RGR - 0.19.CPI - 400.5$
     $(1.07) (1.59) (1.79)$

(4) $IME2 = 0.88.IMES - 0.1.ERV + 0.04.RGR - 0.72.CPI + 101$
     $(0.02) (0.1) (0.2) (0.16)$

(5) $IME2 = -0.46.CPI + 214$
     (1.99)

(6) $IME2 = 0.14.ERV - 0.58.CPI + 216$
     $(1.4) (2.4)$

(7) $IME2 = 0.88.IMES - 0.094.ERV - 0.73.CPI + 105$
     $(0.015) (0.09) (0.15)$

(8) $IME2 = 0.876.IMES + 7.6$
     with F = 879
     D = 0.984
     SR = 10.4
     DW = 2.4
     Value of the coefficients of the explanatory variables in this equation (*t* test)
     ERV = 2.4
     GRC = 0.09
     RGR = 0.46
     WPI = 5.7

(9) $IME2 = 0.88.IMES - 0.81.CPI + 106.2$
     $(57) (6.2)$
     with F = 1627
     D = 0.996
     SR = 5.44
     DW = 2.4
     Value of the coefficients of the explanatory variables in this equation (*t* test)
     ERV = 1.06
     GRC = 0.04
     RGR = 0.07
     WPI = 1.54

(10) $IME3 = 0.89.IMES - 0.017.ERV - 0.49.WPI + 67.8$
     $(51) (0.5) (4.1)$

(11) $IME3 = 0.98.IMES - 2.36$
     (17)

Table 2.6 continued

$$\text{with } D = 0.96$$
$$SR = 20.2$$

(12) $\quad IME3 = \underset{(19)}{0.998.IMES} - \underset{(2.1)}{0.59.WPI} + 68.4$

$$\text{with } F = 182$$
$$SR = 18$$
$$DW = 1.64$$
$$D = 0.96$$

(13) $\quad IME3 = \underset{(18.4)}{0.997.IMES} - \underset{(0.4)}{0.14.ERV} - \underset{(1.3)}{0.49.WPI} + 70$

(14) $\quad IME3 = \underset{(20)}{0.987.IMES} - \underset{(2.6)}{1.08.CPI} + 129.3$

$$\text{with } F = 208$$
$$SR = 17$$
$$DW = 2.35$$
$$D = 0.97$$

Value of the coefficients of the explanatory variables in this equation (t test)
ERV = 0.55
GRC = 1.2
RGR = 1.3
WPI = 0.04

(15) $\quad IME4 = \underset{(17.1)}{1.14.IMES} - \underset{(2.9)}{1.66.CPI} + 181.8$

$$\text{with } F = 149$$
$$SR = 23.5$$
$$DW = 2.2$$
$$D = 0.95$$

Value of the coefficients of the explanatory variables in this equation (t test)
ERV = 0.75
GRC = 0.9
RGR = 1.3
WPI = 1

Abbreviations
F = F test
DW = Durbin-Watson test
D = Coefficient of determination
SR = Standard deviation of the estimate.
Figures between brackets represent the standard deviation of the coefficients.

Continued on page 42

Table 2.6 continued

WPI = Wholesale Price Index
CPI = Consumer Price Index
RGR = Real Growth Rate
GRC = Growth Rate Per Capital
ERV = Exchange Rate Variation

IMES = Index for the increase in military expenditures from 1970 to 1973 (SIPRI)
IME2, IME3, IME4 = indices for the trend in military expenditures according to the conversion ratios used, respectively. PPP(GDP) Purchasing Power Parity for Gross Domestic Product, PPP(GE) Purchasing Power Parity for Government Expenditures, PPP(PSI) Purchasing Power Parity for Public Sector Indices.

---

military expenditures in international dollars for the different countries by taking equations (9), (14) and (15). As our calculations were based on the SIPRI national currency estimates, the explanation of the explanatory value of this variable is evident. Conversely, it is interesting to note that the price indices have a negative influence on military expenditures expressed in international dollars. This appears doubly logical at the theoretical level, in regard to inflation being taken into account mainly by the consumer price index (closer to the concept of purchasing power than the wholesale price index) and also in regard to the negative sign expressing the depreciation of the national currency in relation to the reference currency.

The standard deviations for the regressions selected are comparatively small, bearing in mind that the time interval is three years. It is therefore enough to know, for each country, the SIPRI military expenditures estimate and the wholesale price index trend to obtain an estimate of military expenditures suitable for international comparison over a very short period.

Clearly, the sample of countries is not significant and the problem of price formation in Eastern countries has not yet been broached. But studies of this type would encourage a fuller understanding of the comparative military commitment of states in the economic sphere and most important of all, would reduce the technical alibis for politicians in the crucial issue of reducing military expenditures.

NOTES AND REFERENCES

1. United Nations, *Report by the Group of Experts on the Reduction of Military Budgets*, 11 March 1982, Working Paper No. 3.
2. Kravis, I. B., Heston, A. and Summers, R., *The International Compari-

son Project Phase III, *World Product and Income: International Comparisons of Real GDP* (Johns Hopkins University Press, 1982); Kravis, I. B., Heston, A. and Summers, R., *International Comparisons of Real Product and Purchasing Power* (Johns Hopkins University Press, 1978); Kravis, I. B., Kenessey, Z., Heston, A. and Summers, R., *A System of International Comparisons of Gross Product and Purchasing Power* (Johns Hopkins University Press, 1975).
3. EUROSTAT: *Comparisons in Real Values of the Aggregates of ESA, 1975* (Luxembourg, 1978); Salazar-Carrillo, J., 'Price, Purchasing Power and Real Product Comparisons in Latin America', *Income and Wealth* (March 1973). Ivanov, Y. and Ryzhov, 'A New Stage in the Activities of the Council for Mutual Economic Assistance in the Field of International Comparisons of National Product', *Income and Wealth* (March 1978).
4. Kravis, B., Heston, A. and Summers, R., (1978), *International Comparisons of Real Product and Purchasing Power*, p. 82.

Note on the paper by Fontanel by Frank Blackaby, Stockholm International Peace Research Institute

Whenever the question arises of converting the military expenditure of one country into the currency of another country, it is important to be clear about the question which is being asked.

Sometimes such comparisons are used as proxies for military strength. They are not very good for this purpose, for a large number of reasons: differences in coverage; the difficulty of finding appropriate exchange-rates; the fact that relative prices differ considerably in different countries; the fact that money is spent on ineffective weapons; the fact that defensive preparations do not necessarily cost as much as offensive preparations; and so on. For any such study, it is important to go back to the physical quantities – the numbers in the armed forces, the stocks of major weapons and so on.

Alternatively, such comparisons can be used as measures of the total resources devoted to the military sector – for example, in a world summary table expressed in dollars. Certainly official exchange-rates are not a good way of providing a summation of this kind – as Professor Fontanel's paper shows, this leads to an understatement of the resources devoted to military expenditure in Third World countries.

However, there is a difficulty in the use of purchasing power parities derived from comparative studies of national product in general, or of consumers' expenditure, or of government expenditure. The pattern of military expenditure – and in particular the pattern of relative prices in the military sector – can be very different from that of other kinds of expenditure; this is particularly the case when there is any form of conscription, by which military manpower is obtained at very low rates of pay. This does suggest that, if purchasing power parities are to be used, ideally special parities should be calculated for the military sector.

In order to make such a calculation, it is probably necessary to get a number of physical series – such as the numbers in the armed forces, information on imports of military hardware, and so on. Thus one returns again to the point that more information is needed about the physical quantities involved in military expenditure.

ON MEASURING THE OUTPUT OF THE MILITARY SECTOR

There was some discussion about measuring the output of the military sector. The question was raised whether there was any meaningful measure of output. For Government expenditure on health or education, output measures are conceivable: there are various indicators of the health of a nation, and also of a nation's state of education. It is true that such measures of output of these sectors are as yet relatively undeveloped: certain indicators – such as infant mortality in the health field – are often used, but aggregate indices of the improvement or worsening of the average state of health are not generally available. It is, however, possible to conceive of such aggregate measures. For military expenditure, it is very difficult to conceive of any output measure. The object of military expenditure is presumably primarily security from attack by another country. This is something which cannot be measured.

Those who argue along these lines conclude that it is therefore inappropriate to look for specific price indices for the military sector. The only appropriate use of military expenditure is as a measure of the cost to the nation of providing the military establishment which the country chooses to have; and the proper measure of cost is that of opportunity cost – the alternative output which is forgone because of the regrettable necessity of having armed forces. This is best measured by using either a consumer price index or a gross domestic product price index to deflate the military expenditure series – indicating the loss of consumer goods and services, or alternatively of total national output, which results from the military budget.

The contrary argument points to the fact that – although conceptually there may be output indices for other forms of Government spending such as health and education – in fact they do not exist. Yet purchasing power parity comparisons have been made for these sectors, as between different countries. Thus, for example, comparisons are made of health expenditure in the Soviet Union and the United States. When health expenditures in the two countries are valued in roubles, the USSR/USA ratio in 1976 was calculated at 0.256. When they were measured in dollars, then the ratio was calculated at 0.814.[1] It is possible from an average of these two figures, to derive a comparison of US and Soviet expenditure on health which has certainly not been generally decided as meaningless.

In the same way, comparisons can be constructed between the military expenditure of countries which are not wholly meaningless, according to this line of argument. However, the comparisons do require a great deal of knowledge of physical quantities in the countries compared – so that the physical military inputs are priced at the price structures of both country A and country B (as in the case of a comparison of health expenditure between the United States and the Soviet Union), and some average is then taken of these two figures.

However, these are very complex exercises. Since the physical information about quantities has to be obtained before comparisons of this kind can be constructed, the question does arise how far the conversion of these numbers into an aggregate expenditure figure which can be compared with that of another country does in fact add to the information provided by the physical series – numbers in the armed forces, production of tanks, etc. – on which the expenditure comparisons are based.

REFERENCE

1. Edwards, I., Hughes, M. and Noren, J. 'US & USSR: Comparisons of GNP', in *Soviet Economy in a Time of Change*, Vol. 1 (Jt Econ. Comm., Congress of the United States, Washington 10 Oct. 1979) p. 378.

3 Quantitative and Causal Analysis of Military Expenditures

Louis Pilandon
UNIVERSITY OF CLERMONT FERRAND II

I INTRODUCTION

Recent political events within the international community which have led to armed conflicts display the ever-increasing share of resources that states are devoting to military expenditure.

Although the conflicts are localised geographically, they bear witness to the persisting and increasing tensions on this planet. No area escapes the process, whose acceleration confronts the international community with numerous and serious problems.

Economic thinking, having long ignored this aspect of man's activity, now includes it within the analytical purview for study in the same way as the other public expenditure such as health, education etc.

The present paper accordingly sets out to make a simple contribution to the discussion which has to precede any advance in scientific understanding. Opinions in this paper commit only its author.

The author has other studies under way into the relationships between military expenditures per head and other variables, such as the kind of political regime (military or parliamentary), the economic system (market economy or centrally planned), whether the country is an island or continental, aid received or given, research and development, budget deficit or surplus etc.[1]

The data[2] include population statistics, SIPRI military expenditures per capita, GDP per capita, GDP growth rates, external debt, the rate of inflation and foreign trade.

Although the year 1979 is the statistical basis for this study, the author proposes to test these relationships over a longer chronological series (20 years).

The statistical methods used are essentially:[3] The coefficient of correlation, simple or multiple; the ordinary method of least squares, analysis of variance and standard deviation, the Student and Snedecor-F tests and the Durbin and Watson test.

The analysis, carried out as a first approach, at worldwide level, and then the global division between developed and developing countries showed the disadvantage of having excessively wide groupings in levelling the deviations within the series.

It thus appeared necessary to regroup the countries concerned into geostrategic areas that are the most meaningful so far as regards military expenditures. We therefore distinguished:

(i) Atlantic Alliance (referred to here as NATO and including France although France, while remaining within the Alliance, is not a member of the integrated military organisation).
(ii) Warsaw Pact.
(iii) Rest of Europe (including Albania and Yugoslavia which are not members of alliances).
(iv) Middle East, together with North Africa (Morocco, Algeria, Tunisia, Libya).
(v) Asia, together with Oceania (Australia and New Zealand).
(vi) Latin America from the Rio Grande to Tierra del Fuego.
(vii) Black or Sub-Saharan Africa.

In view of the importance of the 'leader' countries (US and USSR) within their respective groups, it seemed necessary to isolate them first and then reincorporate them, in the interests of better, more accurate findings.

Analysis of the findings obtained from the documents available often required allowing for data at the level of sub-groups or even single countries in the interests of better understanding.

In the sections which follow a number of possible relationships are tested for each of the groups of countries defined above.

II MILITARY EXPENDITURES PER HEAD RELATED TO POPULATION DENSITY

Among the variables likely to affect and thereby explain military expenditures, size of population is certainly the one to be checked first.

Its impact and weight have often been decisive in history (e.g. France versus a Europe in coalition during the French revolution) because this determined how many combatants a government could mobilise. It was also the population which had to and still has to pay the taxes to cover military spending. It is a matter of some interest to a country, even a developing country, from the defence standpoint whether its population is larger or smaller. Taking Brazil and China as examples, suppose they both decided to make an identical extra commitment of $100 million, this would require a levy of 1 dollar per head in Brazil but the same sum would be spread over a group of ten persons in China.

However, we considered that it would be interesting to go further and relate size of population to distribution in terms of kilometric density, to try to ascertain the coefficient of correlation between military expenditures per head and population density.

NATO

As regards the Atlantic Alliance group, i.e. NATO (including France), the coefficients of correlation are not absolutely significant because their value is 0.24 for the group excluding the United States and 0.16 when the United States is included.

These values are all the more expressive in that the probability of deviation according to the Snedecor-F test is under 1 per cent.

It can be concluded, then, that the level of military spending is not linked to population/territory distribution in NATO countries.

REST OF EUROPE

A similar conclusion can be drawn from the results for the second group, 'Rest of Europe', which includes not only the other market-economy European countries but also two centrally planned economy states outside the Warsaw Pact, Yugoslavia and Albania.

The coefficient of correlation, of opposite sign (−0.043) can be regarded as definitely significant, since the probability of its being higher under the Snedecor-F test is less than 1 per cent (0.009).

So for this group of states, level of military spending appears wholly unrelated to population in terms of the head/km^2 indicator. The appearance of a negative value could not, in this case, indicate an inverse relationship between the two variables concerned.

Interpretation of the values obtained for the Warsaw Pact group can be associated with the above conclusions.

WARSAW PACT

The correlation for the series (USSR excluded) with a value of 0.306 is not significant. The Snedecor-F probability of its being higher is well under 1 per cent (0.414) and therefore good.

Including the USSR, very much the leading state in terms of spending per head, size of population and area, leads to a negative correlation of –0.54. This can be explained not only from the previous comments, i.e. the scale of the magnitudes in comparison to all the others, but also by the fact that the USSR has by far the lowest density of population of any of the states in the group.

There can be no doubt that the latter is responsible for reversing the sign. The reliability of the ratio is good, since the Snedecor-F probability of deviation is under 5 per cent (2.13).

MIDDLE EAST

The Middle East, with which North Africa (Morocco, Algeria, Tunisia and Libya) is associated, presents the unusual feature of a fairly high positive coefficient of correlation (0.73). This is a reliable result since according to the Student test, the probability of deviation is under 1 per cent (3.465).

This finding is so completely contradictory to its predecessors, that some explanation for it is worth seeking. Is it a special case, exceptional, accidental even, or is it the outcome of a conscious, deliberate decision, though hard to imagine, on the part of the authorities in the countries concerned?

No one answer can be wholly satisfactory in view of the diversity of situations in each state, but in the absence of any rational explanation it must be assumed provisionally to be accidental.

ASIA AND OCEANIA

Trends for this group are similar to the others apart from the Middle East, since the coefficient of correlation between the same variables has the negative value of –0.084. This result is also very reliable, with a Snedecor-F probability of being higher of under 1 per cent (0.092).

Thus the level of military spending per head presents no visible link with the theoretical spatial distribution of population for these countries. The military commitment is therefore independent of the kilometric population density variable.

LATIN AMERICA

For this geographical zone the overall situation noted above applies. The (linear) coefficient of correlation also has a negative value here (−0.25) showing an inverse trend relationship but of too low a value to be expressive. The Snedecor-F probability of deviation is under 5 per cent (1.347) which means that the result is reliable.

NORTH AFRICA (SUB-SAHARAN)

This group, the last, confirms the absence of any link between military spending per head and density per kilometre.

The coefficient of correlation (−0.34) shows that the military spending level is not linked with population density and that if there were such a link it would be inverse.

Here too the finding is very reliable since the Snedecor-F probability of deviation is less than 1 per cent (2.13).

CONCLUSION

With the exception of the Middle East, for which the explanatory factors do not appear clearly, it can now be asserted that there is no direct, and therefore causal link between the population represented here by density, i.e. spatial distribution, and military spending per head for the various groups of states considered. The reliability of the results obtained would not rule out a reworking of this study for other aspects and variables.

III MILITARY SPENDING PER HEAD RELATED TO GDP PER HEAD

Is the level of resources a determining factor in the level of military spending?

The study using 1979 data offers precise answers to this, based on different results for each of the groups considered.

NATO

The correlation for the two macroeconomic variables, namely military spending per head and GDP per head, for NATO excluding the

USA has a significant value (0.58). That value is reliable since according to both the Student test and the Snedecor-F test the probability of deviation is less than 5 per cent.

When the United States is included the results are reinforced with a coefficient of correlation of 0.61 while the Student probability of deviation is 2 per cent and the Snedecor-F probability 1 per cent.

These results should come as no surprise because evidence has already been found in earlier research[4] of the close relationship between output and military spending over a long period (1961–77), for the world as a whole and for the year 1976. The present study thus confirms the continuity of the ratio, while the difference in value of the coefficients with or without the United States reinforces the hypothesis advanced in earlier work to the effect that members of the Alliance other than the United States have linked up their defence effort to their resources less well, as a result of what I have called the 'protection effect' provided by the United States – a higher relative commitment but one which is more commensurate with their wealth.

REST OF EUROPE

The coefficient of correlation here is higher than for the NATO group (0.77). The result is therefore definitely significant and very reliable (the probability of its being higher is 2 per cent according to the Student test (2.681) and under 5 per cent according to the Snedecor-F test (7.21).

So although this group is composed of disparate economic systems, the combination of states displays a commitment that is more closely linked to its economic resources than the NATO group with the 'protection effect', i.e. superior protection at less cost.

WARSAW PACT

As for NATO, it is interesting to compare the correlation with and without the USSR.

With the USSR, the correlation between the two variables concerned is definitely significant at 0.67, with a Student probability of deviation, however, at under 10 per cent (1.84) and a Snedecor-F probability of less than 5 per cent (3.40). It can therefore be assumed to be reliable.

Including the USSR lowers the correlation figure to 0.62 but it is still significant and reliable, the Student probability of its being higher is 10 per cent (1.8) and less than 5 per cent according to Snedecor-F (3.27).

Although reliability is identical in both cases, the slight variation in the decline of the coefficient of correlation can be explained by the fact that the main partner in the group, the USSR, makes a commitment less commensurate with its resources than the others. In a regression line graph the point representing the USSR shifts appreciably upwards of the y/x line (where x is GNP per head and y is military spending per head) and is responsible for the nearly vertical inclination of the x/y line.

MIDDLE EAST

For this group the coefficient of correlation is one of the lowest in the series (0.46) and at under 0.50 is no longer even significant. However, the result is not very reliable, with a 10 per cent (1.63) probability of being higher according to the Student test, though better, since less than 5 per cent (2.68) according to the Snedecor-F test. The explanation for the low correlation may lie in the high value of military spending *vis-à-vis* resources, this being an area of continuous conflict, latent or open, for decades.

ASIA AND OCEANIA

Although this group is as vast as it is disparate (including China, Japan, Australia, New Zealand, India etc.) the coefficient of correlation found (0.79) was highly significant, especially since its reliability is excellent, the probability of its being higher is under 1‰ (4.73) according to the Student test and under 1 per cent (22.34) according to the Snedecor-F test. For this zone the link between the two macroeconomic variables taken into account is therefore very good, corroborating previous calculations covering other periods.

LATIN AMERICA

This is the group with the lowest coefficient of correlation of the series, 0.45, and therefore the least significant being under 0.50. The reliability of the result is, however, very good since the probability of its being higher is 2 per cent according to the Student test (2.23) and less than 5 per cent for the Snedecor-F test (4.98).

So low a coefficient must be explained mainly in terms of insularity, the isolation of the continent and the fact that armed confrontations are relatively rare and limited, thus accounting for the low expenditure per head. For this is the group with the lowest world average, though signs of higher spending are becoming increasingly apparent both in Central America and in South America (Cuba, Nicaragua, Argentina etc.).

Also, the link between military resources and expenditure has not always been established, to the detriment of the latter.

BLACK AFRICA (SUB-SAHARAN)

While Latin America had the lowest coefficient of the series, Black Africa presents the inverse position since at 0.92, the result is the best encountered up to now. Reliability is very good since according to the Snedecor-F test the probability of deviation is of the order of 1 per cent (92.58). Harmonisation with the reference variables can therefore be regarded as having been achieved for the group as a whole, but the situation there remains unstable and considerable variations can be recorded.

IV MILITARY SPENDING PER HEAD RELATED TO INDEBTEDNESS PER HEAD

These two macroeconomic variables will be studied only for the country groups of the Warsaw Pact, the Middle East, Asia, Oceania, Latin America and Africa.

The developed, market economy countries will not be considered, on statistical documentation grounds. Since the statistics do not present the same definitional criteria as the other zones considered for obvious reasons of comparability, we have stayed with those presenting the same identity characters.

Our few attempts to deal with NATO and the Rest of Europe show no significant relationship, but in future work it is planned to introduce development aid as a factor susceptible to being correlated with military spending.

So these are partial, though on the whole significant results for this series.

THE WARSAW PACT

For the countries combined, excluding the USSR, the correlation appears significant with a coefficient of 0.58. However, the reliability is mediocre, since the probability of being exceeded is over 5 per cent according to the Snedecor-F test (2.077) and 20 per cent (1.44) according to the Student test.

Including the USSR completely changes the coefficient of correlation which then has a non-significant value (0.08) and its reliability is practically nil since the probability of exceeding is between 80 and 90 per cent according to the Student test (0.195) and outside the distribution table according to the Snedecor-F test (0.038).

The constant distortion is perhaps explained by the disproportion between the very large-scale commitment of the USSR to military spending and the low level of its indebtedness, which is much higher in the other Warsaw Pact countries whereas military outlays per head are lower. But the limited reliability of the findings for the Warsaw Pact as a whole permit us to take the explanation no further.

MIDDLE EAST AND NORTH AFRICA

The findings for this group of countries reflect an altogether contrary picture.

The coefficient of correlation is perfectly significant (0.61) thus proving the link at this level between the two macroeconomic variables concerned. The reliability of this result is attested by the low probabilities of deviation, 2 per cent according to the Student test (2.48) and only 1 per cent for the Snedecor-F test (6.161).

It is thus established that there may be a link for this group of countries between indebtedness per head and military spending per head.

ASIA AND OCEANIA

The coefficient of correlation found (−0.10) allows of no conclusion other than that the two macroeconomic variables are independent of one another for this geographical area. However, reliability appears to be excellent, with Snedecor-F probabilities of deviation under 1 per cent (0.156).

The diversity of situation for such countries as Japan, Australia, China etc. is certainly responsible for the impossibility of finding a significant coefficient. A more detailed study for a more restricted group of countries should be undertaken to be able to draw acceptable conclusions.

LATIN AMERICA

As for Asia and Oceania, the coefficient of correlation obtained from comparison of the two variables can by no means be regarded as significant (0.07). It is, however, reasonably reliable since according to the Snedecor-F test its probability of deviation is less than 1 per cent (0.121).

This situation can only be interpreted in terms of the facts, i.e. the very wide distance between the relatively high indebtedness per head and the low level of military spending per head.

BLACK AFRICA

Of all the components studied in the series, Black Africa has the most significant coefficient of correlation (0.96) between the two variables. This can be regarded as reliable since its probability of deviation is 5 per cent (222.45) according to the Snedecor-F test.

Thus Black Africa associates level of indebtedness and level of military spending but as correlation does not necessarily imply causality it is not possible to establish the hypothesis that the countries resort to indebtedness to finance military spending. Although the variables are linked, they do not necessarily explain one another.

V MILITARY SPENDING PER HEAD RELATED TO FOREIGN TRADE PER HEAD

Is the level of military spending associated with the degree to which the economy is open to foreign trade?

NATO

For NATO excluding the USA the relationship is not at all significant (−0.02) but the reliability of the finding is high since the probability of deviation is under 1 per cent according to the Snedecor-F test (0.004).

Including the United States makes no difference since the correlation is –0.06 and the Snedecor-F probability of deviation is under 1 per cent (0.04).

It can thus be concluded for this group from these observations that there is no correlation and hence no relationship between military spending per head and foreign trade per head. The trends for the two variables are independent of one another even though these countries are the leaders in international trade.

REST OF EUROPE

The relationship appears more evident for the two variables since the coefficient of correlation has a significant value (0.52). But this must be treated with considerable caution because the result is unreliable, with a Student test probability of deviation of over 20 per cent. No formal conclusion can be drawn from this observation for this group of States.

WARSAW PACT

For the combined Warsaw Pact countries (excluding the USSR) the relationship concerned appears highly significant since the coefficient of correlation amounts to 0.83. The figure can be regarded as highly reliable since the probability of deviation is under 2 per cent according to the Student test and 1 per cent for the Snedecor-F test.

It seems that the relatively modest level of military spending per head (compared with the USSR) and the greater openness of these economies to international trade are responsible for these findings.

Inclusion of the USSR completely transforms the findings. The coefficient of correlation takes a non-significant and negative value (–0.10) although still reliable, under 1 per cent (0.05) according to the Snedecor-F test.

The high level of military spending per head of the USSR and the low level of foreign trade per head are possible explanations for the spectacular change in the link between the variables.

MIDDLE EAST AND NORTH AFRICA

The coefficient of correlation for this group of countries has no significant value (0.27). However, the figure is reliable since the probability of deviation is under 1 per cent according to the Snedecor-F test (0.820).

This is undoubtedly due to the diversity of the situations of the countries and especially to the energy exports of some within the group. Hence there is no directly measurable link between volume of military spending and foreign trade per head for this group.

ASIA AND OCEANIA

For this geographical area the coefficient is very significant (0.82). The figure can be regarded as highly reliable since the probability of deviation is under 1 per cent according to the Snedecor-F test (28.47) and even 1‰ according to the Student test (5.33).

The fact that this group includes countries with well developed foreign trade (Japan, Australia, New Zealand, Singapore, South Korea etc.) and with generally modest military outlays offsets the opposite situation in such countries as Taiwan, Malaysia, the countries of Indo-China and Pakistan etc.

It is very difficult to go further in the interpretation of these data but military outlays, represented in a good many countries in the area by imports of arms and even, for some, by exports, seem to integrate well within the overall level of trade.

LATIN AMERICA

The relationship between military spending and foreign trade per head only just attains the threshold of significance with the coefficient of correlation equal to 0.50. The validity of this figure is very good since the probability of deviation is under 2 per cent according to the Student test (2.578) and 1 per cent according to the Snedecor-F test.

The correlation is low because of the geostrategic position of these countries, which allows low military outlays per head in comparison with a larger foreign trade per head by value. So the latter cannot play a determining role in the formation of military spending for this region.

BLACK AFRICA (SUB-SAHARAN)

Of all the regions considered Africa again presents the highest correlation of the series (0.96). According to the Snedecor-F test the probability of deviation is 5 per cent (230.00) representing a highly acceptable reliability.

This very remarkable finding is due to the fact that mililtary outlays depend, so far as equipment is concerned, on foreign trade and are therefore influenced by profits earned or credits made available (see results of the previous correlation for indebtedness).

It is in Black Africa that the smallest number of countries is found with armaments industries of their own as compared with other groups in this study. Foreign trade is therefore the main means of acquiring equipment and is therefore a decisive factor in military outlays for this region.

VI MILITARY EXPENDITURE PER HEAD RELATED TO PREVIOUS VARIABLES COMBINED

Having looked at each variable separately, it may be interesting and instructive to group the four elements and compare them with military spending per head within the same groups.

For NATO and the Rest of Europe only three variables are considered since indebtedness is not taken into account for the reasons mentioned.

NATO

Whether or not the United States is included, the correlation is a highly significant 0.82 in the first case and 0.83 in the second.

The figures are also very reliable since the probability of deviation is under 1 per cent according to the Snedecor-F test in both cases (4.31 and 5.16). It can also be noted that including the United States strengthens the value of the correlation.

Relating this to the coefficients for each variable, only one of which could be regarded as significant, it is interesting to note the appearance of a synergistic effect as an explanatory factor for military expenditures.

REST OF EUROPE

The same lesson as for NATO can be drawn from the coefficient of correlation for the three variables together, since the value is 0.83. The probability of deviation here is higher than for the previous group according to the Snedecor-F test since it exceeds 5 per cent

(1.133). Nevertheless, the additivity effect is still notable in comparison with the much less significant findings for each individual variable.

WARSAW PACT

The findings obtained for the four variables feature remarkable values (0.98) with or without the USSR. Reliability is excellent since in both cases the Snedecor-F probability of deviation is under 1 per cent. In this case too, regrouping the variables, which results in an almost perfect correlation (the best of the series) highlights the synergy effect from the combined variables related to military spending.

MIDDLE EAST

As for the groups studied so far, the correlation is much higher than for the same indicators taken individually (0.96) and the probability of deviation according to the Snedecor-F test is under 1 per cent (23.32) so the reliability is excellent. This confirms the synergy effect already encountered.

ASIA OCEANIA

The points made about the other groups are endorsed by the findings for this one (0.84) for the coefficient of correlation with a Snedecor-F probability of deviation of 1 per cent (6.12). The additivity effect appears in the new values though with a smaller margin than in previous instances.

LATIN AMERICA

Another appreciable advance in the value of the coefficient of correlation (0.70) with a good level of reliability (less than 5 per cent probability of deviation according to the Snedecor-F test (3.95). This advance has to be explained in terms of the additivity effect, just as for Black Africa.

BLACK AFRICA (SUB-SAHARAN)

The high value (0.97) of the multiple coefficient of correlation is not surprising since, apart from population, the previous values were the highest in each series.

The reliability is excellent since the Snedecor-F probability of deviation is of the order of 1 per cent.

In seeking a causal explanation of military spending, the specific study of each variable according to the groups defined may be more or less indicative of the role played by each.

But the result of combining all the macroeconomic variables together highlights a synergistic effect owing to their being associated. It allows us to confirm the multicausal nature of military spending whatever group of countries is considered.

VII PERCENTAGE MILITARY EXPENDITURE OF GDP RELATED TO RATES OF INFLATION

As part of this research, still for the year 1979, it seemed interesting to test the relationship often mentioned between military spending and inflation, or military spending and economic growth.

For this purpose we have taken as representative variables the percentage of GDP allocated to defence, and the rates of inflation and of growth for 1979 for the same groups of countries.

NATO

Neither of the two coefficients, with or without the United States, proved significant (0.37 and 0.43). The coefficient incorporating the United States is even slightly weaker. The weakness remains important since it is equal, in the first case, to a Snedecor-F probability of deviation of 5 per cent and of 1 per cent in the second. It is therefore possible to state that the relationship which might unite these two variables is not apparent for the developed market-economy countries.

REST OF EUROPE

The coefficient of correlation of 0.57 shows that there is a link between the two variables. The Snedecor-F probability of deviation is 5 per cent so reliability can be considered good.

This situation may be explained in terms of previous findings showing that military outlays are linked in level to the existing economic potential. These are the countries with the lowest inflation rates, Yugoslavia apart. A tentative explanation for the link encountered may therefore lie in the integration of defence policies in economic policies.

WARSAW PACT

The difficulty of obtaining information about the measurement of inflation in these countries allows no formal conclusions to be drawn from the findings.

With or without the USSR the coefficients of correlation have no significant value (–0.27 and –0.03) although reliability is excellent with a Snedecor-F probability of deviation at 1 per cent (0.41–0.004).

MIDDLE EAST, NORTH AFRICA

The correlation here is significant (0.69) and reliable with a Snedecor-F probability of deviation of 1 per cent (9.26).

The explanation may lie in the increase of resources these countries are enjoying, enabling them both to increase military spending, a process already noted, and to provoke higher domestic inflation for causes of their own outside the scope of the present study.

ASIA, OCEANIA

The negative value of the correlation (0.25) is in no way significant although its reliability is good with a Snedecor-F probability of deviation of 1 per cent.

LATIN AMERICA AND AFRICA

As for the previous group (–0.11 for Latin America, –0.008 for Africa). Reliability is also identical (1 per cent Snedecor-F probability of deviation (0.26) (0.001).

The overall conclusion to be drawn from this review is that there are no evident, consistent links between rate of inflation and proportion of domestic product allocated to military spending. Investigations using the same procedures, but covering the long term and considering the same country groups are currently in hand and may provide material endorsing or impugning this first approach.

VIII PERCENTAGE MILITARY EXPENDITURE OF GDP RELATED TO GROWTH RATE OF GDP

It appeared interesting to compare these two basic variables to measure the relationship if any between the growth in the resources of a group of countries and their use for military expenditures.

NATO

With and without the United States, coefficients of correlation are negative and not significant (–0.44 with and –0.52 without). Although the Snedecor-F probability of deviation is 5 per cent and therefore acceptable in both cases it is impossible to conclude that there is any link between these two variables.

REST OF EUROPE

Conclusions are the same as for NATO, because the coefficient of correlation is positive but not significant (0.34). Snedecor-F probability of deviation is 1 per cent, so the figure is highly reliable.

WARSAW PACT

The coefficients of correlation are not significant (0.44 without the USSR, 0.13 with). So there is no relationship, contrary to what might be expected from centrally planned economies between growth of product and of the share allocated to defence. Equivalent data studied over a long period may perhaps reveal other aspects.

The findings are reliable since in both cases the Snedecor-F probability of deviation is of the order of 1 per cent (0.979 – 0.090).

LATIN AMERICA

There is no relationship in this group since the coefficient of correlation between the two variables is 0.04 with very good reliability (1 per cent Snedecor-F probability).

BLACK AFRICA

The coefficient of correlation for this group could be almost significant inversely (–0.62) proving that the military spending effort can be opposite to or at least very different from the growth in domestic product.

The finding is very reliable with a Snedecor-F probability of the order of only 1 per cent.

In conclusion it can be stated, subject to later detailed studies over longer periods, that there are no direct links between percentage of GDP allocated to defence and growth in GDP. The two variables evolve quite independently from one another.

IX SUMMARY AND CONCLUSIONS

The attempt to identify causality from a quantitative analysis of military spending per head associated with other macroeconomic variables – GDP, indebtedness, foreign trade per head – for the year 1979 highlights several new findings.

A comprehensive study at world level does not allow us to distinguish original behaviour patterns, hence the need and the value of distributing countries by geostrategic zones or clearly defined alliance systems.

Seven groups provided the framework for the study:

The Atlantic Alliance, NATO (with and without the USA).
The Warsaw Pact (with and without the USSR).
Other European non-NATO countries.
The Middle East, and North Africa.
Asia and Oceania.
Latin America.
Black or Sub-Saharan Africa.

The method chosen was based on the study of coefficients of correlation between the variables in pairs, checking the results for reliability by the Student test or Snedecor-F test or both together. The Durbin and Watson test proved that residues were behaving normally. Table 3.1 summarises the correlations found.

The first relationship studied was between military spending per head and population density in the countries grouped as above.

For all groups but the Middle East, there was no significant correlation and the results presented a very acceptable degree of reliability. Population level, therefore, cannot be an explanatory factor for military spending. The fact that the Middle East was an

TABLE 3.1 Summary of correlations for each relationship tested

Zone or alliance	MS/H and Population density Correlation[a]	MS/H and GDP/H Correlation[a]	MS/H and Indebtedness/H Correlation[a]	MS/H and Foreign trade/H Correlation[a]	MS/H and Four variables combined Correlation[a]	Percent GDP Defence percent inflation Correlation[a]	Percent GDP or Defence and % ΔGDP Correlation[a]
NATO							
Without USA	0.249	0.589	no data	−0.021	0.827	0.431	−0.449
With USA	0.166	0.613	no data	−0.062	0.835	0.371	−0.525
Rest of Europe	0.044	0.775	no data	0.529	0.833	0.573	0.345
Warsaw Pact							
Without USSR	0.306	0.678	0.585	0.840	0.988	−0.034	0.443
With USSR	−0.546	0.629	0.087	−0.101	0.985	−0.278	0.133
Middle East North Africa	0.739	0.460	0.617	0.275	0.964	0.693	−0.238
Asia and Australia, New Zealand	−0.084	0.795	−0.109	0.829	0.843	−0.254	0.282
Latin America	−0.257	0.456	0.080	0.509	0.705	−0.118	0.042
Black Africa (Sub-Saharan)	−0.343	0.923	0.966	0.967	0.975	−0.008	−0.653

Notes and abbreviations:
MS = military spending. GDP = Gross Domestic Product. /H = per head. %Δ = percentage growth.

[a]Correct to three decimal places.

exception calls for a further study to confirm or invalidate this finding and draw explanatory conclusions.

The different studies of the relationship between GDP per head and military spending per head carried out previously for other periods[5] are confirmed in their conclusions by the findings for 1979.

Although links are found between the two macroeconomic variables, their intensity varies from group to group. Barely significant correlations for the Middle East and Latin America contrast with those for all the others of which some, such as the Rest of Europe, Asia and especially Africa, show indisputable links. These latter are proved by the high value of the findings and their good reliability.

Anomalies or exceptions are due to specially low military spending per head compared with resources, as for Latin America, or to particularly high availability of resources compared with which military spending per head, though high in absolute terms, remains lower than the potential would allow. This applies to the developed market-economy countries. Thus, overall military spending per head for the great majority of states in the world is more or less directly linked with the amount of resources available to the country concerned.

The study of indebtedness per head as against military spending per head showed highly significant correlations for the Middle East, North Africa and Black Africa and also for the Warsaw Pact without the USSR, though including the USSR meant that neither the Warsaw Pact, nor Asia nor Latin America showed any measurable link.

The lack of measurements for the countries of NATO and the Rest of Europe do not influence the general behaviour, the fragmentary indications in the author's possession tend to suggest that there is no correlation. These observations are highly reliable according to the procedures already used.

Indebtedness and foreign trade often have common points, which was why it seemed interesting to compare foreign trade and military spending per head.

Whereas NATO, with and without the United States, showed negative, non-significant correlations, as did the Warsaw Pact including the USSR, while the Middle East with North Africa showed too small a value to prove a link, all the other zones deserve a closer examination.

Their coefficients were significant and reliable after testing, showing that there is a more or less important link between the two variables. It is then possible to suggest an explanation: for Rest of Europe, the Warsaw Pact without the USSR, Asia–Oceania and Africa, all groups of countries in which armament industries are disparate, incomplete and in some cases non-existent, foreign trade is one of the channels for equipment and, consequently, for spending.

Further research will be undertaken to look more closely at indebtedness and foreign trade. This will be concerned in particular with the origin of the indebtedness, particularly for the developing countries. Its bilateral or multilateral character will be interesting to ascertain and interpret.

The regrouping of the macroeconomic variables considered thus far, related overall to military spending, presents high or very high coefficients of correlation which are thus entirely significant. Since their reliability has been tested too, we can confirm that combining them produces a synergistic effect or additivity for all the groups distinguished, and this is worth emphasising.

This is further proof that the share of national product allocated to military spending depends on a bundle of factors whose totality still remains to be defined and measured. It can be regarded as certain that national product (i.e. wealth), indebtedness and foreign trade together but with unequal weight, play a determining role in the level of states' military spending.

Considering what share of national product each state allocates to military spending and the rate of inflation for the same year, 1979, it has been established that the link between the two variables is very weak, or even non-existent, with only two groups – Rest of Europe and Middle East–North Africa – having significant coefficients. Taken together they do not represent a connection between the two variables.

A similar conclusion can be drawn from the comparison between growth rates and the percentage of national product allocated to military spending, though even more emphatically since no coefficient of correlation is significant. Testing by the Student Fischer Snedecor-F tests proves the reliability of these findings.

These conclusions cannot claim to be full or definitive. They are merely some inputs into the debate and if they can help to raise questions, prompt further studies to endorse or refute them they will have served their purpose, namely to advance this area of knowledge.

NOTES AND REFERENCES

1. The following works by Christian Schmidt may be consulted: *La gestion de la défense*, Paris, Université Dauphine, June 1980. *L'analyse économique comme aide à la décision stratégique*, Défense Nationale, December 1979. *L'économie de la défense en France*, Revue d'Economie Politique no. 6, 1980, pp. 755–71.
2. The data for this paper refer to the year 1979 and are taken from the following sources:

    Country populations: *UN Demographic Yearbook, 1978* (taking whole numbers only).

    Military expenditures per head: *SIPRI Yearbook, 1980–81*
    GDP per head: *World Atlas of the World Bank*, and OECD statistics for its member countries.

    The GDP growth rate: World Tables of the World Bank
    External debt: *The Public Debt of the Developing Countries* (World Bank, 1980). To calculate this per head the *UN Demographic Yearbook, 1980* was used.

    Debts for the centrally-planned economy countries: *La Documentation Française* (CEDUCEE) 1980, calculated per heads as above.

    The 1979 rate of inflation is from the International Monetary Fund. For the centrally-planned countries, estimates are from the *Nouvel Observateur, Faits et Chiffres*, 1981.

    Foreign trade statistics are from the UN 1980 *Manual of International Trade and Development Statistics*, the World Bank's World Tables and the IMF's 1980 International Financial Statistics.

    Calculations per head: the *UN Demographic Yearbook, 1980*.
3. See Fontanel, J., *Etudes formalisées et anlyses économetrique du couple dépenses militaires-développement économique. Les examples d'un pays développé, la France, et d'un pays en voie de développement, le Maroc*, Report to the UN (1980), and Fontanel, J., *Comparisons Between Countries*, Report for the UN Group of Experts for the Reduction of Military Expenditures (New York: July 1981).
4. Pilandon, L., 'Le Rapport Dépenses Militaire-développement Economique á partir de quelques corrélations économiques', *Revue d'Economie Politique*, no. 4 (July/August 1982) pp. 440–73.
5. Communication by the author to the September 1981 Montpellier seminar 'Dépenses militaires et systèmes d'alliance'.

4 Negotiations to Reduce Military Expenditures – Problems and Possibilities

Hans Christian Cars
THE SWEDISH MINISTRY OF DEFENCE

I BACKGROUND

The problems of defining, evaluating, measuring, reporting, comparing and verifying military expenditures have attracted a good deal of interest for quite some time. The purposes of dealing with these kinds of questions may, however, be very different. Some may be mainly interested in military expenditures as an instrument for military balance assessments, the results of which might have an impact on the country's defence policy. Others may want to assess the military expenditures within a group of countries belonging to the same defence organisation in order to arrive at a fair distribution of the social and economic burden imposed by defence obligations. Still others may be interested in military expenditures as an object of disarmament. In this case the main concern may again be to assess a country's relative military capability by comparing military expenditures in different countries, keeping in mind, of course, that military capability is built up during long periods of time and is affected also by many other factors than those that can be accounted for in monetary terms. Great interest may also be devoted to the linkage between disarmament and development as, for instance, the question of imposing some new kind of tax on military expenditures to be used for the benefit of the developing countries. Evidently the purposes may differ rather widely and consequently the problems involved in the different cases enumerated above may also be quite different. However, some of the problems seem to be very similar in all cases. The present paper intends to give a short overview of the problems connected with the use of military expenditures as an object of disarmament.

A number of successive expert groups have worked with the problems and finally achieved the development of an international system for standardised reporting of military expenditures. This system was carefully tested in 1979–80 and subsequently adopted[1] by the General Assembly and introduced on a permanent basis in 1981. Accordingly, international reporting has already started and should now continue with a view to increased participation from an ever-widening set of states in different geographic regions and representing different budgeting and accounting systems. The General Assembly has decided[2] that the Secretariat should make the collection and assembling of data on military expenditures an integral part of its normal statistical practice. The Secretary-General's first report[3] on these matters was presented in August 1981.

The work has then continued through the study of another expert group which has been dealing with the questions of comparing and verifying military expenditures. This group delivered its report to the Secretary-General in March 1982.[4] Some of its main conclusions were:

(a) The reporting instrument represents a viable and practical means for international reporting of military expenditures.
(b) For comparison purposes there is a need to construct military price deflators and military purchasing power parities (PPPs); the construction of such deflators and parities would involve a common understanding among participating states, but given such understanding it should be possible to resolve the technical problems in a way satisfactory to all parties.
(c) The successful demonstration of the feasibility of constructing military price indices and purchasing power parities for different states would contribute much to preparing the ground for future negotiations on the reduction of military expenditures.
(d) In the case of an agreement on the reduction of military expenditures a verification system will be necessary in order to provide assurances that all parties are in compliance with the agreement.

In fact, a variety of means will probably be required and reliable assessments may involve a relatively high degree of political understanding and confidence.

Based on these conclusions the group recommended to the General Assembly that:

(a) The reporting instrument should continue to be used by an ever-increasing number of States from different geographic regions and with different budgeting and accounting systems.
(b) The Instructions contained in the reporting instrument should be modified according to Chapter II, section E.
(c) The Secretary-General, with the assistance of a group of qualified experts and with the voluntary co-operation of States, undertake the task of constructing price indices and PPPs for the military expenditures of participating States. This task should encompass a study of the problem as a whole which would include the following:

— to assess the feasibility of such an exercise;
— to design the project and methodology to be employed;
— to determine the types of data required (such as product descriptions, prices, weights);
— to ascertain the willingness of States to participate and to enlist their voluntary cooperation; and
— to construct military price indices and PPPs.

(d) The General Assembly should invite Member States to participate in the above-mentioned exercise, pointing to the vast political and technical implications that would derive from such a participation for the process of the RME, and disarmament measures as a whole and for international peace and security.
(e) The General Assembly should urge Member States and, in particular, the nuclear-weapon States and other militarily significant States to help create the necessary conditions for fruitful negotiations on agreements on RME and to recognise that in the process of such negotiations a reasonable availability of statistical data would be required. On this basis, Member States should start negotiations as soon as possible.

The group's report was presented and discussed at the Second Special Session on Disarmament when held in New York in 1982. It could also be expected that the issues raised will be further discussed by the General Assembly.[5] As a result of this appropriate decisions should ultimately be taken concerning future activities in this particular field of disarmament.

II THE CASE FOR NEGOTIATING MILITARY EXPENDITURE REDUCTION

The concept of making military expenditures the object of disarmament negotiations constitutes an approach that has several quite interesting aspects. However, many technical and political difficulties are involved which may have been one of the reasons why this concept has never been tested in practice. In view of the fact that so many other approaches have been tried leading only to rather meagre results, and that actually no efforts have been made so far to overcome the difficulties in the course of negotiations aiming at reductions of military expenditures, this possibility should deserve to attract a growing interest. As no such negotiations have ever been tried there remains a chance that they could lead to fruitful results.

The idea of negotiating reductions of military expenditures has also another interesting aspect. While other disarmament concepts are normally concerned with the restriction or abolition of certain types of weaponry, an agreed reduction of military expenditures would have an impact on the whole field of military activities. If an agreement is reached to abolish some kind of weapon there is no guarantee that the money saved is not spent instead on some other kinds of weaponry, the development and production of which would be equally important to prevent or restrain. If this is happening one has, in fact, not really achieved disarmament but merely changed the course of armament.

It is therefore important to make sure that resources released as a result of disarmament agreements are not being used for other military purposes. A way of ensuring that total military efforts are being restricted or reduced is to impose a ceiling above which military expenditures should not be allowed to rise. If such agreements are reached, resources released by separate agreements concerning specific weapons cannot be transferred to other military uses unless in turn other military resources are dispensed with.

Within the framework of an agreement to reduce military expenditures it is possible to prescribe also the kinds of military expenditures that should be reduced in the first place. There are therefore ample opportunities to link such agreements with the kind of agreements one has been working on most of the time so far, aiming at particular restrictions in the use or development of certain weapons such as strategic nuclear weapons, chemical weapons and other weapons with extremely harmful effects.

The two different disarmament approaches are therefore in my view not substitutable but rather very much compatible and should be pursued in a way as to complement each other.

In the context of negotiating an agreement to reduce military expenditures the negotiators would have to face a number of different technical and political problems which may be grouped in the following main categories.

III THREE CATEGORIES OF PROBLEMS

First there are the problems of defining the scope and content of the military sector and the expenditures which should be subject to negotiation. Related to this is the need for data and the problem that relevant data may not always be readily available. This may be because of technical reasons, as for instance inaccurate accounting practices, but in most cases more likely to be because of political considerations concerning the security implications involved by the release of sensitive military information.

The second category of problems concerns the comparison of military expenditures between different periods of time and between different countries. If an agreement to reduce military expenditures is ever concluded it will no doubt deal with real military expenditures in order to avoid undue disturbances caused by differences in rates of inflation. As a consequence of this there is a need to specify the rate of inflation which would be of most relevance to the military sector in each country being party to such an agreement. There is also a need for agreement among the parties about appropriate methods and data to use for this job by which real military expenditures, i.e. military expenditures in constant prices, would be defined.

Another but similar problem within this category is to compare military expenditures of different countries at specific periods of time. This may be desired by negotiating countries in order to help them assess better their relative military capability and present trends affecting its development. Such comparisons may therefore be needed in the context of negotiations concerning reductions in military expenditures. They may also be requested at different times within the period for which the agreement is concluded in order to provide an extra means of checking that the military expenditures of the parties are decreasing in the way stipulated by the agreement.

The third category of problems is that of verifying the compliance of all parties with the stipulations of an agreement to reduce military expenditures. This is very much a question of sufficient access to relevant information but not entirely so. Data must, of course, be available both concerning the expenditures themselves and with regard to a sufficient set of prices and qualities of different military items. As expenditure figures will be given in current prices and therefore – as already mentioned – will have to be transformed into constant prices on the basis of available price data, there will always be room for a certain amount of interpretation. The selection of military items, the assessment of qualities and their changes, the question of weights, are a few examples of such issues that may be subject to discussion. What could be objectively verified, at least theoretically speaking, are the expenditures themselves as they occur at current prices. To verify an agreed reduction of real military expenditures will, however, always involve a certain amount of judgement.

For this reason and in view of the fact that the situation is not likely ever to be perfect with regard to the access to relevant, sufficient and reliable data, the parties will have to accept a level of verification that does not provide proofs but a satisfactory degree of certainty that the other party (or parties) does (or do) comply with the stipulations of the agreement. It should go without saying that any agreement would have to include provisions for verification acceptable to all parties.

Against this general background one might define the problems of verification to be to select and apply appropriate, sufficiently reliable and efficient but not unduly intrusive means and methods for checking the accuracy of relevant data as requested and supplied by the parties according to agreements among themselves.

After this short and very general overview of problems that would arise in connection with agreements to reduce military expenditures we may now return to the first category of such problems, namely the one concerning the definition and valuation of military expenditures.

IV PROBLEMS OF DEFINING THE CONCEPT OF MILITARY EXPENDITURES

It is, of course, essential for all parties to know exactly what is being negotiated and what kind of expenditures should be subject to reduction. As there are great differences between countries in the way they define their military sector, there will be a need at the outset of future negotiations to agree on a common concept concerning the scope and content of military activities and expenditures.

As mentioned earlier, a good deal of work has already been devoted to this subject by several UN expert groups. The international system for standardised reporting adopted by the General Assembly as a result of this expert work contains *inter alia* a very detailed matrix dividing military expenditures into different resource cost categories. These costs are then also distributed with regard to the type of forces like the army, navy and air forces to which the resources have been allocated. The main cost categories are operation costs, procurement and construction and research and development. These categories are also divided into subcategories and sub-subcategories allowing the respondents the option to present their data with different degrees of detail using that level of aggregation which they may find most suitable.

When constructing this matrix, experts had to deal with a number of difficulties of which a few examples may be mentioned below.

Paramilitary forces cannot be easily defined. It may sometimes be difficult to draw the line between such forces and other forces which should not be regarded to be part of the military sector. This question must in each case be subject to judgement.

Basic research is in many cases of great importance for the future development of new armaments. A part of such expenditures could therefore be defined as military expenditures. They are, however, normally included elsewhere in the state budget. It is normally less difficult to define costs of the application of scientific results in the development of new weapons systems and to attribute them correctly to the military sector, although their distribution among the different force groups may still pose some problems.

Technological development and expansion of certain types of infrastructure, as for instance highways, telecommunications, etc. have in many cases also a strong bearing on a country's military capability. It is, however, not normal practice to define the costs of such activities as military expenditures.

Subsidies to the defence industry can be supposed to keep prices of domestically produced arms and other military equipment from rising as fast as they would otherwise do. Although this is to the benefit of the military sector such subsidies are often financed under non-military budgets, which creates a problem that needs to be further considered.

Military services to the civilian economy may in some fields be carried out on a more or less permanent basis and in other cases be called for at special occasions, as for instance in connection with natural catastrophes. The part of the costs for such services that is not reimbursed from other sources is often carried by the military sector. As such costs are not really of a military nature it can be argued that they should be deducted when calculating military expenditures.

This short list of examples shows a number of problems of definition that one would have to deal with when starting to negotiate an agreement to reduce military expenditures. To these problems of defining and measuring the flow of military expenditures the problem of assessing changes in different stock variables may be added. This is illustrated by the following examples.

Stocks of military equipment must of course be considered when assessing a country's military capability. Nevertheless, the proposed system for reporting military expenditures does not envisage any information about the level of existing stocks. Changes in stocks may, however, be deduced by comparing procurement figures with corresponding consumption figures and estimated rates of depreciation.

Stocks of strategic raw materials such as aluminium, oil etc. are of vital importance for industrial production in case of a blockade or war. Such production, especially within the defence industry, contributes strongly to a country's defence capacity. It is, therefore, a matter of opinion whether costs of stockpiling raw materials for such needs ought to be regarded as military expenditures or not. According to the reporting system they are of a non-military nature and thus excluded from the matrix.

Cars: Negotiations to Reduce Military Expenditures 77

Although negotiating countries would be likely to choose somewhat different definitions and solutions than those provided by earlier UN expert groups, the established reporting system could presumably serve as a good basis for the discussions and thereby greatly facilitate future negotiations.

Another purpose of the reporting system is, of course, to promote a greater openness in military matters which would improve confidence among countries and help to create the kind of political atmosphere they would need in order to start negotiations.

V PROBLEMS OF COMPARABILITY

Turning now to the second category of problems, i.e. those of comparability, it should be realised that these problems have not only technical but also strong political aspects.

INTERTEMPORAL COMPARISONS

With regard to intertemporal comparisons the choice of deflator may strongly influence the rate at which real military expenditures would be expected to decrease according to the agreement.

Any deflator would probably be composed by a set of price indices with different weights according to the relative types of expenditure. It must, of course, be desirable to find a deflator which is easy to handle and at the same time reflects in an acceptably accurate manner the price increases in the military sector of the country in question.

An outline for constructing a weighted price index for the military sector was proposed in one of the expert reports back in 1976.[6] This rather ambitious approach represents a serious attempt to provide a well elaborated model for the construction of a deflator. The 1982 report[7] does not contain a similar proposal but instead treats at some depth the theoretical and technical problems involved. Of particular interest in this context are the specific problems relevant to the pricing of military goods and services. Among these could be mentioned:

(a) The rapid technical and technological evolution in the military sector leading to rapid qualitative changes making it particularly difficult to establish price indices for certain military items,

(b) The length of time taken to introduce new products,
(c) The absence of market prices and the monopsonistic position of the government with its nuclear effects on prices,
(d) The general lack of information on prices and qualities of military goods and services.

Besides these and other particular problems of special relevance to the military sector one has, of course, to face all other well-known problems connected with the elaboration of weighted price indices as, for instance, the index number problem, the choice of base period, the selection of data, etc.

The expert group recommends[8] the following steps for the construction of military price deflators: (a) definition of categories, (b) specification of concepts, (c) selection of samples, (d) development of weights, (e) selection of prices and (f) adjustment for quality changes.

INTERNATIONAL COMPARISONS

The problems of international comparisons are by no means of a less political nature than those of intertemporal comparisons. The results of the comparisons may have important political influence on defence policy decisions in several countries. One may in this context recall the impact on American defence policy caused by the reassessment of Soviet military expenditures made by the CIA some years ago.

In order to allow comparisons of expenditure data presented in different national currencies these data have to be transformed to a common currency by some set of exchange rates or parities. Practices in this field are quite different.

Exchange Rates

One usual method is to convert the national figures into United States dollars using a certain selection of exchange rates.

Such rates may reflect the relative value of national currencies at one particular point in time or the average values prevailing during a certain time period. Well known institutions have in this respect preferred to choose different approaches. The International Institute for Strategic Studies (IISS) has picked the set of official exchange rates prevailing at the end of the first quarter of the relevant year. The US Arms Control and Disarmament Agency (ACDA) has instead selected the average/market exchange rates for a particular year. The same principle of using average rates for specific years is also adopted by the Stockholm International Peace Research Institute (SIPRI).

The kind of exchange rates most commonly used are the ones regularly reported to and published by the International Monetary Fund (IMF) in its monthly bulletin *International Financial Statistics* (IFS). The exchange rates that appear in this publication are calculated on the basis of daily data for all countries members of the IMF, i.e. practically all UN Member States. For each IMF country, average or market exchange rates can thus be calculated for every single month. Consequently, average exchange rates can be obtained not only for calendar years but also for any fiscal year.

For the countries not belonging to the IMF – most of which have centrally planned economies – no rates are published by the IMF. The official exchange rates of these countries do not accurately reflect the relative purchasing power of their currencies. To use these rates for comparison purposes would therefore lead to quite distorted results. It is therefore necessary to find another method of comparing available military data of these countries with similar data from other countries.

One option is to use a set of so-called operational rates of exchange that are communicated by Governments of these countries to the United Nations for accounting purposes throughout the UN system. Such operational rates and the par or market exchange rates published by the IMF form together a complete set of exchange rates which embraces all UN Member States. This possible universal application is, of course, a great advantage of using exchange rates for the purpose of converting and comparing military expenditure data. It must not be concealed, however, that this approach has also serious disadvantages.

The main problem in using exchange rates for comparisons of domestic expenditures of different countries is that such rates are influenced by price relations only for such goods and services that are subject to international trade. It is obvious that in most cases such products do not represent more than a small part of all services and commodities being produced in the countries. It is therefore evident that exchange rates resulting from international trade and influenced by a number of other factors as well can only be regarded as approximations to such rates that would prevail if all types of goods and services were taken into account and probably more so, if only military goods and services would not be considered.

This problem of using exchange rates for international comparisons does not only apply to the case of military expenditures but to other domestically accounted expenditure categories as well. The UN Committee on Contributions which is faced with the same problem, has described it as follows:[9]

> In using exchange rates to translate national incomes in national currencies into a common unit, the Committee has always borne in mind that these rates are not necessarily appropriate for estimating the value of those final goods and services included in the gross domestic product which are not normally involved in international transactions. Since countries differ markedly in their economic systems, in the availability of natural resources, in the volume and type of accumulated capital and in the skill and availability of manpower in relation to other factors of production, the price relationship of goods and services not internationally traded may indeed depart greatly from exchange rates. Even in the case of goods entering international commerce, where price relationships may be assumed in the long run to approximate exchange rates, prices to the domestic consumer will differ between countries as a result of variations in net indirect taxes, domestic processing costs and internal transportation and distribution costs. Thus, in any given country, the real value to each inhabitant of his share of the national income may be quite different from the purchasing power which the same amount would represent in, for instance, the United States of America after conversion into United States dollars at the current exchange rate.

General purchasing power parities

The observations made above have led the Statistical Office of the UN to initiate a study aiming at the elaboration of a worldwide set of so-called purchasing power parities (PPPs) that could be used instead of exchange rates for comparisons of data on 'real' GNP per capita. It is possible that such parities would be more suitable than exchange rates to use also for the purpose of comparing military expenditures. These research activities are carried out under the name of the International Comparison Project (ICP) conducted by Professor Irving B. Kravis and his associates at the University of Pennsylvania. Similar activities are also carried out by other projects for certain groups of countries belonging to different economic organisations as the European Economic Communities, the Council for Mutual Economic Assistance and the Latin American Free Trade Area.

The principles of the PPP method are – very briefly described – to select a sample of goods and services that appear in all or most of the countries to be compared, to collect information on the prices of these goods and services in each country, to decide their relative weights and to carry out the calculations leading to a set of relationships between the domestic purchasing power of the national currencies subject to comparison. This process involves a number of choices which may produce certain technical and political difficulties. These problems, which to some extent resemble the problems encountered when elaborating appropriate deflators, are described at some length in the 1982 expert report.[10]

The work of ICP which started in 1968 has so far resulted in the calculation of PPPs for well over thirty countries representing different geographical regions, economic systems and levels of development. These parities – being based on as many as 153 detailed categories of GNP – show great differences in relation to existing exchange rates. The differences are in general negatively related to the level of income per capita. This implies that converting expenditure data from low income countries by means of ordinary exchange rates would tend to underestimate the 'real' value of the reported expenditures compared with an equal amount spent by a high income country. The differences are also affected, but less so, by the extent to which the countries' economies are exposed to international trade. The more open they are the smaller can the differences be expected to be between the purchasing power of the currencies and their nominal value according to the exchange rates.

Altogether, for very poor countries the domestic purchasing power of one unit of national currency has been estimated to be twice or three times as great as it turns out to be according to the exchange rates. This gives another picture of the distribution of income in the world than the one produced by traditional methods. In the same way the choice of conversion procedure will have a vast effect on the perception of military expenditures and their distribution among different countries.

Military purchasing power parities

For the purposes of negotiating agreements to reduce military expenditures one would probably want to develop PPPs with particular relevance to the military sector. In this case one would have to face a number of additional problems of both a technical and political nature. The selection of items would probably be even more difficult in view of existing differences with regard to the defence structures in different countries. Several types of weapons appearing in great numbers in some countries may be totally absent in other countries. It would also be more difficult to assess the differences in quality between technically complex defence systems than between ordinary consumption goods. To these and other technical difficulties could be added the political reluctance to supply information on performance, qualities and prices of different types of military equipment.

The problems of constructing military purchasing power parities should, however, be possible to resolve if there is a sufficient political understanding among the parties involved. Such parities would provide a supplementary method for assessing the relative military strength of negotiating parties and also their compliance with the stipulations of an agreement to reduce military expenditures, if and when such an agreement is concluded. Although international comparisons will most likely be continuously made by the parties, new sets of purchasing power parities may not have to be constructed each year but at certain regular intervals foreseen by the agreement.

VI PROBLEMS OF VERIFICATION

The third and last category of problems, i.e. those of verification, consists in finding such measures that would be both technically applicable, sufficiently determinative, reciprocal among all parties, not unduly interfering and thus politically acceptable. Appropriate measures should be agreed on keeping in mind the purposes of verification which are to protect the security of the parties to an agreement, to deter violation of a treaty, to function as a channel of communication and to evoke a response in the case of non-compliance.

As pointed out by the 1982 expert report, the type or form of an agreement to reduce military expenditures may greatly influence the requirements of verification measures. An agreement could vary in many ways, for instance with regard to the object of reduction (the whole scope of military expenditures or just some part of them), to the manner of valuation and expression (in national currencies or in some common unit of account, in current or constant prices), to a possible linkage to certain force limitations and to the degree of its formality, severity and duration. The compliance with an agreement that does not specify the object of the reduction and/or the terms by which the reductions should be defined and undertaken would be virtually impossible to verify. Clear specifications would not by themselves solve the problems of verification, but would at least provide a realistic basis on which different methods and measures of verification could apply.

It must be expected that such a basis would also comprise a wide exchange of information concerning each party's military expenditures and prices on military goods and services. The methods and measures of verification would then be used to check the reliability of the information at hand. For this purpose they would most likely have to apply not only to economic indicators such as those recently mentioned but also to physical units in terms of troops, planes, vessels, tanks etc.

In view of this, verification may be carried out by means of inspection on-site or by remote sensing with the use of national technical means. There must be ample room for consultations among the parties whereby questions and possible complaints could be dealt with properly in order to affect the behaviour of the parties or to avoid misunderstandings which could otherwise give ground for unnecessary mistrust. Such consultations might, for instance, be carried out by a special consultative committee of experts established by the parties with the task of studying and solving such questions of verification that would arise in connection with the implementation of an agreement to reduce military expenditures.

VII CONCLUDING REMARKS

What has been said above concerning the problems of comparability and verification leads to the conclusion that no single measure of verification could suffice but that a set of different methods and measures would have to be used. It would also be concluded that the process of verification should include a strong element of discussions and negotiations among the parties which would be largely facilitated in an atmosphere of openness and confidence between the parties. One should not be wrong, however, to expect that the problems of verification both could and would be dealt with in such a positive atmosphere because in the absence of it there would probably be no agreement at all.

One main conclusion that may be drawn from the work carried out by UN experts since 1973 is that there are means and methods to define, compare and verify military expenditures. It could also be stated that these means and methods do not provide a unique solution to each problem but a variety of technically feasible options the choice of which would have political implications. Thus, in order to achieve meaningful further developments in this field, the political element must be carefully considered and clearly incorporated in the work that remains to be done. The major powers and other militarily significant states should therefore be encouraged to discuss at least a possible general framework of a future agreement to reduce military expenditures. On this basis further discussions or negotiations could then be carried out by the governments assisted by economic experts taking into account *inter alia* the UN studies on the subject and the means and methods investigated by successive UN expert groups.

NOTES AND REFERENCES

1. United Nations, Resolution of 35th Session of General Assembly, No. 142B, A/RES/35/142B.
2. United Nations, 35th Session of General Assembly, 1st Committee, Paper L39, A/C.1/36/L39.
3. United Nations, 36th Session of General Assembly Paper 353, A/36/353, Add 1 and 2, Corr. 1 and 2.
4. United Nations, Group of Experts on the Reduction of Military Budgets, *Refinement of International Reporting and Comparison of Military Expenditures* (United Nations: 1982). Submitted to UN Second Special Session on Disarmament, A/S-12/7.
5. The General Assembly decided to designate a new group of experts under a new mandate and this group is expected to submit its report in summer 1985 (note added Jan. 1985).
6. United Nations, *Measurement and International Reporting of Military Expenditures*, Report of Expert Group A/31/222 (New York: United Nations, 1976).
7. Ibid., note 4.
8. Ibid., note 4, para 90.
9. United Nations, *Report of the Committee on Contributions*, General Assembly, Official Records: 33rd Session, Supplement No. 11, A/33/11 (New York: United Nations, 1978) para. 11.
10. Ibid., note 4.

Part Two
Macroeconomic Analysis of the Impact of Military Expenditure

Part Two
Macroeconomic Analysis of the Impact of Military Expenditure

5 Military Expenditures and Economic Growth: Some Theoretical Remarks

Hendrik de Haan
UNIVERSITY OF GRONINGEN

I INTRODUCTION

Only a few economists are interested in the economic aspects of the military sector and military expenditures. The political and strategic considerations of military expenditures are, perhaps, so overwhelming, that economists are not encouraged to investigate the economic consequences of these expenditures. This is also true for the economic causes of military expenditures. Some economic factors, like the uninterrupted flow of strategic commodities, determine the international security situation and, therefore, the level of military expenditures. If one realises that military expenditures account for 6 per cent of GNP this lack of interest of economists is not defensible. There are for example, many more specialised development economists working in the industrialised countries, while development expenditures are less than 1 per cent of GNP!

Several questions are of interest for economists, such as the impact of military expenditures on employment, economic growth, inflation, the balance of payments and international capital flows.

This paper deals only with the consequences of military expenditures on economic growth. The main concern is how the traditional growth theories can be applied to this subject. The reason for this limitation of the scope of this paper is that, in my opinion, these simple theories can be used as a first methodological approach to the problem. Moreover, the theoretical basis of some empirical studies on the impact of military expenditures on economic growth is rather weak. Most of those empirical studies consist of regression analyses. This is especially true for the study by Emile Benoit (1973).[1] With another specification than the Benoit's hypothesis it is possible to find a negative relationship between military expenditures and economic growth. Other studies, like those of Smith and Smith, Russett and Sylvan and Fontanel, with a negative correlation are subject to, more or less, the same critique.[2] In all these studies one or another form of regression analysis is used. That does not mean that these studies are not important and interesting, on the contrary, they shed light on very important economic aspects of the consequences of military expenditures in economic growth and other relevant variables in the economic process. The same is true for the famous study of Leontief and Duchin, in which with use of the input–output model designed for *The Future of the World Economy* several (disarmament) scenarios have been computed.[3] This study is a unique one, because it shows the implications of a limitation on military expenditures for all regions of the world and for many production sectors. The major advantage of input–output method is, of course, the computational and practical elegance in comparison with regression analysis. Nevertheless, this method of analysis has well-known limitations due to the matrix of fixed input–output coefficients, although those coefficients can be changing from period to period.

The purpose of this paper is not to analyse the qualifications of those empirical studies but to investigate how the conventional post-Keynesian and neo-classical growth theories can be used as a basis for the analysis of the impact of military expenditures on economic growth.

II THE IMPACT OF MILITARY EXPENDITURES IN POST-KEYNESIAN GROWTH MODELS

From a theoretical point of view the Harrod–Domar version of the post-Keynesian growth models is an elaboration of the traditional Keynesian multiplier–expenditure model. One of the essential features of the multiplier model is that investments have an effect on income but not on production capacity, so the capital stock is constant. In the long term this assumption has to be rejected. This is done by the introduction of the accelerator principle in the investment equation: investments are dependent of the difference between the warranted and the actual capital stock.

Another essential quality of this growth model is that the capital–labour ratio is constant. In the Harrod model this is due to rigid prices (interest and wages), while in the Domar model the capital–labour ratio is fixed by technical factors (as is the case in input–output models). The most simple version of the model is:

$$K_{t+1} = aX_{t+1} \tag{1}$$

in which K is the capital stock, X the national product and a the capital coefficient. Investment I is by definition the increment in the capital stock:

$$I_t \equiv K_{t+1} - K_t \tag{2}$$

Combination of the equations (1) and (2) result in the investment equation

$$I_t = a(X_{t+1} - X_t) \tag{3}$$

Savings S are proportional with X:

$$S_t = sY_t \tag{4}$$

The equilibrium condition is

$$S_t = I_t \tag{5}$$

Substitution of (3) and (4) in (5) gives the equation of warranted growth

$$g_x = \frac{X_{t+1} - X_t}{X_t} = \frac{s}{a} \tag{6}$$

So, the growth rate of production depends on the savings ratio and the capital coefficient.

If one introduces a government sector and imports and exports in this model this growth equation becomes

$$g_x = \frac{s - b - c}{a} \tag{7}$$

where b is governmental expenditure as a proportion of national income and c is imports minus exports as a proportion of national income. In this case the growth rate will be determined by the savings ratio, the government budget ratio, the current account ratio and the capital coefficient, all parameters in the expenditure equations.

The question how military expenditures influence economic growth in a post-Keynesian world, therefore, depends on the impact of military expenditures on s, b, c and a.

In the long term the savings ratio is a rather stable parameter. Nothing can be said on *a priori* considerations on what happens with s as a result of, for example, disarmament measures. I believe the best we can assume is that s is independent of changes in military expenditures.

The parameter b is a quantity that is highly dependent on political discussions. If a reduction of military expenditures is accompanied by a proportionate reduction of taxes, b will remain unchanged and so will the growth rate of national product. Only when disarmament will lead to a reduction of the budget deficit, will there be a positive impact on economic growth.

With regard to the effect of disarmament on c, the question is whether the country is a net importer or exporter of arms. For a country like the Netherlands, a net importer at the moment, c will decrease as a consequence of disarmament, and so, the growth rate will increase. For countries such as the United States, France, Great Britain and the Soviet Union the opposite will be true.

What happens with the capital coefficient a is, as is the case with the other growth parameters, a purely empirical question. It follows from equations (6) or (7) that the growth will be improved when the capital coefficient decreases. In our problem that will be the case only when the capital coefficient in the military sector exceeds that of the civil sector. Or, to put it in other terms, is military production more capital intensive than civil production? I agree fully with Duisenberg[4] that nothing can be said without a thorough empirical study on the capital intensity in both sectors. Referring to the increasing capital intensive character of military production, and especially that of modern weapon systems, is not sufficient, because the same holds for many civil goods like chemicals, cars, etc. Growth will be fostered only if the resources released by disarmament measures are allocated to those sectors of civil production that have a lower capital coefficient than in military production. Certainly, there are such sectors, but without any policy intervention there is no mechanism to ensure that this will happen.

My conclusion of this part of the paper, dealing with the effects of disarmament on economic growth in the post-Keynesian world is that no firm statements on the positive growth effects of disarmament are theoretically founded, except that for net importers of weapons and countries with a budget deficit (that will decrease by disarmament measures) the growth rate maybe improved. There are no *a priori* agreements for a change in the savings ratio and the capital coefficients as a consequence of disarmament. In general, in a post-Keynesian world growth is determined by demand factors. Supply factors, like the growth of the labour force, do not play a significant role. On the contrary, in such a world there is no mechanism in order to make the warranted growth rate g_x equal to the natural rate of growth. There is no stable growth path (the so-called knife-edge problem), so that the labour released by disarmament measures will increase unemployment, if the warranted rate of growth remains unchanged.

III MILITARY EXPENDITURES AND GROWTH IN A NEO-CLASSICAL SYSTEM

In a neo-classical world growth is generated by the supply side conditions: growth of the labour force, capital accumulation and technical progress.

$$X = X(L, K, A) \tag{8}$$

in which L is labour force, K is capital and A is the parameter for the state of technology. As contrasted with the production function in a Keynesian world labour and capital are substitutes. Moreover, the price mechanism is flexible so that all markets are cleared.

The most simple model for closed economy is the following:

$$X = L^\alpha K^{1-\alpha} A \tag{9}$$

This is the well known Cobb–Douglas production function. Labour is growing with a constant ratio g_L

$$L = L_0 e^{g_L t} \tag{10}$$

Moreover, technology is a function of time

$$A = A_0 e^{g_A t} \tag{11}$$

Substitution of (10) and (11) in (9) leads to

$$X = L_0 e^{\alpha g_L t} K^{1-\alpha} A_0 e^{g_A t} \tag{12}$$

Transforming this equation in its logarithmic form and differentiating to t gives

$$g_x = \alpha g_L + (1-\alpha)g_K + g_A \tag{13}$$

The growth rate of the production in a neo-classical world is determined by the growth rate of the production factors labour and capital and the growth of technology.

Investments are defined by the increase in the capital stock

$$I \equiv \frac{dk}{dt} \tag{14}$$

Savings are proportional to national product

$$S = sX \tag{15}$$

The equilibrium condition is

$$I = S \tag{16}$$

So that, by substitution of (14) and (15) in (16)

$$\frac{dk}{dt} = sX \tag{17}$$

Substitution of (17) in the growth rate of capital leads to

$$g_k = \frac{dk/dt}{K} = \frac{sX}{K} \tag{18}$$

A necessary condition for balanced growth is that the growth rate of capital is constant. This can be realised only if, according to (18), the growth rate of production equals that of capital

$$g_x = g_k \tag{19}$$

Insertion of (19) in (13) gives

$$g_X = g_K = g_L + \frac{g_A}{\alpha} \tag{20}$$

The growth rate of production is equal to the growth rate of the labour force (the natural rate of growth) plus the growth of technology divided by α, which is under competitive conditions and profit maximisation equal to the share of wages in the national income.

It is remarkable, that, in contradistinction to the post-Keynesian model, the savings ratio has no impact on the growth ratio. Any increase of this ratio will, according to equation (19), lead to an unbalanced growth, so that savings will decrease to the equilibrium level. This does not mean, however, that this savings ratio has no influence on the *level* of the growth path of production.[5] A higher savings ratio means a higher level of the growth path, but the growth rate of production is unchanged.

The same can be said of the budget ratio b and the current account ratio c of the former section. In the appendix it is proved that in the model with the government budget and imports and exports the growth path of production is

$$X_t = A_0^{1/\alpha} N_0 \left[\frac{(s-b-c)\alpha}{g_L\alpha+g_A} \right]^{1-\alpha/\alpha} \exp\left[\left(g_L + \frac{g_A}{\alpha} \right) t \right] \quad (21)$$

In this equation the exponent $g_L + g_A/\alpha$ is the growth rate of production, while the rest of this expression contains factors that are relevant only for the level of the growth path.

How does disarmament influence the growth process in a neo-classical world? As appears from equation (21), a distinction has to be made between factors determining the growth rate and the level of the growth path. With regard to the rate there are three quantities: the growth rate of the labour force g_L, the growth rate of technical progress and the wage share in national income x.

If we assume that x is the parameter for the distribution of income between wage-earners and non-wage earners, there is no reason why disarmament will change this distribution. We assume, therefore, that x is independent of changes in military expenditures.

Disarmament will increase the supply of labour. This increase can be gradual over a period of many years or once and for all in the case of general and complete disarmament in one period. But this will not determine the growth rate of labour, because this rate depends on factors like the birth-rate and death-rate, the age groups of the population and participation of women in the labour process. The increase in the supply of labour is important for the level of the growth path. There will be no doubt that this level will be higher than in the case of a continued arms race.

The impact of the coefficient g_A, the growth rate of technology, gives more difficulties. The question is, whether military research and development is a more or less important stimulus for economic growth than research and development for civil purposes. Again, this is an empirical question. The difficulty is, however, that there are no econometric studies available within a couple of years, because it is extremely difficult to collect reliable statistical data and to compute equations which are from a statistical point of view significant. Therefore, the true impact of technological innovation as a consequence of military research and development is clouded in myth. The drive for a continuous improvement in weaponry is in one opinion the most important spur to technological progress, and without the urgency of military demands no sufficient funds would be forthcoming. In this opinion the spin-offs from military research to the civilian sector are remarkable. In the other view it is stressed that most inventions of the greatest civilian importance have nothing to do with military research and development. Military spin-offs from civilian research are in that view larger than civilian spin-offs from military research. This discussion is particularly relevant for countries with an important military complex. It is, of course, questionable whether sufficient funds for research will be available without the driving force of military demands. This depends first of all on a political decision of the government. If the government decides that after disarmament the same funds are available for comparable research projects in the civilian sector, there will be no reason to expect a lower growth rate. But is this a realistic assumption?

Secondly, if the civilian spin-offs are greater than the military spin-offs, the growth rate will improve, assuming that the total research fund will be the same after disarmament measures.

With regard to the first part of equation (21), which deals with the level of growth path, the factor α will not be taken into account because α is independent of changes in military expenditures. If g_A will decrease or increase, the level of the growth path will be higher or lower, but the relative magnitude will be low in comparison with the exponent in the second part of the equation. The factor A_0 is invariant to disarmament. It is not plausible that disarmament will change the state of technology.

With regard to N_0, the supply of labour in the base period, one can say, that if this base period coincides with the period of disarmament, the supply of labour will increase. However, there are some statistical pitfalls, because military personnel belong to the labour force and their services are part of the national product.[6]

The impact of the savings ratio s, the budget ratio b and the current account ratio c is the same as in the post-Keynesian model, with this difference, that these parameters are in the post-Keynesian model important for the growth *rate* of production, while they determine in a neo-classical world only the *level* of the growth path.

IV CONCLUSIONS AND REMARKS FOR EMPIRICAL RESEARCH

The main purpose of this paper was to give a theoretical basis for the consequences of disarmament on economic growth. Two conventional growth models, the post-Keynesian and the neo-classical, were investigated. Of course, there are many versions and elaborations of these models, but I do not think that the main conclusions will change if one takes into account all the refinements.

In a post-Keynesian world, with no possibilities of substitution between the production factors labour and capital, growth is determined by demand factors: the savings ratio, the budget ratio, the current account ratio and the capital coefficient. The savings ratio is invariant to changes in the military expenditures. The capital coefficient will decrease if this coefficient is higher in military production than in civil production. In that case growth will be improved by disarmament. The same is true when the budget and current account ratios will decrease as a consequence of disarmament. So, in a post-Keynesian world the final answer depends heavily on empirical considerations.

In a neo-classical world substitution of production factors is possible and the market mechanism will clear all markets (the labour market included). In this case the supply factors (the growth of the labour force, capital accumulation and technical progress) are the major forces determining the growth rate of production. The demand factors are only relevant for the level of the growth path of production. The same is true for the initial supply of labour and the state of technology. In this model the impact of disarmament on technological progress is of particular importance. Whether disarmament will improve the growth rate of production by an improvement in innovation, depends heavily on the policy decision of the government of whether the research funds will be unchanged after disarmament measures. Moreover, it is important whether the military spin-offs exceed the civilian spin-offs of research.

The main conclusion of this paper is that on *a priori* considerations one cannot give any answer to the question whether disarmament will have positiver or negative consequences on economic growth. There are positive and negative effects, which will be different from country to country and from case to case. But, if one overlooks the theoretical arguments it may be clear that with an active economic policy the impact of disarmament on economic growth will not be negative. In this respect the research and development policy of the government is of crucial importance. The same is true for the reallocation of investment resources from military production to civil sectors with a low capital coefficient.

In many of the empirical studies there is no emphasis on the above-mentioned theoretical considerations. Especially in regression analysis the formulation of the hypothesis with regard to the impact of disarmament on economic growth is from a theoretical point of view debatable. In my view a lot of empirical research has to be done on the fields of capital coefficients in military and civil production and on military and civil spin-offs of research and development in order to make it possible to give any statistically reliable and theoretically founded opinion on the consequences of disarmament on economic growth.

APPENDIX

The model is

$$X_t = L_0 e^{\alpha g_L t} K^{1-\alpha} A_0 e^{g A^t} \tag{A.1}$$

$$S = sY \tag{A.2}$$

$$I \equiv \frac{dK}{dt} \tag{A.3}$$

$$G - T = gX \tag{A.4}$$

$$E - M = bX \tag{A.5}$$

$$I = S - (G - T) - (E - M) \tag{A.6}$$

Substituting (A.2)–(A.5) in (A.6) gives

$$I_t \equiv \frac{dk}{dt} = (s - b - c) A_0 L_0 e^{\alpha g_L t} K^{1-\alpha} e^{g_A t}$$

Integration of this equation leads to

$$K_t = K_0^\alpha - \frac{pA}{g_L} L_0^\alpha + \frac{pA}{n} L_0^\alpha e^{(g_L \alpha t)1/\alpha}$$

where $p = s - b - c$ and $A = A_0 e^{g_A t}$ (A.7)

Substitution of (A.7) in (A.1) gives

$$X_t = A_0^{1/\alpha} L_0 \left[\frac{(s - b - c)\alpha}{g_L^\alpha + g_A} \right]^{1-\alpha/\alpha} \exp\left[\left(g_L + \frac{g_A}{\alpha} \right) t \right]$$

(A.8)

NOTES AND REFERENCES

1. Benoit, E., *Defense and Economic Growth in Developing Countries* (Mass.: Lexington, 1973).
2. Smith, D. and Smith, R., *Military Expenditures Resources and Development*, Report for the Group of Governmental Experts on the Relationship between Disarmament and Development (New York: United Nations, 1982). Russett, B. M. and Sylvan, D. J., *The Effects of Arms Transfers on Developing Countries*, Report for the Group Governmental Experts on the Relationship between Disarmament and Development (New York: United Nations, 1982). Fontanel, J., *Formalized Studies and Econometric Analyses of the Relationship between Military Expenditure and Economic Development*, Report for the Group of Governmental Experts on the Relationship between Disarmament and Development (New York: United Nations, 1982).
3. Leontief, W., and Duchin F., *Worldwide Economic Implications of a Limitation on Military Spending*, Report for the Governmental Group of Experts on the Relationship between Disarmament and Development (New York: United Nations, 1982).
4. Duisenberg, W. F., *Economische gevolgen van ontwapening* (Economic Consequences of Disarmament) (Assen, 1965).
5. The proof of this theorem of the disappeared influence of savings can be found in any advanced textbook on economic growth, e.g., Wan, H. Y., *Economic Growth* (New York: Harcourt Brace Jovanovich, 1971) pp. 48–9.
6. In the socialist countries the opposite is true, which proves that this is a mere statistical problem.

Note on The Impact of Military Expenditure on Economic Growth and Performance[1] by David Greenwood, Centre for Defence Studies, University of Aberdeen

This essay is divided into three parts. The first is a cryptic and impressionistic *review* of what economists have had to say about the impact of military expenditures on economic growth and performance. The second consists of brief *reflections* on the literature. In the third part some suggestions are offered regarding priorities for a future *agenda* on the subject at issue.

I REVIEW

Within the literature on the economic aspects of defence with which I am familiar – and that means a Western, and almost exclusively English-language, literature – there are numerous texts which examine how defence efforts impinge on general economic growth (i.e. the overall performance of an economy, viewed in medium- or longer-term perspective) and many works which focus on the effect of military spending on economic performance in particular contexts (e.g. achieving technical progress or sustaining balance of payments equilibrium).

A common *objective* is to identify general propositions of extensive, if not universal, validity. By and large, less attention has been paid to the more modest type of undertaking, namely elucidation of how a carefully defined change in military outlays might affect either growth broadly construed or some specific aspect of economic performance (including, for instance, industrial/sectoral or regional/local effects). So far as *approach* is concerned, in their quest for generally valid propositions, due stress has been placed on empirical inquiry employing quantitative methods of differing degrees of sophistication (and I use the word 'sophistication' advisedly in this connection). Likewise, in the more limited and speculative sort of work, for the most part the economics profession has sought conscientiously to employ relevant data and sound technique.

What illumination of the matters at issue have these endeavours provided? In my judgement the general, retrospective, diagnostic inquiries have produced remarkably little that is worthwhile. Among the more specific and tentative exercises in prognosis which have been undertaken there are a few outstanding studies (of which more later); but in this category also there are plenty of examples of shoddy workmanship.

Such an indictment requires elaboration. Put briefly, the problem is that much, if not most, of the 'general, retrospective, diagnostic' investigations have been done by economists who have been *either* committed to a particular point of view about the 'value' of public spending for military purposes *or* wedded to particular techniques of quantitative analysis. The former have allowed political conviction to intrude on their selection of evidence and their inference therefrom. The latter have crunched their numbers happily enough. When proceeding to interpretation, however, they have shown insufficient regard for the plausibility of the explanations to which their statistical manipulations have led them.

The same applies when it comes to 'specific and tentative exercises in prognosis': too much of this work also has been done by either politically committed advocates or analysts preoccupied with technique.

II REFLECTION

So much for my cryptic review. Let me now take up the themes raised and offer some reflections on the literature.

Consider, first, the 'big' question: is military expenditure inimical to economic growth (defined, as it must be for this purpose, in terms of increase in gross national product or gross domestic product)? Attention to this theme seems to have been monopolised by analysts who are transparently *parti pris*. By one faction, data showing low levels of military spending (or low defence/GNP proportions) associated with high growth rates are assiduously sought and displayed: and, we are told, the facts speak for themselves! The other faction parades instances where both substantial defence efforts have been mounted and high growth rates achieved: and we are invited to conclude that military spending is probably conducive to growth. The inconvenient presentation of the latter's 'evidence' to the former (and vice versa) elicits predictable responses. Familiar lines include 'it depends what you mean by growth' and 'some sorts of growth are more legitimate than others'. 'There is much more to their poor growth rate than the high level of defence spending' is a favourite on the other tack.

The truth seems to be that you can find cases of high military expenditure levels associated with high, moderate and low growth rates (not to mention no growth, and even falling aggregate income and output). *What ought to be investigated are the reasons for this diversity*: and I include this item on my 'research agenda' (of which more later). Interestingly, this is the conclusion reached by Professor de Haan – in another contribution to this volume – and I draw encouragement from that.

There is one matter, though, which does not require investigation. This is the logical trap into which many investigators of the defence–growth relationship seem to tumble. Government spending on defence is a component of GNP (however defined). It follows that large or rising military expenditures make income and output higher than they would otherwise be, all other things being equal. It can be argued, of course, that all other things are not equal; and that, in particular, shifts of resources from civil consumption and investment to defence consumption and investment must damage an economy's potential for growth (and there is no need to spell out the details of that argument). But the issue here is the *choice* which governments make as between the security argument in their objective or social welfare function and the other arguments, including future income and output. You can have more defence and less of other things (including future satisfactions) – the familiar opportunity-cost notion – and that is just about all there is to it. The 'price' (or trade-off) is undoubtedly higher in some places than others, at some times than others. But it is always there; and that is *the* enduring, universal generalisation about the relationship between military expenditure and economic growth.

That point has been spelled out in straightforward terms. No doubt it could be made in more complicated mathematical guise, but I shall not attempt that. Let me remind you instead how many formal analyses of the 'determinants' of defence spending detect a 'relationship' (inverse) between military outlays and investment expenditures and make this the foundation of their assertions that such spending is inimical to growth. There is not just a whiff of tautology here: it smells to high heaven! Money for defence means less money for investment, less investment – accepting familiar theses about the determinants of growth – is likely to mean less growth in the civil components of income and output (although, as de Haan indicates, that has to be demonstrated). How much intellectual energy (if that is what it is) has gone into devising regression equations – and how much computer time has gone into solving them – just to establish that? If the big econometric guns are to be brought to bear on the defence–growth problem, surely they should seek out more lucrative targets? Turning now to observations on issues of economic performance in particular contexts. Once again my general impression is that, in our literature, advocacy too often gets the better of analysis, and assertion gets the better of argument. To cite one or two examples. Quite a few apparently reputable economic studies were produced in the 1950s and 1960s laying responsibility for the United Kingdom's international economic problems at defence's door. This diagnosis may even have influenced policy. Yet it is self-evident that 'the balance of payments is fundamentally irrelevant to the economics of defence' (the phrase is Peter Oppenheimer's). In similar vein, not so long ago it was very fashionable – perhaps still is in some quarters – to identify the absorption of scarce technological resources in defence efforts as a principal cause, if not the principal cause, of the United Kingdom's comparatively poor record of technical progress (in the growth theorist's sense). It took the Brookings' studies of the British economy and several investigations of the complexities of innovation to expose this view for the simplistic one that it is. Equally discredited now, of course, are the extravagant claims of what I call the 'Iron Mountain' school: that is, the apologists for defence R & D, whose principal instrument in argument has been semantic. I refer to the use in this domain not of such perfectly sound and non-value laden notions as 'spillovers' or 'by-products' but the expression 'spin-off' (with its connotations of a dynamic, all-action engine of military-technological advancement discharging benefits in the form of new products and processes at every turn). It is noteworthy that, in the essay already cited, Professor de Haan alludes to this same problem, observing that the true extent of technological innovation as a consequence of military research and development is 'clouded in myth'. It is encouraging that, in another contribution to this volume, Deutsch and Schöpp make an attempt to dispel the clouds a little.

Although 'general, retrospective, diagnostic' studies have tended to predominate (in the literature that I know), with the shortcomings emphasised here, the other type of inquiry distinguished at the outset – 'specific and tentative exercises in prognosis' – has not been entirely neglected. Some studies have been done which stand comparison with the most constructive applied economics in any other field of interest. The path-breaking work of Nobel Laureate Leontief and his collaborators – on the use of inter-industry analysis to illuminate the economic consequences of changes in arms expenditure (in the United States) – is one example. I think Rolf Piekarz's analysis of the international payments aspects of military spending (based on earlier work done in collaboration with Lois Steckler) should count as another. In the 1970s my own institution did some pioneering inquiries on the impact of military installations on local economies, applying techniques of regional analysis; and, naturally, I believe that this work represents yet another.

It is a great pity that there has not been much more work of this genre. For, as hinted earlier, the greatest service which economists can render in the defence field is to devise models for – and, better still, to grapple with actual exercises in – the prediction of what impact a given carefully defined change in military expenditures may have on economic growth broadly construed or on some specific aspect of economic performance. This is where policy-makers and planners are crying out for technically sound work, unencumbered by the political prejudices or tautological absurdities which we do not seem able to eliminate from our attempts to take on the grander questions.

III RESEARCH AGENDA

I said I would conclude with a plea to the next generation of researchers on the impact of military expenditure on economic growth and performance; a plea for more, and better, work with certain definite emphases. I have cast this in the form of a research agenda, the elements of which arise naturally from the thoughts just outlined.

- If the quest for universal propositions about the defence–growth relationship is to continue, let it be purged of prejudice; in particular, please could the indisputable fact that high levels of military spending have been associated with high, medium, low (and no) growth be given the scrutiny which it merits?
- If the quantitative analysts are to continue their endeavours in this sort of direction, please could they remember that governments *choose* the levels of military spending that we get; and, in that light, could they heed Frank Blackaby's recent injunctions, namely to 'convert algebraic formulations into behavioural statements' and (his most important one) not to seek 'eternal laws,

valid at all times and in all places'. And spare us, please, the more ridiculous tautologies.
- Could there, please, be more effort applied to the more modest type of investigation, namely elucidation of how, in the actual circumstances of the individual case, a particular hypothetical change in the scale and/or pattern of military outlays may plausibly be expected – on given, explicitly stated assumptions – to impinge on the rate of growth of aggregate income and output or on some specific aspect of economic performance. This is where *disaggregation* is the approach and where *illumination* may be most confidently expected.

Needless to say, endeavour of this latter sort is 'modest' only by comparison with the 'grand designs' of certain other undertakings. But it is a becoming modesty, which some of the economics profession's most distinguished members have – in their wisdom – preferred to the conceit (which is really the deceit) of cloaking personal value judgements in the trappings of objective inquiry.

NOTE

1. This text is based on the author's oral remarks to the conference when introducing the session on the topic in question.

6 The Burden of Defence in Developing Countries

Paul Rivlin
INTERNATIONAL INSTITUTE FOR
STRATEGIC STUDIES, LONDON

I INTRODUCTION

This paper will deal with two themes that have been largely neglected in the literature on defence economics in developing countries. The first is the extent to which developing countries actually pay for their own defence. The second is the role of defence and the preoccupation with it in the economic decision making process.

One of the most commonly used concepts in assessing the military burden is the ratio of defence spending to GNP. This concept fails to capture the effect of foreign aid, both military and civilian, on the economy. Often the static or short term burden of defence will be lower than the declared budget would indicate. In the medium or long term it may be the same or higher. Non-economists rely on these simple ratios but there is a need to refine and qualify them. The International Institute for Strategic Studies (IISS), the Stockholm International Peace Research Institute (SIPRI) and the US Government's Arms Control and Disarmament Agency (USACDA) all make use of them for intercountry comparisons. Other indicators are also used including defence spending per head.[1] This is of very little use in assessing the burden of defence because it is unrelated to income. For example, the UK is often criticised in the NATO context for spending less on defence in absolute terms, measured in say dollars, than West Germany. This may be true but of economic relevance is the ratio of defence spending to national income per head. Such a ratio is of even greater importance in poor countries although the problems of measuring income are greater.

II THE DEFENCE BURDEN: GNP AND TOTAL RESOURCES

The need for a more refined concept stems in part from the international nature of much military expenditure. Approximate estimates based on SIPRI data show that imports of main weapons by developing countries equalled 9.8 per cent of their military expenditures in 1960, 9.1 per cent in 1965, 11 per cent in 1970, 11.1 per cent in 1975 and 22.1 per cent in 1978.[2] According to SIPRI, main weapons account for 40 per cent of total arms sales. The remaining 60 per cent is taken up by related equipment, training, spares and small arms. Total imports on that basis came to 24.5 per cent of military expenditures in 1960 and 55.3 per cent in 1978. Vietnam was excluded from these calculations until 1975 when the war ended; the OPEC states and Israel were included.

Foreign aid may only reduce the burden of defence in the short run because eventually loans have to be repaid, usually with interest. Much of the aid listed in Table 6.1 took the form of loans, the only grants were those to Egypt in 1979. Interest had to be paid without the use of the funds for productive purposes in the conventional economic sense.

Military aid may be accompanied by civilian assistance. The link can be complex as Galbraith has shown:

> Our economic assistance program to India when I was there amounted to about $670m a year, including food; this approximately offset the ill-will that we incurred with our military hardware in Pakistan.[4]

External aid, borrowing on international markets and national income equal total available resources. This, in the short run, is the concept against which defence expenditure is most usefully compared. For many developing countries total resources available exceed national income. Iraq, rich in oil, has partly financed the war against Iran by external borrowing of between $10 bn and $22 bn[5] compared with a GNP of about $35 bn in 1979.[6]

The availability of foreign aid should make spending on defence

TABLE 6.1 U.S arms deliveries and military aid to non-OPEC developing states $m[7]

	(a) Deliveries	(b) Aid	(c) (b) as per cent of (a)
1970	201	20	10
1971	146	159	109
1972	159	164	103
1973	180	145	81
1974	260	272	105
1975	438	389	89
1976	740	795	107
1977	905	544	60
1978	1330	670	50
1979	1500	2000	133
1980	1700	460	27

Note: The recipients exclude OPEC, Israel and Europe.

and imports of military equipment easier for governments to consider. These inflows increase resources in the short run, although such aid is usually tied to imports from the donor. While other resources can thus be freed for alternative uses military aid does mean that the armed forces are guaranteed funds, at least for imported equipment. Civilian sectors seldom get such specific assistance.

The effect of aid has been most dramatic in the Israeli case. Table 6.2 illustrates the concepts which have been discussed. Unlike many developing countries, the opportunity cost of manpower is high in Israel and is an important source of extra-budgetary costs, not covered by the defence budget.

Table 6.2 is not an exhaustive list of definitions of the defence burden but serves to show the need for precision in using the term.

Although the static burden may be substantially lower than that including debt repayments, an increasing number of developing countries have tried to improve their economic and strategic security by manufacturing weapons themselves. This in turn has led to pressures for arms exports. Such exports result from military activity within the producing nation and should be included in any cost–benefit analysis of the military which is broadly defined.

The Israeli case is an extreme one in that the aid received from abroad is large in scale. Egypt is far poorer and therefore less able to

TABLE 6.2 *The burden of defence in Israel, 1979*[8]

1. The defence budget as per cent of GNP	31.1
2. plus non-budgetary manpower costs	41.3
3. as per cent of total resources*	22.8
4. plus interest payments on borrowing for military imports	43.9
5. minus reduction in interest due to military exports	43.6
6. Defence budget as per cent of total resources	17.1
7. Locally funded defence spending as per cent of total resources†	15.4

* Total resources = GNP plus surplus of imports over exports
† Defence spending = that within the defence budget only.

TABLE 6.3 *The gross and net overall defence burden of Egypt 1966/7–1973*[10]

	£Em	%
1. Budgeted defence expenditure	+2997	44
2. Soviet military aid	+2485	37
3. Indirect defence costs*	+1291	19
4. Gross overall defence burden	=6753	100
5. Soviet aid not repaid	+2485	37
6. Arab grants	+882	13
7. Net overall defence burden	=3386	60

*Losses and evacuation costs in the Suez Canal zone, loss of Sinai oil plus tourist revenues.

afford either military expenditure or war. In her case aid from the USSR played an important role in covering part of those costs.[9]

Between 1966/7 and 1973 budgeted defence expenditures in Egypt came to 10.4 per cent of total resources and 13.3 per cent of GNP.[11] If allowance is made for indirect defence costs as defined in Table 6.3, then the share of total resources was 14.8 per cent and of GNP 18.9 per cent. SIPRI's figure for the share of GNP spent of defence was 17.4 per cent for 1966/67–73[12] and the IISS's was 18.4 per cent for 1969–72.[13] Neither distinguish between locally funded spending and that financed abroad. The Egyptian failure to repay the Soviet Union substantially reduced the cost of defence and war but the net cost to Egypt after allowing for this was hardly one she could afford.

In 1973 military expenditure by non-OPEC developing countries excluding Israel came to $16.728 bn.[14] In 1978 it was $36.486 bn. Both figures are at current prices and exchange rates.[15] US military aid in 1973, as calculated in Table 6.1, equalled 0.9 per cent of that spending. If Soviet aid to Egypt alone, estimated for 1973 according to Efrat's calculations, is added then the share was 6.8 per cent. Including Soviet aid to other countries and aid from other developed states then the total share may have been 10 per cent or more. High spending in 1973 was because of the Middle East War and so the estimate of Soviet aid to Egypt, based on the annual average for the period 1966/7 to 1973, is not likely to be biased upwards.

US military assistance in 1978 equalled 1.8 per cent of total military spending of the non-OPEC group excluding Israel. 1979 saw a large increase in aid to the Middle East under the terms of the Israel–Egypt Peace Treaty, so increasing the aid share in military expenditure.

These calculations are of necessity very approximate. In assessing how much developing countries pay for their defence it is therefore necessary to estimate manpower opportunity costs, the cost of borrowing abroad and in certain circumstances war costs. Myrdal has shown how great the latter can be.[16] The effects of the 1962 war between China and India included not only physical destruction but also disruption. The war broke out at a time when the Third Five Year Plan in India was running into problems. Following the start of the fighting defence spending was more than doubled. This increased the need for foreign exchange, something which caused shortages for those sectors already in difficulty. A worsening food balance resulted in higher demand for imports. The government rephased the Plan and increased taxes in order to improve the financial situation. In 1965 war with Pakistan started and this resulted in further costs rises, dislocation and a suspension of aid from the West. The Third Five Year Plan was substantially underfulfilled in part because of the fighting and its successor had to be made much more modest.

There can be gains from military expenditure as well as costs, those from training have been examined by Pye.[17] A full cost–benefit analysis, which should include analysis of all these factors has been carried out by Benoit.[18] There is one important factor which has been ignored by these writers, with the possible exception of Myrdal. This is role of the defence burden in the economic decision-making process. It is an issue at the boundary of economics, as conventionally defined and is not easy to quantify.

III THE DEFENCE BURDEN AND DECISION MAKING IN DEVELOPING COUNTRIES

In considering why developing countries pursue certain policies it is necessary to examine what is almost always the dominant institution in the economy: the state. The nature of the state, the reasons why it chooses a particular policy in the economic sphere and the influences on it are not usually considered to be an economist's task. Analysis of markets, a much more familiar area for them, is not irrelevant but seldom provides a complete understanding of development. It is for this reason that Myrdal's institutional approach is useful.[19] Such a view is based on his conclusion that the social and institutional arrangements prevailing in developing countries often hinder economic development and do not adjust spontaneously to policies restricted to the economic sphere. An important part of the state in these countries is often the military, indeed the two are sometimes synonymous.

Although the burden of defence may be reduced in the short run by foreign aid, the latter, if specifically for defence, helps to maintain a particular activity in the economy. For non-military regimes the need to avoid a military takeover may be an important reason for defence expenditure.

Focusing attention on external enemies may help to overcome domestic problems or at least delay the need to confront them directly. Many developing countries have a system of government dominated by one man. Owing to the lack of skilled manpower in the state bureaucracy or because of the lack of decentralisation or both, decisions on a wide range of issues have to be taken at the top. The greater the pressure the less the attention there is for each. In so far as the *raison d'être* of the military is to fight then, in certain circumstances, a political leader may have to spend his time restraining the army. Budgetary constraints may produce an incentive to try to obtain military aid from abroad, so drawing the leadership and the country into foreign involvements. The enhanced military capacity may increase the desire to make use of the hardware obtained. This in turn may subvert the purpose of the leadership in its attempt to avoid incurring a domestic defence burden.

An extreme example of the subversion of economic goals by military ones has been cited from the Indian experience. A more drawn-out example is Egypt in the period from 1967 to 1973. During those years of economic stagnation the main aim of government policy was to reclaim territory lost in the 1967 War. Hence in 1971 President Sadat declared:

> You expect me to speak to you today about the change and reorganisation of the state. However that is not my aim at all. The aim we must never forget should be that whatever we do, it is reorganising the state, or anything else – anything we build – we must not forget that the aim should be the battle.[20]

What was forgotten or at least ignored was Egypt's appalling economic problems. In 1980 with a Peace Treaty signed with Israel guaranteeing the return of the Sinai, Sadat listed the achievements of the decade:[21]

1970 Sequestrations abolished
1971 'Centres of power' abolished (attempted coup foiled)
1972 Soviet experts expelled
1973 October War
1974 Open Door announced
1975 Suez Canal reopened
1976 Soviet–Egyptian Treaty abrogated
1977 Jerusalem initiative
1978 Camp David negotiations
1979 Peace Treaty with Israel: 80 per cent of Sinai returned to Egypt
1980 Martial law abolished.

Of these eleven achievements two were directly economic, four had potential economic implications and the rest were political or military. Economic matters received little attention in Egypt from the President during the 1970s both because of the pressure of political and military events and because of Sadat's lack of interest in economics. Even with the qualification made by Efrat about the extent of the defence burden, it is clear that military matters impeded the development process. They used scarce resources and distracted the leadership from economic problems. Military expenditure is therefore a symptom of a country's political malaise but not one which the poor can afford.

Since 1945 military conflict has moved from Europe to the developing world, the battlegrounds are now increasingly in poor countries. Not only have conflicts between developing countries increased in number and intensity but civil wars and proxy conflicts between the superpowers, sometimes with the involvement of the latter, have increased. Wars in the Middle East and South Asia followed the move away from colonial domination to independence. The Vietnam war was the worst example of the latter kind of conflict. In Africa and Central America civil wars have played havoc with life and the chances for development. Superpower and regional involvements have meant that when wars end and peace is established, military expenditure does not slow down dramatically. India and Pakistan, Egypt and Israel are examples of this.

SIPRI provides figures[22,23] which show that non-oil developing countries with a 1977 GNP per head of between $80 and $300 (the poorest category) increased their defence spending 1.6 per cent in real terms each year on average between 1965 and 1970. Between 1970 and 1975 the increase was 2.4 per cent and between 1975 and 1979, 4.7 per cent. Richer countries in the group recorded increases in the first two periods and a deceleration in the third. Hence the very poorest fared worst. Assessing the burden of defence on this basis may be misleading if the poorest countries received military aid. On the basis of the analysis in the second part of this paper, however, this is of little real compensation

Diverting attention from economic development has not been given prominence as a cost of defence. Even Myrdal, who recognised the importance of institutional factors, dealt with it to some extent *en passant*.[24] For that reason a socioeconomic perspective is useful.

IV CONCLUSIONS

Developing countries need sufficient stability in the political and general international sphere to be able to concentrate on economic development. This, to some extent, is the aim of policy.[25] Military activity, even in peacetime is a distraction that few can afford. Even though many developing countries receive financial assistance for defence this involves them in debt without production. Defence burdens calculated from budget figures which ignore this international component may overstate the short run cost, but will not necessarily be a misleading guide to the longer term developmental costs.

NOTES AND REFERENCES

1. IISS, *The Military Balance, 1981–82* (London: IISS) p. 112.
2. SIPRI, *World Armaments and Disarmament – SIPRI Yearbook – 1979* (London: Taylor & Francis) p. 168, footnote 1.
3. Department of Defence, *Foreign Arms Sales and Military Assistance Facts*, 1977 and 1980 (Washington DC: Department of Defence).
4. Galbraith, J. K., *A Life in Our Times* (London: Andre Deutsch, 1981) p. 416.
5. *Middle East Economic Digest*, (London: March 1982). BBC World Service Reports on 24 March 1982 and 31 March 1982.
6. CIA, *World Factbook* (CIA Foreign Assessment Center, 1981).
7. SIPRI, *World Armaments and Disarmament – SIPRI Yearbook 1979*, App. 3B.
8. Rivlin, P., *The Burden of Defence in War and Peace: Israel 1967–80*. Unpublished. 'The Burden of Israel's Defence (1967–78)', *Survival* (London: IISS, July/August 1978).
9. See Efrat, M., 'The Defence Burden in Egypt during the Deepening of Soviet Involvement', PhD thesis, London University, May 1981.
10. Ibid., p. 160.
11. Ibid., p. 165.
12. SIPRI, *World Armaments and Disarmament – SIPRI Yearbook – 1980* (London: Taylor & Francis).
13. IISS, *The Military Balance 1973–74* (London: IISS).
14. SIPRI, *World Armaments and Disarmament – SIPRI Yearbook – 1979*.
15. SIPRI, *World Armaments and Disarmament – SIPRI Yearbook – 1980*.
16. Myrdal, G., *Asian Drama* (New York: Twentieth Century Fund, 1968) chs 5 and 7.
17. Pye, L., in Johnson, J. J. (ed.), *The Role of the Military in Underdeveloped Countries* (Princeton University Press, 1962).
18. Benoit, E., *Defense and Economic Growth in Developing Countries* (New York: Lexington Books, 1975).
19. Myrdal, G., *Asian Drama*, Prologue to Volume 1.
20. Quoted in *Summary of World Broadcasts* (SWB) BBC, London, 18 Sept. 1971, 2nd Series, ME/3790.
21. Ibid., 15 May 1980.
22. SIPRI, *World Armament and Disarmament – SIPRI Yearbook – 1979*.
23. SIPRI, *World Armament and Disarmament – SIPRI Yearbook – 1980*.
24. Myrdal, G., *Asian Drama*, p. 537.
25. Caiden N. and Wildavsky, A., *Planning and Budgeting in Poor Countries* (New Brunswick NJ: Transaction Books, 1980).

7 Economic Growth, Military Expenditure, Arms Industry and Arms Transfer in Latin America

Luis Herrera-Lasso
CENTRO DE ESTUDIOS ECONOMICOS Y
SOCIALES DEL TERCER MUNDO AC,
MEXICO

I INTRODUCTION

In order to understand the phenomenon of militarism in Latin America, we can always retake the Clausewitz maxim as a starting point: War is a continuation of politics by other means. The power politics approach and the 'struggle for power' serve us to understand why military force exists and why it is necessary within and among states. Nevertheless, the economic implications of this phenomenon are very often considered only as a result of a political fact.

We often talk about the need to divert resources from the military towards economic development, and about the urgent necessity of satisfying the basic needs of a large percentage of the world's population. In times of discussion, we usually agree on the necessity of this diversion and on the absurdity of the arms race and military expenditure; but, when we face reality, we find that this absurdity is leading history without any sign of change.

The pursuit of armaments, or to coin a word 'armamentism', and development have an intrinsic interrelation. A solely political approach has proved to be insufficient. To explore the economic significance of armamentism seems to be, at least, a necessary effort in the search for ways to correct what we consider 'an irrational' waste of money and resources.

Although the process and dynamics of military expenditures show ample similarities between most countries, the case of Latin America, as a region, has some particular features which make the area interesting for separate study. To consider the economic significance of military expenditure in the region could be an appropriate and very useful way to understand and foresee important aspects of this process.

II GENERAL FRAMEWORK

When we consider the reality of military expenditure in Latin America we notice that its increase has been considerably lower than that of other developing regions of the world. This has political and economic explanations. On the one hand, Latin America has been protected by the strategic–military umbrella of the United States, which assures protection against aggressors from abroad (although the case of the Falkland Islands leads us to new reflections). At the same time, the absence of serious conflicts within the region has served to discourage Latin American governments from having a very strong military apparatus.

Nevertheless, since 1960 military expenditures in the Third World have risen more than fourfold (in constant prices) and Latin America has followed this trend. In the early 1960s, the total military budget of Latin America averaged $1.5 billion yearly; by 1971 this budget had reached $3 billion.[1] In 1980, the military expenditure of the seven leading countries was nearly $8 billion.[2]

Although the average participation of military expenditure in the gross domestic product has not increased very much in Latin American countries, military achievements of the leading countries have been considerable.

In terms of military exports, Brazil, Argentina and Cuba are among the eleven largest Third World major weapon exporters, with Brazil in first place, covering 33.1 per cent of the total Third World's military exports.[3] In terms of military imports for the period 1977–80, Peru, Argentina, Brazil and Chile were among the 24 largest Third World major-weapons importers, with Peru, heading the list of South America, in seventeenth place (995 million dollars).[4]

Military purchases by Latin American countries also grew considerably during the 1970s. According to Andrew Pierre's recent book, *The Global Politics of Arms Sales*, these purchases increased 300 per cent during the period of 1969–78.[5]

Another significant fact which is reflected in military exports is the continuous growth and success of indigenous arms industries. Argentina and Brazil have the lead in this field. Peru and Chile are also progressing, but on a smaller scale.

Countries like Brazil and Argentina have made enormous progress in their arms industries. They have achieved self-sufficiency in some areas, and have left an important surplus for exports. These exports go not only to Latin American countries but also to markets outside the continent. For example, in 1980–81, Brazil reported military exports to Belgium, France and to nine developing countries.[6]

The interrelationship between arms transfer and the economies of Latin American countries, can be described for analytical purposes, by the following:

(1) The relationship between economic development, level of industrialisation and military expenditures.
(2) Indigenous arms industry, technology and arms transfers.

In the last part of this paper I will try to establish some conclusions and hypotheses for further research on the wide economic impacts and possible future of the military industry, arms transfer and military technology of Latin American countries.

III ECONOMIC DEVELOPMENT, STAGE OF INDUSTRIALISATION AND MILITARY EXPENDITURE

When we talk about power in international relations we must consider the different components of power as a capability which integrate into a potential power to be used under certain circumstances.[7] If we review the different elements of power, we include such factors as territory, population, natural resources, geographic allocation, economic development and level of industrialisation among others. The interrelation between the aforementioned elements and military strength of a country is usually very strong.

For Latin American countries this applies only to a certain extent. If we consider the five largest countries in terms of each of the indicators of GNP, per capita GNP and population, and we compare

TABLE 7.1. Economic indicators and defence expenditures

Country	Population[b] millions mid-1979	GNP 1979[b] (billions in constant dollars)	GNP per capita[b] dollars 1979	Defence[a] expenditures 1980 (current dollars) millions
Brazil	116.5	207.3	1 780	1 540
Mexico	65.5	107.4	1 640	803
Argentina	27.3	60.8	2 230	3 380
Venezuela	14.5	45.2	3 120	1 118
Chile	10.9	18.4	1 690	984
Cuba	9.8	13.8	1 410	1 100
Peru	17.1	12.5	730	431*

*Because of inflation rates, this is not very reliable data.

SOURCE Elaborated with data from (a) *Military Balance 1981–1982* and (b) *World Development Report 1981* (World Bank).

these basic indicators of economic strength with the amounts of military expenditures, we will not find a direct correlation in all cases. Argentina, Chile and Cuba are spending proportionately more than Mexico and Brazil which are the largest economies of the area (see Table 7.1).

Countries such as Brazil, Argentina and Venezuela can afford important military programmes without the consequence of a significant opportunity cost effect on their economies.

This is especially true in the case of Brazil who has the strongest economy and highest level of industrialisation in the region. It is also the case for Argentina, albeit on a lower scale. Venezuela has also developed military programmes but is more dependent on sales from abroad. The lack of a sophisticated industrial complex makes her weaker, but the foreign currency resulting from oil sales has compensated for this fact.

In the cases of Cuba, Chile, Peru and Mexico, we could argue that they are either below or above a 'rational correlation' between economic potential and military expenditures.

The proportion of military expenditure in the gross domestic product of Latin American countries is higher for Cuba, Chile and Peru, than for any other country in the region, while Mexico has one of the lowest allocations (see Table 7.2).

When we analyse higher or lower military expenditures *vis-à-vis*

TABLE 7.2 *Latin American military expenditures as a percentage of gross domestic product*

Country	1971	1975	1978	1979
Argentina	1.7	1.7†	2.1	2.3
Bolivia	1.4	2.3	2.0	2.0‡
Brazil	1.5	1.1	1.1	0.9
Colombia	2.5	1.0	0.7	1.0†
Costa Rica	0.6	0.6	0.6†	0.5‡
Cuba	4.9	4.1‡	8.4‡	—*
Chile	2.3	3.9	5.8	9.4‡
Dominican Rep.	1.9	1.6	1.9	3.2
Ecuador	1.8	2.3	2.2	2.0
Mexico	0.6	0.7	0.6	0.6
Peru	3.6	4.6	5.5	4.0
Uruguay	2.6	2.6	2.7	—*
Venezuela	1.9	1.9	1.5	1.3

* Information not available or not applicable.
† SIPRI estimates, based on uncertain data.
‡ Imputed values, with a high degree of uncertainty.

SOURCE *SIPRI Yearbook, 1981*, p. 169.

economic potential, we find political–strategic answers. In the cases of Chile and Peru, internal militarism and fear of their neighbours have contributed to accelerate their military expenditures, thus exerting significant pressure on their economies. Cuba's extremely delicate strategic position has bound her to devote more proportional resources to defence than any other country in the region. Although Cuba has important military support coming from the Soviet Union, she has to pay a high cost to maintain her security.

The explanation for Mexico's low proportion of military expenditure is both political and strategic. First, Mexico's security in relation to possible foreign attacks has been considered by the United States to be of strategic priority. This fact has released Mexico from the need to build up a stronger military apparatus. Secondly, the existence of a stable civilian government in Mexico for more than half a century has helped to maintain military expenditures at such a low level.

If we explore the economic impact of military expenditures for most Latin American countries, we find that it is not equally significant for all of them; that is to say, the economic impact is greater on the medium and smaller countries than it is on the large nations of the region. Undeniably the resources devoted by Latin American countries to military expenditure respond to political and strategic variables of security which are independent of their overall economic strength. Table 7.3, which excludes Cuba, reveals that the largest percentage of defence expenditures, compared with total government expenditure in 1978, is to be found in Ecuador, Bolivia, Peru, Chile, Argentina (in fifth place), Paraguay, Guatemala and Uruguay; with Brazil, Mexico and Venezuela far behind.

If we consider the reduced budget (and GNP) of the first four countries mentioned above, their stage of development, the structure of their economies, and their urgency to satisfy basic needs for a large proportion of their population, we can assert that a high percentage of military expenditure has a very high economic and social effect. For example, in 1978, the Ecuador government spent $15 per capita on defence and $6 on health services; for Bolivia the ratio was $10 to $5; for Peru $18 to $8, for Chile $37 to $20 and for Paraguay $9 to $2. For all these countries, we can find a correlaton between a high percentage of military expenditures in their government budgets and a low proportion devoted to health services. In all these cases the difference is greater than for the other Latin American countries.

If we consider defence expenditure as a percentage of GNP, we find that excluding Cuba, for 1978 Chile is leading with 4.4 per cent, followed by Argentina and Uruguay (2.5 per cent), Venezuela (2.3 per cent), Ecuador (2.2 per cent) and Bolivia (2.0 per cent). Although we are taking only one year to illustrate this point, it has been the approximate trend for the last two decades.[8] As mentioned above, the Cuban case represents the extreme on the continent. For 1980, the defence expenditure was $111 dollars per capita superior to all other Latin American countries, and the percentage of military expenditure in the GNP was as much as 8.5.[9]

If we consider military expenditure in absolute terms, we find that Argentina is the leader having the largest military budget in Latin America. In 1981, Argentina spent $2.2 billion, followed by Brazil with $1.2 billion, Chile $1.0 billion, Mexico $0.78 billion and Venezuela $0.75 billion.[10] (These figures exclude Cuba.).

As is shown in Table 7.4 based on a number of sources over a ten year period, Argentina appears for all indicators among the first six places. Brazil and Mexico appear in the first six only in the first category while Cuba appears in four – three times in first place. Notwithstanding, Cuba must be considered a special case because of Soviet support. Chile and Venezuela appear in three categories, and

TABLE 7.3 Defence and social expenditure

Country	Defence expenditure as percentage of:				Central government expenditure per capita (1975 dollars)					
	GNP		Central government expenditure		Defence		Education		Health	
	1972	1978	1972	1978	1972	1978	1972	1978	1972	1978
Argentina	1.5	2.5	9.0	11.9	22	36	29	25	8	6
Bolivia	1.5	2.0	16.1	16.1	7	10	13	18	4	5
Brazil	1.4	1.1	8.3	5.8	13	14	11	14	10	20
Costa Rica	0.5	0.7	2.6	2.7	5	8	48	68	6	10
Chile	2.6	4.4	6.1	12.0	4	37	9	40	5	20
Dominican Rep.	1.5	—	8.5	—	11	—	18	—	15	—
Ecuador	2.0	2.2	16.9	19.2	11	15	20	20	3	6
El Salvador	0.8	1.0	6.6	6.8	4	5	11	14	6	6
Guatemala	1.1	1.2	11.0	11.0	3	8	5	9	2	5
Honduras	1.9	—	12.4	—	7	—	13	—	6	—
Jamaica	—	1.0	—	2.6	—	12	—	83	—	35
Mexico	0.6	0.6	4.9	3.4	8	8	27	47	8	9
Nicaragua	1.9	—	12.3	—	12	—	16	—	4	—
Paraguay	1.8	1.3	13.8	11.3	9	9	8	11	2	2
Peru	2.5	2.1	14.8	13.1	23	18	35	23	10	8
Uruguay	1.4	2.5	5.6	10.5	16	17	28	15	5	8
Venezuela	2.1	2.3	9.7	7.8	41	55	73	101	27	35

— No data available.

SOURCE *World Development Report, 1981* (World Bank).

TABLE 7.4 *Economic indicators related to military expenditures*
(In ranking place)

	1st	2nd	3rd	4th	5th	6th
Total amount	Argentina	Cuba	Brazil	Chile	Mexico	Venezuela
Per cent GNP	Cuba	Chile	Argentina	Uruguay	Venezuela	Ecuador
Per cent Government expenditure	Cuba	Ecuador	Bolivia	Peru	Chile	Argentina
US dollar per capita	Cuba	Venezuela	Chile	Argentina	Peru	Uruguay

SOURCE Estimates based on data from several sources: SIPRI, IISS, World Bank, for period 1971–81.

Ecuador, Peru and Uruguay, in two of the three categories, in which the economic impacts of military expenditure are more significant.

We can conclude in general terms, that the major effects of economic expenditure for Latin American countries are not found on the major countries but rather in those 'medium' countries of the region where military expenditure signifies a relevant economic burden.

IV INDIGENOUS ARMS INDUSTRY, TECHNOLOGY AND ARMS TRANSFER

The production of weapons in Third World countries and their participation in arms trade are two of the most significant phenomena regarding armamentism in the last two decades. We find several explanations for these phenomena, political and economic. The entrance to a multipolar world encouraged developing countries to improve their arsenals in order to uplift security and increase regional power. The ample market of arms supplies, due to economic and political reasons, made it possible for those countries to increase their military power in a short period of time. It has been five countries: the United States, Soviet Union, France, Britain and the Federal Republic of Germany, who have been responsible for most of this trade. From 1977 to 1980, these five sold 77.2 per cent of the total amount of arms.[11] The total imports of arms for the period of 1969–78 amounted to 144.2 billion (US dollars: 1977) of which developing countries imported 106.7 billion (74 per cent) and developed countries only 37.5 (26 per cent).[12]

For Third World countries, the business of arms trade and military support has been to buy – and pay the economic cost – or to accept military aid while paying the political cost. In Table 7.5 we find interesting data about US Military Aid and support towards Latin America. Until the early 1970s there existed a major dependency on the United States. The inevitable dependency derived from arms purchases led Third World countries to attempt an indigenous arms industry in order to reduce this economic and political dependence and, if possible, to participate in the arms business as exporters. In order to develop that strategy, many problems had first to be faced: industrial requirements, raw materials, high level technology, skilled labour force, etc. Only a few countries have reached the capacity to overcome these obstacles and initiate powerful arms industry with an

TABLE 7.5 US Military aid towards Latin America

Country	US military aid fiscal years 1950–79 (current US$ in millions)	Foreign military sales programme	Commercial sales	Training of foreign military personnel by the United States*
		(current US$ in thousands) 1975–9		
Argentina	247.0	200 250	82 859	4 017
Bolivia	244.8	2 066	4 085	4 861
Brazil	646.9	289 747	74 460	8 659
Chile	183.9	190 264	8 760	6 883
Colombia	253.2	39 591	17 700	7 907
Cuba	16.1	4 510	—	523
Dominican Rep.	248.4	2 287	2 248	4 218
Ecuador	112.5	91 554	21 553	5 958
Mexico	8.3	21 648	11 209	964
Peru	214.5	186 345	24 681	7 966
Venezuela	138.9	244 734	45 671	5 540

*Students trained under the military assistance programme and international military education and training programme.

SOURCE M. T. Klare and C. Arnson, *Supplying Repression* (Washington: The Institute for Policy Studies, 1981).

TABLE 7.6 Ten largest Third World producers of major weapons, by
weapon category
(Figures are numbers of weapon types produced)

Producing country	Aircraft	Armoured vehicles	Missiles	Warships	Total
Brazil	19	4	3	1	27
Israel	9	4	4	5	22
Argentina	7	2	2	9	20
India	15*	1	3	5	19
North Korea	1*	—	—	10*	11
Taiwan	5	—	4	1	10
South Africa	3ª	1	1*	—	5
Pakistan	4ª		1*	—	5
Peru	1ª			4	5
Indonesia	4ª			1*	5

*Most of these types are produced under licence.

SOURCE SIPRI Yearbook, 1979.

exporting capacity. In the period 1977–80, the total amount of Third World major weapon exporters was $1271 million in seventh place, immediately after the Federal Republic of Germany. That represented 2.2 per cent of the world total. The 98 per cent went to the Third World and only 2 per cent to industrialised countries.[13]

Brazil was the first major weapon exporter of the Third World with 33.1 per cent ($421 million) during that period; Argentina was seventh with only 35 million, and Cuba was eleventh with 15 million.[14]

Although Latin America traditionally has had the lowest average rate of arms imports and military expenditure, the development of an arms industry in some Latin American countries has been proportionally superior to most Third World regions. Brazil has maintained the lead not only in production but also in clients and its variety of projects. In fact, Brazil and Argentina are quite advanced in missile design projects. In 1973, Brazil (AVIBRAS) began the construction of an air-to-surface missile, the MAS-1 Carcara, and in 1976 a surface-to-air missile. Argentina (CITEFA) developed an anti-tank missile between 1974–8, and the construction of an air-to-surface missile (CITEFA), began in 1978.[15]

The data given in Table 7.6 shows the importance of Argentina and Brazil as arms producers in the Third World, not only in numbers of weapon types, but also in their variety. In aircraft production Brazil

TABLE 7.7 Survey of production of major weapons and components in Latin American countries, 1950-72*

Country	Military aircraft			Guided missiles			Armoured fighting vehicles			Warships		Military electronics		Aero-engines	
	A	B	C	A	B	C	A	B	C	A	B	A	B	A	B
Argentina	×	×		×‡	×‡			×		×	×				×
Brazil	×	×		×‡	×	×				×	×	×	×		×
Chile		×									×				
Colombia											×				
Dominican Rep.											×				
Mexico											×				

A = Licensed production.
B = Indigenous production.
C = Co-development with foreign company.
*Including production planned in 1972, whenever these plans are estimated to be remotely possible.
†Negotiations under way between Argentina and Brazil in 1972.
‡Argentina plans production of surface-to-surface and surface-to-air missiles.
SOURCE SIPRI, *Arms Transfer with the Third World*, 1975.

ranked first with 19 types and Argentina was fourth with 7 types. Brazil was first in armoured vehicles with 4 types and Argentina was second with 9 types.

In total numbers, Brazil was leading the group with 27 types of major weapons while Argentina had third place with 20 types. From the 129 types of weapons produced by the ten largest Third World producers of major weapons, more than 40 per cent (52 types), were produced by Brazil, Argentina and Peru.

In table 7.7 we have the largest producers of major weapons in Latin America. We find Brazil and Argentina leading the list with projects of all kinds. In both cases we can see an effort to develop most types of weapons for the navy, the air force and the army. As mentioned above, both are also developing missile projects. From this point of view, we can assert that they are both working on a complete arms industry with a double purpose: to cover domestic military needs and to become competitive and to increase their participation in the arms market.

For the other Latin American countries, we find a general trend to produce warships. Chile, Colombia, Dominican Republic, Mexico, Peru and Cuba are producing mainly coastal patrol boats. This is very understandable if we consider that most Latin American countries have very large coastal borders that are often troublesome to patrol. In all of these cases, the aim is to satisfy a domestic need. Apart from Brazil and Argentina, Chile is the other country with a special interest in building up a military industry; with production of tank-landing ships and helicopters for export.

As shown in Table 7.7, the largest producers of major weapons in Latin America are Brazil and Argentina. Both countries have a high level of industrialisation in terms of the Third World, nevertheless, Argentina's industry is considerably inferior. If we look at the average annual growth of GNP, GDP, industry and manufacturing of the region (Table 7.8), we will find that for the period 1970–79 all rates for Argentina are 2.5 below. If we take Brazil in the same period, we see an average annual growth rate of 8.7 per cent in GDP, industry 9.6 per cent and manufacturing 10.9 per cent. According to these numbers we can deduce that Brazil has a more consolidated industrial base to sustain a balanced production of arms. Argentina, on the other hand has to make a considerable effort and sacrifice of the rest of the economy to maintain her military production. According to Table 7.8, Chile is in a worse situation, even worse than Argentina. The average annual growth rate for Chile of industry for the period 1970–79 was very close to zero while in the manufacturing sector it was negative. Thus maintaining a military industry is very expensive under these conditions. Peru, according to the same indicators, has to pay a rather high price for its arms industry.

A very significant variable in considering the effects of military expenditures and the arms industry on the economy, is the relationship between the necessity of military expenditure and arms production given by political and strategic variables, and the capacity of each country to satisfy their military needs without very much affecting the whole of the economy. It is in this context that a high level of economic development and advanced stage of industrialisation play a determinant role. It seems that those countries with a high industrial output will be more able to sustain a military industry and to reduce economic and political dependence from abroad. In Latin America, Brazil appears as the only country with the capacity to develop an arms industry to satisfy most of its military needs, and increase its participation in arms markets, without a great impact on her economy. Argentina has reached a significant arms industry and it is also an active arms exporter, but the impact of military expenditure is much greater than in Brazil. For the rest of Latin American countries with a high proportion of military expenditure, their dependency

TABLE 7.8 Basic economic indicators for Latin America

Country	GNP per capita		Average annual growth rate (per cent)					
	Dollars 1979	Average annual growth	GDP		Industry		Manufacturing	
			1960–70	1970–79	1960–70	1970–79	1960–70	1970–79
Argentina	2 230	2.4	4.2	2.5	5.9	2.4	5.7	1.9
Bolivia	550	2.2	5.2	5.2	6.2	4.8	5.4	6.7
Brazil	1 780	4.8	5.4	8.7	—	9.6	—	10.9
Colombia	1 010	3.0	5.1	6.0	6.0	5.0	5.7	6.6
Costa Rica	1 820	3.4	6.5	6.0	9.4	8.5	10.6	8.4
Cuba	1 410	4.4	1.1	6.0	—	—	—	—
Chile	1 690	1.2	4.5	1.9	5.0	0.3	5.5	−1.0
Dominican Rep.	990	3.4	4.5	7.5	6.0	10.1	5.0	7.4
Ecuador	1 050	4.3	—	8.3	—	13.4	—	10.2
El Salvador	670	2.0	5.9	4.9	8.5	6.0	8.8	4.3
Guatemala	1 020	2.9	5.6	5.9	7.8	8.0	8.2	6.6
Haiti	260	0.3	−0.2	4.0	0.1	8.3	−0.1	7.1
Honduras	530	1.1	5.3	3.5	5.4	5.0	4.5	5.5
Jamaica	1 260	1.7	4.5	−0.9	5.0	−3.1	5.7	−1.3
Mexico	1 640	2.7	7.2	5.1	9.1	6.4	9.4	6.4
Nicaragua	660	1.6	7.2	2.6	11.0	3.2	11.1	3.3
Panama	1 400	3.1	7.8	3.4	10.1	0.5	10.5	−0.6
Paraguay	1 070	2.8	4.2	8.3	—	9.9	—	7.4
Peru	730	1.7	4.9	3.1	5.0	3.7	5.7	3.2
Trinidad and Tobago	3 390	2.4	3.9	5.2	—	—	—	—
Uruguay	2 100	0.9	1.2	2.5	1.1	4.2	1.5	3.9
Venezuela	3 120	2.7	6.0	5.5	4.6	3.1	6.4	5.7

SOURCE *World Development Report 1981*, The World Bank.

from abroad to arm themselves has a rather high economic and political cost. The lack of a dynamic economy and a high level of industrialisation seems to be a determinant variable in the cost to pay for internal and external security.

Most Third World countries have had to face serious technological problems for the building of military industries. In fact, most arms production projects in Latin America have been developed through a significant participation of European scientists and technicians. Most indigenous projects developed by Brazil and Argentina have had important support by European governments, companies or technicians. As we can note in Table 7.7, many projects are under licence or co-developed with a foreign company.

During the late 1960s there was a turning point in the technology supply for Latin American countries. During this period, the United States showed a strong reluctance to provide highly sophisticated weapons and technological support for these countries. Their argument was, on the one hand, that Latin America should not be a region with plentiful arms because strategically this was unnecessary. On the other hand, to restrict the transfer of arms and military technology should contribute to the avoidance of the presence of major weapons in the region.

This attitude of the United States towards Latin America turned the attention of those countries to Europe. The European military establishment works more in economic (business) terms than in political ones. The Europeans had arms and military technology to offer, and the Latin American countries had interest to buy. Thereafter, arms purchases and the acquisition of military technology depended more on Europe than on the United States. If we look at Table 7.9, from a total of 21 major weapons produced under licence in Latin America, only four licences (19 per cent) came from the United States. As is pointed out on the SIPRI's study on arms trade, the criteria for arms sales and military technology transfer, used by military powers, is different for each country. For the United States, the criteria are predominantly political; to Britain, France and the Federal Republic of Germany, they are mainly economic, and for other European countries they are restrictive. If we consider all major arms imports and military technology in Latin America, we will find that in the past decade, most arms purchases and acquisitions of licences for military production have come from Europe.[16]

In other words, military independence from the United States for Latin American countries signifies a higher economic cost.

TABLE 7.9 Register of licensed production of major weapons in Latin America, 1980

Country	Licencer	No. ordered	Weapon designation	Weapon description	Year of licence	Production	Period of production
Argentina	Germany, FR	220	TAM	MT	(1976)	(170)	1979-80
		300	VCI	MT	1976	(125)	1979-80
		6	Mcko-140	Corvette	1979		
		2	Type 1400	Submarine	1977		
		3	Type 1700	Submarine	1977		
	United Kingdom	1	Type 42	Frigate	1971		
	USA	—	Arrow-3	Trainer	1977	(30)	1978-79-80
		120	Model 500M	Helicopter	1972	(48)	1977-78-79-80
Brazil	France	200	AS-350M Esquilo	Helicopter	1978	(26)	1979-80
		30	SA-315B Lama	Helicopter	1978		
		(34)	SA-330L	Helicopter	1980	(6)	1979-80
	Germany, FR	—	Cobra-2000	ATM	1973	(910)	(1975-76-77-78-79)-1980
	Italy	(150)	AMX	Fighter/ground	1980		
		184	EMB-326 Xavante	Trainer/COIN	1970	(172)	1971-72-73-74-75-76-77-78-79-80
Chile	USA	—	EMB-810C	Lightplane	1974	(190)	1975-76-77-78-(79)-80
Colombia	France	2	Batral type	LST	1979		
Mexico	USA	—	Azteca class	Lightplane	1969	(700)	1973-74-75-76-77-78-79-80
Peru	United Kingdom	10	Lupo class	CPB	1975	(10)	1976-79-80-(81)
	Italy	2		Frigate	1974		

Source *SIPRI Yearbook, 1981*.

TABLE 7.10 *Exports and imports of major weapons for the largest Latin American countries, 1977–80.*
US $ million at constant prices (1975)

Country	Imports	Exports
Brazil	641	421
Argentina	642	35
Peru	995	—
Chile	482	—
Cuba	—	15

— No data available.
SOURCE *SIPRI Yearbook, 1981.*

Unfortunately, current events have proved, at least to Argentina, that such independence is necessary. Otherwise, Argentina would have had to accept American terms of negotiation, which have not been seen by the Argentinian government as favourable to its national interest.

The participation of Latin America in total arms sales is still rather low. The share of Latin American countries in the total of major weapons imports is about 7 per cent of the world total. In absolute terms in 1980, it was less than one billion dollars from a total amount close to 9 billion.[17]

For the period 1977–80 the total amount of major weapons imported by Latin America was $3826 million at constant (1975) prices. For the same period, the exports of the main Latin American countries amounted to $471 million. Although this represented 37.1 per cent of the total Third World major weapon exports, it was only 12.3 per cent of the total imports of major weapons by Latin America. According to Table 7.10, Brazil is the only country with a significant amount of exports to compensate for her imports. Brazil's exports of major weapons for the period of 1977–80, represented 65 per cent of her imports. Argentina, in the same period, had to pay almost twenty times the value of her exports to cover the amount of imports. Peru and Chile are paying, proportionally, much more even than Argentina. Although we do not have the data of Chilean exports, the relation between sales and purchases is not less than 1 to 50.

In total and relative terms, Peru is the country with the highest amount of arms imports. For the same period 1977–80, Peruvian purchases of major weapons amounted $995 million, without major weapons exports registered. We can conclude that Argentina is in a worse position than Brazil, but Chile and Peru, medium countries, are in the worst position of all Latin American countries in terms of the money spent in arms purchases.[18]

The dynamics of the arms industry and arms exports of Latin American countries have three main features. Firstly, they produce and provide not very sophisticated weapons in global terms, but sophisticated enough to satisfy a good part of their military internal needs. Secondly, Latin American arms producers have a good market inside and outside the region, which is likely to expand if producer countries keep developing projects and increasing production. Thirdly, producer countries would also have the opportunity to expand their sales to developed countries, if they concentrated on certain types of arms where they could become highly competitive. That is already the case of military aircraft production like the Brazilian EMB-121 Xingu, and the trainer counter-insurgency aircraft 1A-58A Pucara from Argentina, or the new Argentinian medium tank. As we can see from Table 7.11, the main exports from Brazil, Argentina and Chile in 1980 are military aircraft. In terms of the recipient countries, only Brazil has expanded its market to countries of the Third World outside the region. Moreover, Brazil is already exporting the EMB-121 Xingu to developed countries, in 1980 to Belgium and France. For the other Latin American suppliers, the main market has been inside the region. According to the report of the Frost and Sullivan Co. (USA), for the period 1982–5, Latin American countries will purchase approximately 967 combat aircraft. They estimate that Brazil and Argentina will supply 75 per cent of these purchases with their tactical military aircraft: Brazil with the new type AM-X military aircraft and Argentina with the modern 1A-63.[19]

In general terms we could say that the military industry of Latin America will have good chances to increase its participation in the world's arms market. Nevertheless, this will also depend on how they deal with the present economic situation internally and externally, and how much they are prone to spend in the military industry considering the economic effects on the whole of the economy.

V CONCLUSIONS

The approach to militarism in Latin America, in economic terms, presents some interesting preliminary conclusions.

Firstly, the amount of military expenditure for the countries of the

TABLE 7.11 Latin America: export of arms, 1980

BRAZIL

Recipient country	No. ordered	Weapon designation	Weapon description	Year of order
Belgium	5	EMB-121 Xingu	Transport	1980
France	35	EMB-121 Xingu	Transport	1980
Bolivia	12	T-25 Universal	Trainer	1979*
Chile	6	EMB-326 Xavante	Trainer/COIN	1978*
Gabon	3	EMB-110	Transport	1980
Iraq	—†	EE-11 Urutu	APC	1979*
Iraq	—	EE-17 Sucuri	TD	1979
Iraq	—	EE-9 Cascavel	Recce AC	1979*
Libya	200*	EE-11 Urutu	APC	1978
Paraguay	10	EMB-110	Transport	1977
Paraguay	9	EMB-236 Xavante	Trainer/COIN	1979
Paraguay	12*	Uirapuru-122A	Trainer/COIN	1979
Sudan	6	EMB-111	Mar patrol	1979*
Upper Volta	1	EMB-110	Transport	1980*
Uruguay	1	EMB-110B	Transport	1979*

Continued on page 132

Table 7.11 contd

ARGENTINA

Recipient country	No. ordered	Weapon designation	Weapon description	Year of order
Dominican Rep.	×	IA-58A Pucara	Trainer/COIN	1980*
Iraq	20*	IA-58A Pucara	Trainer/COIN	1980*
Paraguay	1	C-47	Transport	1980
Uruguay	3	C-45 Expeditor	Transport	1980
	××	IA-58A Pucara	Trainer/COIN	1980
	9	T-28	Trainer	1980
Venezuela	24*	IA-58A Pucara	Trainer/COIN	1980*

CHILE

Recipient country	No. ordered	Weapon designation	Weapon description	Year of order
Paraguay	1	UH-12E	Hel	1980*

* Uncertain data or SIPRI estimate
† Total number sold: 2000 EE-9, EE-11 and EE-17; being delivered at a rate of 10 EE-9 EE-11/17 per month from July 1979.
× Negotiating.
×× Undisclosed number on order.

SOURCE *SIPRI Yearbook, 1981.*

region, is not affecting the economy of all countries in the same proportion. Brazil, the largest country of the region with the strongest economy, has an important military complex, but its military expenditure does not play a very important role in the economy as a whole. Argentina and Cuba, although in very different conditions, have devoted a greater importance to military expenditure but pay a significant social and economic cost. Chile, Peru, Ecuador and Uruguay have had to pay the highest economic cost to sustain their military apparatus. Mexico, on the other hand, has one of the lowest proportional military expenditures of the region, and the economic effects of that is minimal.

Secondly, the prosperous arms industry of Latin America is concentrated on Brazil and Argentina. Cuba, Chile and Venezuela have started their military industries but they are still at a very low stage. Brazil is the only country of the region with an industrial base strong enough to maintain an important arms industry without a great sacrifice for the rest of the industry, achieving significant competitiveness in the world market. Argentina, Cuba and Chile, have to devote greater efforts and amount of resource from the whole of the economy to sustain their arms industries.

Thirdly, in terms of technological independence, Brazil and Argentina have developed a significant indigenous technology on all types of major weapons, including missiles. To develop their projects they have worked closer with European companies than with those of the United States. In fact, most of their exports derived from indigenous designers.

Fourthly, in terms of arms purchases and sales, although still with deficit, Brazil has the best balance of the region between imports and exports. All other countries, including Argentina, are far behind compensating arms purchases with indigenous arms sales.

On the other side, military industries in Latin America have good expectations to increase their participation in the world market, if they keep developing the types of arms that can be more competitive. It is likely that for a long period, Third World countries will be their main clients.

NOTES AND REFERENCES

1. Stockholm International Peace Research Institute (SIPRI), *The Arms Trade with Third World Countries* (New York: Holmes & Meir, 1975) p. 259.

2. International Institute for Strategic Studies (IISS) *Military Balance 1981–82* (London: IISS, 1981) p. 259.
3. SIPRI, *Armaments and Disarmament Yearbook 1981* (London: Taylor & Francis, 1981) p. 126.
4. In current prices (1975) SIPRI, *Armaments and Disarmament Yearbook, 1981*.
5. Pierre, A., *The Global Politics of Arms Sales* (Princeton: Princeton University Press, 1982) p. 233.
6. IISS, *Military Balance 1981–82*, pp. 114–18.
7. For a good discussion about the definitions and uses of power, see the article by Baldwin, D., 'Power Analysis and World Politics: New Trends versus Old Tendencies', in *World Politics*, vol. 31, no. 2 (1979).
8. SIPRI, *Armaments and Disarmament Yearbook 1979* (London: Taylor & Francis, 1981) pp. 54–7.
9. IISS, *Military Balance 1981–82*, p. 113.
10. Information provided by a SIPRI official and published in *El Universal* newspaper, 22 May 1982.
11. SIPRI, *Armaments and Disarmament Yearbook 1981*, p. xxi.
12. Pierre, A., *The Global Politics of Arms Sales*, p. 11.
13. SIPRI, *Armaments and Disarmament Yearbook 1981*, p. 188.
14. Ibid., p. 196.
15. Ibid., pp. 86–9.
16. SIPRI, *The Arms Trade with Third World Countries*, pp. 21–30.
17. SIPRI, *Armaments and Disarmament Yearbook 1981*, p. 185.
18. Ibid., pp. 110–20.
19. *Armas y Geoestrategia*, vol. 1, no. 4 (1982) p. 25.

Note on the Impact of Military Expenditure on the Japanese Economy by Jun Nishikawa, UNITAR, Waseda University

Some relationships between military expenditure and economic growth have been recognised. Japan is well known for its low expenditure on defence, and for giving up the force of war by its Constitution. It is pointed out that Japan could utilise the factors of production, which are used in other countries for military purposes, in the productive fields.

Among the OECD countries, Japan, Austria and Canada are the countries where the ratio of military expenditure to GNP is the lowest: between 1 and 2 per cent, in the 1970s. In the decade from 1970, these countries have experienced relatively high economic growth: the real rate of growth amounted to 4–5.5 per cent. For the majority of the OECD countries, where the ratio of military expenditure/GNP amounts to 3–4 per cent, the performance of growth was equally 3–4 per cent. In the case of the USA, where 6 per cent of the GNP is used for defence spending, the real rate of growth in the 1970s was 3.3 per cent. We also know that heavy military build-up in the USSR has made the consumers' life in this country stringent. It is a fact that in the case of Japan and Austria, their rates of fixed capital formation have been far larger than the other OECD countries: 27–33 per cent for the former against 20–23 per cent for the latter in the 1970s.

There might be several reasons for this, including the high propensity to save or the high productivity deriving from the adoption of modern technology after the destruction of old productive equipment during World War II. One of the common characteristics of these two countries is, however, their conviction and constitutional status – permanent neutrality in the case of Austria and giving up war as a means for resolving international conflicts in the case of Japan. This common characteristic has limited their military sector and lowered their military spending. And we may presume that the low military expenditure contributed to both of them having a higher rate of investment than other countries.

If Japan had the same level of military expenditure as the main European countries, how much would it affect the rate of economic growth? To calculate this, let the military expenditure of Japan be 4 per cent of GNP, which is the actual defence level of European countries. In this case, assuming the trade-off between the military expenditure and productive investment, the actual rate of fixed capital formation might be decreased by 3 per cent, which makes an annual capital formation of about 27 per cent. In the 1970s, the capital coefficient in the Japanese economy was 6, so that the rate of economic growth would be about 4.5 per cent. Thus, the non-possession of war forces added, according to our calculation, approximately 1 per cent of real economic growth (which corresponds to the 18 per cent of the average annual growth rate in the 1970s) to the economy. This figure may not seem as impressive as one might expect. However, the fact that the Japanese economy could avoid proceeding to an overall militarisation of the economy is far more important than this abstract figure. We understand this when we see the actual trouble in the American economy.

The military build-up of the Reagan administration will add $170 bn in six years to the total defence budgets planned by the preceding Carter administration and increase the defence budget to 32 per cent of the Federal Government expenditure in 1984 (it was 24 per cent in 1981 – in the case of the Japanese budget, 5.3 per cent in 1980). The ratio of military expenditure to GNP would reach 7 per cent, which is comparable to the figure at the time of the Vietnam war.

We are already seeing the impact of this huge military build-up on the American economy in a number of ways:

(1) In spite of the budget cuts in social welfare, education or other fields, the huge deficit in the federal budget continues. It increases the federal borrowing from the domestic financial market, leading to high interest rates and making borrowing difficult for the private sector. It affects domestic investment.

(2) The overall pull of productive resources (especially capital, engineers, R & D capacity and skilled labour) from the traditional industries, located in the Eastern part of the USA, to the growing armament industries, located mainly in the 'sun-belt' area, contribute to the decrease in productivity as well as in international competitiveness of the traditional leading industries: steel, automobiles, electric and electronics, machine tools, etc. Actually, 60 per cent of the Federal R & D expenditure goes to the military field.

(3) The defence and high technology industries are, in general, capital and knowledge intensive. Therefore, the expansion of these industries creates employment for scientists, engineers and trained workers. However, the employment effect of these industries on production related workers has been rather limited. The increase of expenditure in the defence field creates less employment than the

expenditure in the direct production or social fields.[1] The increase of defence expenditure does not resolve the problem of structural unemployment, which will become far more serious as international competition intensifies.

(4) Finally, as the international competitiveness of main traditional industries decreases, there is a mounting pressure for protectionism. Together with the pull of resources to the newly expanding military and high technology industries, where supply has had difficulty keeping up with demand owing to required higher specification and technologies, this fact poses obstacles in the amelioration of the supply side: inflation will continue.

Thus, in the case of the United States, the increase of military expenditure has not strengthened the economy, and is actualy affecting the national security by weakening its economy.

There is some pressure on Japan to increase its defence expenditure, both from the USA and from the domestic industrial/political complex. However, in light of the analysis made on the effect of military expenditure on the US economy, it is better that Japan avoids following the armaments race already developed between the superpowers. Rather, Japan, which is the unique victim of the atomic bombs dropped on Hiroshima and Nagasaki and also has the unique Peace Constitution, should make serious efforts towards realisation of disarmament, in reducing the North–South gap and in building a peaceful international environment in the world, in order that every country can mobilise their resources in the economic and social fields, avoiding waste of the precious resources which may serve the needs of human beings.

NOTE AND REFERENCE

1. See The Council on Economic Priorities, *The Costs and Consequences of Reagan's Military Buildup* (New York: 1982) pp. 24–8.

Further Note on the Impact of Military Expenditure or the Japanese Economy by Isamu Miyasaki, UNITAR, New York

Economic growth of Japan after the Second World War has been characterised by, among other factors, less military spending, free competition among business, free trade with trading partners and peace.

From an economic point of view, military spending is a waste of resources. It is categorised as 'government consumption' which depends for its finance on a burden on people (tax) on the one hand and is spent as 'consumption' on the other. It certainly stimulates the economy when spent for a short while, but weakens the economy by reducing productivity from a longer point of view.

In addition, military purchases and production are, in principle, against the philosophy of a 'market-economy': market forces do not function, the price mechanism does not work, and interventions by the government, who is a sole purchaser, restrains private initiatives. The problem is not a matter of *volume* but of *quality*. Japan's success in economic development after the war presents a good example of this case.

Military spending is often said to have stimulated technological progress, especially in big projects. It may be true in some specific cases but may not be true when 'opportunity cost' is calculated.

Technological progress has been promoted by government assistance in post-war Japan, in the case of atomic development, computer production, construction of a super-express train etc., particularly at their initial stages. Government assistance has been gradually reduced as the competitive power is strengthened, and in recent years technological progress has been promoted by private initiatives. Free competition among businesses, not government guidance nor government spending, is the major driving force of technological progress.

It is urgently necessary for economists to study further the relationship between military spending and economic growth: to define 'military spending', to collect statistics, to make international comparisons, to calculate the direct and indirect effects on the economy and society, without political prejudgements.

Part Three
Strategic/Economic Approaches to Armaments Dynamics

8 Semantic Variations on Richardson's Armaments Dynamics

Christian Schmidt
UNIVERSITE DE PARIS IX DAUPHINE, CASCI

I INTRODUCTION

The international scientific community is preparing to celebrate the thirtieth anniversary of the death of L. F. Richardson who divided his scientific activities between research into mathematical polymology (war studies) and meteorology. The arms race model which won him posthumous popularity among English-speaking specialists was first formulated in 1919[1] barely following the equally famous equations for aerial combat devised by another British pioneer in mathematical polymology, L. F. Lanchester.[2] Later on, Richardson restated the various properties of his model in detail on several occasions.[3] Today one can say that practically all quantitative studies of the arms race at least mention the Richardson model, so much so that two authors of a recent review of the contemporary literature on the subject even made it a point of honour to be the first not to reproduce the Richardson equations.[4] This continuing reference to the Richardson system is all the harder to understand in that several theoretical criticisms, many on decisive points, have been formulated against it.[5] Furthermore, most of the empirical tests to which it has been subjected during the present period have proved disappointing.[6] Empirical studies over recent years seem to establish:

(1) That far from being the rule, Richardson behaviour seems rather to be the exception in the recent international dynamics of armaments.[7]
(2) That the explanatory power of the internal models, drawing on bureaucratic analyses generally proves superior to that of international interactional models like Richardson's to take account of the dynamics of military spending at least in the case of the world's main military powers and the two largest in particular.[8]

This urgently raises the question of whether the Richardson model is nowadays of historic interest only or whether on the contrary, despite its weaknesses, the system Richardson imagined over sixty years ago can still contribute to improving our understanding of the complex process of the armaments dynamic. It will be argued here that in spite of all the studies devoted to Richardson's work, many aspects of it still have not been exploited and that his model can therefore be a point of departure for new, promising research. The argument is based on the observation that while the model's syntax has already been closely and carefully examined, its semantics have been only very slightly explored within the restrictive perspective of usually rudimentary econometrics.[9] The present paper sets out to fill this gap.

Following this introduction the next part of the chapter is devoted to a critical re-reading of the model itself, in the form in which Richardson presented it. This leads on to establishing the model's theoretical status and then to a systematic classification of the various derivatives it has prompted in the specialist literature (Intriligator listed no fewer than 40[10]).

The third part proposes to distinguish, following a semantic analysis of the different possible interpretations of the model's variables and parameters, an 'economic' and a 'polymological' version. The scope of the different implications of this distinction are then discussed.

The fourth part examines the possible meanings of the model's equations, revealing a 'mechanistic' and several 'decisional' variants and then drawing out the 'positive' and 'normative' interpretations possible.

By way of conclusion, a fifth part presents a general table of the different model categories compatible with the Richardson equations and sets out the ways of moving from one to another. It ends by explaining why the Richardson approach remains to some extent irreplaceable because of the possibilities it offers for varied linkages in a complex system with other models, of war, international negotiations and even domestic economic growth.

II INTERPRETATION OF A THEORY OR EMPIRICAL REPRESENTATION OF A PROCESS

The term 'model' had not yet been developed so far as it has today when Richardson proposed his system of intersecting differential linear equations to represent the processes he had set out to study. He himself defined his objective in *Arms and Insecurity* like this:

> The preparations for war of the two groups may be regarded as the rectangular co-ordinates of a particle in an "international plane," so that every point in this plane represents one conceivable instantaneous international situation. The differential equations are then the equations of motion of the particle.[11]

This quotation prompts several comments. In the first place, Richardson constructed his representation of the international situation by analogy with physics.[12] This reference back to physics lies behind the interpretations he chose for two of the coefficients in his system of equations (coefficients of 'defence' and of 'social viscosity').[13]

Secondly, Richardson's aim appears both wide ranging and yet highly concentrated in its expression, setting out to describe international situations (broad field) with variations in preparations for war (restricted definition) as the only variables in the state of the system. As regards measurements it is noteworthy that although Richardson himself tried to test his system using statistical series of military expenditures evaluated in monetary units,[14] he was careful to make it clear that war preparations are theoretically measurable either in men or in money.

The framework within which Richardson develops his interpretation remains incomplete in relation to his objective, because it does not allow him to identify the nature of the relationships between international situations (tension, war, peace) and the variables through which he proposed to identify them (variations in preparations for war). This gap is perhaps the source of frequent semantic confusion, especially since the introduction of nuclear armaments between what Moll and Luebbert have called the 'arms building' and the 'arms using' models.[15] Numerous contributions attest this.[16] For us, only the 'arms building' category is representative of the arms race. The 'arms using' category deals with another class of processes requiring, in our view, different models concerned with the outbreak and/or development of war.

Thirdly, Richardson's term 'preparations of war' to qualify the two explanatory variables in his system encourages the kind of ambiguity referred to above. It assumes that the amount of military expenditure or the volume of armaments are only approximations of a more general concept of expenditure (or attack) potential and most of all, implies that the two groups, i.e. the countries or country groups (alliances) to which they refer are at least potential adversaries. So war, which does not appear explicitly in Richardson's representation system, is nevertheless implicitly introduced into it through the choice of countries or country groups in the study.[17]

Lastly, the field of interpretation for variations in preparations of war does not reduce, for Richardson, to positive values. Not only does he allow in his system for the hypothesis of unilateral disarmament, but he proposes a bold interpretation of the negative values in terms of international co-operation, which he endeavours to bring out by trying to establish correlations between these negative war preparation values and positive indices for increasing foreign trade. He infers that contrary to what common sense might suggest, the opposite of war is not peace but international co-operation. But even if this latter conjecture is generally rejected as insufficiently worked out, the fact remains that the term arms race is wrong when applied to the Richardson model, whose subject is in fact the international dynamics of war preparations or more simply, the dynamics of armaments. The latter expression will therefore be used in the remainder of this paper.

Leaving aside, now, the analysis of Richardson's aims to consider the status of his model from the standpoint of contemporary epistemology, it is important to distinguish between two possible meanings which might at first sight be attributed to it.

(i) a possible interpretation of a theory of the dynamics of armaments,
(ii) a framework of coherence with which to link up empirical data about the process with one another.

To decide between these two points of view, we must first specify:
(a) the theory of which the system of equations might constitute a

logical interpretation (model in the sense of (i) above), (b) the empirical space for which the system of equations might provide the means for an empirical specification (model in the sense of (ii) above).

(a) The theory on which the Richardson model depends can be summed up in the following proposition: For any country (or group of countries) that is potentially an adversary, any variation in the armaments of one depends on the amount of armaments of the potentially adversary country or countries, on the weight of its own amount of armament and on an intrinsic factor independent of the amount of armaments of either (and vice versa). It is a full theory in the sense that variations in the armaments of the countries analysed are entirely explained by the endogenous variables and parameters of the system. Its 'closed' character even gives it a kind of autonomy. Its subject is clear, the dynamics of armaments. Lastly, it is sufficiently explicit in choice of variables and parameters to be distinguishable from alternative theories also aiming to account for the dynamics of armaments with different variables, especially relating to countries' internal bureaucratic functioning conditions.[18] Its semantic, however, remains somewhat imprecise, because it leaves something indeterminate in the definition of the terms and expressions 'armaments', 'amount of armaments', 'weight of armaments', not to mention the metatheoretical question of what criterion could be used to define 'potentially adversary' countries.

(b) The empirical space to which the Richardson model corresponds makes it possible to identify each point as describing the international situation at a given date. The differential equations permit derivation of variables with respect to time, thus providing a temporal expression of their associated parameters. In fact, though, this is a pseudo-temporality because in the model the parameters are constant coefficients and consequently, defined independently of time. The empirical coherence framework associated with the model is indeed suitable for describing the consequences of the armaments dynamic (representation of the states of the system), but not for explaining the empirical functioning of its mechanism. In particular, there is no room for identifying adjustment lags. This key gap in permitting an empirical interpretation cannot be filled by interpreting the model as free of any assumption as to adjustment lags, i.e. compatible with any such assumption whatever. This shortcoming affects the scope for a causal interpretation of the empirical data. This is because even if we do not consider that the recursive form constitutes the only expression of causality, a causal analysis of the data requires the introduction of further assumptions about the absent time series, the definition of the set of empirical structures, implicitly used by Richardson and is liable even to enter into contradiction with them.[19]

One preliminary conclusion emerges from this examination. In contrast with an opinion shared by the majority of specialists,[20] the Richardson model constitutes a mathematical coherence test for drawing out the logical implications of the initial theoretical assumptions about the dynamics of armaments (model in the sense of (i)) rather than a relevant framework for an empirical representation of the concrete functioning of those dynamics. This does not mean, indeed the opposite is the case, that it would be impossible to conceive of one or more statistical models compatible with the theoretical assumptions in the Richardson model.[21] But these are then different models because, as we have seen, it is logically impossible to infer an acceptable statistical interpretation. Furthermore, construction of such empirical models derived from Richardson's theory, requires beforehand a full semantic investigation of the model components. Without that preliminary stage, empirical work referring to Richardson is liable to go no further than trying to find correlations between military outlays for country pairs ultimately amounting to what Malinvaud regards as econometric exercises without any model.[22]

Closer analysis of the relationship between Richardson's theory and his model discloses three degrees, analytically distinct, in the range of model families grouped together in the literature under the somewhat vague heading of 'Richardson's'.

(i) The first degree is represented by the families of models whose syntax is exclusively constituted of all or some of the variables and equations in the Richardson model. So each model in this family corresponds to a semantic variant, made possible by the imprecision of the definitions mentioned above. Several examples of these variants will be introduced in the third part of the paper.

(ii) The second degree is represented by the family of models whose syntax is constituted wholly or partly of Richardson model variables and equations supplemented by some extra variables and equations with respect to the mathematical structure of the original model. Every model in this family corresponds to an extension compatible with Richardson's logic. Some of these extensions will be described in the fourth part of this paper. These extensions combine with the semantic variations in the third part.

(iii) The third degree is represented by the family of models whose syntax is constituted by an equation system differing from that of Richardson's model but nevertheless reflecting, in a different formal presentation, the same general theoretical assumptions about the international dynamics of armaments as Richardson's model. Every model in this family thus represents a different interpretation of what can by extension be called the Richardson 'paradigm'. One example of this category is provided by lagged adjustment models which illustrate the theory summarised above, but using mathematical apparatus that is syntactically and semantically distinct from the Richardson model apparatus. It seems that attempts to design statistical models for armaments dynamics should be aimed more in this direction. Nevertheless, no such model will be discussed here as that would be outside the scope of the present paper.

The fact remains that theory of armaments dynamics itself, of which the Richardson model provides the first sketch of a formalised interpretation, remains hazy on a number of points.[23] Is it an economic theory or a polymological theory, which we should try at a later stage to link up with econometric or 'polymometric' models? Before these questions can be answered, the semantic imprecisions referred to must be cleared up by drawing out successively:

(a) The possible significances of the model variables and parameters.
(b) The possible interpretations of the model equations.
(c) The possible types of statement to which the model may give rise.

III ECONOMIC VERSION AND POLYMOLOGICAL VERSION

The Richardson model can be written as follows:

$$\dot{x} = a_1 y_{(t)} - a_2 x_{(t)} + a_3 \tag{1}$$
$$\dot{y} = b_1 x_{(t)} - b_2 y_{(t)} + b_3 \tag{2}$$

The fields of interpretation for the values of the x and y variables can be defined either economically or militarily. If the former, $x_{(t)}$ and $y_{(t)}$ represent the amounts of military spending by countries X and Y at time t. If the latter, they represent the armaments volumes of the two countries at time t.

The state of the system is thus defined by expenditures in the former and by volumes in the latter.

The objection that only an economic interpretation of x and y is acceptable, on the grounds that military expenditures can easily be evaluated in economic units but no relative units are readily available to measure armaments volumes, is based on a twofold misunderstanding.

In the first place, strategic units can be theoretically defined with which, for example, to evaluate a country's armament stocks in terms of the losses it could inflict on a potential adversary country. Such units have been proposed for the special case in which x and y represent the nuclear arsenals of countries X and Y.[24] Secondly and more fundamentally, the definition of the fields of interpretation for x and y and the units in which they are measured are two different questions even though their solutions may be linked. Thus, resorting to the monetary unit for an economic interpretation of x and y does not preclude us from providing a definition of the economic cost of military outlays.[25] Similarly, in the military field, adopting the simplifying assumption of a stock of missiles of just one kind in the special case of nuclear arsenals does not permit us directly to define a military performance index except in some very special cases.[26] Generally, some strategic use assumptions must be attached.

From another angle, the economic and military units selected depend on the economic theory and the strategic doctrine in which the economic and/or military variables of the model are interpreted.[27] This has the consequence that the economic and polymological versions of the Richardson system cannot be treated as a straightforward duality between prices (economic x and y) and quantities (military x' and y'). In fact it is a matter of different models, analysis of whose relationships is not trivial but requires a study of the transformation conditions (see Appendix).

Let us just now consider the parameters. It is important at the outset not, like Richardson, to confuse the formal properties inherent in the mathematical structure of its equations with their semantic content. If $a_3 = 0$ and $x = 0$ we can write $1/a_1 = y/x$. However, Richardson deduces the following definition 'apparent catching-up time in an arms race from zero with no grievances'.[28]

However, that definition is unacceptable for three reasons. It has no generality and corresponds to particular values for the variables and parameters. It introduces a further assumption of equality between the armaments of the two countries which does not belong to the model. It implies that the units of measurement for x and y are the same, i.e. that x and y represent either amounts of military expenditure expressed in the same units or armaments volumes expressed in the same units, which introduces a further constraint outside the model. The same argument applies against Richardson's definition of a_2 as representing the delay which is politically necessary for country X to reduce its level of armaments to 0 when its aggressiveness is nil.[29]

In accordance with the predominant convention in the specialist literature, let a_1 and b_1 represent only the coefficients of reaction of one of the countries to the armaments of another. In accordance with the previously introduced definitions of x and y, a_1 and b_1 can theoretically give rise to four different interpretations, subject to the availability of a transition key providing a strategic equivalence of the amount of military expenditures and/or an economic equivalence of the armaments volume (transformation problem). These interpretations correspond to the following four cases:

(1) x and y both represent amounts of military expenditure.
(2) x and y both represent volumes of armaments.
(3) x represents an amount of military expenditure and y a volume of armaments.
(4) x represents a volume of armament and y an amount of military expenditure.

While there is no reason why the values of a_1 and b_1 should be the same in all four cases, their meaning is identical. The expressions $a_1 x$ and $b_1 y$ in fact reflect two distinct ideas: the values X and Y estimate of the other's armaments and the strategic interpretation of these values in terms of threat. Allowing for this distinction makes it possible to introduce an imperfect information into the model, for example by letting a_1 reflect the reaction of X to $\hat{y}$, where $\hat{y} = y$ represents the information available to X about Y's armaments. Similarly, b_1 reflects the reaction of Y to $\hat{x} \neq x$. The Richardson model can then be reformulated as follows:

$$\dot{x} = a_1 \bar{y}_{(t)} - a_2 x_{(t)} + a_3 \tag{3}$$

$$\dot{y} = b_1 \bar{x}_{(t)} - a_2 y_{(t)} + b_3 \tag{4}$$

$$\bar{x}_{(t)} = a_4 x_{(t)} \tag{5}$$

$$\bar{y}_{(t)} = b_4 y_{(t)} \tag{6}$$

However, this reformulation raises an awkward problem of interpretation. It is only of interest if equations (5) and (6) reflect the perfect information that could be available to an independent observer. Without this assumption, arguable from the standpoint of realism, there is no way of linking $\hat{x}$ to x and $\hat{y}$ to y and another model must be constructed to translate, into an adequate mathematical language, the estimates of X and Y leaving the strictly deterministic Richardson framework.[30]

We have still to define the set of possible values for a_1 and b_1. As against a restrictive interpretation which seems to prevail today, according to which $a_1, b_1, > 0$, Richardson does not exclude the case where $a_1 < 0$, $b_1 < 0$. He thinks this case to the introduction of submissive behaviour within the armaments dynamic.[31] The hardest case to interpret is where $a_1 b_1 = 0$, since $\dot{x}$ and $\dot{y}$ now depend only on $a_2 x$, and $b_2 x$, and on a_3 and b_3. For this assumption the Richardson model is somewhat akin to a stock adjustment model,[32] always provided though that the interpretation of a_3 and b_3 is not incompatible with the idea of a relationship between the dispositions of each country towards the other and the definition of a desired amount of military spending or of an armaments volume (cf. below). Let x^* and y^* be armaments desired by X and Y, it can easily be shown that $x^* = a_3/a_3$ and $y^* = b_3/b_2$. The desired level corresponds to the equilibrium values $\dot{x} = 0$, $\dot{y} = 0$ for the system:

$$\dot{x} = - a_2 x^*_{(t)} + a_3 \tag{7}$$

$$\dot{y} = - b_2 y^*_{(t)} + b_3 \tag{8}$$

However, the Richardson character of equations (7) and (8) can be disputed in so far as they move away from the international interactionist system which, as we have shown, constitutes the quintessence of Richardson's theory of armaments dynamics.

In the literature, a_2 and b_2 are conventionally interpreted as coefficients of fatigue or effort linked to the armaments held by X and Y. It is noteworthy though that Richardson uses the formula coefficient of 'fatigue and expense' to qualify a_2 and b_2.[33] This expression is revealing about the ambiguity which it is proposed to dispel by distinguishing the two interpretations, economic and military, of x and y.

If x and y represent volumes of armament, a_2 and b_2 are only the quantified expression of the physical cost of the stock of weapons at each country's disposal. When the armaments dynamics model is generalised to n countries, Richardson even goes so far as to interpret these coefficients as the equivalents of coefficients of each country vis-à-vis itself.

If x and y represent amounts of military expenditure, a_2 and b_2 can take on two different meanings. The first, of a microeconomic kind, reflects only the evaluation in economic units of the cost stocking. The second, macroeconomic, corresponds to a broader measurement of the national economic effect in terms of specific indicators, for example share of military spending in overall public spending (either GDP or GNP), expressed as a percentage of those aggregates. This second meaning of a_2 and b_2 seems more in line with the general spirit of the Richardson model, at least if we adopt a mechanist interpretation of its equation system (cf. below). Consequently, if a_2 and b_2 are given this macroeconomic meaning, the difference between the economic and polymological versions of the model no longer relates only to the measurement units used (measures of the cost in economic or military units) but also bears upon the objects being measured (macroeconomic effort or military effort).

Conversely, however, we decide to interpret a_2, b_2, $a_2 b_2 > 0$, negative or nil coefficients of fatigue appear to be ruled out as it is hard to see what their economic or military significance could be.

a_3 and b_3 are interpreted as coefficients representing the dispositions in which X finds itself relative to Y and Y to X respectively, independently of x and y. Although the determination of a_3 and b_3 does not involve the definitions of x and y, it is formally possible to express $a_3 b_3$ in the units chosen to measure x and y since if, for example $a_1 y = 0$ and $a_2 x = 0$, $a_3 = \dot{x}$. But that must not be confused with a definition of a_3, as has already been shown for a_1 and a_2. More generally, the meaning of a_3 and b_3 is given by a different theory, outside the model itself. This is why examining it involves a metatheoretical kind of investigation which will not be pursued here.

The possible values for a_3 and b_3 depend on the field of interpretation assigned to the theory of the international dynamics of armaments, and to the significance attached to the term 'potential adversary'. a_3 and $b_3 > 0$ correspond to mutual grievances while a_3 and $b_3 < 0$ reflect 'benevolent' dispositions. We could also add that a_3 and $b_3 = 0$ showed 'neutral' dispositions. This latter, however, seems hard to reconcile with the objective Richardson assigned his model to describe what would occur if instinct and tradition were allowed to act uncontrolled.[34]

One can, however, follow the majority of contemporary authors in adopting a more restricted definition of the field of interpretation for the Richardson theory, in which the armaments dynamic described by the model applies only to countries, or groups of countries, that are *potential* adversaries. It is this limited definition of the field of the theory that the present author has himself adopted. Ultimately, a_3, $b_3 > 0$ coincides with the restrictive definition of the entities to which the theory is applicable. That is why admitting that a_3 and b_3 can take any value whatever is tantamount to saying that the armaments dynamic the model describes is valid for all countries and groups of countries without exception. Such an extension, which can be seen retrospectively as a vestige of Richardson's initially ambitious project, therefore appears problematical.

The special role of a_3 and b_3 in the model is highlighted when we try, like Richardson, to generalise it to a number $n > 2$ countries. These coefficients then take the form a_{ij} and reflect the dispositions of each country towards every other country considered individually. Formally, the generalisation of a_1 is similar but it takes a different meaning. In the two-country model $a_1 x$ and $b_1 y$ represent the threat from Y's and X's armaments for X and Y. In other words, armaments and doctrines of use are merged there. That simplification is no longer possible in the model extended to n countries. In this general assumption, Richardson chooses to disconnect information about armaments from the doctrine of its use, arguing that 'other nations are supposed not to have definite information about the intentions of the ith nation, they only guess and suspect, and therefore they are disturbed by the total x, rather than by its component parts'.[35]

That is in fact a highly restrictive assumption because it implies that a_1 and b_1 are always coefficients of defensive reaction towards other countries' armaments, whereas a_3 and b_3 reflect, as we have seen, the degrees of aggressiveness of countries towards one another.[36]

The development of this distinction would lead to the reintroduction, in another way, of the criticism of irrationality rightly made by Rapoport[37] and Gillespie and Zinnes[38] on grounds of the mechanistic character of the system designed by Richardson (cf. below). If a_1 and b_1 cannot be interpreted without reference to a military strategy, even an implicit or very vague one, and if moreover a_3 and b_3

necessarily depend on a concept of collective preference, even a very hazy one, the assumption that a_1 and a_2 are independent of a_3 and b_3, which Richardson was attached to, introduces a kind of 'non-rationality' into the system which the present author considers Richardson himself intended.

To conclude, the semantic identification of the variables and parameters allows us to draw out to broad categories of interpretation for the system of equations (1) and (2), representing two different models.

We shall describe as Richardson's economic model (RE) the interpretation of an economic Richardson theory of the international dynamics of armaments, and as Richardson's polymological model (RP) the interpretation of a polymological Richardson theory of the dynamics of armaments.

RP offers an almost exclusively polymological explanation of the dynamics of armaments, because as we have seen, a_1p, b_1p, a_2p, b_2p and at the limit a_3p and b_3p are questions of polymology, whereas RE only offers a partial economic explanation since a_2e and b_2e are questions only of economics.

The theory modelled by RE appears very rudimentary, because it is wholly contained in the expressions $-a_2exe$, $-b_2eye$ of the system. That is why this economic theory has up to now been developed in two different directions.

The first consists of specifying the economic constraint by breaking down the various cost components (cost of maintaining existing equipment and of acquiring new weaponry), introducing ceilings in the budget resources allocated to military spending.[39]

The second corresponds to making explicit allowance for increases in national GNP in the Richardson equations, re-expressed as difference equations.[40]

More ambitious extensions of RE can be contemplated, notably by including, on top of national GNP, every country's expectations about how the other will perform economically, thus making it possible to introduce economic considerations at the very heart of the interactional process.[41] However, all these developments have the disadvantage that they lead to the relinquishment of the closed character of Richardson's model, which reduces its explanatory power by as much. This comes about because it seems difficult to take account of variables as complex as economic growth rates from a single model of the economic dynamics of armaments. Hence the reason why future developments here should be sought in a linkage between two distinct theoretical models, respectively representing the dynamics of armaments and of economic growth.[42]

The theory modelled by RP is hardly less rudimentary since it is based essentially on the expressions $a_1 p\ yp$, $b_1 p\ xp$. Most of its development has been obtained by transforming the mechanistic interpretation implicit in equations (1) and (2) into a decisional kind of interpretation (cf. below) $a_1 p$ and $b_1 p$ then reflect the result of optimisation procedures for military performance indices.[43] The main limitation on these extensions lies in the definition of these military performance indices which can only be deduced from a war simulation model, taking explicit account of assumptions about the strategic and tactical use of armaments. This direction has been explored for the instance of a nuclear conflict.[44]

But it comes up against two objects. One, methodological, stems from the impossibility of treating two distinct phenomena by means of one and the same model. Thus, variations in missile stocks resulting from the nuclear exchange in the nuclear war model described by Intriligator cannot have the same significance as variations arising out of the arms race process. Similarly, the linearity of the equations cannot be justified in the same way for the two phenomena. The other objection applies specifically to the nuclear instance which most researchers have concentrated on. Nuclear dissuasion, when based on doctrines of use, is not solely to protect the country against the risk of nuclear attack by the adversary country but is also to deter conventional attack. That is why the information provided by a nuclear war is not sufficient to define the military performances it is desired to introduce into the model of armaments dynamics. Here again, the solution must be sought in analysis of the possible linkages between two distinct models, drawn respectively from a polymological theory of the dynamics of armaments and a war theory.[45]

RE and RP do not belong to two mutually exclusive categories since as we have already seen, variables and parameters of both kinds can be combined in the same model as soon as a transition key has been defined between the two. This means that in the interests of realism we could, for example, choose from among all the possible combinations the following economic/polymological formulation:

$$\dot{x}e = a_1 pyp - a_2 exe + a_3 \qquad (9)$$

$$\dot{y}e = b_1 pxp - b_2 eye + b_3 \qquad (10)$$

More ambitious attempts, aiming to integrate international military and political factors together with internal economic and bureaucratic factors into one 'metamodel' have recently been undertaken.[46] But these do not come within the framework of the Richardson equation system under discussion here.

That is why it is not certain that a decisional interpretation of the system, intellectually satisfying though it might be, adds more to our understanding of the armaments dynamics process than a mechanistic interpretation.

Whatever their respective advantages, it is now time to specify the main implications of their differences.

The first concerns the definition of countries. In the mechanistic variant this usually involves just a simple partition defined over the set of system variables and parameters (first case). Another definition of the countries in the mechanistic variant (second case) stems only from the attempt to draw a possible but not necessary analogy with the decisional variant. In the decisional variants, the countries are always treated as decision units as in conventional economic theory of foreign trade.

The second relates to time. For each system state there corresponds one t and only one, but that is a mere indexing and as we have seen, time plays no explanatory role in the international dynamics of armaments as described by a mechanistic model. Time steps in rather differently in the decisional variants. The objectives of the armaments policy-makers can be formulated as follows: (1) to a fixed time horizon, (2) independently of any time specification or (3) taking time itself as the target. Objectives (1) and (3) require a time interpretation. Thus, for example, the integral form generally given to the performance index is defined over the whole time interval T in the case of a fixed horizon.

The third difference relates to the problem of normativeness. We must start by clearing up any confusion between the observed or hypothetical origin of the values attributed to the variables and parameters and the positive or normative status of the statements they interpret. The concept of norm in the mechanistic variant does not have the same sense as in the decisional variants. It is worth pointing out at once that from a strictly logical standpoint, neither the statements of the mechanistic variant nor those of the decisional variants are 'prescriptive' in kind. But whereas the mechanistic model norms do not distinguish rules hypothetically governing the armaments dynamics system, the decisional model norms take the form of what von Wright calls 'technical norms' or 'directives'.[47] For on the one hand, the truth of the decisional model statements has to be assessed independently of the units of choice adopted by the country's arms policy decision-makers, but on the other the relevance of the consequences of those choices clearly depends on there being a norm represented by a performance index, economic or military. That technical norm can have either a positive meaning, when it reflects policy-makers' observed behaviour, or a hypothetical meaning when it contains a prescription for them. It is in this latter sense that the term 'normative' can be used to designate a sub-category of decisional models.

IV MECHANISTIC VARIANT AND DECISIONAL VARIANTS

After the interpretation of variables and parameters, the question arises of the meaning of the Richardson system equations. Two interpretations are possible.

'MECHANISTIC' INTERPETATION

Equations (1) and (2) describe the theoretical adjustment conditions for variables in a self-regulating system, under the parameter restrictions discussed above. The state of the system thus conceived results from an automatic response mechanism. This means (1) either that the armaments dynamic is independent of the choices and preferences of armaments policy-makers in countries X and Y or (2) that the policy-makers in fact have no discretion about the decisions they are obliged to take. The two hypotheses are not identical because, for example, only the latter is compatible with the variable estimation concept introduced in the second part. In the first instance, equations (1) and (2) have no meaning except by reference to the system considered as a whole and parameter values depend exclusively on macroscopic considerations. Coefficients a, b, a_2 and b_2 are interpreted as 'propensities' and coefficients a_3 and b_3 as indicators. In the second, equations (1) and (2) become policy-makers' behaviour, assimilated to the countries whose arms policy they direct, it being understood that their behaviour is wholly determined by the constraints represented by the set of parameters which can be interpreted in various ways (cf. above).

In both cases, the armaments dynamic will be said to be the expression of a mechanistic system.

'DECISIONAL' INTERPRETATION

Equations (1) and (2) describe the theoretical consequences of the interaction of decisions bearing upon system variables controlled by the armaments policy-makers in countries X and Y. Understanding them takes us back to further equations representing the policy-makers' behaviour (assessment functions). Values of a_1 and b_1 may be the outcomes of policy-makers' choices, so that their interpretation depends on the assessment functions selected, whereas $a_3 b_3$ may correspond to constraints on the system regardless of those choices. This means that the armaments dynamic is in the main subject to the control exerted upon the system either by just one or by the two armaments policy-makers of the countries.

In both cases, the armaments dynamic will be said to be the expression of a decisional system.

The original variant Richardson chose was that of a mechanistic dynamic. This thoughtout option was based, so he said, on the assumption that the countries 'follow their traditions, which are fixtures, and their instincts, which are mechanical and because they have not yet made a sufficiently strenuous intellectual and moral effort to control the situation'.[48]

So it was on grounds of realism that Richardson preferred the interpretation he had adopted. We can therefore question the contemporary value of this presupposition, with an eye to the effectiveness of armaments policies as defined and applied in recent times, and to the scope of the efforts put into disarmament negotiations. But to go into that would stray outside the range of this paper. However, it is also arguable that models of the international dynamics of armaments need not necessarily be assessed from a positive standpoint, but lend themselves just as well to a normative interpretation.[49] Then their outcomes take on the value of normative statements in the sense of norm logic.[50] However, the debate about whether to go for a mechanistic or a decisional interpretation boils down neither to a straightforward philosophical postulate about the real nature of the armaments dynamic process,[51] nor to the issue of whether statements have a positive or a normative meaning. The restricted number, and the quality of the items of information processed by the model are also factors to be taken into account.

Now is the time to specify the meaning of the equations under the two variants, mechanistic and decisional. In the mechanistic variant, the interpretation of equations (1) and (2) is in a way direct, so this brings us back to the earlier discussion about the semantics of the variables and parameters they contain. In the decisional variant, though, their intepretation requires an analysis of the supplementary equations describing the objectives in the minds of X and Y countries' policy-makers. Then we have to distinguish the case where only one policy-maker's objectives are taken into account[52] from that in which the model takes account of both countries' policy-makers' objectives.[53] But we may feel that the interpretation of the first case remains incomplete, from the decisional standpoint, in so far as it introduces a decisional semantic asymmetry within the Richardson theory still stated symmetrically (cf. above).

This translation of the Richardson system into the terms of optimum control theory, for the first case, or differential games theory for the second[54] entails a distinction between state variables and control variables and introduces one or two performance indices corresponding to the assessment functions of the X and Y armaments policy-makers. Economic or military interpretations can be proposed of these new components, by reference to the economic and polymological versions. Three levels have to be taken into consideration:

(i) choice of control variable or variables evaluated in economic units or strategic equivalents,
(ii) choice of performance indices, interpreted economically or polymologically,
(iii) choice of objectives selected by policy-makers which may be either economic or military or economic and military.

This simple enumeration is enough to illustrate the wealth of the combinations warranted by the decisional variants of the Richardson system.

V CONCLUSION: A PROVISIONAL TYPOLOGY OF THE INTERPRETATIONS

The 'economic/polymological' categories drawn out by semantic analysis of the variables and parameters in the second part of this paper, and the 'mechanistic/decisional' categories shown by investigation of the meaning of the equations in the third part are not, as we have already seen, mutually exclusive. Their combinations can be summarised by Figure 8.1 below.

Moreover, the procedures for passing from one family of models to another can be described by Figure 8.2 which, for the sake of simplicity, takes only the 'normative/positive' sub-categories within the family of decisional models. Each line in this diagram links one

Interpretation of equations	Mechanistic	Decisional Positive	Normative
Interpretation of variables and parameters			
Economic (level of expenditure in economic units)	REM	RED_p	RED_n
Military (stock of arms in strategic units)	RPM	RPD_p	RPD_n

REM   Richardson's Economic Mechanistic System
RPM   Richardson's Polymological Mechanistic System
RED   Richardson's Economic Decisional System
RPD   Richardson's Polymological Decisional system
p   positive
n   normative

FIGURE 8.1

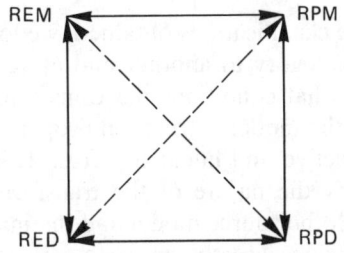

For abbreviations see Figure 8.1 above.

FIGURE 8.2

interpretation family to another, according to the two main category sets analysed.

The direction of the arrows symbolises the order in which passage can be effected. It will be noted that passing from economic to polymological (and vice versa) for a given family of mechanistic or decisional models (horizontal lines) requires that one be sure of the existence of a transformation T, of which an illustration is offered in the annex. Passage from the mechanistic to the decisional (and vice versa) for a given economic or polymological family (vertical lines) is effected immediately by simple addition or elimination of evaluation functions. Then the only problem is of the existence of a solution, which is not guaranteed for all possible forms of evaluation function, having regard to the system state equation linearity constraint. The broken diagonals represent double operations.

This general sketch of the main possibilities offered by the Richardson equation system shows that the research programme the British pioneer set out over sixty years ago is far from having been exhausted. In this author's view it still presents an undeniable advantage over competing programmes mentioned in the introduction. To put it briefly, it constitutes the best approach to rigorously linking up the dynamics of armament with on the one hand, the domestic economics of the countries participating and on the other, the risks of international conflict thereby engendered.

APPENDIX: THE TRANSFORMATION*

The above discussion brought out the different semantic categories according to which Richardson's armaments dynamic could be interpreted.

Starting from the classifications obtained, we look into the ways of passing from one category to another and more generally, into the question of under what conditions the transformations we perform allow any or all of the model's structural properties to be conserved, especially its interactive and linear features. This will require us in particular to specify the nature of the transformation, considering how it links up with the source model and the image model, and the possibilities of passing directly between adjacent categories, i.e.

* I gratefully acknowledge the assistance of Michel Rudnianski in preparing this appendix.

differing in respect of only one feature (e.g. mechanistic economic source model and mechanistic polymological model image).

We shall be mainly concerned here with transformations between mechanistic models, whose treatment appears simpler. We could, in principle, distinguish instances in which the only sources or images are purely economic or purely polymological models, from instances in which one or other model is mixed, such as the economic/polymological model defined in equations (9) and (10) in the preceding chapter. We shall not do so here, but instead broach that distinction in the case of decisional models, where it appears particularly relevant. Discussion of this latter problem requires definition of the command variables, performance indices and targets adopted by the decision-makers, and refers to a detailed analysis of the decisional models which is held over until the following chapter. As regards the other links indicated in Figure 8.2 they do not require the definition of an intrinsically associated transformation since, as remarked above, either the existence of such transformations serves no purpose, as when source and image are on the same vertical of the rectangle, or they can be associated with composite applications one of whose elements is already a transformation, as when source and image models are at the extremities of the same diagonal of the rectangle.

The status of the transformation must be specified. It can be understood in three different ways:

(1) As a simple technical operation making it possible to translate the units in which the variables of one model (the source model) are expressed in the units corresponding to another model (the image model).
(2) As a procedure by means of which, knowing a determined initial model (the source model) a different model can be constructed whose detailed properties are unknown at the outset (image model).
(3) As a representation of a real process corresponding to the passage through time from a situation identified by means of an initial model (source model) to a situation identified by means of a final model (image model).

These meanings are not mutually exclusive – the first, in particular, being implicated in the two others and representing what might be called the *minimal* meaning of the concept of transformation. However, each poses the problem of interpretation in terms of its own.

According to (1), it is only a mathematical operator not requiring any interpretation.

With (2) the choice of the form of the relation depends on the meaning attributed to the procedure. Thus in the first example to be considered below, an economic source model is transformed into a polymological image model by means of an application. The interpretation of the transformation then depends wholly on the existence of a cost function associating a determined volume of arms with any increase in armaments spending. Incidentally, the cost function can be either positive, for example on the basis of empirical observation, or normative in accordance with the definition proposed above (cf. p. 156).

In case (3) the transformation in fact corresponds to a new model, distinct from the source and image models. Consequently, interpretation of that transformation is deduced from the definition of the system state continuum it represents.

The two examples to be considered now both refer to meaning (2). Just a few comments will be made in connection with meaning (3).

DEFINITION OF THE TRANSFORMATION

Let x_s and y_s (x_i and y_i respectively) be the state variables for the source model $1R_s$ (of the model image R_i respectively). The combination $X_s \times Y_s$ (X_i and Y_i respectively) of the pairs $x_s y_s$ ($x_i y_i$ respectively) then constitutes the *state continuum* for source model R_s (of image model R_i respectively).

The transformation passage from mechanistic source model R_s to mechanistic image model R_i is called an application T_{sr} defined over $X_i Y_i$ and with values in $X_s \times Y_s$.

Notice that instead of the application introduced above, we could have thought of taking a relationship of field $X_i \times Y_i$ and value $X_s \times Y_s$ which would have made it possible to deal with cases of a transformation making several equation systems representing the image model correspond to the system of equations defining the source model. The semantic particularity and the complexity of the necessary mathematical treatment, especially to study problems of stability, have, however, prompted us to reject this very general approach, at least temporarily. Another point is that specification of the mechanistic character of the models envisaged in the definition taken appears necessary in view of the remarks in the introduction. For it is clear that except in special cases, the definition of a transformation for passage between decisional models requires the intervention of components other than the state variables.

In either case, the application T_{si} can be interpreted as an assessment function (or cost function) for model R_i variables in terms of model R_s (or the converse for the reciprocal $t_i \triangleq T_{si}^{-1}$ of T_{si} where such reciprocal exists). More generally, then, we have to consider the case where the transformation is a vectorial application $T_{is} \triangleq (T_{si}^x, T_{si}^y)$ the first component bearing solely on the x variable, the second on the y variable.

Transformation of Richardson source model in sense (1) to a Richardson image model in sense (1)

Here we consider the case of an affine transformation characterised by:

$$x_s = T_{si}^x(xi) \triangleq \alpha x_i + \beta, \qquad (\alpha, \beta) \in \mathbb{R}^+ \times \mathbb{R} \tag{1}$$

$$y_s = T_{si}^y(yi) \triangleq \gamma y_i + \delta, \qquad (\gamma, \delta) \in \mathbb{R}^+ \times \mathbb{R} \tag{2}$$

The form of the transformation shows that each model R_i variable can be associated a unique 'cost' or 'evaluation' in model R_s, a non-decreasing function of the variable concerned. In the case of an economic source model and a polymological image model, this means that any given increase in armaments spending corresponds to a determined increase in the volume of arms.

Supposing, further, that α and γ are not nil, T_{si} admits a reciprocal $T_{si}^{-1} \triangleq T_{is}$ possessing the same properties, and that to any given increase in the volume of arms there corresponds a determined increase in armaments spending.

The concept of correspondence introduced, if it refers to a precise mathematical definition, may introduce an underlying problem about its own context, as mentioned in the preceding chapter, of temporality within models. In the particularly simple case being treated here, that problem disappears since the meaning of the transformation and the form of the equations selected to explain it have as their only purpose the translation units into military units. That this is not generally so becomes clear when we note that the passage between models must in fact be interpreted within a process, for example, of production, thereby implying a transformation of time, which may be either a simple translation (a lag) or a more complex relation perhaps associated with a change of scale. We shall return to this point in discussing the movements between decisional models and the delay problems.

For the moment, let us return to source model R_s whose condition equations can be written in the form:

$$\begin{cases} \dot{x}_s = a_{1s} y_s - a_{2s} x_s + a_{3s} & (3) \\ \dot{y}_s = b_{1s} x_s - b_{2s} y_s + b_{3s} & (4) \end{cases}$$

Replacing x_s and y_s in (3) and (4) by their expressions as given in (1) and (2) we obtain:

$$\begin{cases} \dot{x}_i = \dfrac{\gamma}{\alpha} a_{1s} y_i - a_{2s} x_i + \dfrac{1}{\alpha}(a_{1s}\delta - a_{2s}\beta + a_{3s}) \\ \dot{y}_i = \dfrac{\alpha}{\gamma} b_{1s} x_i - b_{2s} y_i + \dfrac{1}{\gamma}(b_{1s}\beta - b_{2s}\delta + b_{3s}) \end{cases}$$

In other words, the image model is a Richardson model in sense (1) (cf. pp.   and   ), i.e. a model of the armaments dynamic whose condition equations are:

$$\begin{cases} \dot{x}_i = a_{1i} y_i - a_{2i} x_i + a_{3i} & (7) \\ \dot{y}_i = b_{1i} x_i - b_{2i} y_i + b_{3i} & (8) \end{cases}$$

$$a_{1i} = \frac{\gamma}{\alpha} a_{1s}; \quad b_{1i} = \frac{\alpha}{\gamma} b_{1s} \qquad (9)$$

with:

$$a_{2i} = a_{2s}; \quad b_{2i} = b_{2s} \qquad (10)$$

$$a_{3i} = \frac{1}{\alpha}(a_{1s}\delta - a_{2s}\beta + a_{3s}); \quad b_{3i} = \frac{1}{\gamma}(b_{1s}\beta - b_{2s}\delta + b_{3s}) \qquad (11)$$

Supposing again that the source model is economic and the image model polymological, formulae (9), (10) and (11) can be interpreted as follows:

(1) For a given coefficient of 'economic reaction a_{is}, country X will have a 'military' reaction coefficient all the higher if the marginal cost α of its armaments is lower and if the marginal cost γ of its adversary's armaments is higher. In particular, if α exceeds γ, the military reaction coefficient of Y is lower than its economic reaction coefficient. In other words, the country's determination to respond, as it shows this in armaments spending will, other things being equal, have

attenuated impacts upon the development of its military power. The results will obviously be the opposite for country Y. If γ exceeds α, the above inequalities reverse.

More broadly, the product of the two countries' reaction coefficients can be seen to remain the same when moving from one model to the other. Adding to this the fact that the effort coefficients conserve their values, it is easy to conclude that the stability conditions $a_i b_i < a_2 b_2$ (cf. Intriligator, 1975) also remain the same.

(2) In the polymological model, i each country's aggressiveness coefficient depends on its three coefficients in the economic model, on the marginal cost of its armaments and on the incompressible costs β and δ relating to the armaments of the two adversary countries. More precisely, the aggressiveness coefficient in the polymological model equals the ratio of the rate of variation in the armaments spending of the country concerned to the marginal cost of its armament, in other words, to the rate of variation in the arms volume, when its own spending level and that of its adversary are equal to their respective incompressible costs.

By way of example, let us consider the aggressiveness coefficient of country X in the polymological model and consider the three-dimensional continuum of coefficients a_{1s}, a_{2s}, a_{3s} in the economic source model. In that continuum let plane $X_{\beta\delta}$ have as its parameters β and δ and equation:

This plane divides the useful half-continuum (i.e. corresponding to $a_{2s} > 0$, cf. p. 151) into three regions:

(i) Region I_x corresponding to the points in the half-continuum for which, for any I_x point, the lower the marginal cost α the higher the 'military' aggressiveness coefficient of X.
(ii) Region II_x corresponding to points in the half-continuum for which $X_{\beta\delta}(a_{1s}, a_{2s}, a_{3s}) < 0$
For any II_x point, the lower the marginal cost α, the greater the 'military' benevolence of X.
(iii) Half-plane $X'_{\beta\delta}$ corresponding to points in the half-continuum for which $X_{\beta\delta}(a_{1s}, a_{2s}, a_{3s}) = 0$.

For any point in this half-plane the 'military' aggressiveness coefficient of X is nil, irrespective of the value of the marginal cost.

In other words, according to whether the point representing the characteristics of X in the economic model belongs to region I_x or region II_x, the same variation in the marginal cost of armaments for X will have contrary effects on X's 'military' aggressiveness, the half-

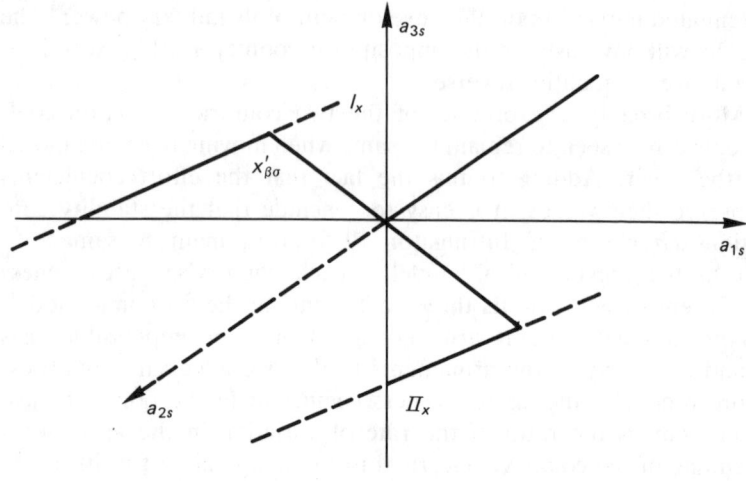

FIGURE 8.3

plane, $X'_{\beta\delta}$ representing the frontier between fields of opposite behaviour.

The sensitivity of this behaviour to alterations in other cost parameters can, in accordance with the foregoing, be evaluated directly by considering the trend for the armaments expenditure variation rate as a function of incompressible costs β and δ, and from the previous chapter's assumptions about the sign of the economic model characteristics (cf. p. 151). Thus it can easily be seen that the rate of variation for X's armaments spending is:

(i) A constantly decreasing function of incompressible cost β of its own armaments, which declines all the more rapidly the higher the economic sensitivity coefficient.
(ii) Either a decreasing or an increasing function of the incompressible cost γ of the adversary country's armaments, depending on whether the economic reaction coefficient a_{1s} is negative (submissive behaviour) or positive. Rate variations in either direction are all the more rapid the higher the absolute value of a_{1s}.

Notice that the relations introduced here between rates of variation of the level of armaments spending and armaments costs are only possible to the extent that one has considered a transformation between models: in other words, a transformation of an economic source model into a polymological image model has the curious consequence, once it can be grasped from a cost function, of specifying the structures of the source model through the relationships of dependence between its coefficients and the cost parameters introduced.

The above discussion of the case of country X obviously applies to that of country Y. Thus a half-plane $Y'_{\beta\delta}$ can be defined in the useful half-continuum of coefficients b_{1s}, b_{2s}, b_{3s} and regions I_y and II_y. If we then consider the (six-dimensional) continuum and in particular, its useful part, nine 'product' regions can be distinguished whose elements belong respectively to the sets $(I_x, II_y, X'_{\beta\delta})$ and $(I_y, II_y, Y'_{\beta\delta})$. The interested reader may be left to consider the detailed characteristics of all these regions, here we merely discuss product region $X'_{\beta\delta} \times Y'_{\beta\delta}$ which seems particularly interesting: it corresponds to nil variations in spending levels both for country X and country Y. More specifically, this surface of separation between fields of opposite behaviour for each of the two countries is the set of the points of the useful part of the product continuum for which incompressible costs β and δ constitute the components of the equilibrium condition of the source model.

It follows that if $a_{1s} b_{1s} < a_{2s} b_{2s}$, the two countries' arms spending levels stabilise around the equilibrium value, i.e. the value corresponding to the incompressible costs.

(3) It is also easy to determine the sensitivity of the military aggressiveness coefficients of the source model from their values corresponding to the equilibrium introduced in (2). Supposing that in each of the (11) formulae, only one coefficient varies at a time, the military aggressiveness coefficient of each country evolves:

(i) In the same direction as its economic reaction coefficient, and all the more rapidly the higher the incompressible cost of the adversary country and the lower its own marginal cost.
(ii) In the opposite direction to that of the trend of its economic effort coefficient, and all the more rapidly the higher its incompressible cost and the lower its marginal cost.
(iii) In the same direction as its economic aggressiveness coefficient and all the more rapidly the lower its marginal cost.

It follows from the above that:

(i) Reaction coefficients have the same sign in the source model and image model.
(ii) Effort coefficients conserve their value when moving from source model to image model.

(iii) Aggressiveness coefficients may or may not change sign when moving from one model to the other. For this to happen it is enough for there to be, for instance, a high economic effort coefficient and a high ratio between incompressible cost and marginal cost for the country concerned. More specifically, the condition vector for the economic model has as its components the incompressible costs of the two adversary countries in equilibrium, the aggressiveness coefficients in the polymological model cancel out, even if they do not do so in the economic model.

In the very special case in which the costs functions are the same for both countries, i.e. where $\alpha=\gamma$ and $\beta=\delta$ some of the preceding interpretations can be affined:

(i) The military reaction coefficients no longer depend on the marginal costs of the two adversary countries, but are simply equal to the economic reaction coefficients.
(ii) The military aggressiveness coefficient of country X and country Y are the same functions of the triplets (a_{1s}, a_{2s}, a_{3s}) and (b_{1s}, b_{2s}, b_{3s}), respectively,

$$a_{3i} = \frac{1}{\alpha} [(a_{1s} - a_{2s})\beta + a_{3s}]$$
$$b_{3i} = \frac{\lambda}{\alpha} [(b_{1s} - b_{2s})\beta + b_{3s}]$$

so that when the coefficients for the two adversary countries are the same in the source model, they are the same in the image model.

NOTES AND REFERENCES

1. Richardson, L. F., *Mathematical Psychology of War* (London: British copyright libraries no. 2, 1919).
2. Lanchester, F., *Aircraft in Warfare: The Dawn of the Fourth Arm* (London: Constable, 1916).
3. Richardson, L. F., 'Mathematical Psychology of War', *Nature*, 135, 830 (1935). Richardson, L. F., 'Mathematical Psychology of War', *Nature*, 136, 1025 (1935). Richardson, L. F., 'The Arms Race 1909–1913', *Nature*, 142, 792 (1938). Richardson, L. F., 'Generalised Foreign Politics', British Association Report of Meeting at Cambridge, 1938. Richardson, L. F., 'Generalised Foreign Politics', *British Journal of Psychology* Monograph Supplement no. 22 (1939). Richardson, L. F., 'Stability after the War', *Nature*, 154, 240 (1944). Richardson, L. F., 'The Number of Nations on Each Side of a War', *Journal of Royal Statistical Society*, 109 (1947).

4. Moll, K. and Luebbert, G. M., 'Arms Race and Military Expenditure Models', *Journal of Conflict Resolution* no. 24 (1980).
5. Rapoport, A., 'Lewis Fry Richardson's Mathematical Theory of War', *Journal of Conflict Resolution*, no. 1 (1957). Boulding, K. E., *Conflict and Defense* (New York: Harper & Row, 1962). Gaspary, W. M., 'Richardson's Model of Arms Race: Description Critique and Alternative Model', *International Studies Quarterly*, 11 (1) (1967).
6. Hollist, W. L., 'Alternative Explanations of Competitive Arms Processes: Tests of Four Pairs of Nations', *American Journal of Political Science*, no. 21 (1977). Hollist, W. L., 'Analyses of Arms Processes in the United States and Soviet Union', *International Studies Quarterly*, no. 21 (1977). Rattinger, R., 'Armaments, Détente and Bureaucracy: the Case of the Arms Race in Europe', *Journal of Conflict Resolution*, no. 19 (1975). Schrodt, P. A., 'Statistical Problems Associated with the Richardson Arms Race Model', *Journal of Peace Science*, no. 3 (1978).
7. Majeski, S. and Jones, D., 'Arms Race Modelling: Causality Analysis and Model Specification', *Journal of Conflict Resolution*, no. 25 (1981).
8. Hollist, 'Alternative Explanation of Competitive Arms Processes: Tests of Four Pairs of Nations'. Wallace, M. D. and Wilson, J. M., 'Non-linear Arms Race Models', *Journal of Peace Research*, no. 15 (1978). Moll and Luebbert, 'Arms Race and Military Expenditure Models'.
9. Rattinger, R., 'Armaments, Détente and Bureaucracy: The Case of the Arms Race in Europe', *Journal of Conflict Resolution*, no. 19 (1975). Cioffi-Revilla, C. A., 'Theory of Arms Race and Mathematical Structures', *International Relations*, mimeo, Chicago: April 1979. Majeski and Jones, 'Arms Race Modelling: Causality Analysis and Model Specification'.
10. Intriligator, M. D., 'Research on Conflict Theory', *Journal of Conflict Resolution*, vol. 26, no. 2, June 1982.
11. Richardson, L. F., *Arms and Insecurity* (Pittsburgh: The Boxwood Press, 1960) p. 16.
12. Rapoport, 'Lewis Fry Richardson's Mathematical Theory of War'.
13. Richardson, *Arms and Insecurity*, p. 18ff.
14. Richardson, L. F., 'Generalised Foreign Politics', *British Journal of Psychology*, Monograph supplement, no. 23 (1939). Richardson, *Arms and Insecurity*.
15. Moll and Luebbert, 'Arms Race and Military Expenditure Models'.
16. Boulding, K. E., *Conflict and Defense* (New York: Harper & Row, 1962). Abelson, R. P., 'A Derivation of Richardson's Equations', *Journal of Conflict Resolution*, no. 7 (1963). Intriligator, M. D., 'Strategy in Missile War: Targets and Rates of Fire', Los Angeles, Security Studies Papers, no. 10 (1967). Intriligator, M. D., 'Strategic Consideration in the Richardson Model Arms Races', *Journal of Political Economy*, no. 83 (1975).
17. Rapoport, 'Lewis Fry Richardson's Mathematical Theory of War'. Rapoport, A., Editor's Introduction to Clausewitz, C. V., *On War* (Penguin, 1968).
18. Allison, G. T., 'Questions about the Arms Race: Who's Racing Whom? A Bureaucratic Perspective', in Pfaltzgraff, R. L. (ed.), *Contrasting*

Approaches to Strategic Arms Control (Lexington, Mass.: D.C. Holt, 1974). Rattinger, R., 'Econometrics and Arms Races: A Critical Review and Some Extensions', *European Journal of Political Research*, no. 4 (1976). Spielmann, K. F., *Analyzing Soviet Strategic Arms Decisions* (Boulder: Westview Press, 1978).
19. Pierce, D. A. and Haugh, L. D., 'Causality Intemporal System: Characterizations and Survey', *Journal of Econometrics*, no. 5 (1977).
20. McGuire, M. C., *Secrecy and the Arms Race* (Cambridge: Harvard University Press, 1965).
21. Schrodt, P. A. 'Statistical Problems Associated with the Richardson Arms Race Model'. Majeski and Jones, 'Arms Race Modelling: Causality Analysis and Model Specification'.
22. Malinvaud, E., *Méthodes des Statistiques de l'Econometrie* (Paris: Dunod, 1969) p. 4ff.
23. Huntingdon, S. P., 'Arms Races: Prerequisites and Results', *Public Policy*, no. 8 (1958).
24. McGuire, *Secrecy and the Arms Race*. McGuire, M. C., 'A Quantitative Study of the Strategic Arms Race in the Missile Age', *Review of Economics and Statistics*, no. 59 (1977). Schmidt, C. and Rudnianski, M., 'Courses aux armements et guerre nucléaire: une approche formalisée', mimeo, Fondation des Etudes pour las Défense Nationale (Paris: 1983).
25. Russet, B. M., *What Price Vigilance?* (New Haven: Yale University Press, 1970). Burns, A., 'The Defense Sector and the American Economics', in Melman, S. (ed.) *The War Economy in US* (New York: St Martin's Press, 1971). Smith, R. P., 'Military Expenditure and Capitalism', *Cambridge Journal of Economics* (1977). Smith, R. P. and Smith, D., 'Military Expenditure Resources and Development' (London: Birkbeck College Discussion Paper no. 87, 1980).
26. Intriligator, 'Strategic Consideration in the Richardson Model Arms Races'.
27. McGuire, 'A Quantitative Study of the Strategic Arms Race in the Missile Age'.
28. Richardson, *Arms and Insecurity*, p. 20.
29. Ibid., pp. 20–21.
30. McGuire, *Secrecy and the Arms Race*. McGuire, 'A Quantitative Study of the Arms Race in the Missile Age'.
31. Richardson, *Arms and Insecurity*.
32. Intriligator, M. D., 'Formal Models of Arms Races', *Journal of Peace Research*, no. 2 (1976).
33. Richardson, *Arms and Insecurity*, p. 15.
34. Ibid., p. 12.
35. Ibid., note no. 8.
36. Rapoport, 'Lewis Fry Richardson's Mathematical Theory of War'. Rapoport, 'Editor's Introduction to *On War*'.
37. Rapoport, 'Lewis Fry Richardson's Mathematical Theory of War'.
38. Gillespie, J. V. and Zinnes, D. A., 'Embedded Game Analysis and International Conflict Control', *Behavior Science*, no. 22 (1977).
39. Gaspary, W. M., 'Richardson's Model of Arms Race: Description, Critique and Alternative Model', *International Studies Quarterly*, vol. 11 (1) (1967).

40. Hollist, 'Alternative Explanation of Competitive Arms Processes: Tests of Four Pairs of Nations'.
41. Schmidt and Rudnianski, 'Courses aux armements et guerre nucléaire: une approche fomalisée'.
42. Ibid.
43. Brito, D. L., 'A Dynamic Model of an Armament Race', *International Economic Review*, no. 13 (1972). Intriligator, M. D., *Mathematical Optimisation and Economic Theory* (Englewood Cliffs, NJ: Prentice-Hall, 1971). Simaan, M. and Cruz, J. B., 'Formulation of Richardson's Model of the Arms Race from Differential Game Viewpoint', *Review of Economic Studies*, no. 42 (1975). Gillespie, J. V. and Zinnes, D. A., 'Progressions in Mathematical Models of International Conflict', *Synthese*, no. 31 (1975).
44. Intriligator, 'Strategy in Missile War: Targets and Rates of Fire'. Intriligator, 'Strategic Consideration in the Richardson Model Arms Races'.
45. Schmidt and Rudnianski, 'Courses aux armements et guerre nucléaire: une approche formalisée'.
46. Orstrom, C., 'Evaluating Alternative Foreign Policy Decision-making Models: An Empirical Test between an Arms Race Model and an Organizational Politics Model', *Journal of Conflict Resolution*, no. 21 (1977). Orstrom, C., 'A Reactive Linkage Model of the US Defense Expenditure Policy-making Process', *American Political Science Review*, no. 72 (1978).
47. von Wright, H. G., *Norm and Actions: A Logical Enquiry* (London: Routledge & Kegan Paul, 1963) p. 9–A–11.
48. Richardson, *Arms and Insecurity*, p. 12.
49. Intriligator, M. D. and Brito, D. L., 'Formal Models of Arms Races', *Journal of Peace Science*, no. 3 (1976).
50. von Wright, *Norm and Actions: A Logical Enquiry*.
51. Rapoport, 'Editor's Introduction to *On War*'.
52. Brito, 'A Dynamic Model of an Armament Race'. Brito, D. L. and Intriligator, M. D., 'Some Applications of the Maximum Principle to the Problem of an Armaments Race', *Modeling and Simulation*, no. 4 (1973).
53. Simann and Cruz, 'Formulation of Richardson's Model of the Arms Race from Differential Game Viewpoint'.
54. Ibid. Gillespie, J. V., Zinnes, D. A. and Tahim, G. S., 'Foreign Military Assistance and the Armaments Race – A Differential Game Model with Control', *Peace Science Society Papers, International*, no. 25 (1975). Zinnes, D. A., Gillespie, J. V. and Rubinson, M., 'A Reinterpretation of the Richardson Arms Race Model', in Zinnes and Gillespie (eds), *Mathematical Systems in International Relations Research* (New York: Praeger, 1977).

BIBLIOGRAPHY

Abelson, R. P., 'A Derivation of Richardson's Equations', *Journal of Conflict Resolution*, no. 7 (1963).
Allison, G. T., *The Essence of Decision: Explaining the Cuban Missile Crisis* (Boston: Little, Brown, 1971).

Allison, G. T., 'Questions about the Arms Race: Who's Racing Whom? A Bureaucratic Perspective', in Pfaltzgraff, R. L. (ed.), *Contrasting Approaches to Strategic Arms Control* (Lexington, Mass.: D. C. Heath, 1974).

Allison, G. T. and Mollis, F., 'Armaments and Arms Control: Exploring the Determinants of Military Weapons', in Long, P. A. and Rathjens, G. W. (eds), *Arms, Defense Policy, and Arms Control* (New York: Norton 1976).

Boulding, K. E., *Conflict and Defense* (New York: Harper & Row, 1962).

Brito, D. L., 'A Dynamic Model of an Armaments Race', *International Economic Review*, no. 13 (1972).

Brito, D. L. and Intriligator, M. D., 'Some Applications of the Maximum Principle to the Problem of an Armaments Race', in *Modeling and Simulation*, no. 4 (1973).

Burns, A., 'The Defense Sector and the American Economics', in Melman, S. (ed.), *The War Economy in US* (New York: St. Martin's Press, 1971).

Cioffi-Revilla, C. A., 'Theory of Arms Race and Mathematical Structures in International Relations', mimeo, Chicago, April 1979.

Desai, M. and Blake, D., 'Modeling the Ultimate Absurdity, a Comment on "a Quantitative Study" of the Strategic Arms Race in Missile Age', *Review of Economics and Statistics*, vol. 63, no. 4 (Nov. 1981).

Gillespie, J. V. and Zinnes, D. A., 'Progressions in Mathematical Models of International Conflict', *Synthese*, no. 31 (1975).

Gillespie, J. V. and Zinnes, D. A., 'Embedded Game Analysis and International Conflict Control', *Behavior Science*, no. 22 (1977).

Gillespie, J. V. (ed.), *Mathematical Systems in International Relations Research* (New York: Praeger, 1977).

Gillespie, J. V. and Tahim, G. S., 'Foreign Military Assistance and the Armaments Race: a Differential Game Model with Control', *Papers of Peace Society (International)*, no. 25 (1975).

Gillespie, J. V., Tahim, G. S., Schrodt, P. A. and Rubison, R. M., 'An Optimal Control Model of Arms Races', *American Political Science Review*, no. 71 (1977).

Gillespie, J. V. and Rubison, R. M., 'Accumulation in Arms Race Models: a Geometric Lay Perspective', *Comparative Politics Studies*, no. 10 (1978).

Gregory, P. R., 'Economic Growth, US Defense Expenditure and the Soviet Defense Budget: a Suggested Model', *Soviet Studies* (Jan. 1974).

Hollist, W. L., 'Alternative Explanation of Competitive Arms Processes: Tests on Four Pairs of Nations', *American Journal of Political Science*, no. 21 (1977).

Hollist, W. L., 'Analyses of Arms Processes in the United States and Soviet Union', *International Studies Quarterly*, no. 21 (1977).

Hollist, W. L. (ed.), *Exploring Competitive Arms Processes* (New York: Marcel Dekker, 1978).

Huntington, S. P., 'Arms Races: Prerequisites and Results', *Public Policy*, no. 8 (1958).

Intriligator, M. D., 'Some Simple Models of Arms Races', *General Systems*, no. 9 (1964).

Intriligator, M. D., 'Strategy in Missile War: Targets and Rates of Fire', Los Angeles, *Security Studies Papers*, no. 10 (1967).

Intriligator, M. D., 'Strategic Considerations in the Richardson Model of Arms Races', *Journal of Political Economy*, no. 83 (1975).
Intriligator, M. D. and Brito, D. L., 'Formal Models of Arms Races', *Journal of Peace Science*, no. 3 (1976).
Lambelet, J. C., 'A Dynamic Model of the Arms Race in the Middle East 1953–1965', *General Systems*, no. 16 (1971).
Lambelet, J. C., 'Do Arms Races Lead to War?', *Journal of Peace Research*, no. 12 (1975).
Lambelet, J. C., Luterbacher, U. and Allen, P., 'Dynamics of Arms Races: Mutual Stimulation vs. Self Stimulation', *Journal of Peace Science*, no. 4 (1979).
Lanchester, F., *Aircraft in Warfare: the Dawn of the Fourth Arm* (London: Constable, 1916).
Lucier, C., 'Changes in the Values of Arms Race Parameters', *Journal of Conflict Resolution*, no. 23 (1979).
Majeski, S. and Jones, D., 'Arms Race Modelling: Causality Analysis and Model Specification', *Journal of Conflict Resolution*, no. 25 (1981).
Malinvaud, E., *Méthodes statistiques de l'Econometrie* (Paris: Dunod, 1969).
Malinvaud, E., 'Sur la spécification des modèles économiques' Les entretiens de Monaco, 1966 – Monograph.
McGuire, M. C., *Secrecy and the Arms Race* (Cambridge: Harvard University Press, 1965).
McGuire, M. C., 'A Quantitative Study of the Strategic Arms Race in the Missile Age', *Review of Economics and Statistics*, no. 59 (1977).
Moll, K., 'International Conflict as a Decision System', *Journal of Conflict Resolution*, no. 18 (1974).
Moll, K. and Luebbert, G. M., 'Arms Race and Military Expenditure Models', *Journal of Conflict Resolution*, no. 24 (1980).
Orstrom, C., 'Evaluating Alternative Foreign Policy Decision-making Models: an Empirical Test between an Arms Race Model and an Organizational Politics Model', *Journal of Conflict Resolution*, no. 21 (1977).
Orstrom, C., 'A Reactive Linkage Model of the US Defense Expenditure Policy-making Process,' *American Political Science Review*, no. 72 (1978).
Pierce, D. A. and Haugh, L. D., 'Causality Intemporal System: Characterizations and Survey', *Journal of Econometrics*, no. 5 (1977).
Rapoport, A., 'Lewis Fry Richardson's Mathematical Theory of War', *Journal of Conflict Resolution*, no. 1 (1957).
Rapoport, A., *Fights, Games and Debates* (Ann Arbor: University of Michigan Press, 1961).
Rapoport, A., Editor's introduction to Clausewitz, C. V., *On War* (Penguin, 1968).
Rattinger, R., 'Armaments, Détente, and Bureaucracy: The Case of the Arms Race in Europe', *Journal of Conflict Resolution*, no. 19 (1975).
Rattinger, R., 'Econometrics and Arms Races: A Critical Review and Some Extensions', *European Journal of Political Research*, no. 4 (1976).
Richardson, L. F., 'Mathematical Psychology of War', *Nature*, no. 135 (1935).
Richardson, L. F., 'The Arms Race of 1909–1913', *Nature*, no. 142 (1938).
Richardson, L. F., 'Generalized Foreign Politics', *British Journal of Psychology*, Monographs Supplement, no. 23 (1939).

Richardson, L. F., *Arms and Insecurity* (Pittsburgh: The Boxwood Press, 1960).
Rummel, R., 'The Relationship between National Attributes and Foreign Conflict Behavior', in Singer, D. (ed.), *Quantitative International Politics* (New York: Macmillan, 1968).
Russet, B. M., 'Who Pays for Defense?', *American Political Science Review*, no. 63 (1969).
Russet, B. M., *What Price Vigilance?* (New Haven: Yale University Press, 1970).
Saaty, T. L., *Mathematical Models of Arms Control and Disarmament* (New York: John Wiley, 1968).
Schmidt, C. and Rudnianski, M., 'Courses aux armements et querre nucléare: une approche formalisée,' Mimeo, Fondation des Etudes pour la Défense Nationale (Paris: 1983).
Schrodt, P. A., 'The Richardson Nation Model and the Balance of Power', *American Journal of Political Science*, no. 22 (1978).
Schrodt, P. A., 'Statistical Problems Associated with the Richardson Arms Race Model', *Journal of Peace Science*, no. 3 (1978).
Simaan, M., 'Nash Equilibrium Strategies for the Problem of Armament Race and Control', *Management Science*, no. 22 (1975).
Simaan, M. and Cruz, J. B., 'Formulation of Richardson's Model of the Arms Race from Differential Game Viewpoint', *Review of Economic Studies*, no. 42 (1975).
Simaan, M. and Cruz, J. B., 'Equilibrium Concepts for Arms Race Problems', in Gillespie and Zinnes (eds), *Mathematical Systems in International Relations Research* (New York: Praeger, 1977).
Singer, J. D. and Wallace, M., 'Intergovernmental Organization and Preservation of Peace, 1816–1964 – Some Bivariate Relationship', *International Organization*, no. 24 (1970).
Smith, R. P., 'Military Expenditures and Capitalism', *Cambridge Journal of Economics* (1977).
Smith, R. P. and Smith, D., 'Military Expenditure, Resources and Development', London: Birkbeck College Discussion Paper, no. 87 (1980).
Smoke, R., *War Controlling Escalation* (Cambridge: Harvard University Press, 1977).
Smoker, P., 'A Pilot Study of the Present Arms Race', *General System*, no. 8 (1963).
Smoker, P., 'Fear in the Arms Races: A Mathematical Study', *Journal of Peace Research*, no. 1 (1964).
Spielmann, K. F., *Analyzing Soviet Strategic Arms Decisions* (Boulder: Westview Press, 1978).
Wallace, M. D., 'Arms Races and Escalation – Some New Evidence', *Journal of Conflict Resolution*, no. 23 (1979).
Wallace, M. D. and Wilson, J. M., 'Non-linear Arms Race Models', *Journal of Peace Research*, no. 15 (1978).
Wold, H., 'Causality and Econometrics', *Econometrica* (April 1954).
Wold, H., *Econometric Model Building: Essays on the Causal Chain Approach* (Amsterdam: North-Holland, 1964).

von Wright, H. G., *Norms and Actions: A Logical Enquiry* (London: Routledge & Kegan Paul, 1963).

Zinnes, D. A., Gillespie, J. V. and Rubison, R. M., 'A Reinterpretation of the Richardson Arms Race Model', in Zinnes and Gillespie (eds), *Mathematical Systems in International Relations Research* (New York: Praeger, 1977).

Note on the Paper by Schmidt by Michael D. Intriligator, Department of Economics and Political Science, University of California, Los Angeles

Christian Schmidt's paper provides a detailed and thorough treatment of the nature of the Richardson model of arms races, one of the most important models of international relations theory. The Richardson model dates back to 1919, but it was not widely known until the publication of his book *Arms and Insecurity* in 1960 and the publication of Anatole Rapoport's 1957 article 'Lewis Fry Richardson's Mathematical Theory of War' and his 1961 book *Fights, Games, and Debates*.[1] Nevertheless the model is very frequently used in the literature. My recent survey of the literature on conflict theory identified, as noted by Christian Schmidt, more than 40 articles on the subject of the Richardson model.[2]

An important aspect of the Richardson model that, in part, accounts for its popularity, is the fact that it can be interpreted in various ways. As Christian Schmidt has noted, it can be interpreted as a model of an arms race, as a model of war, or as a model of dynamic interaction. Richardson treated the model primarily as one of an arms race, but he also used it to study war. In particular, he treated the case of dynamic instability of the model leading to higher and higher levels of weapons in both countries as one that would lead to war. In my view this is not a useful or valid representation of the outbreak of war. Dynamic instability upward would eventually result in countries meeting resource constraint limits, as noted by Boulding.[3] Furthermore the process of war outbreak is one explained more by factors other than arms level, including historical, psychological, economic, and other factors. War can break out at low levels of weapons stocks, for example the Korean War. Conversely, weapons stocks can be at very high levels over long periods without the outbreak of war, for example the post-1945 situation for the USA and the USSR or the situation in Korea since 1965. Schmidt treats the model as one of general dynamic interaction, and it is probably the case that it can be used to study other dynamic processes.[4]

Yet another interpretation of the Richardson model is a system of demand equations resulting from the maximising behaviour of individual agents, the defence planners.[5] This interpretation is a particularly attractive one since arms races are *behavioural* phenomena, which, unlike meteorology (Richardson's own field), should be represented in terms of individual behaviour. The Richardson model gives the impression of being a purely mechanistic one, devoid of behaviour, with mechanical responses of arms (or budget) increases to arms levels. Richardson himself provides such an interpretation. This type of 'black-box' reasoning that emphasises inputs and outputs is acceptable for physical systems but not for social systems, where one would like to penetrate the black box to see the individual behaviour that reacts to the inputs and results in the outputs, i.e., one would like a 'grey box' or, ideally, a 'white box' rather than a black box. Fortunately, some recent literature, identified in note 5, has moved in this direction by studying the arms acquisition process as a dynamic one, using the tools of control theory. The Richardson equations then emerge as optimising responses of defence planners, given specific defence objectives and specific resource constraints. In fact, the linearity of the Richardson model lends itself to the interpretation of a linear decision rule, resulting, for example, from optimising a quadratic objective functional subject to the constraints of a linear model.[6]

Christian Schmidt provides yet another interpretation, distinguishing between the economic and polymological model. These models have different interpretations, and the parameters of the models have different meanings. The distinction is similar to that between stocks and flows. In the Appendix a linear transform is used to move from one type of model to the other. This is a promising first step. Other transforms might also be treated, for example integral and differential transforms.

The Richardson model is one that has been or could be extended in many directions, some of which are identified by Christian Schmidt. A partial list of some of these extensions would include:

(1) Many countries (perhaps including the possibility of alliances)
(2) Many different weapons
(3) Stochastic elements
(4) Time lags
(5) Technical change
(6) Nonlinearities
(7) Bureaucratic behaviour
(8) Imperfect information
(9) The nature of deterrence
(10) Arms limitation agreements
(11) Inventory-theoretic considerations

(12) Game-theoretic considerations
(13) Endogenous forcing (grievance) terms
(14) A complete economic sector

The Richardson model is thus clearly one in which there has been and will continue to be widespread interest, one which is susceptible to various interpretations, and one which can be extended in many different ways. Christian Schmidt's paper provides a valuable in-depth treatment of this important model, which, as he notes, still provides a valuable point of departure for research on the arms race.

NOTES AND REFERENCES

1. See Richardson, L. F., *Arms and Insecurity* (Pittsburgh: The Boxwood Press, 1960) and Rapoport, A., 'Lewis Fry Richardson's Mathematical Theory of War', *Journal of Conflict Resolution*, no. 1 (1957) pp. 249–304, and Rapoport, A., *Fights, Games and Debates* (Ann Arbor: University of Michigan Press, 1961). Kenneth Boulding recalled at the conference that the rediscovery of the Richardson model was, in part, due to Richardson's son, who visited the Center for Advanced Study in the Behavioral Sciences at Stanford, California, when both Boulding and Rapoport were fellows there in 1954–5.
2. See Intriligator, M. D., 'Research on Conflict Theory: Analytical Approaches and Areas of Application', *Journal of Conflict Resolution*, no. 26, pp. 307–27, where the literature on conflict theory is cross-classified by eight analytic approaches and eight areas of application. The Richardson model, using the analytic approach of differential equations as applied to the area of application of arms races, generated more references than any other of the 64 possible cross-classifications.
3. See Boulding, K. E., *Conflict and Defense* (New York: Harper & Row, 1962). See also Intriligator, M. D., 'Some Simple Models of Arms Races', *General Systems*, no. 9, pp. 143–7.
4. For some possible applications to other dynamic processes, see Sandberg, I. W., 'A Mathematical Theory of Interaction in Social Groups', *IEEE Systems*, M4, (1974) 432–45; Sandberg, I. W., 'Some Qualitative Properties of Nonlinear Richardson-Type Arms Race Models', in Gillespie, J. V. and Zinnes, D. A. (eds), *Mathematical Systems in International Relations Research* (New York: Praeger, 1977).
5. See Brito, D. L., 'A Dynamic Model of an Armaments Race', *International Economic Review*, no. 13, (1972) pp. 359–75; Intriligator, M. D., 'Strategic Considerations in the Richardson Model of Arms Races', *Journal of Political Economy*, no. 83, (1975) pp. 339–53; Intriligator, M. D. and Brito, D. L., 'Formal Models of Arms Races', *Journal of Peace Science*, no. 2, (1976) pp. 77–88; Zinnes, D. A., Gillespie, J. V. and Rubison, R. M., 'A Reinterpretation of the Richardson Arms Race Model', in Gillespie, J. V. and Zinnes, D. A. (eds), *Mathematical Systems in International Relations Research* (New York: Praeger, 1977) and Gillespie, J. V., Zinnes, D. A., Tahim, G. S., Schrodt, P. A. and

Rubison, R. M., 'An Optimal Control Model of Arms Races', *American Political Science Review*, no. 71, (1977) pp. 226–44.
6. The model can be extended to the stochastic case providing the stochastic terms are normally distributed. As is well known in the stochastic control literature, maximising a quadratic functional given a model with a linear system of equations of motion and with normally distributed stochastic terms leads to a linear decision rule, with the controls (e.g. arms acquisitions) being linear functions of the state variables (e.g. arms levels).

9 Can Arms Races Lead to the Outbreak of War?[1]

Michael D. Intriligator
UNIVERSITY OF CALIFORNIA
and Dagobert L. Brito
TULANE UNIVERSITY

I INTRODUCTION

The relationships between an arms race and the outbreak of war have been debated over many years. Indeed, the question of war outbreak is the most basic and fundamental one in any study of arms races. This question obviously carries much more urgency when it becomes that of whether a *nuclear* arms race might lead to a *nuclear* war. That is the focus of the present paper: the relationships between a nuclear arms race and the outbreak of nuclear war in a bipolar world of two nuclear powers. The paper also presents a specific application to the United States–Soviet Union arms race of the post-war period.

In his classic study of arms races Lewis F. Richardson identified an unstable arms race with war. He concluded that an unending upward spiral of armaments in two nations must inevitably culminate in war.[2] Neither Richardson's model nor his analysis, however, warrant this conclusion. His model lacks any explicit treatment of war, so treating upward instability as a situation of 'war' appears no more than a convenient label to apply to a particular case of instability. His analysis includes no formalisation of the basis for war outbreak, so there is no justification for treating the upward unstable case as one of war. By contrast, the model to be developed here provides an explicit formalisation of the initiation of war, facilitating analysis of the possible relationships between an arms race and the outbreak of war.

More recent work on the relationships between arms races and war outbreak has been conducted by Lambelet, Smith, and Wallace.[3] This work, however, lacks the formal structure of an analytic model of war outbreak as presented below. Lambelet discusses two extreme hypotheses: the Richardson view that an unstable arms race can only end in war and the hypothesis that arms races and war outbreak are largely independent. He does not explicitly consider the hypothesis suggested below that in certain circumstances arms races can prevent war outbreak (or that a disarming race can result in war outbreak), but he does present some historical cases illustrating these possibilities, for example, '. . . at a more fundamental level, the Korean War may have broken out partly *because* the US had disarmed unilaterally . . .' (pp. 124–5, emphasis in original),

> there are also on record several arms races which were *not* followed by an open conflict. Thus the larger South American countries were, at various times in the century, involved in a clear-cut naval armament race . . . yet, none of the capital ships involved were ever sunk as a result of hostile action . . . [T]he pre-1914 Anglo-German naval race suggests a somewhat similar conclusion . . . (p. 125, emphasis in original).

Lambelet goes on to provide a general framework of a theory of the relationship between an arms race and the outbreak of war. The theory presented below can be considered a realisation of the Lambelet framework, in which arms races affect and are affected by potential war outcomes.

Smith rejects both of the hypotheses advanced by Lambelet in their more extreme variants, that arms races always end in war and that arms races and war are totally unrelated. She then attempts to identify those arms races that are particularly war-prone using statistical methods. She estimates the Richardson model and infers stability or instability from the estimated coefficients of this model. Thus she, in effect, uses the Richardson approach of identifying unstable arms race with the outbreak of war. She presents no formal analysis of the outbreak of war.

Wallace compares the 'preparedness' hypothesis ('if you seek peace, prepare for war') and the 'arms race' hypothesis (that arms races lead to war) using data on 99 serious great power disputes since 1816. He concludes that 'International conflicts and disputes which are accompanied by arms races are much more likely to result in war than those in which an arms race does not occur' (p. 44) on the basis of comparing arms races with a war outcome (23 of 28 cases) and no arms race with a no-war outcome (68 of 71 cases). It should be noted, however, that of the 19 cases he cites of arms races in the nuclear era (since 1945) none have ended in a war outcome, suggesting an opposite conclusion, namely that arms races in the nuclear era do not lead to war. The remainder of this paper provides a formal analysis of the relationships between arms races and war outbreak.

II ARMS RACES

An *arms race* refers to the interactive acquisition of weapons by two or more nations. Assuming only a single weapon, called a 'missile' (more precisely, a warhead of a missile), and only two nations in a bipolar world, an arms race can be represented by movements in the weapons plane. Letting $M_A(t)$ and $M_B(t)$ be the numbers of missiles in country A and B respectively at time t, the weapons plane (M_A, M_B) is shown in Figure 9.1. An arms race is described by the level of weapons on both sides over a time interval, for example over the interval from t_0 to t_1, so the arms race is summarised by

$$\{M_A(t), M_B(t) \mid t_0 \leq t \leq t_1\} \tag{1}$$

Geometrically the arms race is described by a *weapons trajectory* in the weapons plane, and various such trajectories are shown in Figure 9.1. A weapons trajectory can involve increases in weapons on both sides, decreases in weapons on both sides, increases on one side but decreases on the other side, and other complicated changes, such as cycles or loops. The parametric representation in (1), in which numbers of missiles M_A and M_B are functions of time over a relevant time interval allows for all possible trajectories of weapons in both countries.

In order to relate arms races, represented algebraically by (1) and geometrically by a trajectory in the weapons plane, to the outbreak of war it is necessary to specify the nature of war initiation. Section III presents a model of a missile war, while Section IV applies this model to the problem of war initiation. Section V identifies regions of deterrence and of war initiation, and these regions are used in Section VI to relate arms races to war initiation. Conclusions, including applications to the United States–Soviet Union arms race in the post-war era, are presented in Section VII.

Intriligator and Brito: Arms Races and War?

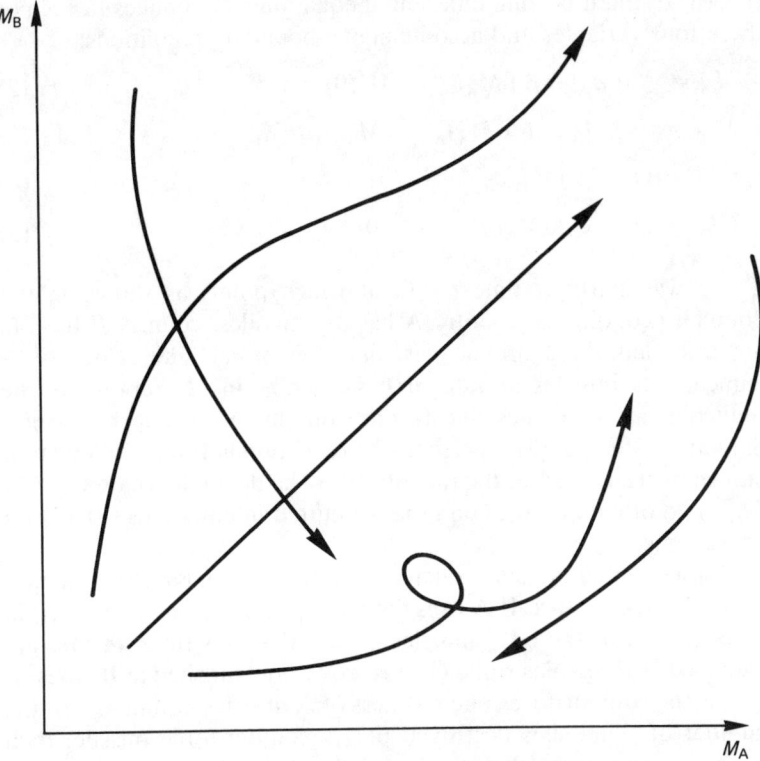

FIGURE 9.1 *Weapons plane and various weapons trajectories*

III A MODEL OF A MISSILE WAR

The model of a missile war to be presented here analyses the causes of changes over time in the number of missiles and casualties in both countries during a possible war.[4] The model consists of a system of four differential equations with initial boundary conditions. The model determines the evolution over time of the war as a result of initial numbers of weapons on both sides, strategic decisions made by both countries, and the effectiveness of weapons against both counterforce targets (enemy weapons) and counter-value targets (enemy cities).

The variables of the model are $M_A(t)$ and $M_B(t)$, which, as before, represent the missiles in country A and B at time t. The model consists of the following differential equations for changes in each of these four variables and accompanying boundary conditions:

$$\dot{M}_A = -\alpha M_A - \beta'\beta M_B f_B \qquad M_A(0) = M_A^0 \qquad (2)$$

$$\dot{M}_B = -\beta M_B - \alpha'\alpha M_A f_A \qquad M_B(0) = M_B^0 \qquad (3)$$

$$\dot{C}_A = (1-\beta')\beta M_B v_B \qquad C_A(0) = 0 \qquad (4)$$

$$\dot{C}_B = (1-\alpha')\alpha M_A v_A \qquad C_B(0) = 0. \qquad (5)$$

The war starts at time $t = 0$, at which point, as shown in the boundary conditions, country A has M_A^0 missiles, country B has M_B^0 missiles, and there are no casualties on either side. Country A launches its missiles at rate $\alpha(t)$, so $-\alpha M_A$ in (2) represents the reduction in A missiles due to decisions by A to launch missiles. Similarly, $-\beta M_B$ in (3) represents the reduction in B missiles due to B launching its missiles at the rate of $\beta(t)$. (The dependence of M_A, M_B, α, β, and other variables on time is omitted in equations (2)–(5) for convenience.)

Missiles can be targeted counter-force at enemy missiles or counter-value at enemy cities. If A uses the counter-force proportion $\alpha'(t)$ at time t, then, of the αM_A missiles launched at this time, $\alpha'\alpha M_A$ are launched at B missiles while $(1 - \alpha')\alpha M_A$ are launched at B cities. If $f_A(t)$ is the counter-force effectiveness of A missiles at time t, i.e., the number of B missiles destroyed per A counter-force missile, then $\alpha'\alpha M_A f_A$ represents the B missiles destroyed by A counter-force missiles, as shown in equation (3). Similarly, the term $\beta'\beta M_B f_B$ in equation (2) represents the A missiles destroyed by B counter-force missiles, where $f_B(t)$ is the counter-force effectiveness of B missiles. If $v_A(t)$ is the counter-value effectiveness of A missiles, i.e. the number of B casualties inflicted per A counter-value missile, then $(1 - \alpha')\alpha M_A v_A$ represents the B casualties inflicted by A counter-value missiles, as shown in equation (5). Similarly, the term $(1 - \beta')\beta M_B v_B$ in equation (4) represents the A casualties inflicted by B counter-value missiles, where $v_B(t)$ is the counter-value effectiveness of B missiles.

The evolution of the war over time, as summarised by the dynamic model (2)–(5), thus depends on the initial levels of missiles M_A^0, M_B^0; strategic decisions on both sides regarding rates of fire, $\alpha(t)$, $\beta(t)$; strategic decisions on both sides regarding targeting $\alpha'(t)$, $\beta'(t)$; the effectiveness of missiles of both sides against enemy missiles, $f_A(t)$,

$f_B(t)$; and the effectiveness of missiles of both sides against enemy cities, $v_A(t)$, $v_B(t)$.

From the viewpoint of either one of the countries, the problem of *grand strategy* is that of choosing both a rate of fire and a targeting strategy. For country A, the rate of fire α can range between zero and some maximum rate $\bar{\alpha}$, determined on the basis of technical characteristics of weapons. Similarly, the counter-force proportion α' can range between 0 and 1, where $\alpha' = 1$ is pure counter-force targeting (no cities) and $\alpha' = 0$ is pure counter-value targeting (only cities). Omitting intermediate values, the two extreme values for each of the two strategic variables for country A yield four alternatives for grand strategy for A:

  (i) *Maximum rate/counter-force*, where A fires its missiles at the maximum rate ($\alpha = \bar{\alpha}$) and targets only B missiles ($\alpha' = 1$), destroying as many enemy missiles as possible – a *first-strike strategy*.
 (ii) *Maximum rate/Counter-value*, where A fires its missiles at the maximum rate ($\alpha = \bar{\alpha}$) and targets only B cities ($\alpha' = 0$), inflicting as many enemy casualties as possible – a *massive retaliation strategy*.
(iii) *Zero rate/Counter-force*, where A holds its missiles in reserve ($\alpha = 0$) and targets only B missiles ($\alpha' = 1$), threatening to strike enemy missiles – a *limited strategic war strategy*.
(vi) *Zero rate/Counter-value*, where A holds its missiles in reserve ($\alpha = 0$) and targets only B cities ($\alpha' = 0$), threatening to strike enemy cities – a *war of nerves strategy*.

Assuming that country A treats the country B strategy as fixed, rather than trying to influence it, and that A has the goal of maximising a payoff function

$$P_A = P_A[M_A(T), M_B(T), C_A(T), C_B(T)],$$

$$\frac{\partial P_A}{\partial M_A(T)} > 0, \quad \frac{\partial P_A}{\partial M_B(T)} < 0, \quad \frac{\partial P_A}{\partial C_A(T)} < 0, \quad \frac{\partial P_A}{\partial C_B(T)} \lessgtr 0 \quad (6)$$

which depends on missiles and casualties in both countries at the end of the war, time T, it has been shown that country A will select at any one time in the war t (where $0 < t < T$) one of these four grand strategies.[5] In particular, while A could choose some rate of fire intermediate between 0 and $\bar{\alpha}$, it is optimal for it to choose only one of these extreme values, firing missiles at either the zero or the maximum rate. Similarly, while A could choose some counter-force proportion intermediate between 0 and 1, it is optimal for it to choose only one of these extreme values, firing missiles at only enemy cities or enemy missiles. Thus, A is confined to the above four possibilities for grand strategy, (i)–(iv). Furthermore, given the payoff function in (6) and the differential equations and boundary conditions describing the evolution of the war in (2)–(5), it is optimal for A to make a single switch in its rate of fire, namely a switch from the maximum rate $\alpha = \bar{\alpha}$ to the zero rate $\alpha = 0$. Similarly, it is optimal for A to make a single switch in its targets, as summarised by the counter-force proportion, namely a switch from pure counter-force targeting $\alpha' = 1$ to pure counter-value targeting $\alpha' = 0$.

If country A uses its optimal strategy the war therefore proceeds in three stages: it starts the war with a first-strike strategy ($\alpha = \bar{\alpha}$ and $\alpha' = 1$), the situation in which it has not yet switched either strategic choice variable, and it ends the war with a war of nerves strategy ($\alpha = 0$ and $\alpha' = 0$), the situation in which it has switched both of the strategic choice variables. The middle stage of the war can be either one of a massive retaliation strategy ($\alpha = \bar{\alpha}$ and $\alpha' = 0$) if the switching time for targets precedes that for the rate, or it can be one of a limited strategic war strategy ($\alpha = 0$ and $\alpha' = 1$) if the switching time for the rate precedes that for targets. Country A thus starts the war using only counter-force targeting at the maximum rate of fire so as to destroy as many as possible of the enemy missiles; ends the war by holding enemy cities as hostages, placing itself in the best possible position for extracting concessions or a desired settlement of the war; and, depending upon which switching time occurs first, during the middle stage of the war either inflicts massive casualties in country B or holds its missiles in reserve, threatening enemy missiles.

IV A MODEL OF WAR INITIATION

Having developed a model of a missile war in the previous section, this model will be speciaiised to treat the case of war initiation. The model is, in fact, reinterpreted in an essential way. It is treated not as a model of an *actual* war but rather as a model of a *hypothetical or potential* war, i.e. a war that might break out at any time. Thus the model is treated not as a representation of actual missiles, casualties, strategic choices, etc. but rather as a representation of *plans* for a war, including expected missiles, casualties, strategic choices, etc. that are foreseen as possible situations by defence planners. The model is thus a representation of war simulations or war scenarios used by defence analysts, for example those in the Pentagon or the Kremlin.

From the vantage point of defence analysts in country A the model can be used to simulate various possible scenarios. Of particular importance are two cases. The first case is that in which B attacks A, in which A simulates the effect of the B attack and its own retaliation. In this case defence analysts in A would seek to have enough missiles to deter B by threatening it with unacceptable levels of casualties in its retaliatory strike. The second case is that in which A contemplates a first strike attack on B, in which its defence analysts would seek to destroy enough B missiles to disarm it and render a retaliatory strike ineffectual. These two cases are that of country A as a *deterrer* and country A as an *attacker* respectively.

In the first case, of country A as a deterrer, its defence analysts should anticipate, as in the last section, that B will strike first using a first-strike strategy ($\beta = \bar{\beta}' = 1$) over the time interval from 0 to θ_B, before A can retaliate. They would then retaliate using a massive retaliation strategy ($\alpha = \bar{\alpha}$, $\alpha' = 0$), inflicting casualties in B over the retaliation time interval from θ_B to $\theta_B + \psi_A$.[6] If defence planners in A simulate the result of this scenario they can solve the differential equations (2)–(5) using these strategic values if, in this simulated war outbreak f_B can be assumed to be constant over the first strike interval θ_B and v_A can be assumed to be constant over the retaliation interval ψ_A. These are reasonable assumptions if both intervals are relatively short. The solution for the casualties in country B at the end of the retaliatory interval is then

$$C_B(\theta_B + \psi_A) = v_A[M_A^0 - f_B(1-\exp(-\bar{\beta}\theta_B))M_B^0][1-\exp(-\bar{\alpha}\psi_A)], \quad (7)$$

showing explicitly the dependence of simulated casualties on initial number of missiles M_A^0, M_B^0; rates of fire $\bar{\alpha}$, $\bar{\beta}$; missile effectiveness ratios f_B, v_A; and the time intervals θ_B, ψ_A. If this expected number of casualties is sufficiently large then A would deter B. In particular, if the minimum unacceptable number of casualties in B is $\bar{C}_B$ then solving

$$C_B(\theta_B + \psi_A) \geq \bar{C}_B \quad (8)$$

for M_A^0, the number of A missiles required to deter B (by threatening an unacceptable level of casualties) is given as

$$M_A \geq f_B (1-\exp(-\bar{\beta}\theta_B))M_B + \frac{\bar{C}_B}{v_A(1-\exp(-\bar{\alpha}\psi_A))}. \tag{9}$$

(Here M_A^0 and M_B^0 are replaced by M_A and M_B respectively since the model is one of a simulated war which can start at any time). This inequality shows the number of missiles required for A to deter B as an explicit function of the number of B missiles (and also the technical parameters $\bar{\alpha}$, $\bar{\beta}$, f_B, v_A; timing parameters θ_B, ψ_A; and the minimum unacceptable number of B casualties $\bar{C}_B$). Geometrically this inequality is the area to the right of the line marked 'A deters' in the weapons plane in Figure 9.2, with intercept $\bar{C}_B/[v_A(1-\exp(-\bar{\alpha}\psi_A))]$ on the M_A axis and with slope $1/[f_B(1-\exp(-\bar{\beta}\theta_B))]$.

In the second case, of country A as an attacker, defence analysts in A anticipate attacking B using its first strike strategy ($\alpha = \bar{\alpha}$, $\alpha' = 1$) over the time interval from 0 to θ_A before B can retaliate. They then have to consider the effects of B retaliating using a massive retaliation strategy ($\beta = \bar{\beta}$, $\beta \leq 0$) over the retaliatory time interval from θ_A to $\theta_A + \psi_B$. Solving the differential equations once again assuming the time intervals are sufficiently short that f_A can be treated as constant over the first strike interval and f_B can be treated as constant over the retaliation time interval, the casualties defence planners in A anticipate in this simulated war outbreak is $C_A(\theta_A + \psi_B)$ which is similar to (7) interchanging the roles of A and B. If defence planners in A regard $\hat{C}_A$ as a maximum acceptable level of casualties then, solving

$$C_A(\theta_A + \psi_B) \leq \hat{C}_A \tag{10}$$

for $M_A(=M_A^0)$ yields

$$M_A \geq \left[\frac{1}{f_A(1-\exp(-\bar{\alpha}\theta_A))}\right] M_B$$

$$- \frac{\hat{C}_A}{f_A(1-\exp(-\bar{\alpha}\theta_A))v_B(1-\exp(-\bar{\beta}\psi_B))} \tag{11}$$

This inequality shows the number of A missiles required for A to attack B as an explicit function of the number of B missiles (and also the technical parameters $\bar{\alpha}$, $\bar{\beta}$. f_A, v_B; timing parameters θ_A, ψ_B; and the maximum acceptable number of A casualties $\hat{C}_A$). Geometrically this inequality is the area above the line marked 'A attacks' in the weapons plane in Figure 9.2, with intercept $\hat{C}_A/[v_B(1-\exp(-\bar{\beta}\psi_B))]$ on the M_B axis and with slope $f_A(1-\exp(-\bar{\alpha}\theta_A))$.

Figure 9.2 also shows 'B deters' and 'B attacks' lines, indicating regions in which defence analysts in country B, on the basis of their

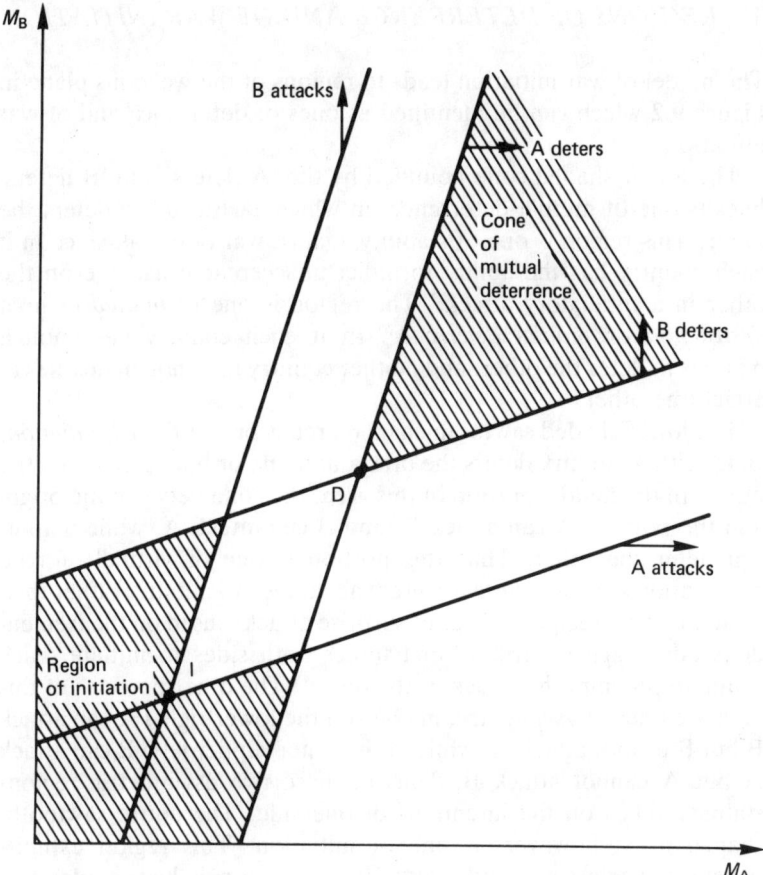

FIGURE 9.2 *Deterring and initiating regions in weapons plane*

simulated war outbreak using the same model of a missile war, have enough missiles, respectively, to deter A from attacking (by threatening unacceptable casualties) and to attack A (suffering an acceptable level of casualties). If the technical and timing parameters are estimated to be the same in both countries then the 'B deters' line is parallel to the 'A attacks' line and the 'B attacks' line is parallel to the 'A deters' line. For example, the common slope of the 'B deters' and 'A attacks' line is $f_A(1-\exp(-\bar{\alpha}\theta_A))$. If defence planners in the two countries have different assessments of these parameters (f_A, f_B, $\bar{\alpha}$, $\bar{\beta}$, θ_A, θ_B) then the lines need not be parallel.

V REGIONS OF DETERRENCE AND OF WAR INITIATION

The model of war initiation leads to regions of the weapons plane in Figure 9.2 which can be identified as ones of deterrence and of war initiation.[7]

The upper shaded cone bounded by the 'A deters' and 'B deters' lines is one of mutual deterrence, in which each country deters the other. This region is one of stability against war outbreak since in it each country has the ability to inflict unacceptable damage on the other in a retaliatory attack.[8] The region is one of *mutual assured destruction* or *mutual deterrence*. In it each country has enough missiles to deter the other, and neither country has enough missiles to attack the other.

The lower shaded sawtooth-shaped area is one of *forced initiation*. In it neither country deters the other, and one or both can attack the other. In the middle portion of this area, the cone between the origin and the point I, A can attack B, and B can attack A, while neither can deter the other. Thus this portion is one of virtually forced preemption in which there is a great advantage to initiate, rather than retaliate. The 'reciprocal fear of surprise attack' based on the tremendous advantage in striking first forces both sides to initiate, each trying to preempt the attack of the other.[9] The other portions of this area are ones of asymmetry; in one (on the lower right) A can attack B but B cannot attack A, while in the other (upper left) B can attack A but A cannot attack B. Thus in these two asymmetric regions stability relies on the intentions of one side. The entire sawtooth-shaped area, however, is one of initiation. This region exhibits instability against war outbreak in that neither side has an adequate retaliatory capability to ensure deterrence and one or both countries has enough capabilities, relative to the missiles held by the opponent, to attack the other.

The deterring and attacking lines for both countries that define the upper cone of mutual deterrence and the lower sawtooth-shaped area of initiation are themselves defined in (9) and (11) in terms of:

f_A, f_B: the effectiveness of missiles in destroying enemy missiles (which depend on missile accuracy and yield and enemy missile dispersion and hardness against attack).

v_A, v_B: the effectiveness of missiles in inflicting enemy casualties (which depend on missile accuracy and yield and enemy civil defence and dispersion).

$\bar{\alpha}$, $\bar{\beta}$: the (maximum) rates of fire of missiles (which depend on missile characteristics and the command and control structure).

θ_A, θ_B: the time intervals during which one country can attack the other without a response from the other (which depend on detection capabilities and command and control).

ψ_A, ψ_B: the time intervals for a retaliatory strike (which depend on missile characteristics and command and control).

$\bar{C}_A$, $\bar{C}_B$: the minimum unacceptable level of casualties which would deter each country, as estimated by the other country.

$\hat{C}_A$, $\hat{C}_B$: the maximum acceptable level of casualties which each country could accept in a retaliatory strike, as estimated by itself.

To give a numerical example, if it takes two missiles to destroy an enemy missile ($f_A = f_B = 0.5$), each missile can inflict 250 000 casualties ($v_A = v_B = 250\ 000$), the maximum rate of fire is 10 per cent per minute ($\bar{\alpha}_1 = \bar{\beta} = 0.10$), the first strike interval is 15 minutes ($\theta_A = \theta_B = 15$) the retaliatory strike interval is 10 minutes ($\psi_A = \psi_B = 10$), the minimum unacceptable level of casualties is 40 million ($\bar{C}_A = \bar{C}_B = 40$ million), and the maximum acceptable level of casualties is 5 million ($\hat{C}_A = \hat{C}_B = 5$ million) then point D in Figure 9.2, the minimum number of missiles required for mutual deterrence is 414 missiles on each side, while point I in Figure 9.2, the maximum number of missiles in the area of forced preemption (where each can attack the other) is 52 missiles. Thus in this symmetrical example if each side has more than 414 missiles there is the stability of mutual deterrence while if each side had fewer than 52 missiles there is the instability of forced preemption.

Obviously all the numbers used in these calculations are subject to uncertainty, particularly the estimates of the minimum unacceptable/maximum acceptable level of casualties. Thus it would be more appropriate to refer not to a cone of mutual deterrence and a region of initiation but rather to equal probability contours of war outbreak, showing relatively high probability of war outbreak in the region of initiation and relatively low probabilities of war outbreak in the cone of mutual deterrence. Alternatively the lines of deterrence and attack in Figure 9.1 can be replaced by bands, reflecting the uncertainty in the values of the parameters defining deterring and attacking regions. For purposes of exposition, however, the lines, the core of mutual deterrence and the region of initiation will be used in the next section to analyse arms races and war initiation.

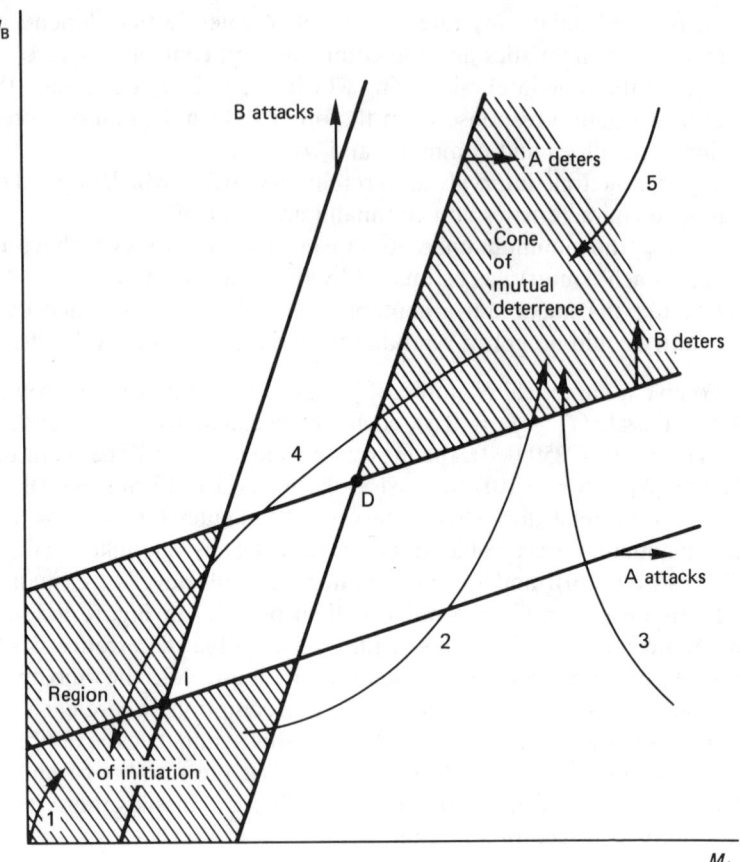

FIGURE 9.3 *Weapons trajectories and regions of deterrence and war initiation*

VI ARMS RACES AND WAR INITIATION

The analysis of arms races and war initiation combines the weapons trajectories describing an arms race in Section II, as shown geometrically in Figure 9.1, with the regions of deterrence and of war initiation in Section V, as shown geometrically in Figure 9.2. The result is Figure 9.3, which shows several trajectories and the regions of deterrence and of war initiation.

Trajectory 1 starts from the totally disarmed state of the origin and, as a result of an arms race both countries move to a highly unstable situation of forced initiation. This is an example of the case in which an arms race leads to war.

Trajectory 2 involves an arms race that, as a result of a weapons build-up in both countries moves the situation from one in which A could attack B to one in which each side deters the other. This is a situation in which an unstable situation is stabilised as a result of an arms race.

Trajectory 3 is one in which country A reduces its arms from an extremely high level while country B simultaneously increases its arms from a relatively low level. The result is a reduced chance of war outbreak, moving from a situation in which A can attack B to one in which each deters the other.

Trajectory 4 is one in which both sides disarm with the result that they move from a stable situation in the cone of mutual deterrence to an unstable one in which each can attack the other. This trajectory illustrates the potential dangers of bilateral disarmament.

Trajectory 5 is one in which, like the previous case, both sides reduce their level of armaments but, unlike the previous case they stay within the cone of mutual deterrence. Such selective reductions in arms need not cause instability as long as the situation remains in the cone of mutual deterrence.

Thus, the answer to the question 'Can Arms Races Lead to the Outbreak of War?' is not a simple one. The frequently expressed opinion that arms races lead to war is neither right, nor wrong; it depends on the circumstances. In certain situations an arms race *can* lead to war (as in Trajectory 1) while in other situations an arms race can lead to peace (as in Trajectory 2). Conversely, a *dis*arming race can result in war (as in Trajectory 4) or can preserve peace (as in Trajectory 5). In fact, the contrast between Trajectories 4 and 5 illustrates the differences between disarmament, which, despite its lofty goals, can be highly dangerous in leading to unstable situations, and arms control which, by selectively reducing weapons but retaining mutual deterrence can promote greater stability, for example in eliminating obsolete or unstable weapons systems but retaining enough weapons for deterrence.

VII CONCLUSION

The result of this analysis is that, by considering arms races in the context of a model of a possible war, arms races can possibly lead to war or to peace while, conversely, disarmament can also lead possibly to war or to peace. The result depends essentially on a comparison of the starting and ending points of the arms race relative to the regions of deterrence and war initiation. Points close to the totally disarmed state are highly unstable, so an arms race starting from the disarmed state would be highly dangerous but, conversely, a disarming race moving close to the disarmed state would also be highly dangerous (as illustrated in Trajectories 1 and 4 in Figure 9.3). Arms control can be interpreted not only as selective decreases in arms which retain mutual deterrence but also selective *in*creases in arms leading to the situation of mutual deterrence (as illustrated in Trajectories 5 and 2 in Figure 9.3).

To relate this analysis to the post-war situation for the United States and the Soviet Union, perhaps the trajectory that comes closest to describing the history of superpower arms since 1945 is that of Trajectory 2. Before the Soviet Union had a significant weapons capability the situation was an asymmetric one in which the US (country A in the figure) could attack the Soviet Union, but the Soviet Union could not attack the United States. In this asymmetrical situation the peace was preserved because of the commitment by the United States not to initiate a war (although some, including Bertrand Russell, advocated that the US strike the Soviet Union during its nuclear monopoly period). The 1950s and 1970s witnessed a major build-up of weapons on both sides, leading to the present situation of mutual deterrence, as illustrated in Trajectory 2, a situation of stability against war outbreak. In fact, the greatest instability was probably in the late 1950s and early 1960s, particularly the 1962 Cuban missile crisis, in which neither side could deter the other. The result of the arms race between the United States and the Soviet Union over the 1960s and 1970s was therefore a *reduction*, rather than an increase, in the chances of war outbreak.

NOTES AND REFERENCES

1. This research was completed under collaborative grants on 'Behavioral and Economic Foundations of Arms Races' from the National Science Foundation, whose support is gratefully acknowledged. A preliminary version of this paper was presented at the International Political Science Association World Congress in Rio de Janeiro, Brazil, August 1982.
2. See Richardson, L. F., 'Could An Arms Race End without Fighting?' *Nature*, 29 (Sept. 1951) pp. 567–8. Richardson, L. F., *Arms and Insecurity* (Pittsburgh: The Boxwood Press, 1960). See also Rapoport, A., 'Lewis Fry Richardson's Mathematical Theory of War', *Journal of Con-*

flict Resolution 1, (1957) pp. 249–304. Intriligator, M. D. and Brito, D. L., 'Formal Models of Arms Races', Journal of Peace Science, 2 (1976) pp. 77–78. Intriligator, M. D., 'Strategic Considerations in the Richardson Model of Arms Races', Journal of Political Economy, 83 (1975) pp. 339–53 for analysis and interpretations of the Richardson model. Richardson in Arms and Insecurity (1960) identifies an unstable arms race with war outbreak but Richardson in his 1951 article provides a qualification to allow for 'submissiveness'.
3. See Lambelet, J. C., 'Do Arms Races lead to War?', Journal of Peace Research 12 (1975) pp. 123–8. Smith, T. C., 'Arms Race Instability and War', Journal of Conflict Resolution 24 (1980) pp. 253–84. Wallace, M. D., 'Armaments and Escalation: Two Competing Hypotheses', International Studies Quarterly 26 (1982) pp. 37–56. See also Huntington, S. P., 'Arms Races: Pre-requisites and Results', Public Policy 8 (1958) pp. 41–86. Saaty. T. L., 'A Model for the Control of Arms', Operations Research, 12 (1964). Saaty, T. L., Mathematical Models of Arms Control and Disarmament (New York: John Wiley, 1968). Pruitt, D. G. and Shyder, R. C., Theory and Research on the Causes of War (Englewood Cliffs, NJ, Prentice-Hall, 1969). Gray, C. S., 'The Arms Race Phenomenon', World Politics 24 (1971) pp. 39–79. Gray, C. S., 'Arms Races and their Influence upon International Stability with Specific Reference to the Middle East', in Sheffer, G. (ed.), Dynamics of Conflict (Atlantic Highlands, NJ; Humanities Press, 1975). Gray, C. S., The Soviet Arms Race (Lexington, Lexington Books, 1976). Lambelet, J. C., 'A Dynamic Model of the Arms Race in the Middle East, 1953–65', General Systems, 16 (1971) pp. 145–67. Lambelet, J. C., 'Towards a Dynamic Two Theatre Model of the East-West Arms Race', Journal of Peace Science, 1 (1973) pp. 1–38. Lambelet, J. C., 'Complementary Analysis of the Anglo-German Dreadnought Race 1905–1916', Papers of the Peace Research Society (International), 26 (1976) pp. 49–66. Holsti, O. R., Crisis, Escalation, War (Montreal: McGluen-Queens University Press, 1972). Russet, B. M. (ed.), Peace, War and Numbers (Beverly Hills: Sage Publications, 1972). Wallace, M. D., War and Rank among Nations (Lexington: Lexington Books, 1972). Wallace, M. D., 'Arms Races and Escalation: Some New Evidence', Journal of Conflict Resolution, 23 (1979) pp. 3–16. Singer, J. D., 'Accounting for International War: The State of the Discipline', Journal of Peace Research, 18 (1981) pp. 1–18.
4. See Intriligator, M. D., Strategy in a Missile War; Targets and Rates of Fire, Security Studies Project, Security Papers no. 10 (Los Angeles: University of California, Los Angeles, 1967). Intriligator, M. D., 'The Debate over Missile Strategy: Targets and Rates of Fire', Orbis, 11 (1968) pp. 1138–59. Intriligator, 'Strategic Considerations in the Richardson Model of Arms Races'. Saaty, Mathematical Models of Arms Control and Disarmament. Brito, D. L, and Intriligator, M. D., 'Some Applications of the Maximum Principle to the Problem of an Armaments Race'. Modeling and Simulation, 4 (1973) pp. 140–44. Brito, D. L. and Intriligator, M. D., 'Uncertainty and Stability of the Armaments Race', Annals of Economic and Social Measurement, 3 (1974) pp. 279–92. Intriligator and Brito, 'Formal Models of Arms Races'. Intriligator, M. D. and

Brito, D. L., 'Strategy, Arms Races and Arms Control', in Gillespie, J. V. and Zinnes, D. A. (eds), *Mathematical Systems in International Relations Research* (New York: Praeger, 1977).
5. See Intriligator, *Strategy in a Missile War: Targets and Rates of Fire*, for proofs of this result and the subsequent results reported in this paragraph.
6. This retaliation strategy is consistent with the switching strategy outlined in the last section; in this case the switch in targets occurs at the time θ_B, so after θ_B the A grand strategy is one of massive retaliation with $a = \bar{a}$, $a' = 0$.
7. For related diagrams see: Kybal, D., 'Remarks', in *Proceedings of the National Security Seminar*, Asilomar, California, 24–30 April 1960. Beaufre, A., *Deterrence and Strategy*, translated from the French by Barry, R. H. (New York: Praeger, 1965).
8. See also Szilard, L., ' "Minimal Deterrent" vs. Saturation Parity', *Bulletin of the Atomic Scientist*, 20 (1964) pp. 6–12.
9. See Wohlstetter, A., 'The Delicate Balance of Terror', *Foreign Affairs*, 37 (1959) pp. 211–234.

---

* Martin C. McGuire, 'US Assistance and Israel Allocation', *Journal of Conflict Resolution*, vol. 6, no. 2 (June 1982) pp. 199–235. Reprinted by permission of Sage Publications, Inc.

10 US Foreign Assistance, Israeli Resource Allocation and the Arms Race in the Middle East: An Analysis of Three Interdependent Resource Allocation Processes[1]

*Martin C. McGuire
UNIVERSITY OF MARYLAND

I INTRODUCTION

In many areas of the world, both developing and developed, the United States and a local ally have a common interest in the ally's security and survival in an environment of escalating and/or volatile challenge and threat. The demands of client states for US help, together with the opportunities they create to influence political texture and events is also likely to be a continuing phenomenon on the international scene. This being the case, continued improvement in our understanding of how the various participants in these conflict processes interact is desirable. Since these processes have been going on for twenty years or more, considerable data may be around to allow for more quantitative description of the processes and of their interactions. As candidates for such an analysis, Israel and the Middle East are notable; Israel for the ambition of its security and development objectives and for its success in obtaining external finance; the Middle East region for the persistence and virulence of its arms race. Moreover, especially in the case of Israel, reliable statistics extending back twenty years are available.

The first ambition of this paper is to build a model or set of models of the behaviour of Israel, the USA, and Israel's surrounding Arab neighbours. The models must be statistically testable, since the second purpose is to test them using a comprehensive body of data which has been assembled for the period 1960–79.

Several insights which should have direct utility for policy makers will emerge from our analysis. First, we will produce a better understanding of how US assistance to a foreign ally, Israel in this case, is effectively used, i.e., whether or not such aid is diverted away from purposes for which it was legally intended. Second, we will have a structured understanding of how US assistance influences Israel's allocations between the public and private sector, and within the public sector between defence and non-defence purposes.[2] Third, the analysis will yield a better grasp on how other external and internal factors determine Israel's allocative behaviour. The allocations have occurred over the past twenty years in a context of volatile growing security threats as perceived from Tel Aviv in part matched by growing US assistance. Throughout this period, Israeli population and per capita income have also grown rapidly. Thus, any analysis of Israeli allocations must disentangle the interrelated effects of Israel's population and income growth, US foreign assistance, and Arab military effort on Israel's allocative behaviour.[3] Fourth, as a policy insight to emerge from our statistically estimated models will be the relative degrees in which US and Arab and Israeli arms expenditures have sustained the arms race in the Middle East.

As already stated, a comprehensive body of data on the Israeli economy and budget allocations over the period 1960–79 has been assembled to address these questions. Table 10.1 shows selected data on Israel and the surrounding Arab states over the time period under study. Several trends are noteworthy. First, it appears that while Israel was able to maintain defence expenditures at a level of about one-third of that of its surrounding Arab neighbours over the period 1960–75, since 1975 Arab outlays have accelerated much faster than Israel's ability or willingness to keep up, so that by 1979 the ratio was

TABLE 10.1 Selected data on the Israel economy and defence outlays, and Arab GNP and defence outlays, 1960–79

Year	1960	1961	1962	1963	1964	1965	1966
Population in millions[1]	2.154	2.234	2.332	2.430	2.526	2.598	2.657
	Per capita outlays in 1975 Israeli pounds						
	To convert to 1979 $ US multiply by 0.203						
All foreign 'assistance' – Net[2] borrowing and grants from external sources	843	1 007	1 264	1 106	961	915	625
Gross exports[2]	1 845	1 965	2 765	3 018	2 978	2 987	3 192
Gross national expenditures[2]	12 850	13 805	15 462	15 973	16 844	17 244	16 416
Investment[2]	3 020	3 458	4 113	4 014	4 647	4 322	3 288
Consumption[2]	9 830	10 347	11 349	11 959	12 197	12 922	13 128
Private[2]	7 778	8 109	8 721	9 200	9 495	9 937	9 815
Public – Non-Defence[2]	1 264	1 303	1 380	1 536	1 467	1 714	1 884
Defence (including US assistance)[2]	788	935	1 248	1 223	1 235	1 271	1 429
US military assistance disbursements[3]							
Gross, including loans	1.7	0.3	0.1	1.1	3.7	71	81
Net of loan repayments	0.8	–0.06	–1.5	1.0	–1.0	53	53
US economic assistance disbursements[3]							
Gross, including loans	176	216	405	325	380	285	231
Net of loan repayments	115	148	289	210	248	157	181
	Total outlays billions of 1975 Israeli pounds						
Combined military expenditures of[4] Jordan, Iraq, Syria, Egypt and Saudi Arabia	5.11	5.14	8.02	8.57	9.15	10.0	10.9
Total Israeli defence expenditure	1.69	2.08	2.91	2.97	3.11	3.30	3.79
Ratio 'Arabs'/Israel	3.02	2.47	2.75	2.88	2.94	3.03	2.87
Arab's GNP[4]	72.2	71.8	108	109	116	116	118

Continued on page 200

TABLE 10.1 – contd

Year	1967	1968	1969	1970	1971	1972	1973
Population in millions[1]	2.776	2.841	2.930	3.022	3.121	3.227	3.332
	Per capita outlays in 1975 Israeli pounds						
	To convert to 1979 $ US multiply by 0.203						
All foreign 'assistance' – Net[2] borrowing and grants from external sources	2 016	1 345	1 207	2 353	1 969	2 019	4 733
Gross exports[2]	3 416	4 680	5 086	5 063	6 212	6 849	6 802
Gross national expenditures[2]	16 140	18 511	21 179	22 384	23 611	25 027	28 599
Investment[2]	2 415	3 644	4 662	5 131	6 094	6 784	7 188
Consumption[2]	13 725	14 867	16 517	17 253	17 517	18 243	21 411
Private[2]	9 529	10 260	11 193	10 828	11 004	11 832	12 297
Public – non-defence[2]	1 789	1 790	1 853	1 884	2 037	2 113	2 304
Defence (including US assistance)[2]	2 407	2 817	3 471	4 541	4 476	4 298	6 810
US military assistance disbursements[3]							
Gross, including loans	21	120	375	186	1 063	734	352
Net of loan repayments	−1.9	46	295	134	959	607	246
US economic assistance disbursements[3]							
Gross, including loans	210	254	220	264	347	380	433
Net of loan repayments	140	153	111	158	219	122	309
	Total outlays billions of 1975 Israeli pounds						
Combined military expenditures o[c4] Jordan, Iraq, Syria, Egypt and Saudi Arabia	13.8	16.2	19.1	22.0	25.1	27.5	42.2
Total Israeli defence expenditure	6.68	8.00	10.17	13.72	13.96	13.86	22.69
Ratio 'Arabs'/Israel	2.06	2.02	1.87	1.60	1.79	1.98	1.85
Arab's GNP[4]	119	124	150	152	163	186	200

Year	1974	1975	1976	1977	1978	1979
Population in millions[1]	3.409	3.493	3.575	3.647	3.719	3.794
		Per capita outlays in 1975 Israeli pounds				
		To convert to 1979 $ US multiply by 0.203				
All foreign 'assistance' – Net[2] borrowing and grants from external sources	2 751	4 171	3 723	2 583	4 188	3 337
Gross exports[2]	7 124	7 305	8 487	9 648	10 856	9 940
Gross national expenditures[2]	29 246	30 124	28 630	26 331	28 956	28 672
Investment[2]	7 123	7 123	5 932	5 176	5 921	6 539
Consumption[2]	22 123	23 001	22 698	21 155	23 035	22 133
Private[2]	13 238	13 286	13 678	13 302	14 228	14 346
Public – non-defence[2]	2 296	2 302	2 450	2 649	2 695	2 844
Defence (including US assistance)[2]	6 589	7 413	6 570	5 204	6 112	4 943
US military assistance disbursements[3]						
Gross, including loans	2 037	1 913	2 603	2 094	1 782	1 488
Net of loan repayments	1 961	1 845	2 471	1 918	1 613	1 287
US economic assistance disbursements[3]						
Gross, including loans	191	902	1 248	1 336	1 564	1 654
Net of loan repayments	109	814	1 103	1 203	1 472	1 576
		Total outlays billions of 1975 Israeli pounds				
Combined military expenditures of[4] Jordan, Iraq, Syria, Egypt and Saudi Arabia	52.1	76.2	99.0	95.9	110	104
Total Israeli defence expenditure	22.46	25.89	23.48	18.97	22.73	18.75
Ratio 'Arabs'/Israel	2.31	2.94	4.21	5.05	4.83	5.54
Arab's GNP[4]	304	432	544	605	731	770

SOURCES 1. Statistical Abstract of Israel. 2. Bank of Israel Annual Reports. 3. *International Finance: Annual Report to the President and Congress* by the National Advisory Council on International Monetary and Financial Policies. 4. *World Armaments and Disarmament*, Stockholm International Peace Research Institute (SIPRI) Annual Reports.

almost one to six. Second, while Israel was able to maintain continued per capita real growth in all expenditure categories throughout 1960–75, since 1975 real per capita defence outlays as well as real per capita investment have declined to allow continued growth in real per capita consumption (both public and private). This shift may reflect Israel's policy objective of maintaining continued immigration. Third, US governmental assistance has grown from a small fraction of all foreign transfers and loans in the early 1960s, to over 80 per cent of such transfers by 1979.[4]

The models explaining Israeli, Arab and US allocations are supply and demand models. Models of this type are usually based on a supposition, explicit or implicit, that the allocation process is the result of utility maximising behaviour on the part of agents or actors on the scene. The epistemological status of such assumptions has been much debated. In recent years, a number of authors have emphasised the multisided, bureaucratic, or committee nature of government decision processes. These are examples of alternative models which may explain the behaviour of the participants in the Middle-East equally well; for instance, models of coalition formation between US and Israeli defence ministries; models which distinguish between the utility function of the country and the interests of the government bureaucracy; models which emphasise the bargaining, game theoretic and/or negotiating styles of Arabs, Israelis, and US officials.[5] In this work it has not been possible to construct formulations which would allow us to identify, from the data, which social choice theoretic processes predominate. Consequently, I have held to the more conventional conceptual structure that governmental allocative behaviour can be legitimately represented as if the government were a monolithic entity which faithfully behaves as if it were maximising the 'representative citizen's' utility.[6] This 'as if' assumption is explicit in our model of Israeli allocations, while more implicit in the model of US and Arab behaviour. For a strong defence of this assumption see work by Silberberg.[7]

II A DESCRIPTIVE MODEL OF THE ISRAELI RESOURCE ALLOCATION PROCESSES: THEIR RESPONSE TO ARAB FORCE LEVELS, THEIR UTILISATION OF US ASSISTANCE, AND THE PROBLEM OF FUNGIBILITY OF US FUNDS

We will assume that Israel's resource allocations between public and private sectors and within the public sector between defence and non-defence in any one year depend systematically on the following factors:

(a) per capita income in Israel, including private remittances from abroad;
(b) population of Israel;
(c) size of the defence capability of their threatening Arab neighbours;
(d) amount of US military assistance and economic assistance in the same year;
(e) the proportion of US assistance to Israeli defence effort.

Obviously, a great many factors influence internal resource allocation decisions made by the political and bureaucratic structure of any country. With a limited number of years' data, however, the foregoing five factors are suggested as a minimum for capturing the essentials of a highly complex process.[8] As stated above, we will assume that resources are allocated among programmes as in a model of individual consumer utility maximisation. This approach, with its shortcomings and advantages, has been extensively scrutinised and evaluated in the economics literature on the fiscal behaviour of state and local governments.[9] Given our intention of utilising the consumer demand approach, our current task is to adapt it from a state-local context to an international context and then to introduce the foregoing explanatory factors into the utility function.

1 ISRAEL'S UTILISATION OF US ASSISTANCE: THE PROBLEM OF FUNGIBILITY

I have argued elsewhere that

> when governments set up large and complicated subsidy programs to influence allocative decisions of individuals or of other governments, acceptance of the face value provisions of the subsidy programme as reflecting true constraints is suspect. In the first place even nominal constraints introduced by a grant or subsidy may be practically impossible to observe. Government programs are typically complicated; nominal grant constraints may vary widely with the characteristics of the recipients; and program administrators may have wide latitude as to which contingencies and constraints to impose. Moreover, as programs grow so do the bureaucracies both of givers and receivers. Increasingly therefore the nominal constraints placed on grants are the outcome of

evolving bargains struck between giver and receiver in a legislative executive cycle . . . .

In the second place, even if it were possible to discover the nominal conditions of a grant, there are strong arguments for expecting the effective conditions to differ . . . . Essentially there are a variety of steps a recipient, especially if it is a local government, can take to transform a conditional or categorical grant into fungible resources. The subsidized good may be resold or traded to some one else. Alternatively an equivalent non-subsidized good may be exchanged in the market for fungible resources. Trades through time may be made among local agencies with capital expenditures. And by judicious redefinitions of expenditure categories or allocations of overhead costs, local officials may in part convert a contingent grant into a pure budget supplement. Accordingly some method to infer the degree of such circumvention of nominal grant restrictions must be constructed to interpret the recipient's response to the grant.[10]

Although this argument was made in the context of US domestic grant and loan programmes to States and local governments, it is equally or more valid in an international context. All the perfectly legal techniques open to the States and localities in the USA are open to other nations which receive US assistance. Thus the Israelis with an active domestic arms industry can substitute US arms for their own while selling their own in export markets. In an environment calling for stringent internal security the line between defence and police, military and civil transportation, military and civilian health services is obviously ambiguous. If it becomes advantageous to draw this line one way rather than another for financial aid purposes, then one might reasonably expect a foreign aid recipient to do so. Consequently, it is likely that at least a part of a grant or loan can be converted into fungible resources and used for any purpose seen fit by the foreign recipient. One output of this study will be an estimate of the degree to which US assistance has been, in effect just another source of fungible revenue to the Israelis.

2   AN ECONOMIC MODEL OF THE INTERACTION BETWEEN INTERNAL RESOURCES AND FOREIGN ASSISTANCE AS DETERMINANTS OF THE RECEIVER'S ALLOCATIONS

Elsewhere,[11] this author has constructed models which allow one to use reported data on expenditures and grant/loan receipts to infer how much (the percentage of) a grant or loan was converted into fungible resources by a receiving government. Statistical estimation of these models provides an estimate of how those fungible resources were spent by the receiver (allocated among various public and private uses), and how the non-fungible portion of a grant/loan influences the receiving government's spending on the aid-targeted programmes (defence, non-defence, etc.). The basic idea underlying these models is that allocations are explained by supply–demand considerations where supply depends upon costs and demand depends upon income and price. The idea is easily explained with the help of supply–demand diagrams. In Figure 10.1, the economy of Israel is shown as consisting of two sectors: defence, and for illustration, everything else lumped together. Dotted lines show demand curves for each sector before US foreign assistance. Supply curves before and after foreign assistance are shown by the curves S. These are horizontal lines to reflect our assumption that average costs of supply in either sector are constant. The allocations before receipt of foreign assistance are shown at the intersection of supply and demand. Now imagine a certain amount of foreign *military assistance*, $\$G$, is disbursed by the US in a given year – presumably to be spent on *military* purposes. Suppose, nevertheless, that, for reasons just cited, a certain amount of that grant (A and B), is effectively converted into fungible resources. This increment to the local resource base will shift demand curves out just as would any addition to the local resource base, with some of the resources (B) devoted to defence and the remainder (A) to 'all else'. This is shown in Figure 10.1(a) (b) by the solid lines. The remainder of the $\$G$ of foreign military assistance is channelled directly into defence. This amount, (G–A–B), has the effect of reducing the *price* of defence capability to the Israelis. Price changes show up as movements *along* the demand curve rather than shifts in that curve (shifts show the effects of income changes) Figure 10.1(c) and (d) show the effects of the price change induced by the non-fungible portion of the grant or loan. Now, the Israelis are effectively paying a lower price for defence; the price declines from P^0 to P^1, although the average *cost* (we assume) of defence is unchanged at $P^0 = P^T$ ('total' price paid for defence). For convenience we can and will define a unit of defence and of 'all else' so that its average cost equals unity ($P^0 = P^T = 1$).

So the total cost of Israel's defence is equal to:

P^T (total price) × Q (quantity of defence) = (G–A–B) + ($E + H$).

Of this total, the Israeli contribution equals:

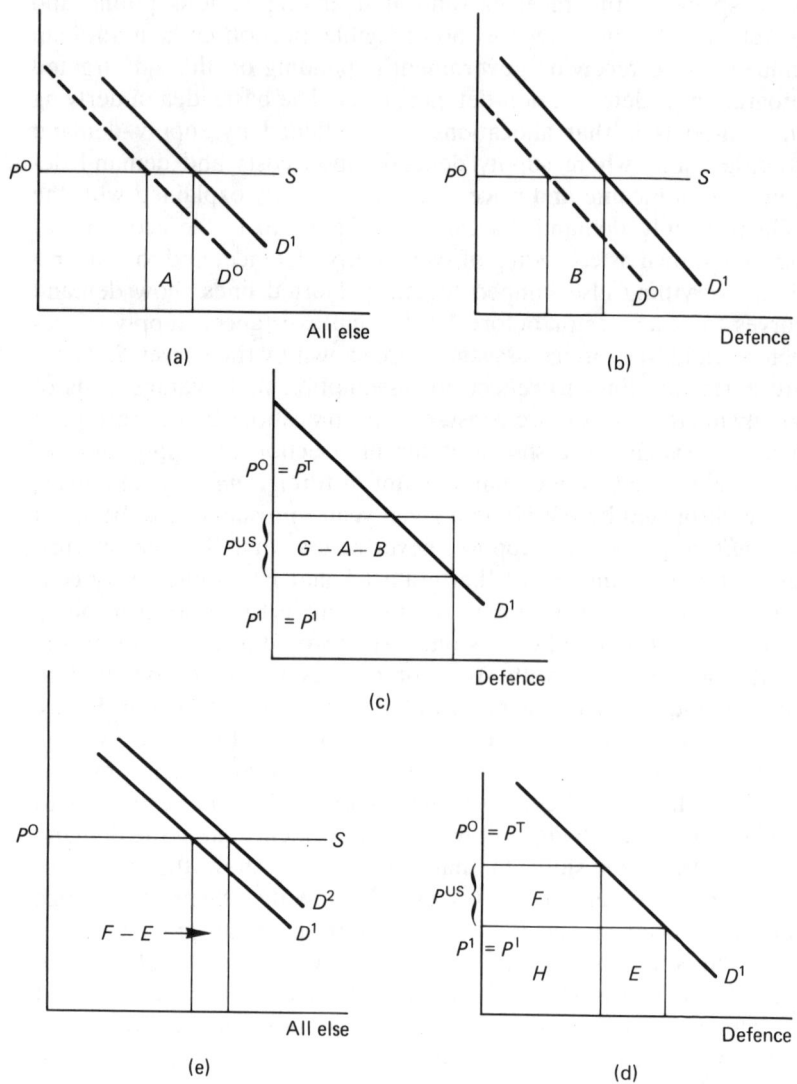

FIGURE 10.1 *Suppy-demand analysis of the allocative effects of foreign assistance*

P^I (Israeli price share) × Q (quantity of defence) = $(E + H)$,

and the US contribution equals:

P^{US} (US price share) × Q (quantity of defence) = $(G-A-B)$.

Of course, the combined price shares must add to the total

$P^T = P^I + P^{US} = 1$.

When the USA intervenes with foreign economic and/or military assistance, we expect Israel's defence budget to change, the exact change depending on the shape of the demand for defence capability curve. Figure 10.1(d) illustrates the effect of the non-fungible portion of aid on Israel's defence outlays. Before intervention Israel would spend area $(F + H)$ on defence; after US intervention area $(E + H)$. The difference in Israel's own defence outlays is the difference between F and E, which may be positive or negative depending on the shape of the demand curve. If the demand curve is very inelastic then area F is large and E small, implying decline in Israel's own expenditures on defence as a result of US assistance. Conversely if the demand curve is elastic, then area E will be large and F small, implying an increase in Israel's own defence outlays. Either way, the shift in resources of $E-F$ into or out of defence entails a corresponding decrease or increase of resources in the remainder of Israel's economy. Accordingly, Figure 10.1(e) shows a shift in demand and resources ($F-E$ positive is illustrated) into the remainder of the economy, as a result of (illustrated) inelastic demand for defence. The final disposition of resources resulting from the income changing (fungible) effect of the grant and the price changing (non-fungible) effect of the grant shows up in terms of the areas A to H as follows:

Change in defence = $G - A - B + E - F + B$
Change in non-defence = $+ A + F - E$
Total change = G

The statistical innovation employed in this study consists in a method for estimating how much of G is *effectively converted* into fungible resources $(A + B)$. I stress 'effectively converted' because the assumption of the method is that in an accounting sense *all* of G shows up as having been spent on defence (or for whatever category it was designated), but that the receiving government adjusts the allocation of its own funds so that the net effect is as portrayed in Figure 10.1. This point is discussed by the author in greater detail elsewhere.[11]

3 THE EFFECT OF ARAB DEFENCE EFFORT ON ISRAELI DEMAND FOR DEFENCE

Several measurement problems arise in the attempt to capture this effect. Ideally one would not want to lump all the Arab states surrounding Israel into one category; each Arab state would count separately. However, the number of observations is not sufficient to accommodate such disaggregations. Also, one might hope to distinguish between the qualitative effectiveness of various Arab forces (through a system of weights, for instance) and between offensive and defensive weapons, with the likelihood that Israel reacts differently to different types of Arab weaponry emphasised. And of course our postulate that Israel reacts to the current flow of Arab expenditures on defence rather than the stock of Arab military strength is suspect. In addition to all these measurement difficulties, the major conceptual problem in capturing Israel's resource allocation response to Arab arms build-up concerns how the Arab defence variable influences Israeli decision. Specifically, should one assume that Israel tries to anticipate and manipulate Arab defence postures with its own, or more simply, that Israel myopically reacts year by year to Arab force postures? Probably neither of these simplifications adequately describes reality. Nevertheless, I have chosen the latter assumption that Israel follows 'Cournot behaviour' reacting myopically to the current Arab force levels so as to maximise its own utility on the assumption that Arab defence effort will not change (despite the fact it does repeatedly change). For all its naiveté, a Cournot process is known to be sufficient to generate and sustain an arms race.[12]

Operationally, therefore, we will assume that the effect of an increase in Arab defence outlays is to change the position of Israel's demand curves – demand for defence and demand for all other goods – shifting some curves in and others out as in Figure 10.1. Using E_D^A for real Arab defence expenditures and E_i^I for Israeli expenditure in category i (defence, public non-defence, private consumption etc.), it follows that since Israel's national income is exhaustively apportioned among the categories, then when E_D^A changes, the resulting changes in E_i^I must sum to zero. Algebraically, this can be expressed as:

$$\sum_i \left[\partial E_i^I / \partial E_D^A \right] = 0$$

We will incorporate this assumption in our choice of a utility function in Section V.

4 THE EFFECT OF POPULATION ON ISRAELI OUTLAYS

The general expectation concerning any governmental allocative behaviour is that allocations to an expenditure category depend on per capita income, population size, price, and other socioeconomic, political, and strategic factors, etc. In the case at hand, we assume that per capita expenditure on defence E^I_D, on public non-defence, E^I_{ND}, and on private consumption E^I_{PVT} each depends in a systematic way on per capita income, price, the magnitude of the Arab 'threat', and Israeli population. The specific question I want to pose here is whether an increase in population with *per capita income held constant* will increase per capita expenditures on defence differently from per capita expenditures on public non-defence or private consumption.

Now, if we were talking about milk or eggs and population doubled while average per capita income, prices and all other factors remained the same, we would expect per capita expenditures on milk/eggs to remain the same (provided average costs of production are constant), and total expenditures to double. Such is the expected outcome for most private good type expenditures, whether they actually occur in the private or in the public sector. Defence, however, is not technically a private good at all; it is the paradigm of a pure public good. In the case of a pure public good, the total amount of defence protection is enjoyed by everyone in the population. As population increases the cost per person of providing an unchanged amount of the public good declines. Therefore, each person would want more of the public good, and a competent 'utility maximising' government would meet this demand. Whether the total outlay on defence increases less than, more than, or just in proportion to the increase in population, will depend on the price elasticity of demand for defence. If demand is price elastic, then an increase in population will bring about a greater than proportionate increase in defence outlays. On the other hand, if demand is price inelastic, defence outlays will increase less than in proportion to the population.

Between the extremes in which defence might be a pure private versus a pure public good there may be some middle ground. An ingenious formulation to discern the degree of publicness or privateness has been developed by Bergstrom and Goodman[13] and will be incorporated in our formulation. Specifically, if the *per capita amount* of a governmentally provided good (defence) is Q_D^I and total population is Pop, the amount consumed by the average individual is $Q_D^I/(\text{Pop})^\varepsilon$. For $\varepsilon = -1$ the entire amount of defence is consumed by each individual, and defence would be a pure public good; for $\varepsilon = 0$ the total quantity of defence is divided equally among all individuals and defence would be a pure private good; for values of ε between -1 and 0 defence is intermediate between pure public and private.

III THE US SUPPLY OF ECONOMIC AND MILITARY ASSISTANCE

Another actor in the drama of the Middle-East arms race is America with its provision of military and economic assistance. What determines the amount of this assistance? No pretence is made here of an exhaustive explanation; political factors are obviously crucial. However, at a minimum we propose that US assistance is dependent on two factors: (a) the magnitude of the 'threat' Israel faces, and (b) Israel's ability to deal with the threat alone. As a measure of the magnitude of the threat we will use surrounding Arab defence outlays; and as a measure of Israel's ability to deal with the threat we will use its gross domestic product. Another candidate explanatory variable might be Israel's own defence effort. Owing to data limitations, this further elaboration was rejected. Moreover, exploratory statistical analysis showed that when this variable was included in the model, it produced no significant explanatory improvement.

IV ARAB DEMAND FOR DEFENCE

The Arab states in the region are the third set of actors in our model. Just as we have assumed that Israel reacts to Arab expenditures, it is reasonable to suppose similar behaviour on the part of the Arab states. Future investigation may show significant differences between Israeli and Arab responses to each other's defence efforts and/or to increased wealth, as well as expected or unexpected divergences between the two adversaries with regard to their reaction to external political events (the Iranian revolution, for instance). For this study, data limitations plus the rather precise quantitative nature of our objectives suggests that we assume Arab defence expenditure depends on Arab GNP as well as on the security 'threat' the Arabs perceive from Israel. As a measure of the Israeli threat we have taken the total Israeli defence effort whether financed from internal or external sources.

V A MATHEMATICAL SPECIFICATION OF THE THREE ALLOCATION PROCESSES: ARAB AND ISRAELI ALLOCATIONS TO DEFENCE, PLUS US ALLOCATION TO FOREIGN ASSISTANCE

The model just outlined must be specified in mathematical form in order to estimate quantitatively the impacts of US assistance, and the allocative behaviour of Israel and its Arab neighbours.

v.a.

1 ISRAELI ALLOCATIVE BEHAVIOUR

Our mathematical specification assumes that Israel allocates its resources among three categories, namely (a) defence, (b) public non-defence, (c) private consumption, so as to maximise *the average person's utility*.[14] To represent this utility we use the well-tested Stone – Geary functional form.[15] This form is written for the average citizen as

$$U = \beta_D \log (Q_D^I - \gamma_D^I E_D^A) + \beta_{ND} \log (Q_{ND}^I - \gamma_{ND}^I E_D^A) \qquad (1)$$
$$+ (1 - \beta_D - \beta_{ND}) \log (Q_{PVT} - \gamma_{PVT}^I E_D^A)$$

Figure 10.2 gives a picture of this utility function in the two dimensions 'defence' Q_D^I and 'non-defence' Q_{ND}^I. The utility function is a Cobb–Douglas form displaced to the origin ($\gamma_D^I E_D^A$, $\gamma_{PVT}^I E_D^A$). We might reasonably expect γ_D^I to be positive and γ_{PVT}^I to be negative meaning that increases in the Arab threat make defence needs more important (increase its marginal utility) and public non-defence less so (decreases its marginal utility). In this case the displaced origin of the Cobb–Douglas function is in the second quadrant, and, as shown in the Figure 10.2, an increase in Arab defence outlays would move the origin from points like Γ_1 to one like Γ_2.[16]

Terms in (1) and derived from (1) are defined as follows:

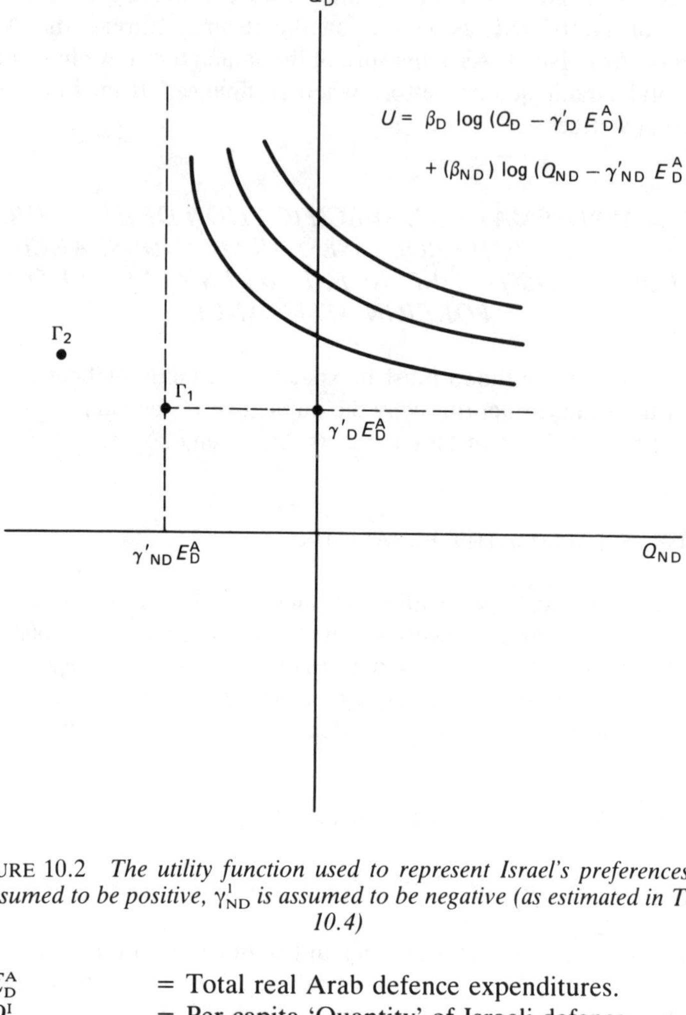

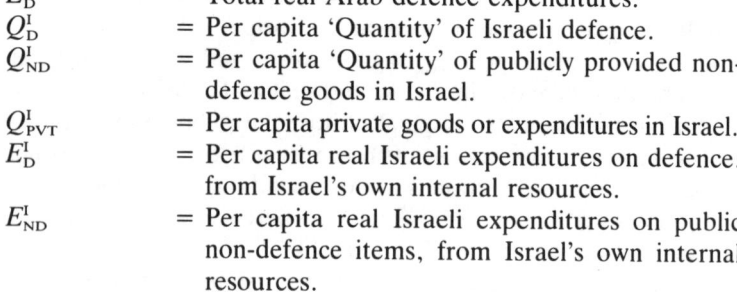

FIGURE 10.2 *The utility function used to represent Israel's preferences. γ'_D is assumed to be positive, γ'_{ND} is assumed to be negative (as estimated in Table 10.4)*

E_D^A = Total real Arab defence expenditures.
Q_D^I = Per capita 'Quantity' of Israeli defence.
Q_{ND}^I = Per capita 'Quantity' of publicly provided non-defence goods in Israel.
Q_{PVT}^I = Per capita private goods or expenditures in Israel.
E_D^I = Per capita real Israeli expenditures on defence, from Israel's own internal resources.
E_{ND}^I = Per capita real Israeli expenditures on public non-defence items, from Israel's own internal resources.

E^I_{PVT}	= Per capita real Israeli expenditures on private goods, from Israel's own internal resources.
γ^I_D	= The rate at which $1 of Arab defence outlays reduces the average Israeli citizen's benefit from Israel's own defence outlays.
γ^I_{ND}	= The rate at which $1 of Arab defence outlays reduces the average Israeli citizen's benefit from public non-Defence per capita outlays.
γ^I_{PVT}	= The rate at which $1 of Arab defence outlays reduces the average Israeli citizen's benefit from private per capita consumption.
β_D	= Israel's marginal propensity to spend fungible resources on defence.
β_{ND}	= Israel's marginal propensity to spend fungible resources on public non-defence purposes.
$1 - \beta_D - \beta_{ND}$	= Israel's marginal propensity to spend fungible resources on private goods and services.

The average citizen's utility function (1) is maximised subject to the budget constraint:

$$R_T = R_L + \phi_D \text{MILAID} + \phi_{ND} \text{ECAID} \qquad (2)$$

$$= P_D Q^I_D N^\varepsilon_I + P_{ND} Q^I_{ND} + Q_{PVT}$$

where:

R_L	= Per capita 'internal' resources, gross domestic product plus transfers from abroad exclusive of US government financial aid;
R_T	= Per capita total fungible resources available to Israel from all sources, domestic and foreign, *including the fungible part of US aid*;
N_I	= Israeli population;
ε	= Parameter indicating degree to which defence is a pure public good. If $\varepsilon = -1$ defence is a pure public good. If $\varepsilon = 0$, defence is a pure private good;
MILAID	= Per capita US security assistance grants and loans;
ϕ_D	= The proportion of MILAID 'converted' to fungible resources by Israel, that is, the proportion which has the same effect on resource allocations as would a grant of fungible unconditional money.[17]
ECAID	= Per capita US economic assistance grants and loans;

ϕ_{ND} = The proportion of ECAID 'converted' to fungible resources by Israel, that is, the proportion which has the same effect on resource allocations as would a grant of fungible unconditional money.[17]

P_D^I = The price of defence after being reduced by the non-fungible part of defence aid (as in Figure 10.1(c)); the Israeli price share of its defence;

P_{ND}^I = The price of public non-defence goods and services after being reduced by the non-fungible part of ECAID (as in Figure 10.1(c)); the Israeli price share of its public non-defence.

Maximisation of (1) subject to (2) produces a system of three demand equations, corresponding to the three sectors: private consumption, public non-defence consumption, and defence. Price and quantity data for defence, non-defence, etc., are not separately observable, whereas expenditure data is available. For this reason expenditure functions rather that demand functions (which require physical quantity data) are used in the model. Since private goods are taken to have a unit price of one, private good quantities and expenditures are identical. The detailed equations are provided in Section VII. For present purposes, however, it is sufficient to write the equations schematically as follows where E_D^I stands for Israeli expenditure in sector i.

$$E_D^I = F_D(R_L, E_D^A, \text{MILAID}, \text{ECAID}, P_D, P_{ND}, N_I) \qquad (3)$$
$$E_{ND}^I = F_{ND}(R_L, E_D^A, \text{MILAID}, \text{ECAID}, P_D, P_{ND}, N_I) \qquad (4)$$
$$E_{PVT}^I = F_{PVT}(R_L, E_D^A, \text{MILAID}, \text{ECAID}, P_D, P_{ND}, N_I) \qquad (5)$$

Since the 'utility' of an average individual depends on real consumption, all variables in (3)–(5) are expressed in constant Israeli pounds. The Stone–Geary utility function implies that the three expenditure functions F_D, F_{ND}, F_{PVT} must be linear in their arguments.

2 US SUPPLY OF FOREIGN ASSISTANCE AND ARAB MILITARY EXPENDITURES

The schematic outline of Section V.a(1), above, completes the demand side of the model. Now we take up the supply side. There are two external entities which influence Israel's needs for allocating its own resources to defence: these are the US and the 'threatening' Arab states. Over the years, the Israelis facing Arab military forces have combined US assistance with their own resources and made their allocations between defence and non-defence. It would not be logical to assume, in this context, that US and Arab defence outlays have been random or unrelated to Israel's economic and military posture nor to each other. Rather a more reasonable assumption is that Arab allocations, US allocations, and Israeli allocations have all been interdependently determined. Therefore, as we argued above, it becomes necessary to incorporate the 'supply' behaviour of both Arabs and the USA. It is easily shown on theoretical gounds that an appropriate form for Arab supply is[18]

$$P_D^A Q_D^A = E_D^A = B_0 + B_1 E_D^I N_I + B_2 R_I^A, \tag{6}$$

where total Arab and Israeli per capita expenditures on defence are denoted by E_D^A and E_D^I, respectively, while the constants B_0, B_1, and B_2 represent the Arab responsiveness to the threat from Israel on the one hand and their own growing wealth on the other. R_I^A indicates total 'Arab' wealth or resources and N_I as above indicates total Israeli population.

In a similar vein, US supply behaviour is assumed to depend on the threat seen from Tel Aviv and on Israeli resources. One might reasonably expect that an Arab arms build-up would stimulate US assistance to Israel, whereas growing Israeli affluence would reduce it. Accordingly, a supply equation of the following form is assumed:

$$\begin{aligned} \text{AID} &= A_0 + A_1 E_D^A + A_2 R_L^I N_I: \\ \text{AID} &= \text{MILAID} + \text{ECAID} \end{aligned} \tag{7}$$

Statistical estimates of equations (6) and (7) are of inherent interest themselves, moreover without them our statistical work will produce biased estimates of the Israeli allocation process.

In summary, the model consists of three internal allocation equations for Israel and two external 'supply' equations. The detailed econometric formulation of the model is set out in Section VII of this paper.

VI OVERALL RESULTS AND INTERPRETATION OF MULTIPLE REGRESSION ANALYSIS

Detailed regression results are reported in Section VII including the outcomes from various estimating procedures and various mathematical formulations of the equations. The purpose of this section is to present an overall 'average' picture of the Israeli allocation process and of the effects of US assistance on it. Similarly, the allocative behaviour of the USA and of Israel's surrounding Arab neighbours is described in 'average' terms.

Tables 10.2 and 10.3 present a best estimate range of results. Specifically, Table 10.2 relates to Israeli allocative behaviour and Table 10.3 to the interdependence between Israel, and USA and the Arab states. Each table is organised in three columns. In the first column is the symbol for the behavioural characteristic (parameter) which has been statistically estimated, in the second column is a word-description of the characteristic, and in the third column is a range of numerical values for the parameter. These numbers are taken from Table 10.5 (p. 229) which gives the statistical results in greater detail. For instance, examination of Table 10.5 row 4 shows that the parameter Φ_D has a low value of 0.036 and a high value of 0.185. In Table 10.2 this is reported in the first line as 4 per cent to 18 per cent. For some parameters, the entire range of estimates is not reported. This reflects my judgement that some values in Table 10.5 are implausible.

Table 10.2 introduces a new parameter not defined in Section V (1), namely the parameter π. This parameter is incorporated in the actual equation system which was estimated (eqns (8)–(12) on pp. 223-4). The additional parameter is necessary because it frequently has been found that communities which receive an unconditional grant or loan will spend it differently if the grant is made directly to the citizens than they will if the grant is made to their government. It is convenient to define π indirectly as follows:

$\pi\,(\beta_D + \beta_{ND}) =$ The proportion of government-to-government aid receipts retained in the public sector by the receiving government. If government-to-government fungible aid is handled the same as internal income growth (or government to citizen aid) then $\pi = 1$, and $(1 - \beta_D - \beta_{ND})$ of the aid is returned to the private sector as tax relief. If all government-to-government aid is retained in the public sector then $\pi\,(\beta_D + \beta_{ND}) = 1$ or $\pi = 1/(\beta_D + \beta_{ND})$ and none is returned as tax relief.[19]

Several rather striking results stand out in Table 10.2. First, all parameter estimates reported yield results which are entirely reasonable from a theoretical viewpoint. The detailed outcomes of re-

TABLE 10.2 *Israeli resource allocation behaviour and utilisation of US assistance, 1960–79 (behavioural parameter)*

Symbol		Description	Range of values*
	I	**Fraction of US loans and grants used as fungible resources by the Israelis**	
ϕ_D		(A) 'Military' loans and grants	4% to 18%
ϕ_{ND}		(B) 'Economic' loans and grants	90% to 100%
	II	**Utilisation of fungible resources by the Israeli economy**	
		(A) Proportion of internal GNP growth	
$\beta_D + \beta_{ND}$		(1) Taxed away for use in the public sector	11% to 32%
$1 - (\beta_D + \beta_{ND})$		(2) Retained in the private sector	89% to 68%
		(B) Proportion of fungible US assistance	
$\pi(\beta_D + \beta_{ND})$		(1) Retained in the public sector	0% to 90%
$1 - \pi(\beta_D + \beta_{ND})$		(2) Turned over to the private sector as tax relief	100% to 10%
	III	**The Israeli division of resources**	
		(A) Percentage of public resources allocated to	
$\beta_D/(\beta_D + \beta_{ND})$		(1) Defence	88% to 95%
$1 - (\beta_D/(\beta_D + \beta_{ND}))$		(2) Non-defence	12% to 5%
		(B) Percentage change in Israeli defence† expenditures caused by a 1%	
$(1 - \beta_D)\gamma_D[1 + (\phi_D - 1)q_D]R$		(1) Decrease in the price of defence relative to private consumption goods (due to the price effect of US military assistance)	−1/4% to −1/2%
$1 - \{(1 - \beta_D)\gamma_D [1 + (\phi_D - 1)q_D]R\}$		(2) Increase in Israeli population	+3/4% to +1/2%

*Taken from Table 10.5.
†R = total 'Arab' + total Israeli defence expenditures.

TABLE 10.3 *The interaction between Arab defence outlays, Israeli defence outlays, and US assistance behavioural parameters (behavioural parameter)*

Symbol		Description	Range of values*
	I	Determinants of US assistance Change in total US military and economic disbursement caused by a $1 increase in	
A_2		(1) Israeli GNP	−$0.05 to −$0.13
A_1		(2) The combined defence expenditures of Egypt, Iraq, Jordan, Saudi Arabia, and Syria	$0.0 to +$0.14
	II	Determinants of Israeli Defence Expenditure Changes in total Israeli defence expenditures caused by a $1 increase in	
β_D		(1) Israeli GNP	$0.05 to $0.31
γ_D		(2) The combined defence expenditures of Egypt, Iraq, Jordan, Saudi Arabia, and Syria	$0.25 to $0.49
	III	Determinants of 'Arab' (Egypt, Iraq, Jordan, Saudi Arabia, and Syria) defence expenditure Change in 'Arab' defence outlay caused by a $1 increase in	
β_2		(1) 'Arab' GNP	0.01 to 0.11
β_1		(2) Israeli defence outlays	0.05 to 2.5

*Taken from Table 10.5.

gression analyses reported in Table 10.5 show high statistical reliability.

Second, the estimates on fungibility (Line I(B)) confirm what we conjecture anyway – that US *economic* assistance is an integral part of Israel's annual budget planning. The estimates show that the vast majority if not all US economic assistance is treated as a fungible resource by Israel. This confirmation lends credibility to the other result (Line I(A)) that a slight but significant fraction of military assistance is diverted into the fungible category.

Third, inspection of Lines II(A) and II(B) suggests some discrepancy in the way Israel allocates resources generated internally compared with fungible resources received from the USA. As confirmation of this behaviour, many studies of US state and local fiscal behaviour have shown that US state and local governments return very little of the grants they receive from other levels of government to their constituents in the form of tax relief. (This effect has become known as the 'flypaper' effect of grants.[20]) Similar comparisons in Table 10.2 indicate that the same may be true for Israel's utilisation of fungible grants (although at an extreme of the range the estimate of 100% in II(B)(2) says that all of fungible grants are returned as tax relief). Possibly the most telling feature of this estimate is the very wide range of uncertainty which surrounds it. In the case of US state and local governments it seems quite plausible that local governments which receive grants/loans from the federal government will have a strong incentive to add such funds to public sector consumption and thus, have every incentive not to use federal grants to reduce local taxes. Moreover, if federal 'bureaucrats' deplore having federal grants used for tax relief the incentive is reinforced. However, when it comes to grants and loans between nations the incentives may be the reverse; since a national government in a centralised unitary system such as Israel is the only tax collector, it may more readily get credit for tax reduction. In fact, government-to-government economic or military assistance could simply be a politically viable way to transfer resources to the *private* sector. In this connection, we point out that the lower the price elasticity of demand for a subsidised good, the more effective is a price subsidy as an indirect means to transfer fungible resources to the receiver.[21]

Fourth, Table 10.2, in fact, indicates a rather low price elasticity of demand for defence in Israel, meaning defence is a necessary with few substitutes rather than a luxury good. The regression estimates in Table 10.5 show that allocations to defence in Israel are much better explained if we take defence to be a pure public good. In combination with the result that the price elasticity of demand for defence capability is low, this implies that defence outlays will increase with population growth but less than in proportion. Thus, line III(B)2 shows Israeli defence will grow with population increases (with per capita GNP constant) but less than in proportion to the population increase.

We now turn to the interaction among the three actors in the Middle East. Actually, the allocative behaviour of Israel (as an instance of the allocative behaviour of a foreign assistance receiving ally) was originally the sole concern in undertaking this study. And in order to obtain statistically unbiased estimates of Israel's allocative behaviour, the 'supply behaviour' of other elements in the system had to be included in the structure to be estimated. As the study proceeded, however, the nature of the competitive supply behaviour of the Arab states and the 'collaborative' supply behaviour of the

USA became increasingly of interest. Table 10.3 focuses on these relationships.

First, Table 10.3 shows that US supply of assistance to Israel is positively correlated with Arab defence outlays, and negatively correlated with Israel's GNP growth. Whether this supply behaviour was derived from conscious US policy choices is open to doubt, but the signal it provides to Israel makes sense – the USA will assist Israel by matching part of Arab defence increases (up to 14 per cent at the margin) but the support will diminish as Israel grows richer. (–5 per cent to –13 per cent at the margin.) These *partial*[22] correlations raise the question of whether the signal issued by the USA is desirable. Further study of these phenomena is in order, especially to discern whether this signal corresponds to any conscious policy, or balance of power among competing US agencies, or among competing interest groups and lobbying entities.

Second, Table 10.3 shows that when the Arabs increase their outlays by $1 Israel ups its expenditures by $0.25 to $0.49 while US assistance increases by up to $0.14 (assuming no change in other factors such as Israel's population or GNP).

Third, Israel's marginal propensity to spend increases in real per capita GNP on defence is in the range +5 per cent to +31 per cent.

Fourth, Table 10.3 indicates that just as the Israelis react to Arab defence expenditures, the Arabs react to increases in Israeli defence outlays by increasing their own outlays. Curiously, the Arabs appear to be much more reactive to Israeli military expenditures than vice versa. The Arabs allocate, at the margin, a somewhat lesser increment of income growth to defence. Thus, the net outcome of Lines II and III in Table 10.3 could be portrayed as a stable arms race as shown in Figure 10.3. For illustration we take the value of γ_D as $0.30 and the value of B_1 as $1.00. The lines $I°$ and $A°$ indicate Israeli and the Arab reaction curves respectively in say 1960, implying a stable solution at $S°$. Over time the Arabs' curve $A°$ has shifted out due to their increased wealth, say to A^i, A^{ii}, etc. Over the same period, Israel's reaction curve has shifted out due to its internal GNP growth and at the same pivoted to a higher slope because of the addition of US assistance. (I have illustrated the case where US assistance as indicated by the parameter A_1 comes to $0.10 for each additional $1.00 of Arab expenditures. As a result the new shifted curves I^i ... I^{ii}, etc., have an assumed slope of 0.40.) The solution point consequently shifts out to S^i, S^{ii}, etc.

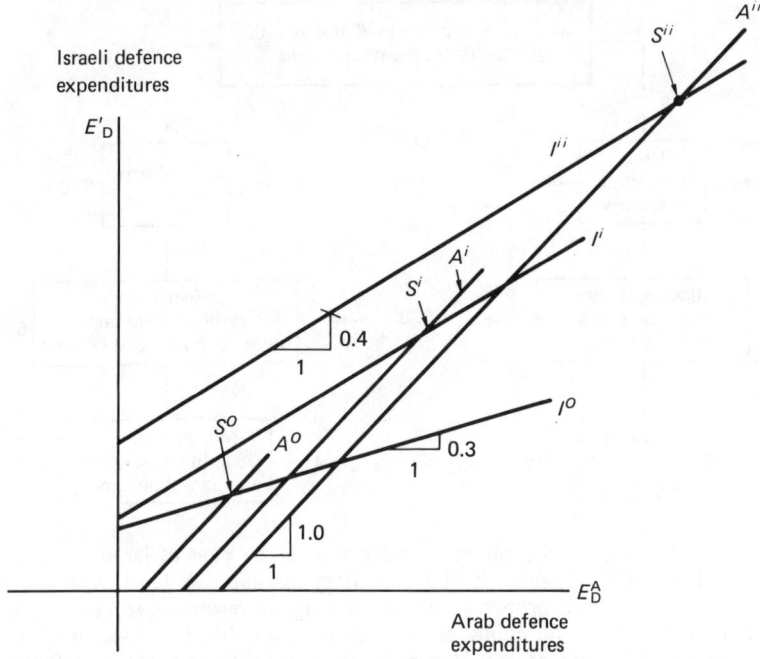

FIGURE 10.3 *Arab–Israeli defence expenditures as an arms race process. A°, A^i, A^{ii} shows Arab reaction curve shifting over time because of increases in wealth. I°, I^i, I^{ii} shows Israel's reaction curve shifting over time because of increased wealth and US assistance*

VII A POLICY APPLICATION OF THE MODEL

These parameter estimates not only yield an overall picture of the Israeli allocation process, they also allow one to trace through the effective allocation of US assistance. As an example we will trace through the allocative effects of $100 in security assistance.

The ultimate disposition of military assistance depends in a rather complex way on four factors: (a) the fraction 'converted' to fungible resources as above, ϕ_D, (b) the Israeli propensity to allocate fungible outside resources to the public sector, $\pi(\beta_D+\beta_{ND})$, (c) the division of the public budget between defence and non-defence, β_D/β_{ND}, (d) the proportion between US security assistance and Israeli defence outlays[23] or q_D and (e) the Israeli demand for defence as a function of

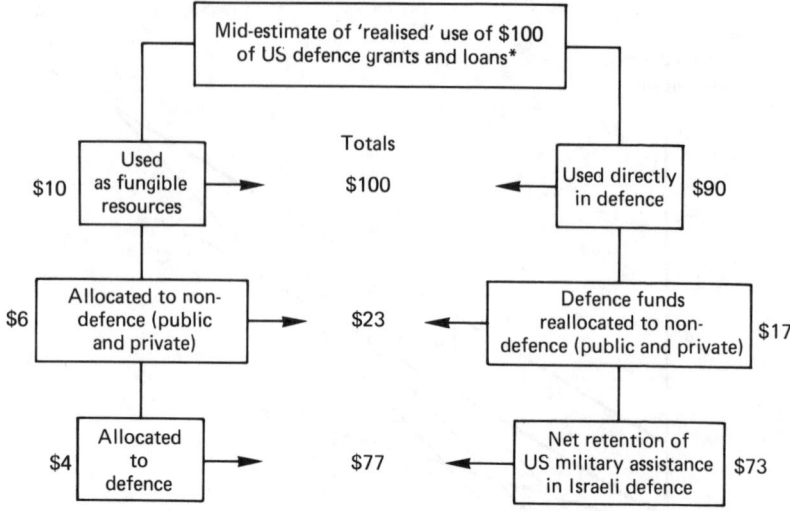

*Assumptions. (a) US Military Assistance is 25 per cent of Israeli defence expenditure. (b) 10 per cent of US military assistance is used as fungible resources. (c) Israeli propensity to spend fungible resources received from external sources in the public sector is 50 per cent. (d) The division of the public budget at the margin is 80 per cent defence to 20 per cent non-defence. (e) Israeli price elasticity of demand for defence is −3/4.

FIGURE 10.4

the price (i.e., Israeli price share) of defence, i.e., $dE_D^1/dP^1 \cdot P^1/E_D^1$. Figure 10.4 gives a 'best guess' estimate for the ultimate disposition of US *military* assistance for the mid to late 1970s.

Figure 10.4 indicates that US military assistance *substitutes* in part for Israeli resources. Combining all the above factors would indicate that Israel diverts between 9 and 30 per cent of US military assistance to non-defence purposes; Figure 10.4 gives a mid-estimate of 23 per cent. How do we evaluate this calculation? When compared with the performance of US federal grants to the states, an estimate of 23 per cent 'leakage' seems remarkably small.[24] The figure also suggests that of $100 in *economic* assistance about $40 will be allocated to defence, though a large degree of uncertainty is attached to this number. So, if $200 is given to Israel and in any one year 50 per cent is military and 50 per cent is economic assistance, these estimates predict that about $117 or roughly 60 per cent ends up as increased defence outlay.

VIII ECONOMETRIC MODEL AND RESULTS

In this section of the paper we report on the detailed statistical model, how it was derived and how it was estimated or fitted to the data.

Equation (1) represents the much studied Stone–Geary utility function which is widely used in empirical analyses of consumer demand, adapted to the economic behaviour of aggregate government units. The terms $\gamma_D^I E_D^A$ and $\gamma_{ND}^I E_D^A$ represent minimum subsistence Israeli consumption requirements for defence and for public non-defence goods and services; these are assumed to depend on the Arab 'threat'. This utility function is maximised subject to the total resource constraint given by equation (2). In the usual statistical demand study, the analyst *knows* the resources (or income) available to the consumer and the prices which he faces for the various goods. However, when transfers or subsidies are involved, as in foreign assistance, the analyst *does not know* in advance how much of such subsidies are effectively converted into fungible resources. In this study, that means that we do not know in advance precisely how US grants and loans change the Israeli resource constraint. That is, we do not know how much of the US military aid reduces the *price* of defence to Israel (Area $G - A - B$ in Figure 10.1) and how much is converted into fungible money (Areas A and B). We assume that $(A + B)/G$ is a constant ϕ, and estimate this parameter statistically.[25]

Equations (8)–(12) represent the entire system of demand (expenditure) and 'supply' equations derived from maximisation of (1) subject to (2).

Israeli expenditure on defence

$$E_D^I = \beta_D R_L^I + \beta_D \pi \phi_{ND} G_{ND} + (\beta_D \pi - 1)\phi_D G_D \qquad (8)$$
$$+ (1 - \beta_D)[1 + (\phi_D - 1)q_D]\gamma_D E_D^A N_I^{\alpha-1}$$
$$- \beta_D[1 + (\phi_{ND} - 1)q_{ND}]\gamma_{ND} E_D^A - \beta_D \gamma_{PVT} E_D^A$$

Israeli Governmental expenditure on non-defence

$$E_{ND}^I = \beta_{ND} R_L^I + \beta_{ND} \pi \phi_D G_D + (\beta_{ND} \pi - 1)\phi_{ND} G_{ND} \qquad (9)$$
$$+ (1 - \beta_{ND})[1 + (\phi_{ND} - 1) G_{ND}]\gamma_{ND} E_D^A$$
$$- \beta_{ND}[1 + (\phi_D - 1)q_D]\gamma_D E_D^A N_I^{\alpha-1}$$
$$- \beta_{ND} \gamma_{PVT} E_D^A$$

Israeli private expenditures

$$E^I_{PVT} = (1-\beta_D-\beta_{ND})R^I_L + \{(1-\pi(\beta_D+\beta_{ND}))\}(\phi_D G_D + \phi_{ND} G_{ND}) \quad (10)$$
$$- (1-\beta_D-\beta_{ND})[1+(\phi_D-1)q_D]\gamma_D E^A_D N^{\alpha-1}$$
$$- (1-\beta_D-\beta_{ND})[1+(\phi_{ND}-1)q_{ND}]\gamma_{ND} E^A_D + (\beta_D + \beta_{ND})\gamma_{PVT} E^A_D$$

US supply of economic and military assistance

$$G = A_0 + A_1(R^I_L N_I) + A_2(E^A_D) \quad (11)$$

Arab defence expenditure

$$E^A_D = B_0 + B_1(R^A_L) + B_2(E^I_D N_I) \quad (12)$$

The notation in this system remains as defined above, except that G_D is substituted for MILAID and G_{ND} for ECAID and $G = G_D + G_{ND}$. The expression $P_D = [1 + (\phi_D - 1)q_D]$ represents the *price* of defence capability as adjusted for the price effect of grants and loans. In terms of Figure 10.1, $P_D = P^1$ (for defence). Similarly for public non-defence expenditures $P_{ND} = [1 + (\phi_{ND} - 1)q_{ND}]$.[26]

The Israeli population variable is entered in the equation as N^ε_I, where $\varepsilon = \alpha - 1$ is a parameter to be estimated, representing the degree to which defence corresponds to a pure public good (in which case $\alpha = 0$), a pure private good ($\alpha = +1$) or something in between.

The system of equations (8)–(12) is non-linear in both variables and parameters; non-linear in variables because q_D is defined as $G_D/(E^I_D + G_D)$ and analogously for G_{ND}. Therefore, in equations (8) and (9) the expenditure variable E^I_D or E^I_{ND} necessarily appears on both sides of the equation. The system is non-linear in parameters because of the public good parameter 'ε'. This system[27] therefore has been estimated using full information maximum likelihood (FIML) techniques.[28] Owing to the probability of autocorrelation, the equations have been estimated in first difference form. To illustrate using the schematic equations (3), the estimated form is:

$$E_t = F_t + \varrho[E_{t-1} - F_{t-1}] + v_t \quad (13)$$

which follows from the assumption of first order autocorrelation in the error terms:

$$e_t = \varrho e_{t-1} + v_t \quad (14)$$

Selected results from FIML estimation are presented in Table 10.4. The estimates were obtained using the time series processor (TSP) version 3.5. The statistical reliability and stability of these estimates is impressive. Given only twenty years of data, corners had to be cut in the number of parameters to estimate. In particular, the values of A_0 and B_0, i.e. the intercepts of the two 'supply' equations, and the subsistence parameter γ_{PVT} were assumed to be zero. Making these assumptions is unfortunate but necessary since the TSP software in many cases was unable to estimate the entire set of parameters and since the number of data observations severely limits the number of parameters that is reasonable to estimate.

Table 10.4 is organised to show various relationships among the parts of the equation system. As noted above, because of insufficiency of data and the complexity of the system it was sometimes not possible to estimate all parameters and all structural equations simultaneously. The table shows how partial estimation was used to make various simplifying assumptions which then led to more comprehensive estimates. Most of the estimates are based on the assumption that defence is a pure public good. Columns 5 to 7 in Table 10.4 show that $\varepsilon(\alpha)$ does not differ significantly from $-1(0)$, and, therefore, that the pure public good paradigm best approximates national defence for the average Israeli.

All estimates of ϱ decidedly and robustly indicate that a simple first order autoregressive process is going on. Therefore, we set ϱ equal to a constant of 1 when this was necessary to estimate the full system.

Inspection of Table 10.4 also shows that in most cases the proportion of economic aid used as fungible resources, ϕ_{ND}, is close to unity. Thus, when it was necessary to set $\phi_{ND} = 1$ as a constant so as to obtain other estimates (for instance estimating $\varepsilon = -1$), we did so.

The table also clearly indicates the reason for building the two auxiliary supply equations – US supply of assistance and Arab defence expenditures. The introduction of these supply relationships rather dramatically improves the plausibility and reliability of estimates on Israel's allocative behaviour. For example, the parameter π determines how much more or less of aid from the outside will be returned to the private sector as tax relief in comparison with internal GNP resources. In row 8 column 8 of Table 10.4, π is estimated to have the very implausible value of -23, although this value is not significantly different from zero. However, the value of $\pi = -23$ was estimated in the absence of the supply behaviour of the USA and the Arabs. Once the entire system is included the estimated value for π becomes more plausible, though still not significantly different from zero (columns 10 and 11).

Lastly, the reader's attention is directed to columns 1 to 4 of

TABLE 10.4 Full information maximum likelihood (FIML) estimation results

Equations included in the FIML estimation + indicates included: − indicates excluded	Comparison of results when loans are calculated at their gross value (a) or at their value net of interest and principal payments (b)				Estimates of 'public' versus 'private' good nature of defence outlays			Comparisons of parameters for different sizes of the system and different equations included in the system to be estimated				
	(1)[a]	(2)[a]	(3)[b]	(4)[b]	(5)	(6)	(7)	(8)	(9)	(10)	(11)	(12)
Israeli defence expenditure	+	+	+	+	+	+	+	+	+	+	+	+
Israeli non-defence public expenditure	+	+	+	+	+	+	+	+	+	+	+	+
US assistance	+	+	+	+	+	+	+	−	+	+	+	+
Arab defence expenditure	−	+	−	+	+	+	+	−	−	−	+	−

Parameter estimates/(t-statistics)

Parameter symbol													
1	ϱ	0.953 (22.9)	1.00 **	0.943 (23.2)	0.972 (34.1)	1.00 **	1.00 **	1.00 **	0.940 (21.1)	0.943 (23.2)	0.950 (25.0)	0.972 (34.1)	0.915 (20.3)
2	β_D	0.211 (2.8)	0.212 (2.7)	0.206 (2.9)	0.189 (2.6)	0.200 **	0.200 **	0.200 **	0.100 (1.6)	0.206 (2.9)	0.224 (2.9)	0.189 (2.6)	0.213 (3.0)
3	β_{ND}	0.010 (2.2)	0.007 (6.2)	0.012 (2.6)	0.012 (3.1)	0.007 (8.5)	0.008 (8.6)	0.008 (9.0)	0.013 (2.4)	0.012 (2.6)	0.011 (2.7)	0.012 (3.1)	0.014 (3.0)
4	ϕ_D	0.114 (2.1)	0.099 (2.0)	0.111 (1.6)	0.112 (1.8)	0.100 Const	0.145 (2.5)	0.083 (5.8)	0.058 (1.1)	0.111 (1.6)	0.185 (1.7)	0.112 (1.8)	0.956 (9.9)*
5	ϕ_{ND}	1.00 (6.7)	1.00 **	0.822 (6.7)	0.907 (10.3)	1.00 **	1.00 **	1.00 **	0.597 (2.8)	0.822 (6.7)	1.00 **	0.901 (10.4)	

		γ_D	γ_ND	π	A1	A2	B1	B2	α=ε+1
6		0.326 (5.2)	−0.003 (0.7)	−2.74 (0.9)	0.138 (5.2)	−0.070 (1.7)	—	—	0.0**
7		0.361 (5.6)	−0.007 (2.7)	−2.68 (1.0)	0.134 (5.1)	−0.085 (1.9)	1.39 (5.2)	0.121 (8.2)	0.0**
8		0.264 (4.7)	−0.008 (2.1)	−2.24 (.64)	0.144 (5.9)	−0.059 (1.6)	—	—	0.0**
9		0.316 (5.9)	−0.013 (3.9)	−1.92 (0.6)	0.128 (5.1)	−0.054 (1.3)	1.49 (6.9)	0.112 (8.3)	0.0**
10		1.53 (0.8)	−0.010 (4.6)	+1.70 (3.5)	0.106 (5.1)	−0.062 (2.4)	1.53 (7.1)	0.115 (8.7)	−1.37 (1.2)
11		0.781 (0.8)	−0.212 (56)	1.00**	0.071 (2.8)	−0.054 (1.8)	0.136 (4.2)	0.012 (4.5)	−0.55 (0.5)
12		1.01 (1.1)	−0.232 (67.4)	1.00**	0.028 (1.3)	−0.109 (4.0)	0.089 (3.2)	0.010 (4.7)	−0.73 (1.0)
13		0.492 (7.2)	−0.010 (2.2)	−23.1 (.8)	—	—	—	—	0.0**

*ϕ_D and ϕ_{ND} constrained to be equal; ** Parameter set at this value as a constant

227

Table 10.5. These regressions were made to determine whether *gross* economic and military loans, or these loans net of annual interest and principal payments were the best indicators of US aid, and gave the best explanation of Israeli allocative decisions. These year to year decisions are, of course, in reality interdependent. Israeli planners and resource allocators must realise when they receive a loan that some interest and principal will be due in the future (some interest and principal will not be forgiven). To capture this effort precisely would require a complicated multiperiod planning model with explicit anticipatory behaviour by Israel decision makers. The amount of data available, however, would not support such a theoretical excursion; so instead, we have run the regressions under two alternative assumptions and have chosen the assumption which gives more satisfactory results. The two assumptions are:

(a) Interest and loan repayments on military loans *are not* a 'military' expense. This corresponds to the actual accounting practices in the Israeli government. In this case annual Israeli allocations to defence *from their own internal resources* are calculated as *total* defence expenditures less *gross* receipts of military grants and loans.

(b) Interest and loan repayments on military loans *are* 'military' expenses. Under this assumption despite accounting and budgeting procedures to the contrary, the interest and principal repayments on debts are perceived as a defence expenditure, i.e. the future burden of present borrowings from the USA is assumed to be perceived as a military burden. In this case, annual Israeli allocations to defence from their *own internal resources* are calculated as total defence expenditure less *net* receipts of military grants and loans (gross receipts less interest and principal repayments). Obviously, in this second case, Israel is counted as spending more of its own money on defence.

Now, compare columns (1 and 2) representing (a) with (3 and 4) representing (b) in Table 10.4. The comparison especially with respect to π suggests that option (b) gives more plausible results. For all the other regressions reported in Table 10.5 we, therefore, have taken interest and principal repayment as a specific military expense in the case of 'military loans' and as a specific public non-defence expenditure in the case of 'economic loans'.

Table 10.5 below gives a format which defines the two alternative assumptions. Lines I, II and III(a) show how the variables E_D^1, E_{ND}^1

TABLE 10.5 *Alternative (a) gross and (b) net definitions of US foreign assistance and how they fit in with the econometric model*

Dependent variables	Independent variables		
Local resources allocated to:		Military grants and loans gross	Economic grants and loans gross
I. Defence II. Public non-defence III. Private expenditures	Local resources	G_D^a or Net G_D^b	G_{ND}^a or Net G_{ND}^b
I(a) (Total defence) (G_D^a)	Case (a) R_L = I(a) + II(a) + III(a)		
I(b) (Total defence) ($G_D^a - I_D - RP_D$)	$G_D = G_D^a$ $G_{ND} = G_{ND}^a$		
II(a) (Total public non-defence) (G_{ND}^a)			
II(b) (Total public non-defence) ($G_{ND}^a - I_{ND} - RP_{ND}$)	Case (b) R_L = I(b) + II(b) + III(b) (same as Case (a))		
III(a) (Total private expenditure)	$G_D = G_D^b = G_D^a - I_D - RP_D$		
III(b) (Total private expenditure) ($I_D + I_{ND} + RP_D + RP_{ND}$)	$G_{ND} = G_{ND}^b$ $= G_{ND}^a - I_{ND} - RP_{ND}$		

I_D = Interest payments on military assistance loans.
I_{ND} = Interest payments on economic assistance loans.
RP_D = Principal repayments on military assistance loans.
RP_{ND} = Principal repayments on economic asssistance loans.

and E_{PVT}^I are defined when we assume interest and principal repayment *are not* 'specific' (i.e. military, or public non-defence) expenditures. Lines I, II and III(b) show the definition of the variables when interest and principal repayments *are* counted as 'specific' expenditures.

IX CONCLUSIONS AND DIRECTIONS FOR FURTHER RESEARCH

1 CONCLUSIONS

This study has drawn a number of conclusions, some of which may apply to other recipients of US assistance in addition to Israel, and others may not to the extent Israel is a special case from the US perspective.

At the most general level first we have demonstrated that a model of government allocation behaviour based on an 'as if' utility maximising assumption about the motivation for this behaviour can indeed explain the data. Second, we have demonstrated that an identification of the ultimate impact of programme targeted aid whether to military or economic categories can be made.

At the specific level of Israel and the Middle East the paper suggests several intriguing conclusions.

1. In the case of Israel there is a very high net retention of military assistance in the military category. Here the difference in allocative processes as between Israel's military and civilian departments is remarkable. Israel uses economic support as essentially another source of fungible revenue while military support is reserved for military use. This fact suggests some significant distinction between the military and civilian bureaucracies in Israel, in the USA, or in both countries although we cannot at this stage identify just what these differences are. While we might have conjectured that it is easier to get military support voted for Israel in the USA, it does not appear that military funds are used as a general budget support obtained through the back door.

2. Keeping to the specific case of Israel, the signals which the USA seems historically to have emitted suggest a more logical pattern than one might have expected. There have been both efficiency and equity objectives operating with respect to US aid allotments – efficiency because the USA has augmented its defence support to offset (in part) Arab arms increases, equity because the USA has cut back its defence support as Israel has grown richer (*other factors being held constant*).

3. Within the Middle East region since the US marginal propensity to spend in reaction to Arab defence outlays is about $0.10 of US aid for $1.00 of Arab outlay, it is difficult to accuse US assistance of fuelling the arms race in that region – assuming, of course, that $0.10 of US aid does not buy such high quality weaponry as to surpass that bought by the Arab $1.00.

2 DIRECTIONS FOR RESEARCH

Econometric analysis such as this necessarily has important limitations. The usefulness of the work probably is greatest when the statistical insights gained for Israel are used as a tool to explore actual, real-time defence planning, budgeting, and financial planning processes within that country, and how these interact with the US decision-making. Several possible extensions include:

(a) Detailed examination of the process of defining defence 'requirements' in Israel. How do requirements depend on the quality and quantity of weaponry in the various Arab states? How does Israel evaluate its own qualitative superiority?
(b) Examination of offensive versus defensive weapons acquisition choices with a view to discovering if some are: (i) more reactive to Arab defence issues; (ii) more responsive to US assistance; or (iii) essentially determined by internal economic or political forces.

The purpose of such investigations would be to verify in a concrete way the statistical trends suggested by the model. This investigation should uncover the mechanism whereby some 'military' aid is treated as a fungible resource, whether this occurs for specific weapons systems for specific types of aid, particular services, etc. With information of this nature the model might be expanded (e.g. to discriminate between offensive and defensive capabilities) and or solved under various new conditions to *simulate* Israeli allocative responses to new situations.

Econometric analysis such as this also might usefully be extended to other countries. Korea, Taiwan, and the Philippines, are obvious candidates because of the quality and quantity of data available. The object of replicating the work for one or more other countries would be to discover whether the relationships uncovered for Israel apply generally to other countries. Israel is often thought to be a 'special case' throughout the Executive Branch. Comparative analysis of other countries would shed light on whether our special treatment of Israel makes a difference in how assistance is actually utilised.[29]

APPENDIX A Basic data on Israel and surrounding Arab states, 1960–1979

	1960	1961	1962	1963	1964	1965	1966
Arab defence expenditures* (millions of current US $)							
Egypt	229.8	255.6	244.1	253.0	308.2	409.4	460.0
Iraq	118.7	125.4	135.0	163.2	185.1	225.7	234.9
Jordan	53.4	52.9	57.7	58.8	59.1	60.2	72.8
Saudi Arabia	57.5	73.5	95.0	120.1	117.9	124.5	233.1
Syria	70.1	72.9	73.0	80.3	90.5	95.5	82.7
Israeli Data[†]							
Exchange Rate US $ per Israeli £	0.556	0.556	0.345	0.333	0.333	0.333	0.333
GNP deflator	5.3713	4.9270	4.5762	4.2275	4.0062	3.6496	3.3533
Population	2.154	2.234	2.332	2.430	2.526	2.598	2.657
Billions of current Israeli pounds							
Total resources	5.893	7.151	9.288	10.916	12.498	14.425	15.536
Investment	1.211	1.568	2.096	2.307	2.930	3.077	2.605
Consumption							
Private	3.119	3.677	4.444	5.288	5.987	7.074	7.777
Public	0.823	1.015	1.339	1.586	1.704	2.125	2.625
Non-defence	0.507	0.591	0.703	0.883	0.925	1.220	1.493
Defence	0.316	0.424	0.136	0.703	0.779	0.905	1.132
Total foreign loans and grants	0.338	0.457	0.644	0.636	0.606	0.651	0.495
Exports	0.740	0.891	1.409	1.735	1.878	2.126	2.529

	1974	1975	1976	1977	1978	1979
*Arab defence expenditures** (millions of current US $)						
Egypt	3 910.7	4 168.8	3 997.6	4 715.8	3 322.8	2 142.9
Iraq	2 232. 7	1 889.0	1 669.3	1 664.2	1 986.9	1 985.9
Jordan	156.6	172.8	180.7	239.3	307.3	379.3
Saudi Arabia	1 677.0	4 774.0	8 933.4	8 984.4	10 635.5	14 225.3
Syria	451.9	886.5	934.9	1 047.1	1 146.5	2 024.8
Israeli Data[†]						
Exchange Rate US $ per Israeli £	0.222	0.156	0.125	0.0956	0.0572	0.0393
GNP deflator	1.3727	1.0000	0.7877	0.5506	0.3607	0.1958
Population	3.409	3.493	3.575	3.647	3.719	3.794
Billions of current Israeli pounds						
Total resources	90.332	130.739	168.454	238.204	411.043	755.344
Investment	17.690	24.880	26.922	34.282	61.048	126.709
Consumption						
Private	32.877	46.408	62.078	88.11	146.696	277.974
Public	22.033	33.985	40.936	51.907	91.371	158.001
Non-defence	5.701	8.041	11.119	17.548	27.783	55.109
Defence	16.363	25.894	29.817	34.472	63.014	95.789
Total foreign loans and grants	6.832	14.568	16.895	17.109	43.180	64.668
Exports	17.692	25.516	38.518	63.905	111.928	192.610

*SOURCE Stockholm International Peace Research Institute, *World Armaments and Disarmament, 1980* (Annual Report)
[†] Bank of Israel Annual Reports

APPENDIX B Basic data on US assistance to Israel, 1960–1979

	1960	1961	1962	1963	1964	1965	1966	1967	1968	1969
US assistance to Israel (millions of current $US)*										
Economic assistance										
Loans										
Authorisations	41.8	29.8	63.5	57.4	32.2	43.9	35.9	5.5	51.3	36.1
Disbursements	35.157	41.341	60.537	56.584	70.724	62.382	57.466	55.092	61.240	54.683
Principal repayments	13.542	16.983	20.390	22.180	27.663	30.284	13.324	19.394	25.837	28.384
Interest payments	0.020	—	0.011	—						
Grants										
Obligations	13.4	18.3	7.2	6.0	4.8	4.9	0.9	0.6	0.5	0.6
Disbursements	4.038	13.047	10.730	5.715	9.008	5.189	3.593	3.172	3.681	3.524
Military assistance										
Loans										
Authorisations	0.5	—	13.2	13.2	—	12.9	90.0	7.0	25.0	85.0
Disbursements	0.379	0.075	0.026	0.211	0.771	16.830	21.288	5.969	30.473	100.048
Principal repayments	0.193	0.090	0.0298	0.015	0.973	4.289	7.277	6.490	18.767	21.140
Interest payments	0.020	0	0.011	0	0.017	0.484	2.065	1.688	3.269	3.139
Grants										
Obligations	—	—	—	—	—	—	—	—	—	—
Disbursements	—	—	—	—	—	—	—	—	—	—
US GNP deflator										
Overall	0.687	0.693	0.706	0.716	0.727	0.743	0.768	0.790	0.826	0.867
Government sector	0.591	0.600	0.618	0.633	0.648	0.670	0.701	0.726	0.764	0.800

235

APPENDIX B Basic data on US assistance to Israel, 1960–1979 (cont'd)

	1970	1971	1972	1973	1974	1975	1976	1977	1978	1979
US assistance to Israel (millions of current $US)*										
Economic assistance										
Loans										
Authorisations	40.7	55.5	53.8	59.4	—	8.6	239.4	252.0	266.8	265.1
Disbursements	74.529	107.680	68.921	70.261	7.469	57.583	200.618	253.824	288.269	590.556
Principal payments	31.928	41.969	88.770	53.124	44.986	48.026	82.527	89.691	54.134	59.001
Interest payments	18.768	19.620	21.786	21.379	20.014	20.013	22.879	26.143	27.564	38.646
Grants										
Obligations	0.4	0.3	50.4	50.4	51.5	344.5	475.0	490.0	525.0	525.0
Disbursements	4.678	5.711	61.549	115.073	97.713	434.165	507.606	592.106	634.042	659.137
Military assistance										
Loans										
Authorisations	30.0	545.0	300.0	307.5	982.7	200.0	750.0	500.0	500.0	2 700.0
Disbursements	55.758	347.156	251.904	150.661	180.344	406.001	571.088	825.992	550.711	499.995
Principal repayments	15.728	33.971	43.574	45.263	41.721	36.704	74.992	111.719	99.664	151.914
Interest payments	5.236	10.011	22.712	26.945	33.065	37.764	72.005	99.582	169.468	257.151
Grants										
Obligations	—	—	—	—	1 500.0	100.0	750.0	500.0	500.0	1 300.0
Disbursements	—	—	—	—	936.6	636.3	863.9	500.0	500.0	624.6
US GNP deflator										
Overall	0.914	0.960	1.000	1.058	1.160	1.272	1.337	1.417	1.521	1.655
Government sector	0.864	0.926	1.000	1.058	1.159	1.275	1.346	1.436	1.584	1.676

* Source for Loan authorisations and Grant Obligations: Based on data from US Agency for International Development, 'Near East: US Overseas Loans and Grants Obligations and Loan Authorizations', April 1980.
Source for Loan Disbursements and for Interest and Principal Payments: Based on data from US Department of Commerce, Research used in the preparation of Annual Reports of the National Advisory Council in International Monetary and Financial Policies.

NOTES AND REFERENCES

1. An earlier version of portions of this paper appeared in 'US Assistance and Israel Allocation', *Journal of Conflict Resolution*, June 1982, vol. 6, no. 2, pp. 199–235 and appears here by permission of Sage Publications Inc. An early version of this paper was presented at the University of Wyoming Summer Institute on Conflict Theory and National Security, July 1981. I am thankful to Dr Sher Rana of the Department of Defense for his assistance and collaboration in the early stages of the project and to Ray Dacey, Carl Groth, Michael Intriligator, Todd Sandler, Thomas Schelling, and my colleague Ernest Zampelli, for valuable comments. Sponsorship by the Office of the Secretary of Defense (ISA), International Economic and Energy Affairs is gratefully acknowledged. The analysis and opinion in this paper is solely the author's, not that of the US Government. National Science Foundation support under SES-80-14238 is also gratefully acknowledged.
2. Future research will focus on the impact of US assistance upon allocations between investment and consumption.
3. Throughout this study we use 'Arab' to refer to the states of Egypt, Iraq, Jordan, Saudi Arabia, and Syria.
4. Detailed data will be furnished on request. In addition to annual raw data on Israel and the surrounding Arab states, quarterly data on actual US disbursements, Israeli loan repayments, and remissions of interest are available for the 1960–79 period. This data is disaggregated according to whether funds are grants or loans, and whether for military of economic assistance.
5. I am grateful to Thomas Schelling and Michael Intriligator for their comments along these lines.
6. The utility function which is maximised and therefore the demand equatives derived therefrom and later estimated in our regression analysis will all depend on *per capita* incomes and *per capita* allocations among the various categories. In this sense the utility stands for the average or representative citizen's preferences. However, our analysis does not depend on the strict accuracy or validity of the so-called median voter model. I am thankful to Todd Sandler for calling this to my attention.
7. Silberberg, E., *The Structure of Economics* (New York: McGraw-Hill, 1978) 214–15.
8. Todd Sandler has made a most interesting suggestion which I hope to employ in future analysis. 'Since Israeli size and borders changed during the period examined, thinning of forces might be important. Have you considered using Israeli's perimeter as a variable to capture this effect?' Letter of 1 December 1981.
9. See for example: Gramlich, E. M. and Galper, H., 'State and Local Fiscal Behavior and Federal Grant Policy'. *Brookings Papers on Economic Activity*, vol. 1. (1973) and Gramlich, E. M., 'Intergovernmental Grants: a Review of the Literature', *International Seminar on Public Economics* (Berlin, 1976).
10. McGuire, M. C., 'A Method for Estimating the Effect of a Subsidy on

the Receiver's Resource Constraint: with an Application to US Local Governments 1964–1971', *Journal of Public Economics*, 10 (1978) pp. 25–44.
11. McGuire, M. C., 'An Econometric Model of Federal Grants and Local Fiscal Response', in Oates, W. F. (ed.), *Financing the New Federalism* (Washington, DC: Resources for the Future, 1975).
   McGuire, 'A Method for Estimating the Effect of a Subsidy on the Receiver's Resource Constraint: with an Application to US Local Governments 1964–1971'.
12. McGuire, M. C., *Secrecy and the Arms Race* (Cambridge, Mass.: Harvard University Press, 1965).
13. Bergstrom, T. C. and Goodman, R. P., 'Private Demand for Public Goods', *American Economic Review*, vol. 63 (June 1973) pp. 235–48.
14. That is to maximise a utility function in which the arguments are *per capita consumption* of defence, public non-defence, and private goods.
15. See Goldberger, A., 'Functional Form and Utility: a Review of Consumer Demand Theory, or Systems Formulation, Methodology and Policy Workshop Paper 6703' (Madison Wisconsin: Social Systems Research Institute, University of Wisconsin, 1967) and also references cited.
16. The Stone–Geary form nicely meets the requirement that $\Sigma(\partial E_i^I/\partial E_D^A) = 0$. The Israeli expenditure function for category i is

$$E_i^I = P_i \gamma_i E_D^A + \beta_i [R_T - \Sigma_j (P_j \gamma_j E_D^A)]$$

where E_D^A = total real Arab defence expenditures, R_T = total resources as defined below on p. 213, and γ_i and β_i are also defined above on p. 213. Evidently

$$\partial E_i^I / \partial E_D^A = P_i \gamma_i - \beta_i \Sigma_j (P_j \gamma_j)$$

so that:

$$\Sigma_i [(\partial E_i^I / \partial E_D^A)] = [\Sigma(P_i \gamma_i)][1 - \Sigma \beta_i]$$

Since $\Sigma \beta = 1$, the requirement is met.
17. In terms of Figure 10.1, $\phi = (A + B)/G$.
18. Assuming the Arabs maximise a Stone–Geary utility function similar to (1), and that they observe Cournot reaction to Israeli defence, an Arab expenditure equation as in (6) will result.
19. For a complete discussion see: McGuire, 'A Method for Estimating the Effect of a Subsidy on the Receiver's Resource Constraint: With an Application to US Local Governments 1964–1971'.
20. Gramlich, 'Intergovernmental Grants: A Review of the Literature.'
21. This paragraph owes much to Thomas Schelling's comments at the Laramie conference in July 1981.
22. Here it should be emphasised that the parameters estimated in the regression analysis give *partial* derivatives of the dependent variable. The actual increase in Israeli defence expenditures during any year depends on a combination of effects, Israeli GNP, US aid, Arab defence outlays plus an error term.

23. The definition of q_D is:

$$q_D = \text{MILAID}/(\text{MILAID} + E_D^I).$$

24. By comparison, McGuire, 'A Method for Estimating the Effect of a Subsidy on the Receiver's Resource Constraint', reports 40 to 70 per cent leakage for US federal grants to 'education'.
25. Various other assumptions about ϕ could be made, for example, that it depends on the size of the grant received. See McGuire, 'An Econometric Model of Federal Grants and Local Fiscal Response', for a discussion. In this study, the small number of observations dictates that we use the simplest assumption possible.
26. We assume that the *post hoc* accounts will show that all US military assistance for any year was allocated to military expenditures. Therefore, the total per capita cost of Israel's forces in any one year will be $E_D^I + G_D$. On the other hand, Israel will have expended $E_D^I + \phi_D G_D$ of its fungible resources on defence. Therefore, the effective price they will have paid for defence becomes:

$$P_D = \frac{E_D^I + \phi_D G_D}{E_D^I + G_D} = 1 + (\phi_D - 1)\left\{\frac{G_D}{E_D^I + G_D}\right\} = 1 + (\phi_D - 1)q_D$$

27. Actually, only questions (8) and (9) are included in the system to be estimated. Equation (10) was never estimated, because it is redundant. Equation (10) can be derived from (8) and (9). See Parks, 'Maximum Likelihood Estimation of the Linear Expenditure System' and Barten, A. P., 'Maximum Likelihood Estimation of a Complete System of Demand Equations', *European Economic Review*, 1 (Fall, 1969) 7–73 for further explanation.
28. For a technical discussion see, Parks, R. W., 'Maximum Likelihood Estimation of the Linear Expenditure System', *Journal of the American Statistical Association*, vol. 66, no. 336, (1971) 900–04.
29. Ray Dacey has suggested an alternative way to get at the question of whether Israel is a special case, namely to compare Israeli allocative patterns before and after major international events such as oil embargoes.

11 Arms Resupply *During* Conflict: A Framework for Analysis[1]

R. E. Harkavy
THE PENNSYLVANIA STATE UNIVERSITY

I INTRODUCTION

Recent years have witnessed an outpouring of writings on arms transfers, following a lengthy hiatus during the first two decades of the post-war period. That growing literature has been largely reformist in nature, in consonance with the strong normative concern with arms control evidenced in American security studies in the wake of the Vietnam war; indeed, is an echo of the writings of the 1930s around the time of the Nye Committee hearings and the Neutrality Acts.[2] Needless to say, the vast expansion of arms transfers in recent years, largely but not entirely propelled by OPEC's petrodollar recycle capacity, has also helped to sustain interest.

The recent period has also seen some ambitious if rudimentary attempts at classification and conceptualisation concerning the arms trade; more sophisticated and varied approaches to the subject from various angles and at different levels of analysis; and the construction of a fairly adequate unclassified data-base for post-war transfers in the major weapons systems categories, the internecine methodological disputes among scholars notwithstanding.[3] There has been, also, deservedly increased attention to the important interrelationships of arms transfers to many related, staple concerns of international diplomacy, that is, to alliances and other security commitments, nuclear proliferation (the 'doves' dilemma), strategic basing access, raw materials, overall trade, and so forth.[4] In a more theoretical vein, attention has recently been focused on the relationship of arms transfers to various notions of dependency; to an allegedly causal connection to big power interventions; to economic and/or political development; and to the reciprocal power/leverage relationship between arms suppliers and their customers.

One obvious and glaring remaining gap in the arms trade literature, however, concerns the almost complete absence of any focused, comparative analysis of arms transfer diplomacy *after the onset of and during conflict*. That is the case despite the obvious fact that suppliers' control over spare parts, replacements for destroyed or outdated equipments, and qualitative upgrading of arms during conflicts which sometimes see escalated levels of weapons sophistication, is very often a crucial determinant of the outcomes of wars between arms-dependent nations. That same supplier control, incidentally, can also sometimes be an important instrument for moderating or even terminating conflicts, as has often been claimed on behalf of the US handling of the brief 'soccer war' between El Salvador and Honduras in 1969.

There are, of course, numerous histories of individual conflicts in which arms resupply has been discussed within a broader context. In a related vein, William Quandt[5] has written on the uses of resupply policy in providing leverage for major powers in cases such as the US–Israel relationship. An earlier work by Lincoln Bloomfield and Amelia Leiss[6] on controlling small wars cited the importance of resupply in the evolution of several Third World conflicts; more recent work by Geoffrey Kemp[7] has stressed the broader, overall implications of the 'back-end' problems of arms transfers. But, the point made above still holds, namely, that there have been no attempts at elaborating a comparative framework – one which might cut across the dimensions of conflict types, various arms suppliers, and with a longitudinal dimension – for the study of arms resupply.

Though aspiring to a start towards such a framework, this effort must unavoidably remain sketchy, explorative, and heuristic. Data measuring arms movements to combatants during some wars are not readily available, particularly where, as in many cases, small arms and components' spare parts have been crucial. Many such transfers have been clandestine, treated as more politically sensitive than 'normal' peacetime transactions by major powers concerned they will be charged with 'fuelling' conflicts. Then too, it is difficult to draw inferences from a disparate batch of conflict cases, which nearly defy classification. Hence, the modest aim here is to lay out all of the myriad dimensions of the subject, to produce some halting spectra of classification, and to illustrate via some recent, prominent wars in the developing world.

II DIMENSIONS OF ARMS RESUPPLY

A comparative analysis of arms supply/resupply during conflict (the hyphenated term deliberately emphasises that some *new* arms client relationships have been *initiated* during wars) might direct attention to the following cluster of issues, each of which itself subsumes a complex welter of considerations.

> type of conflict, i.e., intensity of fighting, duration, human and *matériel* attrition, numbers and types of actors – interstate conventional, civil, guerrilla wars, etc.;
> pre-conflict arms acquisition patterns of 'styles' and their bases in alliances or other security alignments: sole, dominant and multiple source acquisitions, arms sources wholly from within or across major power blocs;
> generally applicable arms supplier rationales, doctrines, criteria, etc., for resupply decisions, i.e. reasons for and against restraint;
> specific arms supplier policies and decisions during ongoing conflicts, ranging from all-out support to total embargoes;
> the logistics of resupply (air staging transit and overflights);
> suppliers' arms production capabilities for resupply, existing weapons and spare parts inventories, forward pre-positioning of *matériel*;
> extant indigenous LDC capabilities for producing spare parts and component replacements;
> the roles of private arms dealers and 'third countries' in resupply;
> covert or clandestine resupply;
> conflict outcomes as reflective of resupply diplomacy and their post-war ramifications regarding the stability of arms transfer patterns and diplomatic realignments;
> the impact of resupply policies on nuclear proliferation incentives, and/or on new indigenous LDC arms production programmes;
> the impact of changing military technology and of related warfare doctrines (offensive versus defensive, preemptive/blitzkrieg versus attrition, etc.) on arms resupply.

1 TYPE OF CONFLICT

The requirements for arms resupply, as well as the interests and policies of suppliers, will, of course, greatly depend on what kind of conflict is involved: the types and numbers of participants, the duration and intensity of combat, and the extent of combatants' outside dependence for arms. Regarding actors, wars might be classified, as they were by Bloomfield and Leiss[8] as 'conventional interstate', 'unconventional interstate', 'internal with significant external involvement', 'primarily internal', or 'colonial'. Sometimes only two nation-state antagonists or internal factions may be involved; other times three, four or more. Often, too, the actors and alignments will shift even amid conflict, with combatants added or dropped, namely, Mauritania's changing role in the Spanish Sahara war or Jordan's belated token entry on to the 1973 stage. And, some recent wars have involved major or colonial powers on one side, so that arms resupply may have been relevant only to the other, weaker, dependent side.

Cross-cutting the above categories, the dimensions of intensity and duration (protraction) are here germane. In relation to resupply, intensity might here be more appropriately gauged by *matériel* rather than human attrition, though the two will obviously often highly correlate. Generally, measures of the scale or 'seriousness' of conflicts will involve a plethora of considerations, as indicated, for instance, by Butterworth's[9] multivariable classifications. Some wars will be short but of high intensity – as in 1967 – and involve pre-emptive 'short-war' or blitzkrieg strategies intended in part to circumvent the need for arms resupply (as Israel in 1973 and Pakistan in 1971 learned, however, such strategies may not always be conducted as planned). Some will initially be intense, but then be transformed into lengthy low-intensity stalemates (perhaps with periodic intense interludes), as witness the progress of the almost 'broken back' war between Iraq and Iran, or the continuing low level of combat between Ethiopia and Somalia, where a once conventional war has faded into a quiet guerilla conflict. Intense and more than merely abrupt inter-state conventional wars will, of course, crucially involve arms resupply if the participants are arms-dependent and if their war efforts are to be sustained.

For one reason or another, numerous post-war conflicts – certainly a majority – have not significantly involved the issue of weapons resupply, that is, at least not as a visible diplomatic issue. Some – the

1967 war or the brief Syria–Jordan clash in 1970 – have been concluded so quickly as to preclude the need for resupply (though even in 1967, France may quietly have resupplied Israel if only through Belgium or Holland).[10] Others – El Salvador versus Honduras, Mali versus Upper Volta – appear rapidly to have petered out just *because* of the conjunction of low pre-war arms stocks and the denial or absence of resupply, making a case for supplier control over the latter as an instrument of arms control or, rather, conflict control. Also, although a nation may get through a short, intense conflict without *then* needing resupply, it may subsequently require a post-war surge of arms replacements so as to bring inventories back to normal prewar levels.

There have been some wars – note the USSR–PRC border skirmishes – in which antagonists have been large powers, autarchic in arms production (in that case, however, highlighting qualitative asymmetries which would help prod China to seek new external infusions of arms technology). In some of the early post-war colonial wars, insurgent forces often relied primarily on weapons and ammunition scavenged from the Second World War battlefields, perhaps supplemented by private traders and/or clandestine governmental sources (as witness the recent shenanigans of ex-CIA personnel in Libya, the line between these two is often blurred).[11, 12]

What is or is not a 'conflict' is, at any rate, often arguable. Butterworth,[13] construing the term broadly, has amassed a list of more than 300 in the post-war period. SIPRI[14] recently tallied up 133 'armed conflicts' since 1945, utilising a narrower construction. Quite probably, only two or three dozen of these have significantly involved arms resupply requirements and related diplomacy. In some cases – note recently escalated or expedited US arms shipments to North Yemen, Thailand, and Sudan (respectively threatened by South Yemen, Vietnam in Cambodia, and Libya) – arms resupply during low-level conflicts has served more the purpose of an intended deterrent warning by a big power, i.e. a form of signalling, than that of actual replacement of attrited weapons stores.

As already anticipated, most but not all of the prominent or celebrated cases of arms resupply have been the large-scale conventional conflicts between arms-dependent Third World states, for instance, the several serial Arab–Israel, India–Pakistan, and Ethiopia–Somalia wars, and the recent ones pitting the PRC versus Vietnam and Iraq versus Iran. That between China and Vietnam was a good example of an interstate conventional war where only *one* side was reliant on outside resupply, albeit holding a qualitative edge in weaponry as a trade-off.

Some colonial wars have been fought – on one side at least – by virtually weapons-independent nations (Britain, France), while in others, the colonial powers themselves (Portugal, Belgium, Netherlands) along with the contending insurgents have been at least somewhat dependent on arms from major powers, if not directly for the prosecution of the colonial wars, then for fulfillment of broader alliance (NATO) responsibilities: that earlier presented the USA with some tricky political dilemmas.

Not all internal wars, meanwhile, follow the unconventional or small-scale guerrilla pattern. China's civil war in the late 1940s (also Spain's in the 1930s) eventually assumed the dimensions of a large conventional interstate war, with Chiang's once well-armed forces virtually denied replenishment from the USA, and Mao's forces availed of a combination of Soviet, captured Japanese, and then captured Kuomintang *matériel*. Many revolutionary wars in the postwar period have, of course, followed the pattern of a western-aided conservative incumbent regime pitted against insurgents armed by the USSR, China, or their allies. However, South African aid to Jonas Savimbi's forces in Angola, circuitous US and/or Egyptian assistance to Afghani Moslem rebels, and Israel's earlier help for the Kurds, Biafrans, and southern Sudanese insurgents, all demonstrate a variety of other patterns. In Zimbabwe, two rival revolutionary factions were respectively armed by the USSR and China, long after the latter two had come to be bitter rivals. Some internal conflicts, meanwhile – Lebanon, 1985, China in the 1920s, perhaps what is now emerging in Iran – are simply chaotic, which condition is reflected in the complexities of the arming of various contending factions, often defying tracing or political analysis.

2 PRE-CONFLICT ARMS ACQUISITION PATTERNS

Crucial to analyses of resupply – or its denial – are the patterns, that is, the origins, of the combatants' arms acquisitions in the immediate years preceding war. That will obviously largely determine from whom, at least in the first instance, spare parts and replacements will be sought; still, a number of interchangeable possibilities will often remain. For instance, if the volume of spares required is not too great, other nations dependent for arms on the same primary supplier may play roles as resuppliers, that is, if the original supplier is not willing or able to place 'third country' restrictions on them. Sometimes, however, the original supplier will prod an intermediary to play the role of resupplier just *because* it does not itself wish to bear the political onus of such a visible role, or is cross-pressured between contending friends. Hence, Eastern European sources have resupplied Iraq of late with Soviet arms with which to fight Iran, allowing the USSR to retain a (perhaps superficially) low profile.[15] Earlier, Iran and Turkey had played similar roles as conduits for US arms to Pakistan.[16]

Indeed, the prospect of the eventual need to call upon a major power supplier for help if war should break out may be one important criterion for an original choice of supplier, along with price, quality of arms, training support, and the like. For, if a prospective recipient anticipates being embargoed in a crisis – particularly if it cannot afford beforehand (or is not allowed by the supplier) to build up large inventories – then a choice of such a supplier as a primary source of arms would virtually amount to a concession that the arms were being purchased largely for symbolic or prestige purposes. At minimum, they would presumably be intended as a fragile, weak deterrent devoid of actual war-fighting capability. In reality, of course, recipient nations are often not able to gauge such things well in advance. The suppliers' logistical capabilities (including not only arms inventories and production output, but also air staging and overflight access), and more importantly, its long-term political relationships with a variety of countries, cannot easily be predicted well over the horizon, nor can its internal politics which, in some periods, may dictate restraints on arms sales. Israel, in purchasing US arms in the 1960s, could not easily have predicted the growth of OPEC leverage to what it became by 1973, nor either the American post-Vietnam mood of disengagement. Morocco, purchasing US arms over a long period of time in the 1960s and 1970s, could not easily have predicted the moralistic, legalistic policies put into practice by the Carter administration in 1977–8, which jeopardised the sources of arms it needed for counter-insurgency purposes. Iraq, purchasing Soviet arms in the early and mid-1970s, could hardly have imagined the fall of the Shah and, hence, ironically, a more conflicted and vacillating Soviet support of Iraq because of Syrian and Libyan cross-pressures.

In some instances, entirely new arms sources, or the rapid expansion of hitherto only minor ones, may be sought at the outset of or during conflicts. This may be done – if accustomed suppliers are not forthcoming – even in the face of the severe penalties associated with familiarisation on new weapons, retraining, new logistical systems, etc., particularly amidst ongoing conflict. Somalia, cut off from its normal Soviet source at the outset of its recent war with Ethiopia, sought desperately to acquire new western arms while scrounging for replacement Soviet-origin arms in a variety of other nations recently tied to the Soviet orbit, for instance, in Egypt and Iraq.[17] Ethiopia's situation was virtually a mirror-image, as it retrained on Soviet arms while seeking spares and replacements for its US-supplied arsenal in Yugoslavia, Israel, and Libya, among others. Iraq, apparently unsatisfied with Soviet bloc support in 1980–81 (though it obviously was receiving more than a trickle of replacements), moved to expand what had been, *ante bellum*, only peripheral arms client relationships with Brazil, Italy, and France, all oil-hungry nations anxious to please.

Pre-conflict arms recipient patterns may be ranged along a continuum from sole (all arms from one supplier) to predominant (most arms, let us say 60 per cent plus, from one source), to multiple (no supplier accounts for more than 60 per cent) source 'styles'.[18] The latter two patterns may further be subdivided according to whether an arms-dependent state, in dividing its purchases, does so wholly within the western or Soviet blocs or, rather, across both.[19] Needless to say, recent systemic shifts away from Cold War bipolarity have complicated analyses along such lines. China may now be counted almost as constituting a 'third bloc', whereas earlier, many LDCs (Sudan, Guinea, Somalia) acquired arms simultaneously from it and the USSR without severe political complications.[20] Likewise, nowadays, US and Western European diplomatic orientations in some places, for instance, in Iraq or Libya, have evolved so much at variance that a 'within-bloc' or 'cross-bloc' pattern here may now have different political implications than was the case a decade or two ago.

At any rate, there has been a great increase in the number of dependent states which now field arms both from Soviet bloc and western sources. In some cases, this has resulted from simultaneous, 'even-handed' acquisition policies; in others, more segmented patterns may be discerned, whereby presently mixed weapons inventories may reflect sequential periods of dominant western and Soviet security orientations. In the latter type of case (Egypt and Morocco are here good examples), remnant stocks from an earlier but long departed supplier may be a rusting, gradually wasting asset kept alive by cannibalisation and third country spare parts transfers.

Recent history divulges myriad, bewildering combinations of the above patterns where resupply diplomacy has come to the fore. In fact, the classic, expected Cold War pattern pitting sole or predominant Soviet bloc clients against like provisioned western customers has been rare, at least among the very finite number of conventional interstate wars. Iraq and Iran did, as measured by pre-war inventories, almost fit that pattern (Iran had, none the less, a large British-supplied tank force and some Soviet weapons; Iraq had begun acquiring some French arms), but as it turned out, under bizarre and rapidly altered circumstances.[21] The 1973 war also almost fitted such a pattern, as was reflected in the competitive Soviet–US airlifts, though here too, Israel was still substantially reliant on regunned British tanks and French aircraft as well as on a variety of indigenously produced systems.

Most pre-existing, pre-war arms inventories have divulged more complex patterns and, hence, trickier political dilemmas regarding resupply. India entered the lists in 1965 with a complicated mix of US, British, and Soviet matériel (also some from Italy, France, Yugoslavia); Pakistan then predominantly relied on US arms abetted by scattered other western sources.[22] By 1971, India's forces had been shifted further towards a Soviet orientation (though not without considerable additions from the USA and France, mostly produced on licence); Pakistan, meanwhile, had acquired arms in the period 1965–71 from almost everyone – France, China, the Soviet Union, and the USA – origin equipment via Jordan, Libya, Belgium and Italy. Here were two bitter rivals, both of which could be listed in the multiple source cross-bloc acquisition mode.

Nigeria, before 1967 reliant mostly on British arms, was resupplied by the latter but also by the USSR and its friends during the 1967 Biafra secession war, while the insurgents were armed from France, Portugal, and Sweden, among other sources. Also in 1967, Israel, then supplied primarily by France – but also utilising British, US (via the FRG) and Italian matériel – was faced off against Soviet-armed Egypt and Syria and US – and British-armed Jordan. Some wars have, of course, been fought by pairs of nations armed beforehand by the same source. Honduras and El Salvador in 1969, and later the Turks and Greek Cypriots, were all predominant US clients.

Some interesting questions are begged here, again, where the paucity of existing data, particularly as pertains to small arms, ammunition, and a variety of 'non-lethal' auxiliary equipment (trucks, radios, radars) is a barrier to empirical analysis. Most basic is that of whether pre-existing sole or predominant supply relations, particularly if still flourishing just before the onset of conflict – also very often correlated with formal alliances or obvious security commitments – have more often than not assured resupply during conflict by contrast with multiple source pre-war inventories. In the same vein, it might be hypothesised that multiple source acquisitions (in some cases here probably reflecting commercial rather than political supplier motives) might more readily allow a supplier to abjure involvement if conflict should erupt, if only under the cover of moralistically rationalised arms control policies.[23]

On the face of it, the record appears mixed, and one must also recognise that wars may be viewed by major powers as *opportunities* to solidify or even initiate security relationships as well as potentially dangerous or unwanted embroilments. For instance, the USA used the occasion of the Chinese invasion of India in 1962 to move towards the latter with arms aid;[24] at another, later time is eschewed such a purposeful move towards Somalia. The USSR backed Syria and Egypt to the hilt in 1973, as earlier it had backed North Korea and North Vietnam; it was more cautious in 1980 in Iraq's case, and abandoned Somalia in 1977.

Of course, preemptive or preventive wars may result, in part, from a nation's perceptions of the dangers of shifting arms supply relationships.[25] Somalia tried to take advantage of Ethiopia's transition to Soviet arms. Iraq, in attacking Iran in 1980, was fully aware that the latter had virtually sundered its vital US tie over the hostage affair and was, hence, highly vulnerable to an attrition war where resupply would count. Israel preempted in 1967 with French equipment and was subsequently embargoed; retrospectively it appears Israel was aware beforehand of a then imminent shift in French Middle Eastern diplomacy which, as it turned out, may have been eased rather than caused by Israel's effective use of French weapons.[26] France, however, has in other cases backed up pre-existing arms relations with resupply: Chad, Morocco, and Mauritania are recent cases, along with Iraq.

Indigenous production capability is an additional factor here, regarding components and spare parts as well as whole systems. Important also is related capacity for battlefield repair or cannibalisation. The latter can act almost as a force multiplier (attrition mitigator!) in combat. Israel, for instance, while reported to have had some 900 tanks knocked out during the 1973 war, was apparently able to repair or rebuild through cannibalisation or spare components several hundred of those. Its actual losses, therefore, may have been less than first reported, which if so, would substantially have reduced its resupply needs. India appears to have been availed of like capability in 1971, not surprising in view of its burgeoning indigenous arms industry. For a nation unsure of whether it will be resupplied in war, a flexible industrial structure which can extend inventories via spare parts and components is a prized asset.[27]

Often, the extent of such capabilities is obscured in the open reporting of wars outside the realm of intelligence agencies. Iraq has made claims during its recent war of extensive indigenous capability to sustain its forces, of a validity not easily determined.[28] Various analyses differ about what kind of capability South Africa is developing to sustain in combat, if necessary, a military structure still highly reliant on earlier French, Italian and other transfers of weapons and licensed technology.[29] In smaller-scale guerrilla wars, meanwhile, some forces (Eritrean guerrillas, the Viet Cong), have developed surprising infrastructures capable of ammunition and small arms manufacture, repair and component building, etc. Again, the nature and length of combat is important to analysis of a variety of such situations, for instance, regarding industrial conversion in small countries where a modest capability in machine tools might allow for a substantial reduction of resupply requirements, if relatively unsophisticated, small ammunition and component plants could quickly be constructed.

3 GENERAL ARMS SUPPLIER DOCTRINES, RATIONALES

Numerous past analyses of comparative arms supplier behaviour have provided some applicable classifications of rationales or motives for selling arms. Such analyses habitually posit a (partly artificial) division between political and economic rationales; additionally, some major powers are claimed relatively more or less inclined toward the one or the other.[30] Political rationales are variously said to include, among others, the cementing of alliances; forging of close fraternal relationships with clients' officers corps; maintaining regional balances of power, however defined; acquiring access to basing facilities and for overflights; promoting the viability or effectiveness of 'surrogate' or 'forward' fighting forces; controlling recipients' abilities to make war; forestalling nuclear proliferation by providing alternative routes to security, and so forth. SIPRI[31] earlier aggregated these rationales, as they pertained to the USA and the USSR, as a 'hegemonial' style of arms supply. A more 'commercial' style, stressing economic rationales, was said to direct attention to payments balances, domestic employment in arms industries, corporate profits (or their equivalents in 'socialist countries'), raw materials access, and economies of scale for domestic arms industries.

However 'clear' and simple these combined rationales may appear under normal circumstances, once a client state is engaged in combat, its recent and hence most relevant supplier(s) may be faced with a variety of often conflicting rationales and motivations, producing cross-pressures around a decision about whether to resupply. These mixes of political and economic factors will often be congruent with or follow from those within determined earlier *ab initio* transfers in the absence of war, except that they operate in a compressed time frame, and also often involve vague fears about the loosing of unpredictable forces in the fog of war, for instance, expanded wars which might directly involve the suppliers. Worst case scenarios, that is, enter the picture. There is probably some overall inclination towards caution as a result, but not in all cases.

Generally, these criteria or rationales can be stated in contrasting, opposite clusters, divided between those which argue for a less restrained, that is maximalist, resupply effort, and those which, conversely, involve a more restrained or minimalist support posture.

Militating *against* restraint and for a forthcoming resupply effort:

The supplier wishes its client/friend/ally to win, or at least not to lose – this can involve domestic public sympathies, and also the prestige of the supplier and its domestic arms if they predominate in the client's arsenal;

The supplier's credibility and faithfulness as an ally, friend, and arms supplier is inescapably engaged – this will usually be of more than passing interest to other states similarly tied to the supplier;

Pressures from other arms clients friendly to a combatant, and often having considerable leverage (see US–Saudi relationship);

The supplier wishes to maintain the pre-existing arms relationship after the conflict and to forestall a shift in the combatant's politico-military orientation. This may have ramifications related to strategic access, raw materials sources, investments, etc., i.e., all of the usually cited elements of influence and leverage;

The supplier may wish to forestall nuclear proliferation incentives or those for indigenous conventional arms development, either or both of which may be given impetus by unsatisfactory (to the client) support during crises;

In some cases, a supplier may wish to see its new weapons tested on a real battlefield, though this is rarely if ever an openly stated consideration (the Spanish Civil War syndrome).

Militating *for* restraint or for a very limited resupply effort:

The 'slippery slope' anxiety syndrome attributed to the USA as a result of the Vietnam experience, i.e., an assumption that arms resupply leads to direct supplier military engagement. More broadly, as pertains to training and field advisers, some refer to a 'back-end' problem of arms transfers, provoking the imagery of quagmires.[32]

Reluctance to draw down one's own military equipment stocks in a manner jeopardising the preparedness of one's own forces and/or arms commitments to other clients. Variously, for the USA this has involved the 'critical items' list and 'queuing' problems evidenced during and after the 1973 war.

Fears about exacerbating tensions or even military conflict (maybe even catalytic nuclear war) with suppliers of client's rival(s) – at minimum, fears of clouding of *détente* or exposing of failed expectations about 'linkage';

Fears about resupply efforts endangering other important relationships with non-combatants, if only masked by cover rhetoric about 'lack of consultation'. For example, US resupply of Israel in 1973 worsened American relations with Western Europe and non-Arab Muslim states; Soviet movements of arms from Egypt to India in 1971 worsened Soviet relations with the former;

'Moral' or humanitarian rationales (or, at least, concerns about moral image), arms control norms and policies. Arms resupply is a more obvious target of rectitudinous outrage than normal, peacetime supply. Also, supplier may determine, on pragmatic or moral grounds, that a restrained resupply response will foreshorten, terminate, or mitigate conflict;

If escalated qualitative levels of arming are involved or demanded, there may be fears about compromising military secrets, either via capture (note Soviet SAM-6, BMP/AFV in 1973) or through observed use (as with electronic countermeasures) which divulges capabilities;

The logistics of resupply may be politically embarassing or result in the accrual of political debts to nations allowing overflights or air staging (note Portugal, Spain, UK's Diego Garcia in relationship to Middle East). Just possibly, suppliers' unauthorised use of others' air spaces may bring it into conflict with states not directly engaged in the conflict;

The supplier may be convinced that its client will lose the war even if resupplied, hence, reflecting on its (the supplier's) prestige;

The supplier quietly wishes a client to be defeated or overthrown, so as to remove an 'unwanted burden'. Recent US policies regarding Somoza, perhaps also the Shah, have hinted at such a rationale;

The supplier wishes to use the event of a war as an opportunity to completely re-orient regional policies and alignments, as did apparently France during and after the 1967 war.

The foregoing list of reasons, pro and con, for and against a forthcoming resupply posture may, of course, be related to the previously enumerated general set of political and economic criteria. But many such decisions have been merely situational, basically *sui generis*, and have involved a complex and specific set of factors, more often than not involving severe cross-pressures. Hence, overall arms transfer doctrines, or even overall inclinations towards restraint or its lack, may be only a rough guide to actual behaviour.

For the USA in 1973, sentiment, and credibility as an ally or friend, was pitted against crucial political interests elsewhere, in Europe as well as in the Arab world. Internal politics too provided cross-pressures, with an influential ethnic vote on one side, but with powerful economic interests and a potential eruption of public opinion – if oil shortages should have become very serious – on the other. Israel's assumed nuclear weapons were presumably a factor; so too, various calculations about a future 'peace process' in connection with various possible war outcomes.[33] Later, in 1977–8, the US resupply policy towards Morocco was equally cross-pressured. On the one side was credibility as an ally, also Saudi pressures; on the other, arms control rationales (also then involving the issue of credibility, post-PD-13),[34] 'legal' inhibitions regarding United Nations dicta, and relations with oil-and-gas-rich Algeria. Here, there were cross-pressures even as pertained to the sole criterion of overseas energy sources. Earlier,

US resupply policy towards Pakistan in 1965 had had to take into account alliance maintenance, newly developing improved ties with India after 1962, relations with Iran, annoyance at burgeoning PRC–Pakistan ties, intelligence monitoring bases on the Khyber Pass, and fears of new involvements at a time Vietnam was heating up.[35]

The Soviets too have had to face resupply decisions involving conflicting motives and cross-purposes, though where moralistic concerns or arms control 'norms' have rarely been in evidence. Regarding Egypt and Syria in 1973, the political incentives were mostly on the side of all-out resupply, though with some broader risks regarding *détente* (hence, also, the SALT process) and the possibility of serious superpower confrontation. Then too, there was the issue of payment – ironically, Sadat's inability to pay for the massive Soviet resupply effort may have been one major element in the subsequent near-total Soviet–Egyptian rift, coming as it did after Soviet arms transfers policy seemed to shift towards an emphasis on using weapons sales to accrue hard (i.e., western) currency.[36] That shift became more marked in the early 1980s, as Soviet bloc debts to the West, and the USSR's grain purchases, increased the pressures for earning hard currency via arms sales to Libya, Iraq, Algeria, and (financed largely by Saudi Arabia) Syria.

Even in the absence of the arms control inhibitions under which the USA laboured in the 1970s, and even given the ideological compatibility of almost all Soviet clients, some situations involving wars did produce cross-pressures regarding Soviet resupply. We have already noted that political costs incurred in the case of Iraq, where the Soviets tilted towards the Syria–Libya duo, perhaps in part because even before the conflict, Iraq had begun somewhat to reorient its foreign policy towards the West. Earlier too, Soviet abandonment of Somalia and its heavy arms resupply to Ethiopia during the Horn war of 1977–8 had produced severe political cross-pressures, what with Iraq on the other side (along with Saudi Arabia, Egypt, and Iran) but with Libya and South Yemen backing the Marxist Ethiopian regime. This, and other events involving North and South Yemen, hurt the once solid Soviet–Iraq tie.

Second-tier powers too have laboured under some cross-pressures concerning resupply decisions, again spanning the economic and political realms, though their arms sales policies are often claimed largely oriented to the former. In 1967, France had to juggle the factors of credibility, desires for alignments and also arms markets, its prior collaboration with Israel in developing arms, oil, the Israeli nuclear factor, and its own Jewish and Arab domestic constituencies in connection with resupply policies, altogether not brought to a serious impasse because of the abruptness of the war. Later, it backed its clients in Chad, Morocco, Tunisia, and Zaire – variously, credibility, raw materials, and the desire to maintain a remnant African francophone solidarity were involved, countered by political and economic interests in other African nations such as Libya and Angola. Britain, meanwhile, in 1973, refused Israel spare parts for earlier supplied Centurion tanks, no doubt reckoning that its ties with Arab OPEC nations were overriding and the supplier credibility issue here nugatory.

For some smaller suppliers – note Israel in Central America or Brazil in Iraq – arms resupply during conflict, particularly where big power policies are inhibited by intra-regional cross-pressures or human rights concerns, may be one way of establishing a foothold in some arms markets, of acquiring chips which later can be cashed in. They can, in other words, fill gaps where others fear to tread, and where a single new market may represent a big boost to their ambitions as new arms suppliers. Hence, note Israel's concentration of late on South Africa and Chile (as its Central American markets begin to dry up) to compensate for numerous other markets it is shut out of by overwhelming Arab economic leverage.[37] Brazil's resupply, meanwhile, particularly of armoured personnel carriers, to Iraq during its war may perhaps only be understood as one element in a complex web of transactions spanning oil imports and nuclear technology, the latter related to an earlier nuclear deal between Brazil and West Germany.[38]

4 SUPPLIER POLICIES AND BEHAVIOUR

Prior to a conflict, an arms supplier nation may be a sole or predominant provider to a (soon-to-be) combatant, or merely one of several weapons sources. It may also have been altogether absent in that role, but political conditions (demands or entreaties from conflict participant, new political opportunity for supplier, self-perceived 'moral' imperative, etc.) may dictate its entering upon the scene *de novo* once a war starts as did the USSR recently with respect to Ethiopia. As previously indicated, this may also involve medium powers or other licensees, or smaller 'third party' surrogates or retransferers of arms, as well as the superpowers.

It is to be emphasised that resupply behaviour, whether restrained or not, may also depend on the actions of the suppliers to the client's rival(s), that is, the behaviour of the major powers is often reciprocally, causally linked. Virtually unrestrained resupply by one side (as by the Soviets at the outset of the 1973 war) may place tremendous pressures on the other to match the *ante* on behalf of its own clients. Either explicit or tacit bargaining over the flows of arms may be conducted between rival suppliers, as well as between the latter and their respective clients, as a conflict proceeds. Then too, as previously noted, major powers may be subjected to powerful pressures from non-combatants as well; hence, witness Saudi pressures on the USA regarding arms supplies to Morocco and Somalia during their recent engagements.

At the outset of war, a major power arms supplier, in response to a request for resupply (and aside here, for the moment, from matters of timing and escalation in connection with other suppliers' responses) will have to choose from policies located somewhere along the following spectrum, but which cannot describe altogether discrete possibilities. A supplier may, variously,

>declare and enforce a total formal embargo (perhaps on all parties involved, relevant or not), deny all resupply including spare parts, and insist upon matching behaviour by licensees and other potential third party transferers;
>decide to transfer non-lethal *matériel* only, i.e., food, medicine, innocuous means of transport, etc.;
>conduct a measured, low-level resupply effort, perhaps intended merely as a symbolic gesture, involving limited, albeit 'lethal' spare parts and ammunition. As a variant, this may be done clandestinely or through encouragement of third parties so as to maintain a low profile for the major supplier state'(perhaps even in conjunction with a declared embargo);
>resupply spare parts and full systems up to one-to-one replacement levels; or, merely resupply spares and ammunition, but allow whole systems inventories to suffer attrition;
>solemnly announce an embargo, but encourage surrogate suppliers (licensees, other recipients) to fully resupply, up to or beyond pre-war inventory levels;
>first, abjure any resupplies, but commence transfers only if that is not matched on the other side or if the client's situation becomes desperate;

resupply heavily to increase the client's weapons inventories beyond pre-war quantitative levels, but not provide newer, more advanced weapons which might alter the nature of the conflict;
qualitatively upgrade the client's equipment, while maintaining approximately pre-war quantitative levels;
provide an all-out and massive arms resupply, resulting in both enhanced quantitative and qualitative levels of arming for the combatant, i.e., introducing large numbers of new weapons systems.

Responses by various suppliers all along the above spectrum have been evidenced in the wars of recent decades. Some have been largely predictable, signalled by prior policy pronouncements and consistent doctrines. Others have less easily been anticipated, for example, the all-out Soviet resupply effort to Ethiopia in 1977–8 (which fits the last of the above categories), the result of a deliberate calculation by the USSR to give up its major base at Berbera but to establish in exchange a strong position in the inherently dominant state of Africa's Horn.

The USA has experienced a tortuous and often confusing history of resupply policies over the past half century, which has in various circumstances ranged along the entirety of the above spectrum of responses. There has been often unresolvable ambivalence between an inclination to back friends in crises, and a rectitudinous moralism which often surfaces at the outset of conflicts, only sometimes a cover for ducking engagement. There has been a discernible periodicity to such shifts, which has corresponded to overall foreign policy mood cycles.[39]

Before the mid-1930s, American arms transfers were conducted mostly on a *laissez-faire* basis, that is, with an absence of governmental licensing controls. The only exceptions were occasional embargoes, desultorily enforced, usually applied to revolutionary forces in Latin America. But amid the 'merchants of death' controversies in the 1930s (themselves in part sparked by evasions of an embargo on resupply during the Chaco war between Bolivia and Paraguay), the USA enunciated a policy, embodied in the Neutrality Acts, which required it to 'quarantine' any and all conflicts by stopping arms supplies to *both* sides, thus ignoring all distinctions between aggressor and victim.[40] That policy proved unworkable, not to say dangerous, for US interests, and was later voided by the Lend-Lease Act to allow arms assistance to Britain and France in 1940. It reflected, however, a chronic American dilemma: during ordinary times, arms trade business is business, but when the clouds of war form, a horrified moralism is often invoked, often asymmetrically disadvantageous to US friends.

After 1945, the early Cold War period saw few restraints on US arms transfers, even during conflicts. There were exceptions, for instance, the embargo during the Israeli 'War of Independence' (applied to both sides, but effectively disadvantaging Israel) and the very minimal resupply support to the collapsing Kuomintang army during the Chinese Civil War (in part, an economically-based decision, given the enormous quantitative requirements). But others – Guatemala, South Korea, Greece, etc. – were helped during their conflicts.

Later, however, there were the formal embargoes applied to both sides of the 1965 India–Pakistan War (India had been bolstered by US arms after the Chinese invasion of 1962; Pakistan had then long been a US client) and of the 1967 war, which ended before the embargo could assume any real meaning for Israel or Jordan (Israel then relied primarily on France for its arms). Here, one saw fears about additional 'quagmires' as the Vietnam war was being expanded, but also cross-pressures which dictated avoiding problems with first India and then the Arabs. In 1969, the USA also formally embargoed its clients in Honduras and El Salvador during their brief 'soccer war', contributing thereby to halting that conflict. In 1973, of course, the USA withheld resupply to Israel for some 10 days, followed by a massive airlift when Israel's precarious position became clear, and perhaps also because it was feared Jerusalem would have to resort to a nuclear option out of desperation. Towards the end of the war, US threats to halt further resupply were effective in pressuring Israel to accept a ceasefire and to release the surrounded Egyptian 2nd Army east of the Suez Canal.

The Carter administration in 1977 quickly enunciated an ambitious policy of arms transfers restraint, embodied in the vaunted PD-13. Discussed in its various dimensions in numerous other places,[41] that policy clearly involved a predisposition to a very restrained resupply policy – albeit not formally provided for by PD-13 – at great variance with the 'Nixon Doctrine' which seemed to imply a forthcoming arms policy to friends in conflict. But, it was obvious – indeed, made very explicit – that the background of Vietnam and of the later reaction to it with the controversial Angolan restraints policy dictated by Congress, was a major inspiration for the Carter arms policy. Tests of that policy were not long in coming.

As it happened, the unfolding of the Carter administration's sequential decisions in various arms resupply contingencies from 1977–80 was a tale of the gradual unravelling of its moralistic aspirations, as that administration came to face what it came often to refer to as 'geopolitical realities'. That unravelling was, of course, paced and paralleled, by the failure of the multilateral restraints initiative leading to the CATT talks, which were hoped to produce an analogy to the London Nuclear Suppliers' arrangements.[42]

The Carter administration did not actually ever face a major crisis or a large-scale interstate conventional war requiring a resupply decision; nothing on the scale of, or with the enormous implications of, the 1973 Middle Eastern war. Rather, it confronted a variety of such decisions involving smaller though not altogether insignificant interstate and civil wars: Zaire's 'Shaba I' invasion, Morocco's (also, initially, Mauritania's) Spanish Sahara imbroglio, Chad's border problems with Libya which long preceded the latter's takeover, Somalia's war with Ethiopia, Zaire's 'Shaba II', the Nicaraguan civil war, and North Yemen's brief fending off of an attack by South Yemen. Indeed, aside from generally illustrating the various facets of resupply diplomacy discussed above, these cases provided a telling reflection of the gradual unravelling of the Democratic Administration's arms transfer controls policies.

In the first test, the invasion from Angola in March 1977 of Zaire's Shaba Province (locale of much of the West's cobalt sources), the USA – which by the end of the Ford administration had appeared committed to becoming *the* predominant arms supplier to Zaire – decided to assist the endangered Mobutu regime with 'non-lethal' arms only. This was meant, aside from the specifics of Shaba, to provide an early demonstration of the new administration's arms control *bona fides*.[43] At any rate, the invasion of Zaire was eventually repelled by some 1500 Moroccan troops moved by a French airlift; aided by Egyptians, some Belgian arms and even non-military aid from China.

Almost simultaneously, the then new administration had to face the problem of what arms support was to be provided Morocco for its then worsening sandy 'quagmire' in the Western Sahara. A variety of conflicting policy considerations were involved: the international 'legal' aspects of Morocco's occupation as defined by the UN; existing US restrictions on Morocco's use of arms other than for 'defensive' purposes; Saudi promptings of US support to a fellow 'moderate' Arab monarchy; and conflicting US economic interests in Algerian oil and gas, and Moroccan and Spanish Saharan phosphates and iron ore. Morocco, while possessing substantial quantities of French and also earlier (1960s) supplied Soviet weapons, had become reliant upon the USA for F-5 aircraft, Hercules transports, M-48 tanks, and Dragon, TOW and Chaparral missiles, the heart of its defence capabilities. It was to the USA it looked for attack helicopters and armed COIN aircraft to fight the Polisario, and for additional major systems to balance massive new Soviet arms shipments to Algeria. For the time being, arms control norms prevailed – equipment specifically intended for counter-insurgency purposes was withheld.[44]

Later on in 1977, the still infant Carter administration was faced with additional requests for arms during conflicts (one minor, one near-major) from nations which had not previously been American arms clients, but which very much wished to be. Those were Chad – amid a complex civil war which saw Libyan support to Moslem insurgents – and Somalia after the invasion of Ethiopia's Ogaden, in the wake of Ethiopia's shift from American to Soviet arms clientship. In both cases, the administration's response was very cautious indeed. Chad was considered for some 'non-lethal' aid, but which was eventually denied because of fears about new 'slippery slopes'.[45] Somalia, whose forces had long been equipped with Soviet weapons, meanwhile was attempting to extend their useful lives by acquiring spares and replacements from, among others, Egypt and Iraq. Amid the confusion, the USA, under evident Saudi and Egyptian pressure, first hinted at resupplying Somalia, but then declined on the grounds that it could not underwrite an armed cross-border aggression, but left the door ajar in the event an Ethiopian counter-attack should carry into Somalia proper, thus providing a 'just' rationale for 'defensive' arming. Support was provided Somalia by West European 'surrogates', however, and the USA would, only much later, extend military aid to Somalia as a quid pro quo for use of the naval and air facilities earlier provided by the USSR.

In 1978 and 1979, however, the by then wearied and chastened Carter Administration slowly reversed its arms supply policies, and this was reflected as well in its response to several conflict situations where resupply came to be at issue. In Shaba II – in part because of evidence of direct Cuban involvement – the USA responded in a more than 'non-lethal' fashion.[46] True, the administration did completely cut off arms to Somoza's Nicaragua, hastening if not causing its downfall, particularly as the USA also pressured Israel to follow suit. But here, arms control norms – which had explicitly been applied in the cases of Zaire, Morocco, Chad, and Somalia – were virtually absent, giving way to human rights issues and a desire not to have the USA appear to go down with a sinking ship.[47]

Later, in 1979, the Carter administration was to be much more forthcoming in responding to resupply requests from Morocco and North Yemen. A loosening of restrictions on counter-insurgency equipment for the former was slowly brought about, resulting in decisions to provide OV-10 armed COIN aircraft and Cobra helicopter gunships.[48] The *volte-face* on Morocco was followed by a strong response to South Yemen's incursion into North Yemen, resulting in an accelerated shipment of some $500 million of fighter aircraft, tanks, APCs, ATGMs, and SAMs.[49] These moves were to foreshadow the much more aggressive policies regarding trade-offs of basing facilities for arms in Kenya, Oman, and Somalia, and also the massive new arms supplies for Egypt and Pakistan under consideration towards the close of the Carter administration.

The Reagan Administration, coming to office in 1981, lost little time in signalling that it would, for good or worse, be a much more faithful resupplier of arms to American clients and friends in conflict. Of course, more broadly, the PD-13 restraints policy was immediately jettisoned, superseded by what appeared virtually an all-out arms selling policy, with both aggressive economic and political security aims.[50] In its first few months, the new administration moved swiftly to bolster shaky incumbent regimes in El Salvador and Guatemala with fresh military supplies. It also moved towards further forward positioning of *matériel* in the Persian Gulf/Indian Ocean region. Then, hints of 'new' strategic relationships with Israel seemed to anticipate stocking of US *matériel* in Israel which might preclude the necessity for all-out resupply in the event of a new conflict, a policy to be matched by allowing Saudi Arabia to pile up large inventories of spare parts for its newly acquired massive arsenal. Sudan, under pressure from Libya on its western border, was promised the acceleration of arms already in the pipeline as was Egypt in the wake of Sadat's assassination. But, it remained to be seen what resupply responses might be forthcoming with regard to a number of situations – Israel, Pakistan, Taiwan, Kenya, Somalia,

Morocco, etc. – where tricky dilemmas involving severe cross-pressures might yet be encountered if wars were to erupt.

(5) SUPPLIER CAPACITY FOR RESUPPLY: EN ROUTE ACCESS, LOGISTICS CAPABILITIES, AND COMPARATIVE ARMS PRODUCTION BASES

In examining the resupply policies of arms supplier nations – and their clients' perspectives thereon – it is often nearly forgotten that a significant capability to conduct resupply operations by the former is by no means always to be taken for granted. For that very reason, a dependent nation choosing a sole or predominant arms supplier might wish to take into account the latter's access to aircraft staging bases and overflight corridors, its sea and air logistical capabilities, its production base and normal 'excess' inventories for various weapons categories, and its potential vulnerability to political pressures from the clients' adversaries. The importance of these matters, in combination, was underscored in 1973 and in several subsequent conflicts, and has further been brought to prominence by the American search for forward weapons depots with which to assist friends (as well as to provision US forces) in case of a crisis in or around the Persian Gulf.

In order quickly, economically, and effectively to resupply clients during wars – greatly dependent, of course, upon the latter's locales – major powers must often have access to, depending on the circumstances, lengthy networks of air staging and refuelling facilities, and land overflight corridors. As the USA (and Israel) learned in 1973, such access, while *pro forma* in some places during normal peacetime conditions, is not to be taken for granted under more extraordinary circumstances. The Soviets, meanwhile, making effective use of arms transfer diplomacy, have acquired effective chains of access, running along a north–south axis through the Middle East and down into Africa; and along an east–west axis extending virtually all across the Eurasian rimland.[51] Hence, their recent resupply efforts on behalf of India (1971), Egypt and Syria (1973), Angola, Mozambique, Ethiopia and Vietnam (and also the Afghanistan puppet regime) have been enabled in a matter which would not have been possible a decade or two before. (For less time-dependent resupply operations, the Soviets have also developed a vast fleet of weapons-carrying merchant ships, which can provide a surprisingly large sealift capability.)[52]

Dependent arms clients engaged in conflict will often themselves need to join their suppliers in applying leverage to assure access routes for their supplier's arms, and will sometimes be actively engaged in denying such access to their antagonists. For instance, the Arabs were successful in pressuring most of Western Europe (except Portugal, with its Azores bases) to deny the US access for weapons movements in 1973; since then, with the next possible conflict in view, they have worked on Portugal and on others as distantly removed as the Philippines. During the 1973 war, Arab (as well as Soviet) influence over Turkey and Yugoslavia was crucial to providing overflight corridors for Soviet transports. Ethiopia and Somalia struggled for influence over various Middle Eastern Arab states in connection with respective arms resupply routes during their Horn conflict, among other things apparently causing the Soviets to conduct unauthorised overflights over some states – Egypt, Sudan, Pakistan – after Somalian leverage underpinned by Saudi Arabia, proved temporarily effective.[53]

Iraq, its ports near the mouth of the Shatt Al Arab closed to Soviet bloc resupply during its war with Iran, was reportedly provided overland access by friends in Jordan, Saudi Arabia, and Kuwait, apparently triggering some brief Iranian bombing of the latter.[54] Iran, meanwhile, in receiving weapons from Syria, was apparently able to use Soviet airspace (even as simultaneous Soviet resupply of Iraq proceeded); a reported parallel covert Israeli attempt to reprovision Iran with 'Argentinian' aircraft met armed resistance when a plane strayed into Soviet airspace.[55]

The speed and volume of arms resupply may be crucial, as witness the 1973 outcome, after a virtual head-to-head contest between US and Soviet airlift capabilities. Further, to the extent resupply appears contingent or is delayed, combatants' military strategies may have to be adjusted to cope with expected (temporary or more long-term) shortages, as was done by Israel in 1973 concerning emphases between its eastern and western fronts, and the opening of large-scale offensive operations. One must await more detailed histories of the confusing Iraq–Iran conflict in order to ascertain whether similar considerations have affected rival strategies in that contest.

The arms production bases and reserve inventories of major states may have a great bearing on resupply capabilities and decisions, and their comparative (between suppliers) status may be important to the extent significantly unbalanced. In recent years, the USSR's annual unit output of tanks, fighter aircraft, artillery pieces, APCs, and other systems has greatly exceeded that of the USA; also, its faster turnover of weapons 'generations' has spun off a much larger volume of surplus equipment. Hence, the USSR has been able to conduct, without much strain, quantitatively massive resupply operations (Middle East, Ethiopia, Angola), while the US replenishment of Israel's forces in 1973 seriously denuded the *matériel* stocks of US forces in Western Europe; afterwards there was a severe 'queuing' problem involving the requests of numerous clients in a variety of weapons areas. That situation has not changed much since 1973, at which time it became known that US tank production had fallen to a derisory annual figure of 360 units; numerous reports in recent years have pointed to dangerously low US ammunition and spare parts stocks in Europe and elsewhere.

One recent press report cited some of the following figures concerning US and Soviet current annual production of conventional weapons systems which might be involved in resupply operations:[56]

	USA	USSR
Tanks	650	2000
'Other combat vehicles'	1000	5000
Combat aircraft	275	500
Helicopters	200	500

SOURCE *New York Times*, 20 Jan. 1980, p. E3.

Additional data for SAMs, anti-tank weapons and other key systems would undoubtedly divulge comparable ratios. Similar and related conclusions may be drawn from comparative data on weapons inventories; one recent report produced the following figures for 1976 and 1981 inventories in three classes of weapons particularly germane to resupply.

		USA	USSR
Tanks	1976	9 181	42 000
	1981	11 560	48 000
Combat aircraft	1976	3 665	4 740
	1981	3 988	4 885
Artillery	1976	4 955	13 900
	1981	5 140	19 300

SOURCE *Time Magazine*, 20 July 1981, p. 15.

The above numbers, startling by comparison, would, of course, have to be interpreted in the light of the qualitative content of these weapons, to provide an indication of the amount of combat capability or firepower they actually represent. But, in that regard, numerous recent analyses have pointed to a significant narrowing of the once yawning qualitative gap between US and Soviet forces. Generally, even if the relatively higher requirements for the larger Soviet home forces are taken into account, the flexibility given the Soviets for massive supply/resupply efforts on behalf of clients clearly stands out, particularly for large-scale, sustained conventional conflicts which involve significant *matériel* attrition. For the smaller and shorter wars, such considerations are, of course, rendered far less relevant.

Further, the possibility is not precluded that either the USA or USSR might be called upon to conduct more than one resupply effort simultaneously, either to both sides of a single conflict or to clients in separate but simultaneous ones. Such situations can provide severe political and/or logistical dilemmas. For the Soviets, one interesting historical precedent occurred in the late 1930s, when Soviet arms aid to Loyalist Spain was apparently curtailed because of the competing requirements for reprovisioning of China's war effort against Japan at a time the USSR had a vital interest in keeping the latter's army fully occupied.[57]

A future Middle Eastern war could see the USA pressured to mount a resupply effort not only on behalf of Israel, but of Egypt, Jordan, and Saudi Arabia as well. 'Even-handed' denial of resupply to all might then be a likely response, which would disadvantage Israel if the Soviets were, as one would expect, supportive of Syria and Iraq. The USSR for its part has in the recent past – either itself or via thinly disguised surrogates – provided arms to both sides of the Iran–Iraq struggle. The USA might at some point face simultaneous resupply requests from two or more among Pakistan, Thailand, South Korea, and Taiwan, along with the aforementioned Middle Eastern states, if there were more than one simultaneous conflict.

In order to mitigate the possibly sudden and massive requirements for long-distance resupply, both of the superpowers have taken increasingly to forward positioning of *matériel*, or, sometimes difficult to distinguish, the persuading of well-stocked friends to assist resupply of beleaguered clients with the promise of later restocking of the denuded armouries of the former. Sometimes logistics are paramount in such considerations; at other times, a superpower may have reasons to mask or at least make less visible its role as resupplier through use of a surrogate, even with the sure knowledge that its ultimate role will be ascertained by all concerned.

Concerning forward positioning, the Soviets have, in recent years, piled up huge arms caches (under what degree of physical control is not entirely clear) in Libya, Ethiopia, Syria, and South Yemen, usable, for instance, for assistance to Soviet client states further south in Africa, as well as for a major Middle Eastern war. Such forward positioning not only enables more rapid and massive arms assistance further along logistics routes, but in some circumstances, may circumvent the need for tricky diplomacy regarding overflights, say, over Yugoslavia or Turkey. The USA, meanwhile, has tried to interest Egypt and/or Saudi Arabia to act as similar forward depots, so far without notable success. Some recent reports now indicate that US plans for strategic cooperation with Israel may have such purposes in mind, even if masked and at the risk of anxiety in Saudi Arabia, the ironic ultimate intended target of such assistance.[58]

Sometimes, forwardly positioned arms may not so easily be moved for purposes elsewhere, i.e., the hosts' political ties and purposes may not coincide with those of the superpower. The USA was apparently denied permission to move weapons from West Germany (long thought of as a forward depot for contingencies in the Near East or Africa) to Israel in 1973, and assumed a similar hold would be put on NATO weapons stocks if another such war should erupt. The USSR, in 1971, did move weapons out of Egypt to assist India, but only at the cost of considerable Egyptian unhappiness that is now considered by some analysts as one of the factors having led to Sadat's subsequent expulsion of most Soviet advisers.[59]

Concerning 'surrogate' resuppliers, their use has been frequent in a variety of cases. The USA, after embargoing Pakistan after 1965, is widely suspected of having winked later – if not actually connived in – the movement of equipment of US origin from Turkey and Iran (possibly both in 1965 and 1971). Whether the US has tacitly approved Israeli shipments of US equipment to Iran in 1980–81 is an intriguing question. Probably not! The Soviets, meanwhile, have used Eastern European allies to supply Iraq, while looking the other way as Syria and Libya have moved Soviet-origin equipment to Tehran. Similar behaviour was evidenced during the war in the African Horn in 1977–8.

In the realm of long-range, large-scale arms airlift, the superpowers alone field significant capability; here, bipolarity remains virtually undisturbed. For that reason, many LDCs – particularly those at great distance from Europe or those anticipating intense wars of attrition – might well exercise caution in choosing predominant reliance on European arms. Further, the Europeans, though not likely to be hamstrung by arms control or other moralistic criteria in decisions concerning resupply, might well be subject to severe military and economic threats in cross-pressured situations which they might find more difficult to brush aside than would a superpower. The UK, even when near-independent in oil, and even if otherwise inclined would not likely dare an airlift on behalf of Israel or South Africa!

A measure of the much more limited airlift capacities of the second-tier powers can be gauged from the following comparative data in Table 11.1.

Those data fully demonstrate that the USA and USSR, alone, are capable of large-scale arms airlifts. Of course, however, the comparisons will depend on the locales of conflicts – generally, the US capability becomes comparatively advantageous at longer ranges, even relative to the USSR. Then too, in some circumstances, as was the case for France's resupply of Mobutu's Zaire in the Shaba I crisis, or Cuba's Angola airlift, second-tier powers may rely upon airlift assistance from one or the other of the superpowers, where there is a convergence of political aims if not willingness to act upon them.

Thus, too, while several of the second-tier powers have, in recent years, become more significant arms suppliers, their weapons are not as widely distributed around the world as those of the superpowers (in the case of some French systems – Mirage jets, helicopters, air-to-air missiles, anti-tank weapons – this generalisation is gradually fading in validity.)[60] That automatically translates into lesser overall opportunities for acquiring spares and replacements from other than the primary source; from 'third countries', private traders, battlefield abandonments, and so forth. Even in peacetime, of course, second-tier nations are widely considered weak on the 'back-end' of the transfer process, in support, training, and assistance in maintenance. Such problems will be multiplied once combat begins. But, in smaller conflicts, the lesser suppliers can still play a major resupply role, as witness the role of Israel (and perhaps now South Africa) in assisting friendless incumbent regimes in Central America.

(6) POST-CONFLICT RAMIFICATIONS OF RESUPPLY POLICIES

The foregoing has indicated that arms resupply policies will often have a significant impact on post-war political relationships, sometimes resulting in greatly altered diplomatic orientations on the part of dependent nations.

Embittered client states which have been denied satisfactory resupply by erstwhile big power friends may drastically shift alignments

TABLE 11.1 Air lift capacities

Country		Transport aircraft inventory	Maximum payload (lbs)	Range with max. payload (miles)	Range with max. fuel (miles)
USA	*(241)	C-141	90 880	2 935	6 390
	(74)	C-5A	220 967	3 256	7 991
	(276)	C-130 (tactical)	43 310	2 487	4 606
USSR	(600)	An-12 Cub	44 090	2 236	3 540
	(40)	An-24/26 Coke/Curl	12 125	683	1 584
	(20)	IL-14 Crate	10 000	930	1 990
	(20)	IL-18 Coot	29 750	2 300	4 040
	(8)	IL-62 Classic	50 000	4 160	5 715
	(20)	Tu-134 Crusty	18 075	1 174	1 876
	(75)	Il-76 Candid	88 185	3 100	4 163
	(60)	AN-22 Cock	176 350	3 100	6 800
	(1400)	Aeroflot, various			
UK	(11)	VC-10CI	22 200	2 000	3 400
	(45)	C-13OH(tactical)	43 310	2 487	4 606
France	(56)	Transall C-160	35 274	1 151	5 504
	(48)	Noratlas	17 435	760	1 615
	(90)	various (DC-8, Mystere-20, etc.)	—	—	—
FRG	(75)	Transall C-160	35 274	1 151	5 504
	(4)	Boeing 707-320C	88 900	3 625	5 755
	(3)	VFW-614	8 598	414	1 553
PRC	(300)	Y-5/An-2	3 300	NA	562
	(100)	ex-Soviet, variously, IL 14/18, An 12/24/26 – see above data			
	(18)	Triden, C-46	26 800		
	(150)	large transports, various, from Civil Aviation Admin.		1 785	2 360

NOTE   Range data do not account for refuelling capability of some US, UK, and French transports.
SOURCE   Numbers and types of aircraft from recent editions of IISS, *The Military Balance* (London); range and payload date from *Jane's All the World's Aircraft* (London: Marston & Low), annual.

and seek new sources of arms afterwards. The US and British embargoes on both Pakistan and India in 1965 drove them, respectively, to much closer ties and more significant arms relationships with China and the USSR. France's embargo on Israel in 1967 likewise pushed the latter towards a much greater dependence on the USA, one for which it has had, ever since, no available alternative.

Sometimes a nation massively resupplied during a war will have trouble paying for it afterwards – in the heat of conflict, particularly if national survival is at stake, it is unlikely to quibble over cost. After 1973, Sadat was clearly furious at Soviet insistence on full payment for the massive infusion of *matériel* during the war; his later break with the USSR may in part have been explained as a convenient excuse to erase the debts.[61]

Then, too, resupply expenses may be critical to a dependent state's decisions regarding both nuclear and conventional arms developments. Israel and India both have been prodded towards greater indigenous weapons production capability by memories of embargoes or at least difficulties in acquiring sufficient spares and replacements during conflict. Israel's moves towards deployment of nuclear weapons has obviously been hinged on such factors; indeed, may have provided some leverage in persuading the USA to initiate the airlift in 1973 after over a week's delay. Others – Taiwan, South Korea, perhaps Pakistan, may one day hold similar leverage to force or encourage resupply efforts if their situations should appear desperate.

Some nations have, of course, moved to increase weapons and related inventories after having been denied or delayed resupply during conflict, so as to reduce their vulnerability to repetitions of such experiences. Carrying large inventories is, however, as with any enterprise, rather expensive, regarding maintenance, storage, and security, as well as initial purchasing costs.

Generally, data are very scarce regarding most nations' inventories, particularly regarding ammunition and spare parts. The SIPRI and IISS orders of battle and arms transfer registers divulge approximately how many tanks or artillery pieces various LDCs have, but not how many tank or artillery shells, not to mention spare treads or lanyards. The meaning of such data would, if available, depend at any rate on vague and subjective assumptions about whatever *matériel* attrition might be experienced in future wars. Israel, having run short of critical supplies in 1973 after some 10 days, is now commonly assumed to have 20–30 days' stocks of ammunition and spare parts on hand.[62] But, such assumptions are based on the attrition rates of 1973, which might or might not be repeated in a future conflict and which at any rate, might last well beyond 30 days, as so many wars do. Saudi Arabia has also been reported laying away copious inventories, perhaps in part intended for retransfer, say to Jordan during another Arab–Israeli war. Soviet clients probably worry less about such restraints, but even here, recent Soviet behaviour towards Iraq might be taken by some as cautionary.

The political changes wrought by resupply policies may, of course, extend beyond relationships between suppliers and the supplied. Note the strains caused by the 1973 war on US–West Europe relations, which although publicly discussed as a failure by the USA to 'consult' its allies, actually involved a fundamental difference over policy. Likewise, increased US military aid to Portugal after the 1973 war – and countering Arab financial inducements to the nation which controls the strategic Azores Islands – was a direct result of the access diplomacy surrounding the US airlift in 1973. The Soviets, meanwhile, no doubt have had to provide *quid pro quo* in exchange for landing and overflight rights used in resupply efforts to, variously, Vietnam, Angola, Mozambique, and Ethiopia.

(7) TECHNOLOGICAL CHANGE AND THE CHANGING BASES FOR MILITARY STRATEGIES: IMPLICATIONS FOR ARMS RESUPPLY

Two areas of ongoing technological change are particularly pertinent in connection with arms resupply: new conventional weapons developments – particularly as they affect alternating periods of advantage between offensive and defensive warfare – and the previously discussed major powers' long-range logistical capability for transporting military *matériel*.

Regarding the former area, numerous military historians and strategic analysts – van Creveld, Quester, Fuller *et al.*[63] – have depicted the long-term historical alternations of advantage to offensive and defensive strategies and tactics, to strategies of annihilation versus attrition (van Creveld discusses the relationship between three essential elements: striking power, mobility, and protection). For this century, it is a commonplace that the mobile warfare anticipated and planned for by turn-of-the-century strategists such as Foch and Schlieffen became the defensive stalemate and massive attrition of the First World War trenches, featuring the combined dominance of automatic weapons, artillery, and barbed wire. The lessons of the 1905

Russo-Japanese war were ignored. By 1939, of course, another turn of the wheel had given the advantage to the vaunted German blitzkrieg offensives as the combination of armour and tactical airpower became ascendant; then, the lessons of the First World War were no longer valid, as symbolised by the failure of France's Maginot Line strategy.

In the recent past, many analysts have described the Israeli 1967 preemptive blitzkrieg as, in a way, the 'final battle of the Second World War', a belated tribute to Guderian.[64] By 1973 – and this is disputed by some – the emergence of precision-guided munitions (PGMs), particularly with the newer anti-tank and anti-aircraft missiles, is said qualitatively to have changed the nature of modern conventional warfare. Those changes in weaponry have, of course, been paralleled by enormous changes in command, communication and control (C^3) technologies, the implications of which for defensive or offensive advantages are not yet clear. Generally, it is assumed by most analysts that a new period of ascendance for the defence has arrived (hence, almost automatically, enhanced likelihood of much greater battlefield attrition), though this may vary depending upon the nature of combatants, terrain, availability of high-technology weaponry, and so forth. Thus, according to van Creveld:

> Meanwhile the advantages of the defense have been indisputably demonstrated by the Yom Kippur War. Consequently, there is reason to think that battles – though not necessarily campaigns – will become harder to decide in the years to come, and will display a growing tendency to degenerate into slugging matches going on interminably until one or the other side gives way because of sheer exhaustion. Under such conditions, ammunition expenditure is likely to rise enormously as will losses in men and materiel. Fire as opposed to shock action; cover against free movement; slaughter as against maneuver; these, presumably, will characterize the tactics of the near future.[65]

Much of the literature devoted to this subject dwells on the applicability of the lessons of the 1973 conflict to future possible major conflicts in Central Europe as well as between Israel and the Arabs.[66] What the present applicability may be to other cockpits of conflict in the Third World is not clear. It is noteworthy, for instance, that India, only two years before 1973, was able to conduct a rapid, successful war of movement in East Bengal in 1971; the counterpart conflict in the Punjab was much more a stationary slugging match resulting in high *matériel* attrition. The Vietnam–China war appears also to have favoured the defence and attrition; likewise that between Iraq and Iran. In the latter case, however, the protracted stalemate may be due less to the nature of modern weaponry – or for that matter, terrain – than to the skills of the contending forces and to the politically-induced caution of military tactics.

Needless to say, the new PGM weaponry has heretofore had little impact on the resupply requirements associated with guerrilla or counter-insurgency warfare. But, it has been noted that portable SAMs provided the Polisario have wreaked minor havoc on the Moroccan air force, and it is assumed that the same effect could be produced in Afghanistan if the Muslim foes of the USSR were similarly provisioned (particulary regarding attrition of Soviet helicopter gunships).

Generally, the impression is conveyed of increasing resupply requirements as a function of evolving military technology which augurs high rates of attrition. Van Creveld states the assumption as follows:

> While NATO, comprising the richest – in any case, the most advanced – nations on earth still possess the resources at least to prepare for more than the briefest of armed clashes, this is no longer true for most, if not all, other countries. For them, the superiority of the defense and the rates of attrition this imposes means that waging conventional war is simply ceasing to be a feasible option. As the Indo-Pakistani and Arab–Israeli conflicts clearly demonstrated, it will in the future be sheer lunacy for any state except the two superpowers – and if things go on as they do in the present, for any except the Soviet Union alone – to engage in a military adventure on any scale without making sure first of a resupply of ammunition and materiel that, again, only the superpowers and no other state can furnish.[67]

Of course, if such developments were to increase the *deterrent* value of military forces – as they are said also to do with respect to big-power interventions in the Third World – then the overall frequency of conflict might be lessened and the pressures on big powers' arms inventories reduced accordingly.

Surely, the new developments would appear to lessen the prospects for a repeat of Israel's preemptive successes in 1956 and 1967, which, reportedly were explicitly used as models by the Pakistan army in the period preceding 1971. But, if such quick 'victories' are less likely because of emerging weaponry, the kind of 'seize and hold' strategy utilised by Egypt in 1973 – and recently repeated by Iraq – may become a more familiar model, featuring a quick initial offensive of limited depth, followed by reversion to defensive, stationary tactics aimed at causing unacceptable attrition. This has widely been described as a combination of strategic offence and tactical defence. In the Iraq–Iran war, that has resulted in a defensive stalemate, but where the intensity of conflict is so low as to minimise though by no means eliminate arms resupply requirements.

Meanwhile, new technological developments in long-range air transport are also gradually altering the big powers' capacities for arms resupply. The US fleet of C-5 and C-141 transports well demonstrated their astonishing range and load capacities in 1973, even despite the penalties on cargo efficiency caused by the shortage of staging facilities *en route* to the Middle East (since then, the C-141 'stretch' programme and vastly enhanced aerial refuelling capability, along with the C-5 wing strengthening programme have greatly improved the US airlift capability).[68] One recent RAND report has demonstrated that with adequate in-air refuelling, that the C-5 fleet can mount large-scale resupply operations almost anywhere on the globe, so long as access to Diego Garcia and Ascension Island (both British possessions) is maintained.[69] Meanwhile, as noted, the USSR, in its massive airlifts to Angola, Ethiopia, and Afghanistan, demonstrated that it is moving towards equivalent capability hinged primarily on the lumbering but huge Antonov-22. Both sides, meanwhile, are moving ahead with roll-on/roll-off (RO/RO) ships, particularly useful for power projection 'since they deliver military rolling stock in operating condition, reduce cargo-handling time by about 75 per cent, and require no specialised port equipment other than wharves.[70] The US RO/RO capability is growing more slowly than that of its rival, which is expected to deploy some 70 such craft by 1985, constituting a formidable sealift capacity.

But, the impact of increased airlift capacity is also modified by ongoing developments in weaponry. One recent report noted that the new US Abrams tank is so bulky at 60.3 tons, that it cannot be carried aboard any aircraft except the C-5, but which can haul only one at a time. As a result, 'the M-1 can be used only in areas to which it can be sent leisurely by ship, meaning Europe and possibly Korea'.[71] That point could, possibly, be meaningful for resupply contingencies in the future involving users of US tanks, even those who may still be able to afford the likes of the Abrams at $2.5 million apiece.

III CONCLUSION

The previous discussion has illustrated the considerable diversity of the patterns of arms resupply during conflict. Additional data collection and analysis would be required before generalisations might be ventured regarding, for instance, the causal interrelationships between conflict types, pre-conflict arms acquisition patterns, supplier responses during conflict, and post-war shifts of arms clientships and security alignments, not to mention the impact on the outcomes of wars. Then too, further research would be required before generalisations might be established regarding the longitudinal dimensions of these relationships, that is how they have varied in response to such systemic factors as the ebbs and flows of superpower relations, changed power relationships between suppliers and recipients as aggregate groups, the breakdown of alliance bipolarity, and so forth.

Meanwhile, the accompanying summary chart (Table 11.2) is offered for display, if only to illustrate for heuristic purposes what is involved in some of its complexity.

TABLE 11.2 Recent arms resupply patterns

Conflict	Type	Pre-war acquisition style	Supplier resupply policies	Summary impact on war outcome
Iraq v. Iran	Interstate conventional, protracted attrition, initially high- then low-intensity	Predominantly Soviet, some French	Sovs (grudging), Brazil, France, Italy, US. Egypt	Both sides hampered by shortages; Iraq asymmetrically advantaged by resupply diplomacy
		Predominantly US, some UK and Soviet	Soviet-origin arms via Libya and Syria, Israeli	
Morocco v. Polisario	Interstate unconventional, protracted, moderate intensity	Predominantly US, some French, Spanish, Soviet	US restrained supply. France resupplies, no Soviet resupply	Morocco earlier inhibited by US hold on COIN weapons, later relaxed but as yet to no avail.
		Soviet-origin arms via Algeria	Sufficient resupply via Libya and Algeria	
Somoza's Nicaragua v. Sandanistas	Civil war, internal, protracted	US predominantly	US embargoes, pressures Israel to do same–some resupply earlier from Israel and Argentina	US embargo crucial in tipping scales to insurgents.
		Various government and private sources	Well resupplied by Cuba, Iraq, Venezuela, Panama, et al.	
Zaire v. Shaba invaders	Cross-border, combined convention and unconventional; brief but intense	US, France, PRC, Belgium	US restrained in Shaba I, but France and Belgium forthcoming. US less restrained in Shaba II	Zaire sufficiently resupplied to repel invaders after initial setbacks.
		Soviet bloc, probably Cuban conduit in Angola		
Ethiopia v.	Conventional inter-state, changing to unconventional inter-state with much lessened intensity	Predominantly US	US embargo, forces re-equipped with Soviet arms and US-origin *matériel* from	Ethiopian size prevails, abetted by asymmetric advantage of Soviet resupply.

Somalia		Predominantly Soviet	Yugoslavia, Viet, Libya, Israel. Soviet embargo, forces re-equipped with W. European arms plus resupply of Soviet-origin arms from Iraq, Egypt, etc.
PRC v. Vietnam	Conventional inter-state, brief but very intense	Indigenous with old Soviet licenses, some indigenous design	None required
		Predominantly Soviet	Heavy Soviet resupply, basing access as quid pro quo
Rhodesia v. Zimbabwe guerrillas	Guerrilla war, with insurgent side divided in two	Predominantly British, various other	Near-global embargo, but some resupply from S. Africa, private sources
		Soviet and PRC sources, mostly small arms	Soviet, PRC resupply via Tanzania, Mozambique
Arabs v. Israel (1973)	Conventional interstate, short but very intense	Predominantly Soviet	All-out Soviet air and sea lift. Soviet airlift gives initial advantage, later out-balanced by US airlift – crucial to outcome.
		Predominantly US, some French and indigenous	Delayed all-out US resupply, airlift-replacements plus some new weaponry
Pakistan v. India (1971)	Conventional inter-state short but intense	Predominantly US, some PRC, France, USSR	US denies resupply but 3rd party transfers from Iran plus PRC resupply
		Predominantly Soviet significant UK, France, indigenous	Significant Soviet resupply, some from Egypt
			PRC prevails somewhat but at great cost against superior weaponry.
			Soviet arms resupply crucial.
			Embargo assists insurgent victory, but population imbalance overriding factor.
			India asymmetrically advantaged by Soviet resupply.

NOTES AND REFERENCES

1. A different version of this paper was published in the *Jerusalem Journal of International Relations*, vol. 7, no. 3 (1985) and the material used appears here by permission of the Editors. The author gratefully thanks Randy Sones, Catherine Schultz, and Cathy Gees-Larue for research assistance in connection with this article, and also The Liberal Arts Research Office of the Pennsylvania State University for financial assistance.
2. For an elaboration on this point, see the editors' 'The Road to Further Research and Theory in Arms Transfers', in Neuman, S. and Harkavy, R. (eds), *Arms Transfers in the Modern World* (New York: Praeger, 1979), pp. 315–21.
3. See US Arms Control and Disarmament Agency, *World Military Expenditures and Arms Transfers* (Washington DC: USGPO), annual; Stockholm International Peace Research Institute, *The Arms Trade with the Third World* (New York: Humanities Press, 1971); International Institute for Strategic Studies, *The Military Balance* (London: IISS), annual; and Leiss, A. C. et al., *Arms Transfers to Less Developed Countries* C/70-1 (Cambridge, Mass.: MIT Center for International Studies, 1970). For a review of arms transfer data and measurement problems, see Fei, Edward T., 'Understanding Arms Transfers and Military Expenditures: Data Problems', in Neuman, S. and Harkavy, R. (eds), *Arms Transfers in the Modern World* (New York: Praeger, 1979) pp. 37–46; and Lawrence, E. J. and Sherwin, R. G., 'Understanding Arms Transfers through Data Analysis', in Ra'anan, U., Pfaltzgraff, R. and Kemp, G. (eds), *Arms Transfers to the Third World: The Military Buildup in less Industrial Countries* (Boulder, Col.: Westview, 1978).
4. See Neuman and Harkavy, *Arms Transfers in the Modern World* and also various selections in Ra'anan, Pfaltzgraff and Kemp (eds), *Arms Transfers to the Third World: The Military Buildup in Less Industrial Countries*; Cannizzo, C. (ed.) *The Gun Merchants: Politics and Policies of the Major Arms Suppliers* (Elmsford, NY: Pergamon, 1979) and Cahn, A. et al., *Controlling Future Arms Trade* (New York: McGraw-Hill, 1977).
5. Quandt, W., 'Influence Through Arms Supply', in Ra'anan, U. Pfaltzgraff, R. and Kemp, G. (eds), *Arms Transfers to the Third World: The Military Buildup in Less Industrial Countries* (Boulder, Col.: Westview, 1978) pp. 121–30.
6. Leiss, A. C. et al., *Arms Transfers to Less Developed Countries* (Cambridge, Mass., MIT Center for International Studies, 1970).
7. Kemp, G., 'Arms Transfers and the "Back-End" Problem in Developing Countries', in Neuman, S. and Harkavy, R. (eds), *Arms Transfers in the Modern World* (New York: Praeger, 1979) pp. 264–75.
8. Bloomfield, L. and Leiss, A., *Controlling Small Wars: A Strategy for the 1970s* (New York: Knopf, 1969) Appendix.
9. Butterworth, R., *Moderation from Management: International Organizations and Peace* (Pittsburgh: University of Pittsburgh Center for International Studies, 1978).
10. Churchill, R. and Churchill, W., *The Six Day War* (London: William Heinemann, 1967).

11. Thayer, G., *The War Business* (New York: Simon & Schuster, 1969) and Engelmann, B., *The Weapon Merchants* (New York, Crown Publishers, 1964).
12. For a brief recent portrayal of this milieu, see also 'The Private World of an International Arms Dealer', *The New York Times*, 19 January 1980, p. 8.
13. Butterworth, R., *Managing Interstate Conflict, 1945–74* (Pittsburgh: University of Pittsburgh Center for International Studies, 1976).
14. Stockholm International Peace Research Institute, *World Armaments and Disarmament: SIPRI Yearbook 1981* (London: Taylor & Francis, 1981).
15. See, among numerous sources, 'Iraqis Said to Get About 100 Tanks', *The New York Times*, 4 February 1981, p. A4; and 'Focus of Drawn-out Gulf War Shifts Away from the Battlefield', *Washington Post*, 7 December 1980, p. A33.
16. Thayer, G., *The War Business* (New York: Simon & Schuster, 1969).
17. David, S., 'The Realignments of Third World Regimes from One Superpower to the Other', unpublished thesis, Harvard, 1981.
18. Leiss, A. C. et al., *Arms Transfers to Less Developed Countries* (Cambridge, Mass: MIT Center for International Studies, 1970).
19. Harkavy, R., *The Arms Trade and International Systems* (Cambridge, Mass: Ballinger, 1975).
20. Central Intelligence Agency, 'Communist Aid Activities in Non-Communist Less Developed Countries, 1978' (Washington, Sept. 1979).
21. International Institute for Strategic Studies annual, *The Military Balance* (London: IISS).
22. Stockholm International Peace Research Institute, *The Arms Trade Registers* (Cambridge, Mass: MIT Press, 1975).
23. Kemp, G., 'Arms Transfers and the "Back-End" Problem in Developing Countries', pp. 264–75.
24. Brines, R., *The Indo-Pakistani Conflict* (London: Pall Mall, 1968).
25. Harkavy, R., *Pre-emption and Two-Front Conventional Warfare* (Jerusalem: The Hebrew University, 1977) and Rosen, S. and Indyk, M., 'The Temptation to Pre-empt in a Fifth Arab–Israeli War', *Orbis*, vol. 20, no. 2 (Summer 1976).
26. Beattie, K., 'French Policy in the Middle East', Senior Thesis, Kalamazoo College, unpublished, 1973.
27. Moodie, M., *Sovereignty, Security and Arms* (Washington: Georgetown CSIS, 1979) and Neuman, S. and Harkavy, R., 'Into the Crystal Ball: Indigenous Defense Production and the Future of the International Arms Trade', unpublished paper, ISA, Los Angeles, March 1980.
28. See 'Gulf War: Battle of Chiefs', *Washington Post*, 26 April 1981, p. A19, wherein one Iraqi official is quoted as claiming that Iraq was producing 70–80 per cent of the spare parts needed by its army during the war with Iran.
29. Crocker, C., *South Africa's Defense Posture* (Washington: Georgetown CSIS, 1981).
30. Gelb, L., 'Arms Sales', Foreign Policy, No. 25 (1976–7).
31. Stockholm International Peace Research Institute, *The Arms Trade with the Third World* (New York: Humanities Press, 1971).
32. Kemp, 'Arms Transfers and the "Back-End" Problem in Developing Countries', pp. 264–75.

33. Insight Team of the London Times, *The Yom Kippur War* (New York: Doubleday, 1974).
34. For a review and analysis of what is involved in PD 13 and related congressional legislation, see Hammond, P. Y., Louscher, D. J. and Salomon, M. D., 'Controlling US Arms Transfers: The Emerging System', *Orbis*, vol. 23, no. 2 (Summer 1979) pp. 317–52.
35. Brines, R., *The Indo-Pakistani Conflict*.
36. Rubinstein, A., *Red Star on the Nile* (Princeton: Princeton University Press, 1977).
37. See 'Israeli Arms: A Top Export', *The New York Times*, 15 March 1981, p. 9.
38. See 'For Brazil, an Embarrasing Tale of Intrigue', *The New York Times*, 23 June 1981, p. A12.
39. Holmes, J., 'A Liberal Moods Interpretation of American Diplomatic History', paper delivered at ISA meeting, Los Angeles, March 1980, and Klingberg, F., 'The Historical Alternation of Moods in American Foreign Policy', in *World Politics* IV (January 1952) pp. 239–73.
40. Atwater, E., *American Regulation of Arms Exports* (New York: Carnegie Endowment for Peace, 1941) and Stedman, M., *Exporting Arms: The Federal Arms Export Administration 1935–45* (New York: Kings Crown Press, 1947).
41. Hammond, Louscher and Salomon, 'Controlling US Arms Transfers: The Emerging System', pp. 317–52.
42. Louscher, D. and Salomon, M., 'The Failure of CATT: A Bureaucratic Perspective on Policy Reform', paper delivered at ISA, Los Angeles, March 1980.
43. 'US Military Aid to Zaire is Expected to Increase Because of Soviet and Cuban Roles in Other Countries', *New York Times*, 20 June 1976, p. 13; 'Decision Near on Disputed Aid to Zaire', *New York* Times, 21 January 1976, p. 3; and 'US Will Discuss Arms Plan to Aid Kenya and Zaire', *New York Times*, 14 June 1976, p. 1.
44. 'US Appears to Take More Neutral Stance on Sahara War', *Washington Post*, 29 May 1977, p. A12; and 'US Said to Defer Plan for Plane Sales to Morocco', *New York Times*, 28 February 1978, p. 6.
45. 'US Steps Up Offers of Arms to Africans; Ready to Aid Sudan', *New York Times*, 28 July 1977, p. 1; 'Arming Friends to Disarm Foes', New York Times, 31 July 1977, Section 4, p. 1; 'US, Paris Agree to Help Africans Defend Selves', *Washington Post*, 30 May 1978, p. 1.
46. 'US Role in Zaire Grows with Gabon, Senegal Airlift', *Washington Post*, 9 June 1978, p. A21; and 'US Will Fly Moroccan Units to Help Zaire', *Washington Post*, 3 June 1978, p. 1; 'Carter Takes Middle Path in Zaire', *Christian Science Monitor*, 22 May 1978, p. 1.
47. See 'Direction of New Nicaragua Unclear', *Washington Post*, 24 July 1979, p. A10; and an additional *Washington Post* article, 20 August 1979, p. A18.
48. See 'US Allows Single Arms Sale to Morocco', *Washington Post*, 10 February 1979, p. A17; and 'Carter Aides Split on Issue of Arms Sales to Morocco', *New York Times*, 19 October 1979, p. A7. For a recent update, see 'Sahara War: US Rallies Behind Morocco', *New York Times* 18 February 1980, p. A3.

49. Safire, W., 'Saleh in our Alley', *New York Times*, 3 Dec. 1979, p. 25.
50. See, for instance, 'Arms Sales: Boom Time', *The Economist*, 4 July 1981, p. 26.
51. Haselkorn, A., *The Evolution of Soviet Security Strategy: 1965–1975* (New York: Crane, Russak, 1978) and Harkavy R., *Great Power Competition for Overseas Bases* (Elmsford NY: Pergamon, 1982).
52. Dismukes, B. and McConnell, J. (eds), *Soviet Naval Diplomacy* (New York: Pergamon, 1979).
53. For an analysis of Soviet access routes to the Horn, see 'Airlift to Ethiopia', *Newsweek*, 23 January 1978, p. 35.
54. See 'A Year of Iran–Iraq War Seems to Bring Impasse', *New York Times*, 23 September 1981, p. A2; and 'Iraqis Resume Pumping of Oil by Pipeline Across Turkey', *New York Times*, 21 November 1980, p. A14.
55. See 'Israel–Iran Arms Deal Reportedly Exposed', *Portland Press Herald*, 27 July 1981, p. 2.
56. For additional information, reporting on a declassified DIA study, see 'Study: Soviet Arms Output Triple US', *Philadelphia Inquirer*, 7 September 1981, p. 8-B.
57. Whaley, B., Unpublished ms. on Clandestine Soviet Arms Shipments.
58. See 'US–Israel Strategic Link: Both Sides Take Stock', *New York Times*, 2 October 1981, p. A8.
59. Haselkorn, *The Evolution of Soviet Security Strategy: 1965–75*.
60. Kolodziej, E., 'France and the Arms Trade', *International Affairs*, January 1980, pp. 54–72.
61. Rubinstein, *Red Star on the Nile*.
62. See 'Israeli Arms: A Top Export', *New York Times*, 15 March 1981, p. 9.
63. Creveld, M. van, *Military Lessons of the Yom Kippur War: Historical Perspectives* (Washington: Georgetown CSIS, 1975). Quester, G., *Offense and Defense in the International System* (New York: John Wiley, 1977) and Fuller, J. R. C., *A Military History of the Western World*, 3 vols (New York: Minerva Press, 1955).
64. See Creveld, M. van, *Military Lessons of the Yom Kippur War*, p. viii.
65. Ibid., p. 39.
66. Rosen, S. and Indyk, M., 'The Proliferation of New Land-Based Technologies: Implications for Local Military Balances', in Neuman, S. and Harkavy, R., *Arms Transfers in the Modern World* and Hudson, C., 'The Impact of Precision-Guided Munitions on Arms Transfers and International Stability', in Neuman, S. and Harkavy, R., *Arms Transfers in the Modern World*.
67. Creveld, M. van, *Military Lessons of the Yom Kippur War*, p. 48.
68. Joint Chiefs of Staff, *United States Military Posture* (Washington: USGPO, 1981).
69. Dadant, P., 'Shrinking International Airspace as a Problem for Future Air Movements – A Briefing' (Santa Monica: Rand, 1978) R-2178-AF.
70. Joint Chiefs of Staff, *United States Military Posture for FY 1982* (Washington: USGPO, 1981) p. 47.
71. 'Arming for the '80s', *Time Magazine*, 27 July 1981, p. 15.

Part Four
The Anatomy of Arms Industries

12 Efficiency, Industry and Alternative Weapons Procurement Policies

Keith Hartley
UNIVERSITY OF YORK

I INTRODUCTION[1]

NATO weapons markets are by no means Pareto-efficient. They are characterised by government-created monopolies and trade barriers, and are more appropriately analysed as political markets (i.e. a study in public choice). Weapons procurement policy is determined by agents in the political market place, with vote-sensitive domestic governments influenced by budget-maximising defence agencies and industry departments, as well as by producer groups in the form of weapons contractors. Any assessment of efficiency is complicated by two factors. First, procurement policy usually embraces a variety of diverse and often vaguely-specified objectives, including advanced technology, jobs, the balance of payments and the 'avoidance of undue dependence on foreigners'. Second, weapons contracts are usually subject to state imposed profit controls, so that profitability cannot be used as an efficiency indicator. This paper considers some aspects of the efficiency of both weapons industries and procurement policies. Aerospace is taken as a case study. A starting point is an analysis of the differences in efficiency between the American and European aerospace industries. What, for example, are the efficiency implications of alternative market structures and associated national procurement policies? Consideration is then given to two specific hypotheses, relating to labour hoarding and development time scales. Finally, some of the cost implications of alternative procurement policies are presented as part of any information framework for public choices.

II THE EFFICIENCY OF THE US AND EUROPEAN AEROSPACE INDUSTRIES: SOME QUESTIONNAIRE RESULTS

The results of an interview–questionnaire survey are summarised in Table 12.1, where the replies are classified by country of origin.

Most of the respondents agreed that the European aerospace firms were less efficient than their US rivals. Five major explanations were given for this differential efficiency:

(i) *Lower labour productivity and more labour hoarding in Europe.* Considerable emphasis was placed on European labour market problems. These embraced trade union constraints on hiring and firing (hence more labour hoarding), a reluctance to use shift working, immobility and a European concern with job preservation rather than production. The result was that during the 1970s, European productivity was estimated to be between one-third and two-thirds of that in the US aerospace industry (value added per head)[2]. Inevitably, international comparisons of productivity are complicated by differences in inputs, outputs, type and mix of products. It can also be misleading to base comparisons on the best foreign enterprises rather than the average.[3] Nevertheless, the US aerospace industry is reputed to benefit from its hire and fire policy and a mobile labour force which results in a greater employment elasticity. For example, Boeing reduced its labour force from 142 700 in 1968 to 56 300 in 1971, equivalent to a decrease of 61 per cent; similarly, General Dynamics reduced employment from 103 600 in 1969 to 60 900 in 1972, which was a 41 per cent reduction. In contrast, the British Aerospace company reduced employment from 81 200 in 1969 to 71 200 in 1972 (a 12 per cent reduction), whilst the UK aerospace industry required a 16-year period to reduce employment by 35 per cent (311 900 in 1957 to 201 700 in 1973). Such stylised facts are suggestive rather than conclusive and they provide the basis for testable hypotheses about employment behaviour in different nations' aerospace industries.

TABLE 12.1 *Questionnaire evidence on efficiency*

1. European aircraft industry: what are its distinguishing features?

(i) Less efficient than US	YES	NO
US responses	9	2
European responses:		
(a) airframe and helicopter firms	5	3
(b) buyers and suppliers	6	3
Total	11	6

(ii) If *yes*, why:

	Number of responses	
	Europe	USA
(a) Lacks scale economies from long runs.	6	5
(b) Smaller R & D teams.	1	—
(c) Lower labour productivity for a given output.	7	2
(d) More labour hoarding.	4	4
(e) Poorer weather in UK.	1	—
(f) Less capital per worker.	4	5
(g) Behaviour, organisation and attitudes of UK procurement agency.	1	—
(h) Others (specify)	2	6
(i) Lags in technology, especially in production.		
(ii) Reluctance to use shift working.	—	3
(iii) Europeans want job preservation, cannot hire and fire, and labour is immobile.	—	3
(iv) Europeans slower in management decisions and not aggressive sellers.	—	3

2. Main features of US industry as seen by your organisation?

	Europe	USA
(a) More efficient.	7	2
(b) Shorter time scales.	2	1
(c) Cheaper aircraft.	3	1
(d) Higher priced spares.	—	—
(e) More competitive.	3	7

(i) The results are extracts from a longer questionnaire based on an interview survey of five US aerospace companies, the major European airframe, engine and helicopter firms, together with a group of suppliers and officials in NATO, NAMMA and the UK Ministry of Defence. Interviews were conducted during 1977–80.

(ii) Numbers refer to number of responses. The results are based on a sample of 15 European respondents and 11 US respondents. In question 1, the 17 European respondents is explained by 2 who replied *yes* on long runs and *no* on short runs.[16]

(ii) *The European industry lacks the scale economies from long runs.* Output is a major determinant of productivity and unit costs through its effects on both scale and learning economies. For combat aircraft, a US output of 1000–2000 of a type is typical (e.g. F-16, F-18), with over 5000 units not unknown (e.g. F-4); production rates average 12–30 units per month, sometimes reaching almost 60 per month. In contrast, a typical UK domestic order for a combat aircraft might be 200–300 units at a rate of 2–4 per month. Similarly, the initial F-16 order from the four European nations totalled 348 units compared with a USAF planned buy of almost 1400. Such scale differentials emphasise the problems confronting the European producers and also indicate the opportunities for cost savings from alternative procurement policies (e.g. buying off-the-shelf; joint projects).

Learning is a major source of productivity improvements in aerospace. Typically, US labour learning curves have steeper slopes, averaging 75 per cent for aircraft compared with 80 per cent in Europe. Studies of US and UK learning curves show that unit man hours are slightly higher in America during the early stages of output, say up to the 50th unit; but then the USA's steeper learning curve gives them an advantage, especially since the UK curves tend to 'flatten out' when output exceeds 100 units[4]. Certainly some of the firms interviewed claimed that on unit production costs, British producers could be cheaper than the USA up to an output of 150–200 units; but above 200 units, America is superior on both man-hours and unit production costs. Nor is UK experience unique and learning curves for other European firms tend to 'flatten out'. In comparison, it is claimed that US learning curves are 'continuously falling'. The shape and flat portion of European learning curves might reflect the payments system,[5] modifications, reduced productivity at the end of the line and the desire to protect jobs.[6] It might also reflect Europe's general lack of continuous experience in producing large-scale outputs. However, the interview study provided no conclusive support for any of these hypotheses.

(iii) *Less capital per worker.* A substantial number of respondents suggested that the European industry has less capital per worker and the vintage of its capital stock is believed to be older. Once again, there were exceptions to these broad generalisations. For example, a Rolls-Royce study found that in three out of five US firms investigated, the average age of machine tools was greater than in Rolls.[7]

(iv) *Europe lags in technology, particularly in production work.* It was claimed that the US industry has a substantial technical lead, possibly in the region of 7–10 years. In this context, both co-production and joint projects are partly justified in terms of their alleged technical benefits to Europe. Licensed and co-production involves US firms supplying Europe with manufacturing technology, such as the experience of working with new materials, precision machining and new management techniques (e.g. F-16)[8]. But such technology transfers from the USA to Europe (or vice versa) are not 'free gifts'. The initially estimated co-production premium on the F-16 was $1.07 m per copy, so that the Europeans were willing to pay an extra $370m to acquire the technology and other benefits associated with their purchase of 348 aircraft (1975 prices). Aerospace firms will willingly supply technology on the basis of the profitability of the transaction. The result is an international market in technology transfer in which firms aim to establish property rights in their valuable ideas through patents licenses and by associating technology with the sale of aerospace equipment (e.g. co-production; industrial collaboration; work-sharing). In supplying technology, an airframe firm has every inducement to offer a purchasing nation its less valuable (older) knowledge, as well as aiming to shift any technology transfer to its suppliers (i.e. sub-contractors lose technology). However, the international market in technology transfer is affected by governments. Firms generally acquire new technology at zero price through the state funding of new weapons projects. As a result, they are more willing to sell such technology, subject to government constraints on the range of eligible buyers. In addition, firms have considerable opportunities for influencing budget-maximising bureaucracies and vote-conscious governments to fund new advances in technology.

(v) *The US industry is more competitive.* American producers emphasised the competitive nature of their industry, as reflected in alternative sources of ideas (i.e. R & D), the existence of rival suppliers and sub-contractors, and firms which are alleged to be more aggressive and responsive to customer requirements. This has implications for procurement policy in European nations.

TABLE 12.2 Largest companies in Europe and USA, 1980

Company	Sales (millions ECU, current prices)	Employment per man, ECU,	Productivity (sales current prices)
USA			
Boeing	6772	106 300	63 707
McDonnell-Douglas	4358	82 550	52 792
Lockheed	3876	74 600	51 957
Pratt and Whitney	3874(e)	70 000(e)	55 343
General Dynamics	3407	84 400	40 367
Europe			
British Aerospace	2378	77 500	30 684
Aerospatiale	2244	34 422	65 191
Rolls-Royce	2102	58 800	35 748
Dassault-Breguet	1830	15 660	116 858
MBB	1309	26 287	49 797

Notes: ECU = European Currency Units; e = estimate; productivity figures are based on sales: ideally value-added data are required, otherwise comparisons are distorted by differences in the amount of bought-out components.

SOURCE *The European Eurospace Industry: Trading Position and Figures* (Brussels: Commission of the European Communities, October 1981).

The successful US aerospace industry, characterised by large firms with both military and civil activities, has often been regarded as the model or 'ideal' for Europe: hence the major European nations have aimed to create larger firms. Table 12.2 shows the sales, employment and productivity data for the top five companies in America and Europe. Only the state-owned British Aerospace company approached the size of the top US firms (note its relative productivity). But a correlation between size and success in the USA does not necessarily imply causation. Optimum firm size will be determined by technology, relative factor prices, the mix of R & D and production, the type of aircraft (e.g. small, simple fighters or complex supersonic bombers and transports), delivery time scales and the degree of specialisation amongst sub-contractors. Doubts about the simple case for large units are reflected in the example of Dassault-Breguet which is generally regarded as a successful combat aircraft firm, with some 15 000 employees! Nonetheless, evidence from the US industry provides two policy guidelines for European nations. First, large firms with employment ex-

TABLE 12.3 Concentration in the European and US industries, 1979

Country	Percentage of total aerospace industry turnover accounted for by:	
	Largest company (%)	Three largest companies (%)
USA	22.8	49.4
UK	38.5	77.7
France	41.2	77.8
W. Germany	40.9	69.1
Italy	49.3	87.2*
Belgium	36.7	73.9*
EEC	15.3	37.9

*Based on the two largest companies.

SOURCE *The European Eurospace Industry: Trading Position and Figures* (Brussels: Commission of the European Communities, October 1981).

ceeding 100 000 are capable of competing successfully in world markets. On this basis, European joint ventures which aim to achieve US scales of output (e.g. Panavia Tornado) need not necessarily encounter managerial dis-economies. Second, in creating larger domestic firms, the European nations have encountered the classic trade-off between efficient scale and competition. Evidence on concentration ratios is shown in Table 12.3. For the EEC, concentration ratios seem to be comparable with those in the USA, but this gives a misleading impression of the market structure within each European state. In other words, there are possibilities for creating a competitive aerospace market at the EEC level. In the absence of competition, firms have opportunities to pursue non-profit objectives. Indeed, the existence of state subsidies and other forms of government support and protection (including public ownership), might induce aerospace firms to become subsidy-maximisers, seeking revenue from their national governments rather than aiming to sell their products in competitive world markets.[9]

Clearly, the five explanations offered above are not independent. Some are related to the scale of output (e.g. labour productivity; capital intensity), whilst others reflect differences in the structure and competitiveness of labour and product markets in America and Europe. Equally, there were exceptions to the general finding that European firms were less efficient than their US rivals. From the interview study, Europe appears to have a comparative advantage in specific product groups such as avionics, ejector seats, engines, small guided weapons. VTOL technology and possibly helicopters.[10] It was also interesting to note the factors which were *not* mentioned as explanations for any differences in efficiency between the American and European industries. These included the size of European R&D teams, the behaviour of the UK procurement agency, and the UK's weather (e.g. via its effects on flight testing programmes and the necessity to work under cover)!

Questionnaire results are, of course, usually criticised for bias, for reflecting beliefs and for failing to hold constant other relevant influences. Whilst the results of the interview–questionnaire study provide useful insights (especially where data are unavailable), they are no more than the first stage in the process of constructing testable hypotheses about industry performance. Data are available for testing two hypotheses, relating to labour hoarding and development times.

III LABOUR HOARDING

The interview–questionnaire evidence suggested that European aerospace firms hoard labour whilst their US rivals have a competitive advantage from their 'hire and fire' policy. This hypothesis was tested using a standard employment function to estimate employment elasticities and the speed at which labour adjusts to its planned level:[11]

$$\text{Log } L_t = \log a - g\frac{\lambda}{\alpha} t + \frac{\lambda}{\alpha} \log Q + (1 - \lambda) \log L_{t-1} \qquad (1)$$

where L is employment, t is a time-trend, representing capital stock and technology, Q is output, g is a technology coefficient, λ is the speed at which actual employment adjusts to its desired level ($0 < \lambda < 1$) and α is the elasticity of output with respect to employment.

Two employment elasticities can be distinguished. First, an unadjusted elasticity shown by the regression coefficient on output (ε'). Second, a 'true' elasticity (ε'') which does not include the adjustment process (λ) and which is the reciprocal of the short-run returns to labour ($\varepsilon'' = 1/\alpha$). Three sets of hypotheses relating to labour hoarding were tested:

(i) *Hypothesis I: European aerospace firms have lower employment elasticities and adjust more slowly (λ) than their US rivals.* Data

TABLE 12.4 Employment in aerospace industries

Dependent variable: Employment by industry ($\log L_t$)	Coefficient of $\log Q$ (ε')	R^2
Belgium	0.374† (0.144)	0.456
France	−0.028 (0.034)	0.079
Italy	0.294* (0.079)	0.634
Netherlands	0.146 (0.200)	0.062
UK	−0.084 (0.134)	0.047
W. Germany	0.282† (0.113)	0.439
EEC	−0.001 (0.068)	0.00005
Canada	0.774* (0.162)	0.791
USA	0.757* (0.146)	0.769

Notes:
(i) Estimated from equation $\log L = \log a + b \log Q$, where L = employment and Q = output in million ECU, 1975 prices and exchange rates.
(ii) Data from 1970–79 for each nation's aerospace industry.
(iii) Standard errors are shown in brackets. *Significant at 1 per cent level; †significant at 5 per cent level.

SOURCE *The European Eurospace Industry: Trading Position and Figures* (Brussels: Commission of the European Communities, October 1981).

limitations prevented satisfactory tests. However, limited empirical results at the industry level provided tentative support for the hypothesis. Table 12.4 shows that employment in the North American aerospace industries was much more responsive to variations in output. In contrast, the British and French industries showed no statistically significant relationship between output and employment.

Further tests based on the US and UK airframe *firms* are reported in Table 12.5. Some consistency can be seen with the results on industry elasticities. There was, though, substantial heterogeneity amongst the US firms, both in terms of the significance of the coefficient on output and its magnitude. In addition, where the

TABLE 12.5 *Employment in American and British airframe firms*

Dependent variable log L	Coefficients of:			R^2
	t	log Q	log $L_t - 1$	
1. British Aerospace		0.164		0.254
		(0.089)		
2. British Aerospace	0.005	−0.015	0.822†	0.398
	(0.004)	(0.109)	(0.349)	
3. Boeing		0.279		0.044
		(0.305)		
4. Boeing	−0.014	0.259	0.609†	0.581
	(0.014)	(0.366)	(0.253)	
5. General Dynamics		0.815*		0.937
		(0.064)		
6. General Dynamics	0.003	0.963*	−0.197	0.941
	(0.005)	(0.165)	(0.207)	
7. Lockheed		0.549		0.175
		(0.281)		
8. Lockheed	−0.008	−0.159	0.792*	0.776
	(0.005)	(0.237)	(0.166)	
9. McDonnell-Douglas		0.627*		0.396
		(0.183)		
10. McDonnell-Douglas	−0.018	0.445	0.479	0.776
	(0.009)	(0.253)	(0.232)	
11. Northrop		0.492*		0.610
		(0.093)		
12. Northrop	−0.004	0.424	0.277	0.521
	(0.019)	(0.363)	(0.244)	

Notes:
(i) Estimated from equation (1) and from equation log L = log a + b log Q, with output in constant prices, 1975 = 100.
(ii) t = 1969–81 for British Aerospace; 1967–79 for General Dynamics and 1960–79 for remaining firms.
(iii) In equation (7), the output coefficient is almost significant at the 5 per cent level; similarly with the coefficient of L_{t-1} in equation (10).
(iv) R^2 is adjusted for degrees of freedom in all the multiple regressions.
(v) There was positive serial correlation in equations (3), (4) and (9).
(vi) Standard errors are shown in brackets. *Significant at 1 per cent level; †significant at 5 per cent level.

lagged dependent variable was significant, the British firm adjusted more slowly than its US rivals.

(ii) *Hypothesis II: Within an economy, aerospace industries have lower employment elasticities and are slower adjusters than non-defence industries.* This hypothesis was tested for the UK engin-

TABLE 12.6 Labour hoarding in the UK

Industry	Employment elasticities ε'	Employment elasticities ε''	Lagged adjustment λ	$\bar{R}^2$
1. *Vehicles*	0.196†	0.335	0.586	0.942
(a) Aerospace	0.235†	1.263	0.186*	0.949
(b) Motor vehicles	0.339*	0.545	0.621*	0.905
(c) Wheeled tractors, motor cycles, etc.	0.557†	0.557	−0.020*	0.987
2. *Shipbuilding*	0.26	1.033	0.259*	0.942
3. *Metal Goods*	0.371*	0.855	0.434*	0.887
4. *Electrical Engineering*	0.409*	1.207	0.339*	0.804
(a) Electrical machinery	0.394	0.545	0.723	0.866
(b) Insulated wires, cables, electronics, radio and radar.	0.336†	0.939	0.358*	0.873
(c) Broadcasting equipment, domestic appliances.	0.508†	0.527	0.964	0.655
5. *Mechanical Engineering*	0.479*	1.039	0.461*	0.906
(a) Agricultural machinery	0.345†	0.801	0.431*	0.797
(b) Metal-working machine tools	0.599*	0.877	0.683	0.909
(c) Ordnance and small arms	0.397	1.355	0.293*	0.791
6. *Instrument Engineering*	0.255†	0.261	0.976	0.169

Notes:
(i) Time trend 1959–76 based on equation (1) above.
(ii) *Significant at 1 per cent level; † significant at 5 per cent level.
(iii) $\bar{R}^2$ is adjusted for degrees of freedom.
(iv) Equations 4(a) and 4(c) were estimated using Cochrane–Orcutt iteration: where the estimate of rho was significant the CORC result is reported; otherwise OLS was used.

SOURCE Hartley, K. and Lynk, E., *Labour Demand and Allocation in the UK Engineering Industry: Disaggregation Structural Change and Defence Reviews*, (University of York, Mimeo, 1982)

eering industry and the results are reported in Table 12.6. It can be seen that a disaggregated analysis of industrial groupings (e.g. vehicles) reveals a substantial amount of heterogeneity. The unadjusted estimates (ε') show that aerospace has one of the lowest employment elasticities in the group. However, using the true estimates (ε''), the results are reversed and most industries had lower employment elasticities than aerospace. There was, though, support for the slow adjustment process (λ). Aerospace together with the other defence-intensive industries, namely, electronics, shipbuilding and the ordnance group, were relatively slow adjusters. Such slow adjustment might reflect the contractual arrangements for Government defence work. In non-competitive markets with state profit regulation, cost-based contracts can be used to finance labour hoarding.[12]

(iii) *Hypothesis III: A shock effect is required to induce the aerospace industry to release labour.* This hypothesis was also tested for the UK engineering industry. During the years 1965–8 and 1974–5, a series of major UK Defence Reviews aimed to reduce current and future military expenditure and these were used to represent a shock effect. The objective of the Reviews was to release resources, especially skilled manpower, from domestic weapons contractors and the armed forces, so enabling an expansion of civil employment, with apparently favourable effects on exports, import-saving and domestic investment. To test for any once-and-for-all 'shake-out' effects of the Defence Reviews, dummy variables were incorporated into the standard employment function. It was predicted that the defence-intensive aerospace industry would lose labour. Examples of the results are shown in Table 12.7. The defence based sectors of aerospace, electronics, ordnance and shipbuilding provided no obvious support for the shake-out or shock effect hypothesis. In fact, there were indications of the opposite effect with these industries appearing to acquire labour. The aerospace industry responded to cancellations by withdrawing work from sub-contractors, increasing exports as well as by obtaining work-sharing arrangements and new weapons projects (e.g. collaborative ventures). Significantly, UK firms have often claimed that a major 'benefit' of collaborative projects is that they are much more difficult to cancel! Such attitudes and responses might be more consistent with a public choice explanation of the adjustment of military contractors to Defence Reviews. Elsewhere, Table 12.7 shows that only instrument engineering and possibly the wheeled tractors group released labour during the Defence Reviews. At the same time, a number of industries in the electrical and mechnical engineering group gained manpower. However, the absence of a shock effect or shake-out from the weapons industries does not mean that the Defence Reviews have failed to release labour. Table 12.6 provided evidence of a positive relationship between output and employment in the aerospace and electronics sectors. Thus, where the Defence Reviews have reduced future weapons ex-

TABLE 12.7 The effects of UK Defence Reviews on employment

Industry	Coefficients of:				$\bar{R}^2$
	DV1	DV2	DV3	DV4	
1. *Vehicles*					
(a) Aerospace				0.025 (1.774)	0.957
(b) Motor vehicles				−0.014 (1.458)	0.913
(c) Wheeled tractors, motor cycles, etc.		−0.043 (1.959)			0.989
2. *Shipbuilding*			0.019 (1.613)		0.949
3. *Metal Goods*	0.012 (1.418)				0.895
4. *Electrical Engineering*		0.023† (2.798)			0.875
(a) Electrical machinery		0.037† (2.160)			0.967
(b) Insulated wires, cables, electronics, radio and radar.		0.027 (2.082)			0.901
(c) Broadcasting equipment, domestic appliances.			−0.012 (0.757)		0.641
5. *Mechanical Engineering*	0.037* (3.431)				0.951
(a) Agricultural machinery			0.028† (2.236)		0.848
(b) Metal-working machine tools	0.051* (3.753)				0.956
(c) Ordnance and small arms			0.041* (4.019)		0.949
6. *Instrument Engineering*		−0.032* (3.198)			0.530

Notes:
(i) Only the dummy variables are reported. The estimates were derived from log-linear employment equations as in (1) above with the addition of a dummy variable for the Defence Reviews.
(ii) The dummy variables are DV1 = 1 for 1965–8, 1974–5 and 0 elsewhere; DV2 = 1 for 1964–5, 1968, 1974–6 and 0 elsewhere; DV3 = 1 for 1963–4, 1967, 1973–4 (i.e. $DV2_{t-1}$); DV4 = 1 for 1966–9, 1975–6 and 0 elsewhere (i.e. $DV1_{t+1}$).
(iii) Equations (4c) and (5c) were estimated using Cochrane–Orcutt iteration.
(iv) Figures in brackets are *t* ratios.
(v) Remaining details as in Table 12.6.

penditure, they will have achieved a corresponding reduction in the planned manpower requirements of the defence industries.[13]

IV DEVELOPMENT TIME SCALES AND EUROPEAN JOINT VENTURES

It is often claimed that collaborative projects will enable the European nations to compete with the US aerospace industry. Such a claim can be evaluated by considering a variety of performance indicators for joint aerospace projects, including their scale of output, exports, magnitude of cost savings, escalation and development time scales. Pairwise comparisons are one research method enabling a comparative evaluation of collaborative ventures and similar national projects. Difficulties cannot be avoided, especially the need to hold constant other relevant influences. For example, projects are not identical and there differences in the resources allocated to them and in their urgency.[14] Even so, comparisons can be made and this section concentrates on one readily observable aspect of industrial performance, namely, development time scales.

It has been suggested that a joint project takes longer to develop than a national venture. Three indicators can be used to test this hypothesis, namely, pairwise studies and comparisons with the average development time for UK or US aircraft. Table 12.8 shows some of the evidence for aircraft:

(i) On a pairwise basis, Tornado required over twice as long to develop as the US Fl-11 and F-15 aircraft. Similarly, the Alpha Jet required almost an extra four years compared with the UK Hawk, whilst the Airbus needed 15 months longer than the Boeing 747.
(ii) The average development time for joint aircraft projects was about one year longer than required for UK military aircraft. Only the Jaguar was undertaken in a shorter time than the UK average for combat aircraft.
(iii) All the joint projects required longer development periods than the average for US military and civil aircraft.

Thus, it seems that joint European aircraft projects require longer development periods compared with national programmes. But before any conclusions are made about the relative efficiency of joint ventures, other relevant influences have to be considered. Projects

TABLE 12.8 Aircraft development times

Project	Total development time
Joint projects	
Concorde (UK–F)	13 years 2 months
Jaguar (UK–F)	7 years
Tornado (UK–WG–I)	12 years
Alpha Jet (F–WG trainer)	9 years
Airbus	5 years
National projects	
Hawk (UK trainer)	5 years 1 month
Mirage F1 (F)	9 years
F1-11 (USA)	4 years 6 months
F-15 (USA)	5 years 11 months
Boeing 747 (USA)	3 years 9 months
Average development times for (1955–69):	
(a) US military aircraft	6 years 3 months
(b) UK military aircraft	8 years 4 months
(c) US civil aircraft	3 years 7 months
(d) UK civil aircraft	4 years 4 months

SOURCES Elstub *Productivity of the National Aircraft Effort* (London: HMSO, 1969); Taylor, J. W. R. (ed.), *Jane's All the World's Aircraft* (London: Janes Publishing Co., 1981).

differ in their complexity, priority, resource costs, and different governments might be pursuing alternative policy objectives (e.g. the acquisition of advanced technology; entry into the EEC; lengthy development might be the preferred policy).[15]

V CONCLUSION: THE COSTS OF ALTERNATIVE POLICIES

In purchasing weapons, nations are confronted with a set of policy alternatives:

(i) *Independence versus free trade.* Complete independence is costly and involves sacrificing the potential gains from international specialisation and trade. It has been estimated that NATO weapons standardisation policies leading to the exploitation of scale economies and the gains from trade are likely to reduce unit costs by at least 20 per cent. Further savings are available from the aboliton of any 'duplicate' R & D and from economies in life-cycle costs.[16]

(ii) *Licensed production and sharing production work*. These involve the domestic manufacture of another nation's weapons, either wholly or in part. Generally, the result is higher costs than if the weapon had been purchased directly off-the-shelf. The typical cost penalties for any form of shared production work are in the range +10 per cent to +50 per cent, with the lower bound estimate applying to advanced nations and the higher figure to less-developed countries. Usually, the cost penalties reflect the absence of learning economies and relatively short production runs.[16]

(iii) *Joint projects* involving the sharing of both R & D and production work between member nations of the club. In the ideal case, there are reputed to be savings in development expenditures and reduced unit production costs associated with a larger output as nations pool their orders. But actual joint ventures usually involve departures from the 'ideal' case. Compared with a national project, they can result in higher R & D costs, possibly approaching an extra 30 per cent, and production inefficiencies (X-inefficiency) in the region of an additional 1–10 per cent for a given output.[17]

Proposals for improving the efficiency and performance of NATO weapons markets have to recognise that public choices are made in political markets and that governments might regard the existing 'distortions' as worthwhile (cf. second-best). Nevertheless, there are opportunities for efficiency improvements. One possibility would be the creation of a competitive free trade area in both weapons and civil goods, so leading to gains from international exchange based on specialisation and comparative advantage. In this way, resource allocation would not be distorted through restricting free trade to weapons. Such a solution would also have to be associated with internationally agreed arrangements for compensating the potential losers (e.g. labour adjustment policies). In addition, there are opportunities for introducing efficiency incentives into the employment contracts of bureaucrats working in national procurement agencies and the armed forces. The aim would be to provide inducements and rewards for not spending (e.g. to avoid gold plating on weapons) and for providing governments with more information on the cost implications of alternative weapons procurement policies. In this context, each nation's armed forces might be given a fixed budget for a specified period and instructed to buy equipment for its needs, shopping around as a competitive buyer. Other government departments would then be responsible for employment and technology objectives. Without such policy changes, the worry is that proposals for 'improving' the operation of NATO weapons markets will be dominated by equity, rather than efficiency, criteria.

NOTES AND REFERENCES

1. The author is most grateful for comments from Professor E. Deutsch, and participants at the IEA Conference, to Ted Lynk and Eileen Sutcliffe and for support from Dr F. Welter, NATO and from the SSRC Public Sector Studies Programme at York. The usual disclaimers apply.
2. Commission, 'Action Programme for the European Aeronautical Sector', *Bulletin of the European Communities*, Supplement No. 11, (Luxembourg: Commission of the European Communities, 1975). Harvey, R. A., 'Learning to Improve Productivity and Cut Costs', *The Aeronautical Journal*, Royal Aeronautical Society (London, May 1981).
3. Hartley, K., 'Defence and Advanced Technology', in Dosser, D., Gowland, D. and Hartley, K. (eds), *The Collaboration of Nations* (Oxford: Martin Robertson, 1982).
4. Jefferson, P., 'Productivity Comparisons with the USA: Where do we Differ?', *The Aeronautical Journal*, Royal Aeronautical Society, London (May 1981).
5. For example, premium bonuses cannot be revised downwards. In the early stages of production, workers might 'go slow' to obtain favourable bonus rates. Also, the UK does not continuously redesign jobs to reflect organisational learning, since this would involve changing labour rates (upwards). The steeper US learning curves are achieved with little use of payment-by-results systems.
6. Harvey, R., 'Analysis of Contributory Factors in Aircraft Production Learning', *Industrial Applications of Learning Curves and Progress Functions* (London: Institution of Radio and Electronic Engineers, December 1981).
7. Rolls-Royce, *Report on Visit to the USA*, private data (Specifications and Brochures Department, Aero Division, Derby, 1978).
8. Udis, B., 'Technology Transfer in the Case of the F16 Military Aircraft', in Gee, S. (ed.), *Technology Transfer in Industrialised Countries* (The Netherlands: Sijthoff and Noordhoff, 1979).
9. Hartley, K. and Tisdell, C., *Micro-Economic Policy* (London: J. Wiley, 1981).
10. See Table 12.1, Q1(i), where the European responses are classified by buyers and different types of firms.
11. The model is derived from a production function with capital and

technology given in the short run and approximated by an exponential time-trend; also actual employment adjusts to its desired level with a simple lag adjustment (18). Alternative specifications, including factor prices, have been estimated (13).
12. Hartley, K. and Watt, P., 'Profits, Regulation and the UK Aerospace Industry', *Journal of Industrial Economics* (June 1981).
13. Hartley, K. and Lynk, E., *Labour Demand and Allocation in the UK Engineering Industry: Disaggregation, Structural Change and Defence Reviews* (University of York, UK, 1982) mimeo.
14. Hartley, K. and Corcoran, W., 'The Time-Cost Trade-Off for Airliners', *Journal of Industrial Economics* (March 1978).
15. Some of these other factors can be included in a general estimating equation of the form: $T = T(C, X_1, \ldots, X_n)$, where T = development time; C = development cost (negative relationship); $X_1, \ldots, X_n$ = other influences, e.g. whether the project is a national or collaborative venture, and the role of previous experience (e.g. the application of military technology to civil aircraft and the development of successive generations of aircraft). In the absence of data on development costs, weight might be used as a crude proxy.
16. Hartley, K., *NATO and Arms Co-operation: A Study in Public Choice* (London: Allen & Unwin, 1983).
17. Hartley, K., 'Defence and Advanced Technology'.

Note on the Paper by Hartley by Edwin Deutsch, University of Technology of Vienna

This paper has two features which evoke two different kinds of remarks. It contains a very interesting microeconomic account of production efficiencies and market failures in US and European aerospace industries. The comments will first concentrate upon this. Then the paper draws some policy recommendations aiming at a more efficient use of resources. The welfare implications will be subject to critical comments. Since I am not an expert in aerospace industries, I will confine myself to general remarks on economic and statistical methods.

The interview–questionnaire survey reveals the common opinion about labour productivity differentials between USA and Europe. Empirical evidence for the fact, that US firms are more productive than the European ones, is drawn from Table 12.2.

Unfortunately, the productivity measures are not based on value added per man but on sales per man. Therefore the productivity measure contains the value of intermediate inputs. This might cause an upward bias for smaller firms. Additional productivity comparisons based on value added – if available – could yield interesting insights into the degree of vertical integration of US and European firms and into an optimal degree of integration with respect to firm size. For instance, the high productivity of Dassault-Breguet can be attributed partly to purchases of intermediate products.

Dr Hartley cites five major explanations for the productivity differentials. Among these I consider (ii): Scale economies and (iv): Lag in European technology as satisfactory arguments, with interesting insights into learning curves and technology transfer (development time schedules and costly European joint ventures could equally be included here; they supply additional evidence). Scale economies do of course not only depend on the efficient use of labour but also on the degree of mechanisation and automation. In this respect, the capital intensity argument (iii) is treated rather shortly. The argument (i): lower labour productivity and more labour hoarding in Europe refers to the central thesis of the paper. The lack of labour mobility contributes significantly to the productivity differentials. This is illustrated by the reductions in employment around 1970, which were larger in the USA than in Europe. But since no output or value added figures are given, the illustration remains incomplete (the statistical tests performed in the second part of the paper refer to the UK only). The final argument (v): The US industry is more competitive seems well supported by successful decentralisation decisions. I want to mention an additional important fact which is not considered in the paper. After 1971 the dollar-exchange rate declined considerably. This improved US export opportunities with favourable effects on scale and productivity. Thus the arguments should be reconsidered in the light of exchange rates, export prices and export market shares.

The next part of the paper deals with statistical tests on the labour hoarding hypothesis. Let me state first some general comments. In the original economic sense labour will be hoarded as long as expected labour adjustment costs are higher than transitory costs of under-utilised labour; in this sense labour hoarding is rational from the point of view of the profit maximising firm. This has to be contrasted with the main concern in this paper: the lack of labour mobility is attributed to a bargaining situation between capital and labour and to the interference of subsidising vote-sensitive governmental institution. Here Dr Hartley raises an important question. It is interesting to note that the estimates give some support to the hypothesis that defence related industries are slower adjusters than the other ones. Nevertheless, the interpretation of the employment elasticities requires some caution: even if the sectoral elasticities are significantly different from zero, they might not be significantly different between each other (see Table 12.4). Furthermore, the representation of the capital stock by a time trend is restrictive. There is no reason to assume an asymmetry in the adjustment process, since the under-utilisation of capital reduces productivity as well. Hence it would be interesting to compare the results with estimates where the capital stock or the relative price of capital appears explicitly.[1]

In the final part of my comments I turn to policy recommendations and welfare implications. I agree with the proposals directed to cost reductions by using the gains from international specialisation. It is also noteworthy that attention is paid to the role of the armed forces as monopsonist. Here is a considerable way for wasting resources. On the other hand, I cannot agree with the welfare implications of a 'hiring and firing policy'. The notion of Pareto efficiency cannot be simply applied here. The case reminds of Allais'[2] famous work on a mixed economy with a public sector enjoying increasing returns to scale; and a private sector with decreasing returns to scale. A social optimum achieved by marginal cost pricing will yield profit maxima in the private and profit minima – possibly deficits – in the public sector.

Even if resources are used efficiently, occurring deficits must be financed by taxes with unavoidable redistribution effects. Second best considerations of this kind call for a careful use of efficiency and competition notions.

Although I might interpret Dr Hartley's paper from my own point of view, I think that short-term public choice favouring the arms industry inhibits the problems of structural change. Labour mobility is required to perform the latter, although not just in the sense of hiring and firing. But I thank Dr Hartley for providing useful points of discussions.

NOTES AND REFERENCES

1. See for example, Nadiri, I. and Rosen, S., *A Disequilibrium Model of Demand for Factors of Production* (New York: NBER, 1974).
2. Allais, M., *A la Recherche d'une discipline Economique* (Paris: 1943).

13 Re-evaluating Economic and Technological Variables to Explain Global Arms Production and Sales

Edward A. Kolodziej
OFFICE OF ARMS CONTROL, DISARMAMENT AND INTERNATIONAL SECURITY, UNIVERSITY OF ILLINOIS

I INTRODUCTION

The purpose of this paper is to stimulate discussion of the economic and technological incentives currently at play in the decision-making of nation-states that encourage the expansion of national arms production centres and the subsequent diffusion of arms and military technology across national borders. This focus contrasts with currently prevailing notions that emphasise strategic and political factors to explain the upward climb of military spending on arms and the growth of the arms trade. One recent, widely publicised book on the subject, for example, characterises arms transfers as a 'new diplomacy'.[1] Another writer, long acquainted with the arms production in the developing world, argues that 'the primary purpose of a Third World arms industry is enhanced national security'.[2] These writers stress the real and perceived security needs of states, their desire to escape external manipulation by major suppliers, their effort to minimise external dependency on other states, their search for political bargaining leverage, and their pursuit of enhanced national status associated in many minds with strong military forces and indigenous production capabilities.[3]

Without slighting or denigrating these factors, they are not fully persuasive as an explanation of the driving forces behind increased arms spending, production, or transfers. Several states, like Mexico and the Philippines, face weak external threats but continue to produce arms. Others, like the West European democracies, produce more arms than they can absorb. Similarly, the superpowers, which dominate global arms transfers, also draw varied economic benefits from arms sales that tend to be obscured in the polemical exchanges between Moscow and Washington. The Soviet Union has sold Indian railroad rolling stock and cashews, received in exchange for arms, to acquire hard currency.[4] Several American corporations, like General Dynamics and McDonnell-Douglas, are heavily dependent on domestic and foreign arms sales. The Northrop Corporation specifically designed the highly successful F-5 for international sale, and the Pentagon has under study the development of a new fighter only for export, a proposal advanced by the Carter administration, which was ostensibly opposed to increasing arms sales. Developing states, like Israel, India, and Brazil, have also become notable arms producers and, as the discussion below suggests, only part of the growth in this area can be attributed to external threats.

The paper is divided after this introduction Part I into three. The first in Part II sketches the growth in global military power over the past decade and its diffusion around the world, particularly to developing states. It provides a framework for the discussion of arms production, transfers, and acquisition. The second in Part III discusses what might be termed 'bounded' economic and technological rationality as a determinant of arms production and transfers. It refers to the economic incentives for expanded domestic arms production and foreign sales initially arising from the strategic–political considerations that initially prompted an indigenous arms production effort. From this perspective, the development and increasing sophistication of a state's arms production capacity and the active development of a foreign market for its products are seen as a set of dependent variables whose value is initially determined by a state's security needs and diplomatic objectives. However, the strategic–political incentives that led to the organisation of an arms industry and the production of increasingly advanced weapons are gradually modified as the economic constraints of sustaining an indigenous arms production and of responding to the demands of technological modernisation are understood.

In this early phase of 'bounded' rationality, pressures rise to produce and sell arms to cut the costs of production through series runs; to schedule arms production more efficiently through optimal utilisation of the factors of production, especially of highly skilled personnel; to seek foreign cooperation in covering the mounting cost of research and development and in selectively expanding the nation's weapons development and production capabilities; and to limit balance of payment deficits attributable to foreign arms purchases. Gradually, these subsidiary economic–technological considerations assume an independent character and claim on national priorities. These limit realisation of an autonomous arms production system fully and singularly responsive to internal demand for more and better weapons and, accordingly, free of concern for foreign support of an indigenous arms industry. Under terms of 'bounded' rationality in arms production, the resource and technological capabilities of the nation's economic base, demands for internal welfare expenditures, and the need to use scarce weapons producing resources efficiently and effectively set parameters for the independence of the nation's arms complex and its ability to sustain and continuously renovate itself independent of outside assistance through arms sales and cooperative R and D or production arrangements with other states.

One passes from 'bounded' rationality in making decisions about arms production, sales, and acquisition to market and developmental rationality when public welfare and corporate and personal profit considerations gain the ascendancy. In this second or mature phase (the focus of Part IV of the paper), arms are treated like any other good or service that can be made and exchanged to enhance the public good or private gain.[5] While 'bounded' rationality is by and large concerned with the *demand* side of weapons and the ways that the costs and burdens of producing arms can be relaxed and the reliability of supply assured, this market or developmental phase dwells on the *supply* side of arms production, transfers, and acquisition. Factors shaping this phase are principally economic and technological, although the goods and services that are provided for the world market are lethal and destructive. Considerations include competitive pricing for weapons to meet the terms of international competition, assured provision of raw materials, particularly energy resources (e.g., oil) and scarce minerals, access to foreign markets, product leadership through arms sales to penetrate foreign civil markets controlled by competitors, maintenance of high domestic employment, economic growth, and investment opportunities. Balance of payment concerns, moreover, centre on preserving a state's competitive position and the strength of its currency, through increased arms sales abroad, rather than simply on husbanding scarce foreign reserves. These welfare concerns are linked, moreover, to internal political demands for regime stability and party advantage.

II THE GROWTH OF MILITARY POWER AND ITS DIFFUSION THROUGH ARMS PRODUCTION AND TRANSFERS

The decentralisation of military power around the world and its diffusion within the developing world are suggested by several quantitative and qualitative measures.[6] First, military spending is proceeding at a faster rate in developing compared with developed states. Much of the 14.8 per cent growth in world military expenditures between 1968 and 1977 is attributable to the developing states. During this period the military spending of developed states rose from $305 billion to $319 billion in constant 1976 dollars, an increase of 4.6 per cent, while expenditures among developing states jumped from $54 billion to $92 billion or 70.4 per cent. The developing states outstrip the percentage increase in developed state spending in every region. Most prominent is the Middle East, which recorded increases of over 270 per cent, followed by Africa (including the Maghreb), which doubled its military expenditures. In both instances the rate of military spending exceeded the growth in GNP. Meanwhile, North America experienced a decline of 25 per cent. In three instances (Africa, Middle East, and East Asia), a higher percentage of a region's GNP was spent for military purposes in 1977 than in 1968. While the ratio of military spending to GNP fell for developed states by almost two percentage points (7.4 to 5.6 per cent), this same ratio for developing states held almost steady, falling only two-tenths of a percentage point from 6.1 to 5.9 per cent while GNP was increasing by almost 80 per cent. These GNP–military spending ratios are confirmed as might be expected in per capita expenditure data. The developed states declined 2.9 per cent on this scale, while the developing state percentage was a positive 38.1 per cent.

Second, the developing states account for most of the growth of world armed forces since 1968. While the armed services of the developed countries were shrinking by almost 11 per cent between 1968 and 1977, those of the emerging world expanded by over three million or 25 per cent. In this connection Africa has changed most over ten years. Armed forces are estimated to have increased from 635 000 to 1 340 000 or 111 per cent. The Middle East follows with a 76 per cent increase and then, surprisingly, Latin America, which has no outstanding military conflicts similar to those in Africa and the Middle East, registered a gain of almost 36 per cent in personnel under arms.

Third, developing states have significantly increased the firepower, range, and reliability of their ground, sea, and air systems in the past decade. Table 13.1 reinforces the image of an increasingly diffuse international security system, characterised by a rising number of centres of military force. In 1950, SIPRI indicates that no Third World state had supersonic aircraft or missiles, and only one possessed armoured fighting vehicles, such as tanks or armoured personal carriers. By 1960, 38 countries had heavy armour in their inventories; 26 were manning modern warships; and only one state (Taiwan) had supersonic aircraft. By 1977, almost fifty emerging countries had deployed supersonic aircraft, some as advanced as those found in the air forces of developed states. These included MiG 23's (North Korea, Syria, Iraq), Jaguars (India, Oman and Ecuador), Mirage 3's and 5's (17 states), and F-5's (16 states).[7] The trend continues as South Korea and Pakistan has access to F-16's, Israel to F-15's and F-16's, Saudi Arabia to F-15's, and Syria and India, to MiG 25's. By the end of the 1970s, over eighty developing states possessed heavy armour; 42 had various missile capabilities; and 67 disposed modern warships in their navies, largely fast, light attack ships with impressive destructive capabilities.

Fourth, arms imports illustrate the upward rate of military expenditures and weapons acquisition of developing states. Using five-year averages for 1968–72 and 1973–7, the developing states clearly outdistanced the developed states in the amount and in the growth rate of arms imports. In 1968–72, the developing states accounted for 70.1 per cent of all transfers; in the next five-year period of 1973–7, the percentage rose to 73.1. Correspondingly, the rate of growth is also

TABLE 13.1 *Number of Third World countries with advanced military systems, 1950, 1960, 1970, 1977*

	1950	1960	1970	1977
Supersonic aircraft	—	1	28	47
Missiles	—	6	25	42
Armoured fighting vehicles	1	38	72	83
Modern warships	4	26	56	67

SOURCE   SIPRI, *World Armaments and Disarmament: 1978* (New York: Crane, Russak, 1978), pp. 238–53.

impressive since the base for developing state imports is greater to start with than for developed states. The latter increased their imports by nearly 43 per cent; the former jumped 163.1 per cent. The greatest rate of increase in arms imports was in Africa, including North Africa. Over the last five years, imports into Africa leaped almost 450 per cent over the previous five-year period. The Middle East is also a leader with an increase of slightly more than 300 per cent. Latin America is in third place in arms imports, followed by South and East Asia.

More revealing than arms imports perhaps is the increasing tendency of developing states to produce their own weapons either indigenously or under licence. These range over heavy armour, supersonic and subsonic aircraft, helicopters, missiles, and warships. While none of these states has been able to free itself from foreign dependence, they have been able, for a variety of reasons to be discussed below, to increase their bargaining leverage *vis-à-vis* the developed states in acquiring the weapons that they need. Not only are developing states able to produce more weapons than ever before but they are also able to design and fabricate a larger variety of sophisticated weapons systems.

Table 13.2 lists the number of states in Africa, Asia, Latin America, and the Middle East which produce weapons in four major categories – aircraft, armoured vehicles, tactical missiles, and naval vessels. The 28 states which are covered in the survey are not distinguished by the level of independence that they have achieved in each category. These levels, defined by Andrew Ross on a graded six-point scale, range from licensed assembly at the lowest point of capability to licensed component production, licensed system production, system modification and reverse engineering, dependent

TABLE 13.2 Arms production in developing countries, 1960, 1970, 1980

Aircraft	1960	1970	1980
Fighters	1	1	5
Trainers (jet)	2	4	3
Trainers (basic)	5	4	11
Maritime (reconnaissance)	—	—	2
Transports	1	3	7
Aircraft (engines)	1	2	5
Helicopters	—	2	11
Avionics	—	—	3
Total (producing states)	6	7	16
Ground equipment			
Tanks	—	2	5
APC	—	—	2
Armoured cars	—	2	2
Reconnaissance vehicles	—	—	2
Armoured bridgelayers	—	—	1
Total (producing states)	—	4	6
Missiles			
Surface-to-air	—	—	5
Air-to-ground	—	—	3
Air-to-air	—	1	5
Surface-to-surface	—	1	3
Anti-tank	—	1	7
Total (producing states)	—	3	9
Naval vessels			
Frigates	1	1	4
Corvettes	2	1	1
Patrol craft	8	11	20
Submarines	—	—	3
Amphibious craft	1	2	3
Support craft	6	4	7
Total (producing states)	13	15	25

SOURCE Andrew L. Ross, *Arms Production in Developing Countries: The Continuing Proliferation of Conventional Weapons*, No. N-1615-AF, Rand Corporation Note, Santa Monica, California, 1981, pp. 16–19.

R & D and production, and independent R & D and production at succeeding higher levels on the scale.[8]

In each of the weapons categories that are listed in Table 13.2, the number of states producing a particular item has grown; in several cases they have more than doubled in the decade between 1970 and 1980. Several areas bear particular notice. Between 1970 and 1980, the number of states producing fighters grew from one to five; basic trainers from four to 11; and helicopters from 2 to 11. Overall, the number of states in the developing world producing aircraft doubled from 7 to 16.[9] Similarly, naval craft producers climbed from 15 to 25 with a significant increase in the number of states capable of producing patrol and support craft.[10]

Production of armoured vehicles and tactical missiles has grown more slowly. Over the decade since 1970, the number of states producing tanks increased from two to five and armoured personnel carriers from zero to five. The total number of producing states rose from 4 to 6.[11] The producers of tactical missiles tripled in the same period from three to nine.[12] Producers of SAM missiles leaped from zero to five;[13] those producing anti-tank weapons, from one to seven.[14] Five states (Argentina, Brazil, India, Israel, and South Africa) produce arms at some level of independent capability in all four major categories.

These figures also imply a high stage of technological development since aircraft, missiles, electronics, and aircraft engines require a broad scientific, engineering, and industrial base. However much countries like China or India may be still considered underdeveloped, measured by GNP and per capita income figures, they have been able to accumulate the technological systems to produce advanced military equipment. One can metaphorically speak of a 'Belgium' emerging from India or a 'Netherlands' arising from an otherwise underdeveloped China. The same process of modernisation, with military technology as the spearhead, may be seen to be operating in other states, like Brazil, Pakistan, and Argentina.[15] Modernisation is seen to be partially a function of a technologically advanced warfighting and economic system, linked to a capacity to sell arms and military know-how abroad.

The interest in advanced military technology is associated logically with still another indicator of the growing military capability of developing states: the proliferation of nuclear technology and weapons. India's explosion of a nuclear device in 1974 ended any remaining illusions that nuclear proliferation might be arrested in the developing world.[16] Pakistan, according to public reports, is rapidly approaching the explosion of the first 'Islamic bomb'.[17] Other candidates for nuclear status include Iraq, Taiwan, South Africa, South Korea, Brazil, and Argentina. Many analysts assume that Israel has acquired the necessary technology and has assembled, short of testing, several nuclear bombs.[18]

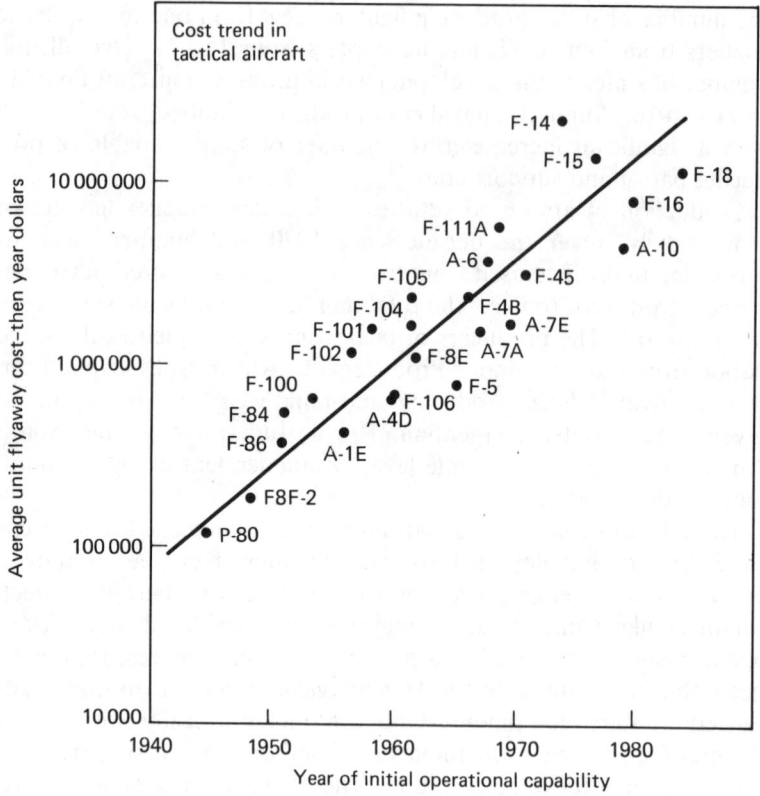

Source US, Department of Defense, *Statement of William Perry, Assistant Secretary of Defense for Research and Engineering*, fiscal year 1980 (January 1979), pp. 1–8.

FIGURE 13.1

III BOUNDED RATIONALITY AND ECONOMIC AND TECHNOLOGICAL INCENTIVES TO PRODUCE, TRANSFER, AND ACCUMULATE ARMS

The mounting cost of new weapons systems is a major problem facing arms producers and military establishments. Figure 13.1 sketches the increasing cost of American tactical aircraft from 1940 to 1980. The trend line is steeply upward, rising from approximately $100 000 a copy in the 1940s to an average of over $10 million in 1980.

Kolodziej: Global Arms Production and Sales 313

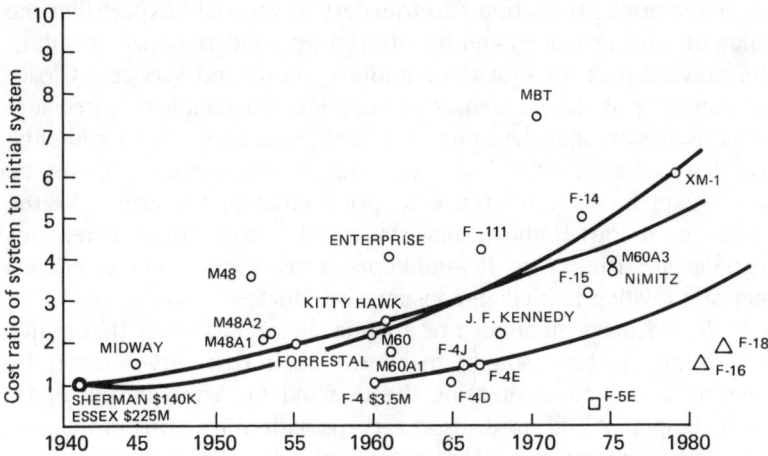

FIGURE 13.2 *The trend in procurement costs of weapons systems. Examples used are aircraft carriers (indicated by names), tanks (Sherman and M numbers), and fighter aircraft (F numbers). Tank data are for 1000th unit, aircraft data for 100th unit. All data are normalised to remove the costs of inflation and quantity changes*

SOURCE Jacques Gansler, *The Defense Industry* (Cambridge: MIT Press, 1980), p. 16.

These same upward cost curves can also be discovered by comparing the cost figures for tanks, carriers, and fighter aircraft between earlier and later models. As Figure 13.2 notes, the Sherman tank which cost $140 000 in 1940 is dwarfed by the estimated price of the newly planned XM-1 tank which will cost almost six times as much. The Essex aircraft carrier cost $225 million in the Second World War; the Nimitz class carrier costs approximately five times as much. Similarly, the price of the F-4 fighter was $3.5 million in 1960 while the F-14 requires an outlay approaching $20 million a copy.

The rising costs of new weapons place great strain on the military establishments and economies of supplier states and recipients. Increased costs mean that fewer systems can be purchased to fulfil a state's strategic needs. Meanwhile, resources are drained from civilian segments of the economy and decision-makers must face a choice of cutting expenditures for public welfare or accepting higher rates of inflation, potentially damaging to the economy. The rising costs of weapons development and production tend to have an ironic impact on global arms production and transfers. One would expect that the value of arms produced and transferred would increase as a result of the upward push of prices for military goods and services. Closer examination of the behaviour of supplier and recipient states suggests, however, that the upward sloping price curve for armaments, whether purchased for home or foreign consumption, cannot be solely explained by reference to price inflation for arms. As the discussion in Part II above suggests, world demand for arms remains high despite rising costs. It would appear that the demand for arms is inelastic relative to civilian consumer products.

If West European states are a guide, it would appear that major arms suppliers have sought to control their cost curves either by meeting and even stimulating the demand for arms abroad or by co-development and production accords with other arms producers, including recipient states. Increasing sales to other countries has a number of economic benefits. It spreads the cost of research, development, and production over a larger number of units, producing downward pressures on the price of a particular weapons system. Production schedules can be arranged in more orderly fashion over longer periods of time if domestic and foreign purchases can be balanced. Maintaining employment also tends to become more manageable.

These positive economic effects were very much on the minds of French policy-makers when the surge in French arms exports first began in the 1970s. In the wake of the 1968 uprising, the government was forced to cut back defence spending and, specifically, arms procurement in favour of greater civilian *and* military welfare. Table 13.3 charts the gradual decline in French military spending relative to GNP between 1960 and 1980. Drops in defence spending are particularly noticeable after the close of the Algerian war in 1962 and after the May events in 1968. Defence spending, as a percentage of GNP, steadily fell from approximately 6.2 per cent in 1960 to 4.2 by 1969. Even this lower level of defence expenditures could not be sustained after 1968, and it continued to fall, first precipitately after 1968, and then gradually through most of the 1970s, reaching a floor of 3.4 per cent for 1974–6. The military programme voted into law in 1976 envisaged a real increase in defence spending both as a percentage of governmental outlays and of GNP. These decisions are evident in the slight upward movement in defence spending since 1976 as a percentage of GNP. By 1980, defence spending represented approximately

3.8 per cent of GNP. It is by no means certain that this level of spending can be sustained in light of high, chronic unemployment, strong inflationary pressures, and a declining franc and balance of trade position. Military expenditures as a percentage of central governmental spending has not been arrested. It has gradually declined from 28.5 per cent in 1960 to slightly less than 17 per cent by 1980.

What is of more interest is the shift within the defence budget between procurement and personnel expenditures. During the 1960s, once the Algerian war was terminated and the Fifth Republic cutback in land forces was achieved in favour of smaller armed forces grouped around a nuclear striking capability, French procurement expenditures as a percentage of the military budget continued to rise from a low of 36.2 per cent in 1962 to a high of almost 52.2 per cent in 1967. It is important to note that much of these purchases for new weapons could not be exported since they involved nuclear forces and their support equipment. This placed an added burden on the defence industry in terms of the cost of weapons. Pressures were bolstered, even before the May events swelled them, to find foreign outlets for excess production capacity. Defence Minister Michel Debré cited specifically several of these economic considerations in justifying his determination to increase French foreign arms sales. Arms sales led to a 'better balance in scheduling orders, an increase in quantities that are produced, [and] therefore the spreading of fixed costs over a longer series [of units]'.[19]

It would appear that not only France but also the principal West European states have adopted a vigorous export policy to control the rising costs of weapons and the burden that they put on defence spending, welfare expenditures, and the efficient management of the arms industry. Except for Italy, all of the states in Table 13.4 can be seen to have increased arms exports at a faster rate than defence expenditures. While other factors may explain these differential rates than a successful response to global demand for arms, the figures do provide *prima facie* evidence that cost-cutting considerations formed a part – and in the French case an important part – of the explanation for increased arms production and transfers. British and German defence spending increased by 77 and 87 per cent respectively, while arms deliveries rose 117 and 191 per cent in each case. French defence spending approximately doubled during this period while arms transfers increased fivefold. Only Italy shows a net decline in

TABLE 13.3 *French defence budget with selected components for procurement and personnel, as a percentage of total governmental spending and GNP, 1960–80*

billion of dollars

Year	Defence total budget (initial)	Procure-ment	%	Personnel	%	Governmental total budget	% of total budget	GNP	% of GNP
1960	3.35	1.21	36.2	2.14	63.8	11.75	28.5	54.03	6.2
1961	3.41	1.15	33.8	2.26	66.2	12.72	26.8	58.79	5.8
1962	3.50	1.17	33.5	2.33	66.5	14.17	24.7	64.81	5.4
1963	3.76	1.57	41.8	2.19	58.2	15.73	23.9	73.73	5.1
1964	4.02	1.84	45.7	2.18	54.3	17.48	23.0	82.04	4.9
1965	4.21	2.11	50.1	2.10	49.9	18.71	22.5	87.71	4.8
1966	4.46	2.28	51.2	2.18	48.8	20.46	21.8	94.89	4.7
1967	4.77	2.49	52.2	2.28	47.8	23.04	20.7	103.70	4.6
1968	5.06	2.53	50.0	2.53	50.0	25.17	20.1	110.00	4.6
1969	5.08	2.49	49.0	2.59	51.0	28.54	17.8	120.95	4.2
1970	4.90	2.31	47.1	2.59	52.9	27.84	17.6	125.64	3.9
1971	5.21	2.37	45.5	2.84	54.5	29.11	17.9	140.81	3.7
1972	6.17	2.83	45.8	3.34	54.2	34.86	17.7	171.39	3.6
1973	7.81	3.58	45.8	4.23	54.2	44.12	17.7	223.14	3.5
1974	7.95	3.55	44.7	4.40	55.3	45.69	17.4	233.82	3.4
1975	10.22	4.45	43.5	5.77	56.5	60.47	16.9	300.59	3.4
1976	10.46	4.38	41.9	6.08	58.1	61.17	17.1	307.65	3.4
1977	11.89	4.87	41.0	7.02	59.0	68.33	17.4	330.28	3.6
1978	14.99	6.31	42.1	8.68	57.9	88.70	16.9	416.39	3.6
1979	18.12	7.83	43.2	10.29	56.8	107.86	16.8	489.73	3.7
1980	20.97	9.44	45.0	11.53	55.0	124.08	16.9	551.84	3.8

SOURCES There is considerable variation among French official sources and those of other national and international agencies with respect to French spending on defence, the division of expenditures between personnel and capital purchases, the total of central governmental spending, and GNP. Compare, for example, these differences in French official sources over a period of five years: France, Assemblée Nationale, Commission de la Défense Nationale et des Forces Armées (1977), *Avis sur le projet de loi de finances pour 1978*, no. 3150, *Défense: Dépenses en capital*, pp. 13–17; *idem*, Commission des Finance (1979), *Rapport sur le projet de loi de finances pour 1980*, No. 1292, Défense, Considérations Générale, pp. 27, 81, 108–110; France, Sénat, Commission des Finances (1980), *Rapport Général: Défense*, no. 98, p. 7; and France, Ministère de Défense SIPRA, *Le Budget de la défense national pour 1981* (Paris, 1981), pp. 5–7. Defence expenditures are taken from *Rapport* No. 1292 (1979), p. 81; the percentage division between personnel and capital expenditures for 1960–74 is drawn from *Avis*, no. 3150 (1977), p. 17 (initial budget figures) and from SIPRA, *Le Budget de la défense national pour 1981*, for 1975–80. Central governmental expenditures percentages are taken from *Avis*, No. 3150 (1977), p. 16 (initial budget figures) for 1960–74 and from Sénat, *Rapport*, no. 98 (1980), p. 7, 1975–80. Percentage of GNP spent on defence, calculated in terms of the defense budget, is based on Sénat *Rapport*, no. 98 (1980), p. 7, for for 1960–80. Percentages are rounded to nearest one-tenth of 1 per cent.

Exchange rates are taken from International Monetary Fund, *International Financial Statistics: 1977*, Vol.xxi no. 5 (May, 1977) pp. 166–7 and May, 1981, pp. 152. Note discrepancies between IMF figures for GNP and those deriving from French parliamentary sources, which are lower. The differences are partly due to the different base on which GNP is calculated. The Parliamentary reports depend on calculations for *produit intérieur brut*, a formula that generally leads to lower estimates of internal gross national product.

Note also that oscillations in the percentage increase in the budget are partly due to the rate of inflation in France and the shifting exchange rate, expressed in dollars. For example, between 1969 and 1970, defence spending (*crédit de paiements*) increased from 26.4 to 27.19 billion francs. However, the rate of the franc declined relative to the dollar and, therefore, the dollar value of defence spending is shown to have fallen. This distorted effect becomes especially acute after 1981 because of the devaluation of the French franc.

These French sources conflict with other open literature sources for French defence spending, GNP, and central governmental expenditures. Compare with US, Arms Control and Disarmament Agency, *World Military Expenditures and Arms Transfers: 1970–1979* (Washington: Government Printing Office, 1982), p. 38; International Institute for Strategic Studies, *Military Balance: 1982–1983* (London, 1982), p. 124; and SIPRI, *World Armaments and Disarmaments Yearbook, 1982* (London: Taylor & Francis, 1982) p. 150. These latter three sources generally cite higher ratios for defence spending relative to GNP and central governmental expenditures than does the French Ministry of Defence or parliamentary reports.

For an alternative calculation of defence spending estimates from 1945–76, see Michel Martin, *Warriors to Managers: the French Military Establishment Since 1945* (Chapel Hill: University of North Carolina, 1981) p. 54.

TABLE 13.4 *Defence expenditures and arms transfers of selected West European states, 1972–7*

(billions of current dollars)

Year	ITALY		FRANCE		UNITED KINGDOM		WEST GERMANY	
	Defence expenditures	Arms transfers	Defence expenditures	Arms transfers	Defence expenditures	Arms transfers	Defence expenditures	Arms transfers
1972	4.2	0.19	10.0	.8	9.3	0.46	12.7	0.32
1973	4.4	0.12	10.8	1.2	10.0	0.6	14.1	0.12
1974	4.8	0.10	12.0	1.4	11.1	0.55	16.1	0.21
1975	4.9	0.7	13.6	1.9	11.9	0.53	17.5	0.42
1976	5.0	0.14	14.9	2.4	13.0	0.68	18.4	0.70
1977	5.7	0.14	16.5	3.0	13.5	0.88	19.4	0.90
1978	6.2	0.15	18.6	3.8	14.6	1.2	21.4	0.95
1979	7.2	0.11	12.1	4.8	16.5	1.0	23.7	0.93

Note that figures for French arms exports are derived directly from French parliamentary reports and subsequently translated into current exchange rates. For French figures see France, Assemblée Nationale, Commission des Finances, de l'Economie Générale, et du Plan, *Rapport sur le projet de loi de finances pour 1981*, No. 1976, *Défense, Dépenses en Capital*, 9 October 1980, p. 196 and International Monetary Fund, *International Financial Statistics*: 1977, XXI, no. 5 (May 1977) pp. 166–7 and ibid., May, 1981, p. 152. Slight differences in citations between table and sources are due to rounding.

SOURCE: US, Arms Control and Disarmament Agency, *World Military Expenditures and Arms Transfers* (Washington, DC, 1982) pp. 58–9, 63, 80, 100–1, 105, 122.

the value of its arms transferred. The high point in transfers was attained in 1972, at the beginning of the period covered in Table 13.4. Italy has since never been able to reach that level.

There is reason to believe that ACDA's arms transfer figures are deflated. Its estimates for France are well below French parliamentary figures by a ratio of approximately 3 to 1.[20] There is also evidence that British arms transfer data are underestimated by a 2 to 1 ratio;[21] similarly one can suspect that the figures for Italy and Germany are undervalued. Even with ACDA data, however, the more rapid rate of arms transfers over defence spending is evident.

A second strategy adopted by developed state arms suppliers is co-development and co-production to cut national, if not overall, programme costs for new weapons and to assure markets for output through purchases by the armed forces of the producing states. Table

13.5 lists selected cooperative accords between France and other European states since 1960. France has entered into more of these arrangements than any other member of the Atlantic Alliance. The French example, as the largest arms producer in Western Europe, is in advance of the trend among other West European suppliers which are turning increasingly to joint development and production schemes as a way out of the impasse of high defence costs.

Rising weapons costs appear to have had the same effect on developing as developed states in encouraging indigenous arms production although the economic considerations underlying this expansion are somewhat different than those driving arms production decisions in developed states. Whereas developed states appear initially concerned about holding weapons costs down, developing states appear more focused on the problem of acquiring weapons and technical know-how despite low hard-currency reserves and, except for oil producing states, an unfavourable position in world trade. Although most developing states do not enjoy a high standard of living, their demand for weapons, including nuclear technology and fissionable materials, steadily grows. Professor Yehezkel Dror also argues persuasively that the Third Word demand for conventional and nuclear arms can be expected to grow in the immediate future even at the expense of domestic welfare and economic growth.[22] In the short-run, however, the foreign reserves of a developing state is one of the principal restraints on its capacity to acquire arms. As one study of Indian defence policy recently observed:

> The dependence of defence production on foreign exchange is only about 10 per cent of the total defence expenditure. But since about 70 per cent of the defence expenditure goes to Pay and Allowances, and Provisions and Stores, the actual dependence relative to the total allocation for the manufacture of weapons and equipment was consequently much higher. And although steady advances had been made since 1964 in reducing external dependence on both components and technical know-how the accelerating pace of development in military technology abroad made such dependence inevitable for the indefinite future.[23]

An arms industry is viewed as a means to relax the constraints of inadequate foreign reserves. It is seen as a reliable source of supply and as a mechanism for preserving and even improving a state's precarious balance of payments position. The problem of high unit

TABLE 13.5 Selected joint military development and production programmes between France and other European states

Programme	Cooperating Nations	Major Contractors	Contracted or start of study*	Service
Transall (transport)	West Germany (G)	Nord Aviation, MBB (G), Fokker (N)	1959	Army/Air Force
Atlantique (marine patrol aircraft)	West Germany (G), Great Britain (GB), Belgium (B), Netherlands (N)	Bréguet, Sud-Aviation Dornier (G), Rolls-Royce (GB), ABAP (B), Fokker (N)	1960	Navy/Air Force
Hawk SAM missile	Italy (I), G, B, N	Consortium under SETEL grouped around Thomson-Houston	1960	Army
Martel ASM anti-radar (AS.37) TV guided version (AJ168)	GB	Matra and Hawker-Siddeley	1963	Air Force/Navy
Milan anti-tank missile	G	Euromissile (composed of Aérospatiale and MBB)	1964	Army
Hot	G	Euromissile	1964	Army
Roland I (clear weather) and II (all weather) SAM	G	Euromissile	1964	Army
Jaguar dual purpose training and attack aircraft (various models)	GB	SEPECAT, grouping British Aircraft Corporation (BAC) and Dassault-Bréguet; motors by Rolls-Royce and Turboméca	1964	Air Force
Helicopters Puma†	GB	Puma/Gazelle, Aérospatiale and Turboméca, Lynx	1967	Air Force/Army

Gazelle Lynx		(Westland and Rolls-Royce)		
Exocet† AM 38 and AM 39, air-to-surface (ASM) SSM naval missile	GB	Aérospatiale, BAC Hawker-Siddeley	1967	Air Force (AM 39) Navy (AM 38, AM 39)
Alpha-Jet	G	Dassault-Bréguet and Dornier (airframe); SNECMA, Turboméca MTU and KHD (motors)	1969	Air Force
Otomat (SSM, ASM) (several successive versions)	I	Matra, Thompson CSF, Thomson-Brandt, Turboméca SNPE, Oto Melara	1969	Navy
NATO-ASSM	G	Euromissile	1977‡	
PAH-2/HAC helicopter	G	Euromissile	1978‡	
AS-2L, ASM	G	Euromissile	1978‡	
Leopard/AMX 30 tank	G	GIAT, Krauss-Maffei and Krupp	1980‡	

* The sources are not always clear on these two points, the official accord between governments and the start of study and design of the project by one or more states.

† Design is French; production essentially licensed by France to Great Britain.

‡ These projects are in the development stage.

SOURCE Various sources have been consulted. Most important is the annual review of world armaments, issued by the Stockholm International Peace Research Institute (SIPRI), *World Armaments and Disarmament: The SIPRI Yearbook, 1962–1980*; *Jane's All the World's Aircraft* (London: MacDonald, 1959–75); *Defense Marketing Systems, Foreign Military Markets, France* (Greenwich, Conn.); and France, Assemblée Nationale, Commission de la Défense Nationale et des Forces Armées, *Avis sur le projet de loi de finances pour 1975, Défense: Dépenses en capital*, no. 1233, pp. 93–6.

costs of production, which more advanced supplier states confront, does not appear as a deterrent to developing states. The number of producing states, as noted earlier have approximately doubled since 1970.

The capability of these states to free themselves increasingly of exterior dependency appears to be growing. Table 13.6 classifies the 28 arms producing states listed in Table 13.2 according to the developmental stage that each has reached along a scale of six levels of increasingly independent arms development and production capability between 1970 and 1980. The growth in indigenous arms production capabilities is impressive. The development is across all major weapons systems, including aircraft, armoured vehicles, tactical missiles, and naval vessels.

Notable are the number of states that have reached the fourth stage of system modification and reverse engineering over the ten-year period. The acquisition and development of technical skills at this level position these states in the next decade to become almost totally independent in producing selected weapons although they are likely to remain dependent on technology transfers in highly specialised and advanced fields, like fighter aircraft, particularly engines and avionics, electronics, and computers. Independent R & D and production capabilities have been achieved in only one area, tactical missiles. Brazil has achieved this status in surface-to-air and air-to-ground missiles; Argentina in air-to-ground missiles; Israel in air-to-ground, surface-to-surface, and, with Taiwan, in anti-tank missiles.

Developing states are also insisting on various licensed agreements and an access to advanced technology as parts of their contract to purchase weapons. Table 13.7 lists the licence accords in force between several developing states and developed state suppliers. Such arrangements are clearly on the rise from what was the pattern in the 1960s when most arms sales were restricted to the sale of end items. This trend is likely to continue into the 1980s as recipient states insist on access not only to arms but also to increasingly more advanced military technology. As these contractual relations are institutionalised, the developing states can be expected to move further along the way towards weapons independence, at least in areas of low or medium technology. New producing centres can also be expected to join the ranks of developed states.

The ironic outcome of this process of acquiring more know-how is that developing state producers will gradually confront the same cost problems and very likely begin to seek similar solutions through

TABLE 13.6 Arms production capabilities of developing states, 1970 and 1980

Type of arms	(1) Licensed assembly		(2) Licensed component production		(3) Licensed system production		(4) System modification		(5) Dependent R and D production		(6) Independent R and D production	
	1970	1980	1970	1980	1970	1980	1970	1980	1970	1980	1970	1980
Aircraft												
Fighters		1			1	3		2	1			
Trainers (jet)		1			3	1		2	1	1		
Trainers (basic)		1				4		2	3	1		
Maritime (recon.)							1	1		1		
Transports		1			1	2		1				
Helicopters				5	1	4		3	2	3		
Aircraft engines				2	1	4		1				
Aeronautics						1				2		
Armoured vehicles												
Tanks					2	1		2		2		
APC						3		1		2		
Armoured cars					1			1	1	1		
Recon. vehicles										2		
Armoured bridgelayer								1		1		
Missiles												
Air-to-air					1	2						1
Surface-to-air						4		2		1		1
Air-to-ground												3
Surface-to-surface						1						1
Anti-tank					1	4	1	2	1			2
*Naval Vessels**												
Patrol craft			1		3	10		2	7	12		
Support craft						1			4	6		

*Only selected naval vessel capability is listed in those cases where growth has been greatest.

SOURCE See Table 13.2

TABLE 13.7 *Licensed arms production accords acquired by developing states, 1970–80*

Country	Aircraft	Naval vessels	Armoured vehicles	Tactical missiles
Argentina	2	4	2	
Brazil	6			1
Chile		1		
Egypt	2			1
India	7	1	1	1
Indonesia	3	1		
Israel		1		
North Korea	1			
South Korea	4		1	
Libya	1			
Mexico		1		
Nigeria			1	
Pakistan	2		1	1
Peru		1		
Philippines	1			
South Africa	2	1	1	1
Taiwan	4			1
Totals:	35	11	7	6

SOURCE SIPRI, *World Armaments and Disarmament* (Cambridge: Oelgeschlager, Gunn, and Hain, 1981) pp. 252–7.

increased export and joint development and production arrangements in imitation of the developed states before them. Advanced weapons producers in the developing world, like Israel, Brazil, and India, are already facing these choices and appear to be adopting the same strategies as the West European states and, to some extent, the superpowers as well in searching for export outlets and in insisting on expanded joint military and civilian ventures to compensate for arms purchases. Increasingly, Ministers of Economics and Finance are joining Ministers of Defence and Arms Production in these discussions.

An additional trend that may reinforce an increase or a bolstering of national arms producing centres is the progressive diversification of supply sources. More states than ever before since the Second World War appear to be consciously attempting to avoid being dependent on any one state or small group of states.[24] This trend will tend to open new outlets for an increasing number of suppliers who will be eager to service these markets and to encourage the extension of this diversification process so profitable to arms suppliers pressed to maintain their arms industrial complexes.

IV MARKET AND DEVELOPMENTAL INCENTIVES TO PRODUCE AND TRANSFER ARMS

Until now, the discussion has concentrated on the derivative economic incentives arising from stratetic-political determinants of arms production and on how these economic considerations are gaining ascendancy in the calculations of national decision-making bodies. Arms production and transfers can also be viewed as a good or service that can be bought and sold like any other economic product. In greater or lesser measure it would appear that developed state suppliers view arms sales in this light. The French are perhaps the most unambiguous about treating arms as a commodity and vehicle of economic exchange. Weapons production and sales have progressively assumed a life of their own detached from the political or strategic objectives that may have initially prompted a decision to develop weapons indigenously. Under this guise, arms are not tools of national defence but goods and services whose sale is beneficial for national welfare, economic growth, and high employment as well as for personal and corporate profit.

If domestic spending for arms is combined with arms deliveries, we can gain some notion of the overall importance of arms production to the French economy. These totals are likely to underestimate the economic impact of arms production since precise data are not publicly available with respect to the contribution of the arms industry to each sector of the French economy or to the economy as a whole. Table 13.8 combines domestic and foreign demand for French arms and relates arms deliveries to business turnover. By these measures of business turnover in arms production, the value of arms produced for sales to French and foreign armed forces doubled from $3.63 billion in 1972 to $7.86 billion in 1977, a rate faster than the index of industrial prices during the same period. Also revealing is the increasing proportion of French arms exports to business turnover. In 1972, this ratio stood at 22.0 per cent and increased steadily at approximately three percentage points a year to 38.1 per cent in 1977.

The gradual replacement of foreign sales for domestic demand may also be measured by the ratio of arms deliveries to the procurement

TABLE 13.8 *Estimated business turnover for French armament industry, 1972–7*

(billions of dollars)

	1972	1973	1974	1975	1976	1977
(1) Domestic procurement	2.83	3.58	3.55	4.45	4.38	4.87
(2) Delivery of arms to other states	0.80	1.175	1.386	1.944	2.435	2.992
Total (1) and (2)	3.63	4.775	4.936	6.394	6.815	7.862
Percentage of arms sales to business turnover	22.0	24.7	28.1	30.4	35.7	38.1
Percentage of arms sales to domestic procurement	28.3	32.8	39.0	43.7	55.6	61.4

SOURCES France, Assemblée Nationale, Commission de la Défense Nationale et des Forces Armées, *Avis sur le projet de loi de finances pour 1978, Défense: Dépenses en capital*, 11 October 1977, and France, Assemblée Nationale, Commission des Finances de l'Economie Générale et du Plan (CFEGP), *Rapport sur le projet de loi de finances pour 1980, Défense: Considérations Générales*, no. 1292, 2 October 1979. Exchange rates from International Monetary Fund, *International Financial Statistics, 1977*, XII, no. 5 (May 1977) pp. 166–7, and (May 1981), p. 152.

budget of the defence budget from 1972 through 1977. This ratio more than doubles over this period. In 1972, the ratio stood at 28.3 per cent. Five years later the ratio of arms sales to domestic demand grew to 61.4 per cent. The implications of these measures is clear enough. While the size of the arms industry has remained relatively static over the past twenty years, the proportion of the industry's resources devoted to export has progressively grown each year.

Table 13.9 relates the business turnover figures calculated in Table 13.8 to GNP. Arms production represented approximately 2.12 per cent of GNP in 1972; it slowly rose to 2.38 per cent by 1977. As these figures suggest the rate of increase in value for arms production was greater than the growth in GNP. During this five-year period, the value of arms production in current prices increased by 117 per cent; GNP rose only 93 per cent. Not only is France's trade position significantly dependent on arms export, but domestic production and employment are tied more tightly than ever to arms production.

Table 13.10 presents several revealing measures of the importance of French arms sales to the French economy. Arms transfers have grown from 3 per cent of overall imports in 1972 to 4.6 per cent in 1977. This is a substantial and growing proportion of French trade. Arms are not merely a supplement to the defence budget, offsetting

TABLE 13.9 *Business turnover for arms as a percentage of GNP*
(billions of dollars)

	1972	1973	1974	1975	1976	1977
Business turnover	3.63	4.755	4.936	6.394	6.815	7.862
GNP	171.39	223.14	233.82	300.59	307.65	330.28
Percentage	2.12	2.13	2.11	2.13	2.22	2.38

SOURCES See Tables 13.8 and 13.3.

the high cost of weapons development and production; they are integral components of France's competitive position in international markets. The importance of this rising dependence on arms transfers is accentuated by France's overall dependency on international trade to sustain economic growth. In 1955 trade represented approximately 20 per cent of GNP; twenty years later, one-third of France's GNP was trade related.

Viewed from the perspectives of oil imports and balance of payments, arms exports are also key elements of French prosperity. The cost to France of oil more than quadrupled between 1972 and 1977, rising from $2.7 billion to $11.9 billion in 1977. Arms sales covered approximately 30 per cent of French oil imports in 1972; this percentage fell to a low of 14 per cent in 1974; and rose again to 25 per cent in 1977. The jump in oil prices, however, required a rapid expansion in French arms sales merely to maintain the ratio of arms deliveries to oil imports of the pre-oil crisis period. While civilian goods and services certainly contributed their share to conserving oil imports, arms sales comprised a larger proportion of the increase. Similarly, arms deliveries account for a notable share of France's efforts to maintain an equilibrium in trade. As Table 13.10 suggests, France's trade balances would have been sizeable if it had not been able to step up its arms deliveries. In the absence of arms deliveries, deficits in 1972 might conceivably have risen from $570 million to $1.37 billion; in 1977 the rise in deficits might have increased from $5.53 billion to $8.52 billion.

Two other features of French arms transfers also bear notice. These refer to the contribution of arms transfers to total capital exports and to the geographic distribution of French deliveries. During the 1970s French arms sales provided significant impetus to the expansion of France's capital goods exports. Overall capital exports are estimated to have increased by 48 per cent between 1974 and 1976 while arms deliveries expanded by 75 per cent.[25] These

TABLE 13.10 Arms transfers related to exports, oil imports and commercial balances

(billion of dollars)

	1972	1973	1974	1975	1976	1977
Exports	26.43	36.48	46.16	53.01	57.16	64.97
Arms deliveries/exports per cent	3	3.2	3.0	3.7	4.3	4.6
Oil imports	2.7	3.5	9.8	9.7	11.5	11.9
Arms deliveries/oil imports per cent	29.6	33.6	14.1	20	21.2	25.1
Imports	27.0	37.55	52.84	53.94	64.46	70.50
Balance: exports and imports	−0.57	−1.07	−6.68	−.93	−7.30	−5.53
Arms sales	0.80	1.175	1.386	1.944	2.435	2.992
Deficit without Arms sales	−1.37	−2.245	−8.066	−2.874	−9.735	−8.522

SOURCES France, Assemblée Nationale, Commission de la Défense Nationale et des Forces Armées, *Avis sur le projet de loi de finances pour 1978, Défense: Dépenses en Capital*, 11 October 1977, and France, Assemblée Nationale, Commission des Finances de l'Economie Générale et du Plan (CFEGP), *Rapport sur le projet de loi de finances pour 1980. Défense: Considérations Générales*, no. 1292, 2 October 1979. Exchange rate export, import, and oil import data drawn from International Monetary Fund, *International Financial Statistics: 1977*, XXI, no. 5 (May 1977) pp. 166–7, and (May 1981), p. 152.

percentages suggest the weaker competitive position of France's civilian capital goods industry relative to its principal competitors within the OECD. Arms deliveries, moreover, account for a significant share of France's trade with the developing world. In 1970, less than 50 per cent of French arms deliveries were outside the Atlantic community and Europe. By 1976, the proportions had significantly shifted to 15 per cent with the developed world and 85 per cent with developing countries.[26] Within this latter sector, it was not surprising to discover that some of the largest gains in trade were with oil producers. The first major breakthrough occurred with Libya in 1970 with the sale of 110 Mirage aircraft to the Kaddafi regime. This spectacular sale was followed by others to Saudi Arabia and Iraq throughout the 1970s and into the 1980s.

The French success in selling arms and military technology can be attributed to several market-related factors besides the attractive price tags associated with French arms and the concessionary financial arrangements and compensations often included in contracts for French arms. American preoccupation with the Vietnam war during the 1960s opened new markets for French arms orders as American arms production was geared to the war and to the needs of selected allies. French arms merchants, encouraged and abetted by governmental officials, were quick to fill growing world demand. Other potential competitors, like Great Britain, West Germany, and Japan, were either unable or unwilling to fill the void. The British government under Labour Party rule in the 1960s hesitated to increase foreign arms sales and relinquished its place as the third largest arms seller to France by the end of the 1960s. West Germany and Japan had developed a profitable export industry based on civilian goods. As defeated powers in the Second World War, expanding arms production would have opened their governments to charges of militarisation from domestic and foreign critics.

The success of French arms, particularly Mirage aircraft in the 1967 Arab–Israeli war, further promoted sales. On the other hand, the weakness of French exports in non-military sectors, relative to its OECD competitors, encouraged increased reliance on military sales. Of particular interest to the French was the sale of capital goods, like heavy complex armaments, whose added domestic value was high relative to consumer products or semi-processed goods. Also the employment opportunities, afforded arms sales for highly skilled, technical personnel, were considerable. These varied economic and political factors gave France a comparative advantage in selling arms abroad.

The size of the defence industry, measured by personnel, remained substantially stable from the late 1960s into the 1980s despite a decreasing demand for procurement by French military forces and continued social and potentially disruptive demands for increased social expenditures, economic growth, and full employment. The arms industry employs approximately 300 000 scientists, technicians, and workers and this number has not appreciably changed over the last decade. The proportion of this work-force devoted to arms sales abroad has of course increased as the French arms industry becomes more export dependent. For French planners, arms sales were progressively viewed as a support for output that could not otherwise be sustained by domestic demand and as a complement to sagging civilian sales abroad. Producing arms is an instrument of economic and social welfare. Arms also act as product leaders to expand trade abroad and to open markets for civilian goods and services.

The French case suggests that the economic notion of comparative advantage still operates in arms production as in civilian economic endeavours. It is by no means restricted to French arms since other states besides the superpowers have been able to carve out selected markets for their specialised products. Among developing states, Israel, Brazil, and, to a lesser extent, India, have enjoyed some success as arms suppliers. Israel has reached world stature as a supplier of quality products, some indigenously produced, like the Gabriel surface-to-surface missile, or adapted from the technology of its suppliers, like the Kfir fighter, patterned after the French Mirage airframe and powered by US-built GE engines.

Israel sells military arms and equipment to a wide range of customers, including West Germany, Indonesia, South Africa, Singapore, Taiwan, Chile, Ecuador, Mexico, Honduras, Guatemala, and, until recently, Nicaragua. It has reportedly sold war *matériel* to Iran although diplomatic relations between the two states have been severed. It also produces civil aircraft, all forms of tactical missiles (listed in Table 13.2), patrol boats, armoured vehicles, artillery and small arms, radar, communication, and navigation systems, industrial and shipborne monitoring and control systems, medical electronics, microelectronics, computers and computerised communications systems, fire control systems, security systems, air and ground crew equipment, ground-support equipment, and microwave components.[27] ACDA lists exports of $360 million in current dollars for 1982, a figure that is likely to be conservative.[28]

Brazil has also captured markets in the Middle East and Africa and must be considered an important arms supplier. In the Middle East, it has sold equipment, especially light armoured vehicles, to Libya, Qatar, and Iraq. The Cascavel, a light armoured vehicle that mounts a 90 mm cannon and carries laser range-finders, has seen service with Iraqi armed forces in the war with Iran. Brazil's state-owned Empresa Brasileira de Aeronautica (Embraer) is the world's sixth largest aviation firm. It sells the twin-engine Bandeirante aircraft worldwide and also manufactures the Xavante jet under Italian licence. Brazilian arms are also attractive to developed states. The United States Marines are studying a Brazilian light tank for possible purchase, and France has already purchased Brazilian light transport aircraft for its armed forces. Brazil is likely to continue to invest in its arms industry in the future. As one close student of Brazilian politics and foreign and security policy observes:

> Brazilian arms are especially attractive to third-world countries since they are comparatively simple, high quality, and free of

ideological ties. Because of the growing demand for Brazilian arms, and given that Brazil must increase exports to compensate for rising petroleum prices, the state continues to assign a high priority to investment in what already is the largest and most sophisticated conventional-weapons industry in South America. As a major arms supplier, Brazil will be able to exert greater pressure on its neighbors and to increase its influence in the emerging commercial markets of black Africa, the Middle East, and Asia.[29]

From two opposing viewpoints – developed state suppliers and emerging developing state arms producers – there appear to be attractive economic gains to be made from producing and selling arms. For the established supplier, like France, there is a comparative advantage to selling military hardware and technology over other possible investment possibilities. For the emerging arms producer, there may also be gain to be had in reducing the loss of foreign reserves and in penetrating markets previously held by more traditional suppliers. These real and perceived economic benefits derive from a logic driven either by the notion of bounded rationality (where strategic–political considerations frame techno-economic decisions) or market and developmental economics (where welfare and profit are the predominant motivations).

There is much force in the argument that spending resources on arms reduces what can be devoted to welfare, and there is considerable documentation comparing expenditures for both objectives.[30] However, this relationship is far from being a zero-sum game as perceived by national decision-makers concerned with security and welfare problems.[31] As this paper has suggested, there are powerful economic and technological incentives that prompt decision-makers to invest in arms production. At least in the short and middle term, marginal gains appear to be forthcoming, justifying the original investment. It does little good to argue with the leadership of these national production centres that they are wasting national resources; much less does the argument cut that global resources are being squandered with the result that regional and world tensions are likely to rise. These considerations apparently have lesser weight when one examines the specific decision taken by decision-makers at the national level where resource allocation goes on. Announced commitment to arms control goals or to a decrease in arms traffic are repeatedly subordinated by arms producing states to the continued expansion of military production and transfers. The effort of the Carter administration to cut American arms transfers had already failed before the Reagan regime further relaxed barriers to sales abroad. The Giscard d'Estaing government and the succeeding Socialist regime in France, while both deploring arms transfers, have presided over the greatest expansion of arms transfers in France's history. Neutralist governments in India and Brazil, while critical of superpower arms policies, are committed to the expansion and improvement of their arms producing and marketing capabilities. India integrates economic and military planning, going further than some non-western states. The Brazilian leadership is no less bent on a policy of military and economic independence, however doubtful or illusory that goal may appear.[32]

Some analysts in the developing world are prepared to argue that economic development can actually be spurred either as a spin-off of military preparedness or, further, as a direct result of military expenditures. The welfare–defence debate may be characterised in these terms. If the predominant opinion within India still views defence spending as an economic burden, influential segments of the security community promote military expenditures and arms production as complements of civilian economic development or as a motor-force of the civilian economy.[33]

From a political and psychological perspective, the economic claims of these schools of thought are not especially relevant. What counts as much, if not more than real economic benefits, in determining resource allocations favouring arms production is the *perception* of economic and technological gain. Further research will be needed to determine the validity of the economic claims of supporters of increased defence spending and arms production as well as the political strength of these advocates at the national level. If the upward increase in global military spending, especially on the part of developing states is any guide, and if reference to specific case studies of the behaviour of national leaders in Western Europe, Israel, Brazil, and India are any indication, the argument that one must sacrifice welfare for military prowess and vice versa is by no means universally accepted. Many go beyond the guns-butter trade-off and argue more butter *because of* guns.

CONCLUSIONS

An examination of prevailing trends in arms production and sales and of the behaviour of élites concerned with arms production, purchases and sales suggests that economic and technological variables play a significant role in explaining the continued expansion of activity in these domains. Strategic-political factors, while important, are insufficient to explain this upward movement. Public welfare and corporate and personal profit are also driving military–industrial complexes forward. We need to know more about how these techno-economic forces are shaping arms production and sales. We also need to know more not only about how welfare and military expenditures are related but also how decision-makers perceive this relationship. There still exists a great deal of uninformed and wishful thinking about economic development and military expenditures. Unless we make greater progress in determining this relationship, we will be hampered in fashioning policy tools to control the diffusion of arms and military technology. A long and hard look at the economic and technological determinants of arms production, transfers, and accumulation, free from ideological barriers to precise analysis, appears overdue.

NOTES AND REFERENCES

1. Pierre, A., *The Global Politics of Arms Sales* (Princeton: Princeton University Press, 1982). See also his article, 'Arms Sales: The New Diplomacy', *Foreign Affairs*, vol. LX, no. 2 (Winter 1981–2) 266–86.
2. Moodie, M., 'Defense Industries in the Third World: Problems and Promises', in Neuman, Stephanie G. and Harkavy, Robert E., *Arms Transfers in the Modern World* (eds), (New York: Praeger, 1979) p. 300.
3. Most of the writers in the Neuman–Harkavy reader on arms transfers, for example, accent strategic-political explanations of arms transfers. See ibid.
4. Thomas, G. C., *The Defence of India* (Delhi: Macmillan, 1978) p. 135.
5. For an initial effort to model the economics of arms production transfers, and acquisition, see Alexander, A., Butz, W. P. and Mihalka, M., *Modeling the Production of International Trade of Arms: An Economic Framework for Analyzing Policy Alternatives* (Rand Corporation, Santa Monica, California, March, 1981) p. 1.
6. These measures are elaborated in Kolodziej E. A. and Harkavy, R., 'Developing States and the International Security System', *Journal of International Affairs*, vol. XXXIV, no. 1 (Spring/Summer, 1980) 59–87.
7. The Stockholm International Peace Research Institute (SIPRI), *World Armaments and Disarmament: 1978* (New York: Crane, Russak, 1978) pp. 238–53.
8. Ross, A. L., *Arms Production in Developing Countries: The Continuing Proliferation of Conventional Weapons*, No. N-1615-AF (Rand Corporation Note, Santa Monica, California, 1981) pp. 16–19.
9. Argentina, Brazil, Egypt, India, Indonesia, Israel, North Korea, South Korea, Libya, Nigeria, Pakistan, Peru, Philippines, South Africa, Taiwan, Thailand.

10. Argentina, Bangladesh, Brazil, Columbia, Dominican Republic, Egypt, Fiji, Gabon, India, Indonesia, Israel, Ivory Coast, North Korea, South Korea, Malagasy Republic (Madagascar), Malaysia, Mexico, Peru, Philippines, Singapore, South Africa, Sri Lanka, Taiwan, Thailand, Venezuela.
11. Argentina, Brazil, India, Israel, South Korea, South Africa.
12. Argentina, Brazil, Egypt, India, Israel, South Korea, Pakistan, South Africa, Taiwan.
13. Brazil, India, Israel, South Africa, and Taiwan.
14. Argentina, Brazil, Egypt, India, Israel, Pakistan, Taiwan.
15. See articles on these three states, respectively, by Professors David Myers (Brazil) Stephen Cohen (Pakistan) and Edward Milenky (Argentina), in *Security Policies of Developing Countries: A Comparative Approach*, Kolodziej, Edward A. and Harkavy, Robert (eds), (New York: Lexington Books, 1981).
16. For a useful review of developing state nuclear programmes; consult John Kerry King (ed.), *International Effects of the Spread of Nuclear Weapons* (Washington, DC: Government Printing Office, 1979).
17. Sintra, P. B., and Subrahmanyam, R. R., *Nuclear Pakistan* (New Delhi: Vision Books, 1980).
18. Harkavy, R., *Spectre of a Middle Eastern Holocaust* (Denver: University of Denver Press, 1977); also Aronson, S., 'Nuclearization of the Middle East', *The Jerusalem Quarterly*, no. 2 (Winter, 1977) 27–44.
19. Ministère de Défense, *Livre Blanc sur la Défense Nationale, I* (Paris, 1972) p. 54.
20. See the author's comparison of ACDA and French data in the author's 'Measuring French Arms Transfers', *Journal of Conflict Resolution*, vol. XXIII, no. 2 (June 1979) 195–227. For a review of French arms transfer policy and its economic consequences, consult the author's 'France and the Arms Trade', *International Affairs* (January 1980), 54–72.
21. This conclusion is suggested by Laurence Freedman in 'British Foreign Policy to 1985. IV: Britain and the Arms Trade', ibid. (July 1978) 377–92.
22. Dror, Y., 'Nuclear Weapons in Third-World Conflict', in *Adelphi Papers* No. 161, *The Future of Strategic Deterrence* (London: International Institute for Strategic Studies, 1980), Part II, pp. 45–52.
23. Thomas, G. C., *The Defence of India*, pp. 110–11.
24. See Mihalka, M., 'Supplier-Client Patterns in Arms Transfers: The Developing Countries, 1967–76', in *Arms Transfers in the Modern World*, pp. 49–76; p. 73 summarises recent bloc changes in arms supplies and provides evidence for the growing multilateralisation of the arms trade.
25. See the author's 'Determinants of French Arms Sales Behavior: Implications for National and International Security', in *Threats, Weapons, and Foreign Policy*, v. Sage International Yearbook of Foreign Policy Studies (Beverly Hills: Sage, 1980), pp. 137–76.
26. Ibid.
27. The list is drawn from Bernard Reich's analysis of Israeli security policy in *Security Policies of Developing Countries*, pp. 216–17.
28. US Arms Control and Disarmament Agency, *World Military Expendi-*

ture and Arms Transfers (Washington DC: Government Printing Office, 1984) p. 73.
29. Myers, D. J., 'Brazil', in *Security Policies of Developing Countries*, p. 69.
30. See ACDA and Sivard, R. L., *World Military and Social Expenditures: 1981* (Leesburg, Va., 1981).
31. Neuman, S. G., 'Arms Transfers and Economic Development: Some Research and Policy Issues', in *Arms Transfers in the Modern World*, pp. 219–45, reviews the literature in arms sales and economic development.
32. Myers, D. J., *Security Policies of Developing Countries*, pp. 53–72.
33. Thomas (see ref. 4) surveys these schools of thought, pp. 125–135. K. Subrahmanyam, *Defence and Development* (Calcutta: Minerva, 1973) presents a spirited brief in support of the view that defence spending can contribute to economic development. Also relevant are Rajesh K. Agarwal, *Defence Production and Development* (New Delhi: Arnold–Heinemann, 1978) and K. Subrahmanyam (ed.), *Nuclear Myths and Realities* (New Delhi: ABC Publishing House, 1981).

14 Civil Versus Military R & D Expenditures and Industrial Productivity

Edwin Deutsch and Wolfgang Schöpp
UNIVERSITY OF TECHNOLOGY OF VIENNA

I INTRODUCTION

This paper centres upon the economic interrelations between civil versus military expenditures for research and development, labour productivity and incomes. It starts from the proposition that in general the average growth of productivity in the economy will not be raised, if the share of military R & D expenditures in government-funded R & D expenditures is increased. This proposition is first discussed on theoretical grounds. Then, by means of an international comparison, some tentative empirical evidence will be presented to this controversial issue.

The main economic arguments in support of military expenditures may be summarised briefly. By and large it is taken for granted that technical progress is stimulated and propelled by military research and development. There are several examples of military experience opening the way for innovations in the civil sector. Hence it is argued that technological spillover from the military sector to the civil sector raises the growth rate of productivity in the total economy. Furthermore there is the argument that defence-related investment good industries must be stabilised by adequate domestic military spending and by promoting exports. Weapons exports are necessary to reduce the costs of procurement of the domestic armies. By removing under-utilised capacities and by expanding defence-related manufacturing activities, it will be possible to reduce the rate of unemployment in the economy.[1]

It is not surprising that political support for the arms race is enhanced when periods of economic crises meet with periods of virtual or supposed threats to national security. As a matter of fact, during the 1970s the growth rates of productivity declined in most OECD-nations, while the rates of unemployment started to increase. This development was accompanied by an accelerated arms race in which the majority of western industrialised nations entered with more or less reluctance. The intensified arms production is reflected most significantly in the volume of exports of major weapons to Third World countries. It was just after the oil crisis year 1973 that it began to increase much faster than the volume of world trade, and it doubled within six years.[2] Parallel to the expanded weapon production the government funded military R & D expenditures accelerated in real terms. In some nations like France the share of military R & D in total government funded R & D rose sharply.[3] In the USA military R & D was bounded under the Carter administration after 1977, but under the Reagan administration it is currently reaching unprecedented levels. The political objective of military spending is clearly to maintain technological superiority of western industrialised nations, and to guarantee national security by expanding the arms production in the defence-related industries.

The following discussion focuses on the validity of the argument, that military expenditures will raise the growth rate of productivity not only in some parts of industry, but also in the economy as a whole. The difficulties of such an analysis are obvious, and a full discussion is far beyond the scope of this paper.

For methodological reasons, the military sector will be separated from the civil sector.[4] This assumption makes it possible to compare the economic effects of military versus civil R & D expenditures. It is surprising that relatively little attention is paid in the literature to this important topic. The considerable literature on R & D does not distinguish between the two types of expenditures, but concentrates upon the overall statistical description of R & D effort and its outcome. There is certainly some difficulty in empirical investigations, since international statistical data splitting up civil and military R & D are rather fragmentary. If not otherwise stated, military and civil R & D are understood to be government funded. The statistical estimates presented below must be seen in this context.[5]

Section II consists of a discussion of macro- and microeconomic aspects of R & D. It raises a central hypothesis concerning the impact of civil versus military R & D on labour productivity for a given structure of remuneration rates. Section III presents a simple model which permits a statistical test of the hypothesis. The empirical results are presented in Section IV. The results are summarised in the concluding Section V.

II ECONOMIC ASPECTS OF MILITARY R & D

Consider first the microeconomic point of view. The weapons industry operates on input and output markets where the degree of imperfection is relatively high. This reminds one of Schumpeter's view that market imperfections are necessary to stimulate economic development by technological progress; temporary quasi-rent, uncertainty and potential rivalry are the driving forces behind the innovation process.[6] These phenomena are not easy to measure in empirical investigations. In general, to grapple with resource market imperfections, firm size and concentration ratios are among the commonly used indicators. The efficiency of the outcome is usually quantified by the number of (important) innovations, or by the subsequent growth of firms.

In their summary of the existing literature on R & D and market structure, Kamien and Schwartz[7] do not deal with military R & D explicitly. On the other hand, they present a number of settled results: In general, there are no economies of scale with respect to firm size in the innovation process. Small and medium size firms and laboratories are likely more efficient than large ones, and small firms are more cost-conscious than large ones. The efficiency curve with respect to firm size shows first increasing, then decreasing returns to scale.

The interpretation of this curve requires of course some caution. In big corporations inventions are often not patented, the same is true for top secret military inventions. The usual measure of number of innovations does not apply here. The technological diffusion from military R & D to the civil use of innovations takes time, ten years or more just in the successful cases like electronic air navigation and telecommunications via satellites. In these fields, among others, military experience generated positive external effects in the civil sector. On the other hand, the extreme specialisation of many military innovations does not allow for civil applications. If these innovations are not considered to increase the public security of welfare, then by consequence there are diseconomies of scale in military R & D expenditures.[8]

The high costs occurring with the development of arms deserve several comments. Leonard[9] for instance showed that private firm-financed R & D spending is correlated with the subsequent growth of firms, while federal financed R & D is not. He drew this conclusion from an analysis of aircraft and electrical equipment industries which belong to the defence related industries. Thus military R & D as part of federally financed R & D is likely to be less efficient than the private R & D. Some lack of cost-consciousness may enhance the existing tendency for wasting resources in bureaucratically administered projects.[10] Other studies have shown that the concentration of R & D effort into a small number of firms reaches a maximum efficiency at a 50–60 per cent concentration ratio, measured in terms of the eight largest firms. A higher concentration ratio reduces efficiency again. This may have consequences for the allocation of military R & D by governmental institutions, which prefer large firms to manage military projects.[11] But, as far as the authors know, little empirical evidence is available on a general and analytical level.

Total costs are augmented by failures in military developments which are often exceedingly expensive. Since the losses are public, a further motive for the arms race may be found here. Public risk bearing for R & D outweighs uncertainty and failures especially when weapons should be sold on risky export spot markets. But public risk bearing for large and uncertain projects is quite a general feature of the current economic situation. Private firms are less willing to undertake R & D projects with a long maturity horizon. A study of the OECD[12] maintains that an increasing number of projects aim at risk aversion and at short developments, which are less costly. On the other hand, there is no general empirical evidence that government funded R & D is increasingly substituted for private R & D. The share of government funded R & D in total R & D is about 50 per cent on average, oscillating over time but not showing a common international tendency upwards or downwards. Table 14.1 shows various R & D expenditures in 1975 for the six OECD nations which are considered here. One recognises that Japan is the only nation with relatively low government funded R & D.

As mentioned earlier, only government R & D will be considered further.

TABLE 14.1 R & D in six OECD countries, 1975

	Canada	France	Germany	Japan	Netherlands	USA
Total R & D in per cent of GDP	0.96	1.45	1.96	1.69	1.87	1.66
Government R & D in per cent of total R & D	56.7	45.4	47.4	29.7	44.9	54.8
Military R & D in per cent of government R & D	6.1	41.7	13.5	1.7	3.6	49.8

The distinction between military and civil R & D is not clear cut; military and civil space research are one among several fields of interference. A certain difficulty for industrial analysis arises because R & D is partly basic research. Civil R & D contains such items as environmental health and social science R & D, which cannot be compared directly with industrial productivity measures. These facts will be reconsidered in Section V.

In the Appendix, the relative shares of military R & D expenditures in total governmental funded R & D are plotted for the six OECD nations considered here: Canada, France, Federal Republic of Germany, Japan, the Netherlands, and USA. The period of observation covers more than two decades; according to the availability of data from about 1955 to about 1979. In Canada, Japan and Germany there was a tendency of declining shares of military R & D. In contrast, the share of military R & D has risen in France (after 1969) and in USA (after 1965). The course of these shares can be compared with the indices of real labour productivity. There is the marked difference between the persistent high growth rates of productivity in Japan and the declining growth rates of productivity in USA.

The microeconomic considerations on military versus civil R & D suggest that a higher share of military R & D would yield decreasing returns to scale as far as large projects are concerned. If the microeconomic consideration were true in general, the theory would predict some trade-off between military expenditures and average labour productivity. One is tempted to argue that the theory applies to the data: Japan with her low scale military spending shows higher growth rates of productivity than the USA where large scale military spending prevails. Of course, this reasoning calls for caution. The index of average labour productivity consists of various components of which R & D and its composition is only a single one. Indeed, in the case of France there is no visible trade-off of this kind.

However, the microeconomic reasoning can be supplemented by the following macroeconomic considerations.

It seems reasonable to view the allocation of R & D to military and civil purposes as an indicator for the long-run development of the economy. An increasing share of military R & D will raise the demand for technologically advanced equipment and for qualified work in the military sector. To some extent resources will be withdrawn from the civil sector. Since the rates of return and the real wages in the military sector are usually above the average remuneration rates in the economy, this will exert the following effects.

In periods of full employment, the civil sector may suffer from a labour shortage. The same will hold true in periods of higher rates of unemployment, if the qualified labour force is attracted by better working conditions in the military sector, and if the civil sector finds itself unable to pay the wages which prevail in arms producing economic activities. Similarly, capital will be attracted in the military sector, giving rise to some capital scarcities in the civil sector. Now, in the short-run and at the given state of technology, the military sector will expand. Then, in the medium-term, technical progress may increase productivity growth in the military sector. Before technological spillover from the military sector to the rest of the economy takes place, productivity growth in civil production will lag behind. Since civil GDP is larger than military GDP, the weighted average of the growth rates of labour productivity is dampened. Whether the average growth rate will increase in the long-run or not, depends on the speed and intensity of civil innovations which are induced by technological spillover from the military sector. Although little empirical evidence exists, there might be an optimal distribution between military and civil economic activities such that technological spillover works out its full effect. If the military sector expands over this optimal share in GDP, it will absorb economic resources even in the long-run such that the average growth rate of labour productivity will fall below the optimal level. This will especially be the case, if an increasing part of the labour force and of capital is absorbed in the production of arms which by their degree of specialisation do not induce civil innovations. Then resources, which might be more productive there in the long-run, measured in terms of total income foregone, are withdrawn from the civil sector.[13]

The arguments presented here depend on sufficiently high differentials of rates of return and of wages between the two sectors. They shed light on existing coalitions between capital and some parts of the labour force which have a common interest in maintaining the level of arms production. These coalitions get political support in periods of economic crises, especially when the national and international solidarity of trade unions is weakened under the pressure of unemployment.

The arguments can be reversed in the following sense: if the share of civil R & D in total government funded R & D is increased, and if technical progress comes into effect in the civil sector without the roundabout innovation process in the military sector, productivity growth in the civil sector may increase. The rates of return in the civil sector will increase, and this will permit the attraction of qualified workers paid at wage rates above the average. If civil R & D is expanded while the volume of economic activities in the military sector is still above the optimal level mentioned above, the average index of labour productivity in the economy will increase.

Since the optimal distribution between the military and the civil sector is rather a theoretical artefact, the arguments will be summarised in the following hypothesis:

Hypothesis: For a given structure of remuneration rates for capital and labour, the average growth rate of labour productivity in the economy will increase in the long-run, if the share of military R & D declines relatively to the share of civil R & D.

III THE MODEL

The following symbols are used:

Y = labour productivity (value added per worker).
k = real capital stock per worker.
w = real wage rate (nominal wage deflated by the manufacturing price index).
σ = elasticity of substitution, $\sigma = 1/(1+\varrho)$.
ϕ = share of civil R & D expenditures.
ψ = share of military R & D expenditures, $\phi + \psi = 1$.
δ = time discount factor.

The other symbols refer to (unknown) coefficients.

The logic to test the hypothesis is presented briefly: the rate of growth of real wages is assumed to be proportional to the rate of growth of labour productivity. An additional influence is exerted by the past pattern of the government funded R & D shares ϕ and ψ. Using coefficients a_i and the time discount factor δ, the model is assumed to be

$$\ln w_t = a_0 + a_1 \ln y_t + \sum_{\tau=0}^{\infty} \delta^{\tau}(a_2 \phi_{t-\tau} + a_3 \psi_{t-\tau}). \tag{1}$$

The equation (1) will be rearranged, although the statistical inference is slightly different. With the use of the identity $\psi = 1 - \phi$ it is written now

$$\ln y_t = c_0 + \sigma \ln w_t + c_1 \sum_{\tau=0}^{\infty} \delta^{\tau} \psi_{t-\tau}, \tag{2}$$

with $\sigma = 1/a_1$ and $c_1 = -(a_3 - a_2)/a_1$.

The main argument concerns the coefficient c_1: If c_1 is negative, then, *ceteris paribus*, a rising share of military R & D decreases the rate of growth in productivity. In the case of a positive c_1, the rate of productivity accelerates.

The economic rationale for equation (2) and coefficient c_1 is presented now. Starting from a neoclassical CES production function with neutral technical progress, an equation between labour productivity, real wages and technical progress is derived on the lines of the original article of Arrow *et al.*[14] Neutral technical progress is defined in a special way: taking a weighted average of past shares of military and civil R & D, the impact of changes in the composition of these shares on productivity growth is investigated. The other effects of technical progress are attributed to an unexplained residual.

Let the unexplained residual be defined by an exponential term $\exp(a_1 t)$. With the use of additional coefficients a_0, a_2 and a_3, the time discount factor δ and a distribution parameter β, the CES function is written as

$$Y_t = a_0 \cdot \exp(a_1, t) \cdot \exp\left(\sum_{\tau=0}^{\infty} \delta^{\tau}(a_2 \phi_{t-\tau} + a_3 \psi_{t-\tau})\right)$$

$$\cdot (\beta k^{-\varrho} + 1 - \beta)^{1/\varrho}. \tag{3}$$

Under marginal productivity conditions, (2) is derived from (3) in the following way. First define a productivity level $\bar{y}_t$ measured in units of the base year:

$$\bar{y}_t = y_t \cdot \exp(-a_1 t - g(t)) = a_0 \cdot (\beta k^{-\varrho} + 1 - \beta)^{-1/\varrho}, \tag{4}$$

with $g(t) = \Sigma_\tau \delta^\tau (a_2 \phi_{t-\tau} + a_3 \psi_{t-\tau})$.

The time index t will be omitted during the next steps. Define constants $\zeta = \beta a_0^{-\varrho}$ and $\eta = a_0^{-\varrho}(1-\beta)$. Solving (4) for k and taking logarithms, one obtains

$$\ln k = \frac{1}{\varrho} \ln \zeta + \ln \bar{y} - \frac{1}{\varrho} \ln(1 - \eta \bar{y}^\varrho).$$

Logarithmic differentiation yields, with the elasticity of substitution $\sigma = 1/(1+\varrho)$:

$$\ln \bar{y} = -\sigma \ln \eta + \sigma \ln \left(\bar{y} - k \frac{d\bar{y}}{dk} \right). \tag{5}$$

Now, wages are assumed to be proportional to $(\bar{y} - k(d\bar{y}/dk)) \cdot \exp(b_1 t + g(t))$, with some unexplained long term growth rate b_1. Inserted into (5), one gets:

$$\ln y = c_0 + \sigma \ln w + (1-\sigma)(a_3 - a_2)\Sigma_\tau \delta^\tau \psi_{t-\tau} + (a_1 - \sigma b_1)t. \tag{6}$$

If $a_1 = \sigma b_1$, one obtains (2). The coefficient c_1 in (2) satisfies the relation

$$c_1 = (1 - \sigma)(a_3 - a_2). \tag{7}$$

For $\sigma < 1$, c_1 is positive if technical progress by military R & D is higher than by civil R & D ($a_3 > a_2$); then the rate of productivity accelerates *ceteris paribus* with a rising share ψ. It declines if $c_1 < 0$.

Although somewhat arbitrary, the assumption $a_1 = \sigma b_1$ was necessary in order to eliminate the time trend t as explanatory variable. (from a statistical point of view, the logarithm of labour productivity depended too much on t and much less on the other explanatory variables). Thus, using this assumption, the final form (2) was brought into ARMAX-form for econometric estimation. Using the lag operator L ($Lx_t \equiv x_{t-1}$):

$$(1 - \delta L) \ln y_t = \sigma(1 - \delta L) \ln w_t + c_1 \psi_t + c_0 + u_t, \tag{8}$$

with $u_t \sim N(0, \sigma^2)$.

The discount factor δ is either set to 0.9, *a priori*, according to US experiences,[15] and (8) is estimated by OLS; or δ is estimated together with the other coefficients by nonlinear maximum likelihood.

Some final remarks on the economic content of model (3) are in order. R & D cannot be considered here as a special kind of capital stock, as it is done, for instance, in Griliches and in Nadiri.[16] Instead, changes in the composition of φ and ψ shift the production function faster or more slowly to the origin, leaving the marginal rate of substitution between capital and labour constant. The shift is induced by a reallocation of resources in favour of civil or military uses. According to the remarks on the final form of the model, at any time t the previous changes in the composition of R & D have a cumulative effect on this shift. In this sense, long-term effects of the distribution of R & D are captured.

In general, R & D, data are highly autocorrelated with regimes of accelerating and decelerating expenditures. This has consequences for the use of resources and for productivity: for instance, an increase in military R & D is usually accompanied by increasing levels of current arms production. Current production at any time is not only influenced by the shares of R & D but also by various compositions of capital and labour. According to the neutrality assumption these effects are assumed to be separable. In practice they are certainly not.

IV EMPIRICAL ESTIMATES

The results from estimating the model (8) are given in Table 14.2. The period of observation differs among the six nations investigated here. It was chosen according to the available length of time series. Because of autocorrelation in the residuals and multicollinearity in the explanatory variables the results must be considered with caution. t-Values of estimated parameters are given in parentheses. The first row corresponding to each parameter refers to the OLS estimation with *a priori* fixed time discount rate $\delta = 0.9$; the second row shows the estimates for nonlinear ML-estimation over c_0, σ, c_1 and δ. The optimal value for δ is noted. Surprisingly, the optimal δ in the case of USA coincides with the *a priori* fixed $\delta = 0.9$, and this result is similar to the estimations of Griliches and of Nadiri.[17]

Apart from the constant c_0, the majority of estimated parameters is significantly different from zero. Relatively poor estimates were obtained only in the case of France, and for the Netherlands, the coefficient c_1 cannot be distinguished from zero. For the Netherlands, Canada and USA a dummy variable 1971–8(79) had to be introduced for removing a break in the R & D data (compare again the data

TABLE 14.2 Empirical estimates for equation (8)

		Period of observation						
		Canada (1955–79)	France (1959–79)	Germany (1956–79)	Japan (1955–75)	Netherlands (1961–78)	USA (1955–79)
optimal δ		0.95	*	0.70	0.75	*	0.90
c_0	δ = 0.9	0.002 (0.28)	0.01 (1.28)	−0.15 (0.24)	0.01 (1.16)	−0.01 (0.76)	−0.01 (3.9)
	δ = opt.	−0.03 (3.67)	—	0.002 (0.29)	0.11 (3.04)	—	—
δ	δ = 0.9	0.14 (0.8)	0.62 (1.68)	0.93 (4.48)	0.89 (5.96)	0.67 (1.3)	0.27 (2.03)
	δ = opt.	(0.15) (0.82)	—	0.94 (15.)	(0.64) (10.8)	—	—
c_1	δ = 0.9	−0.18 (3.90)	0.005 (0.03)	−0.14 (0.86)	1.99 (1.85)	1.37 (0.66)	−0.08 (4.17)
	δ = opt.	−0.11 (2.77)	—	−0.17 (1.03)	−0.54 (0.65)	—	—
dummy	δ = 0.9	0.01 (0.73)	—	—	—	0.06 (1.9)	−0.023 (3.9)
	δ = opt.	0.02 (1.41)	—	—	—	—	—
R^2 adjusted for degrees of freedom	δ = 0.9	0.77	0.40	0.51	0.73	0.41	0.80
	δ = opt.	0.97	—	0.93	0.99	—	—

No minimum for likelihood-function obtained within the interval 0 < δ < 1.

description in the Appendix). For several reasons, the point estimates must not be overvalued. Instead, the interpretation of the results will concentrate upon qualitative issues.

The hypothesis stated in Section II seems not to be contradicted: in no case would an increase in military R & D spending yield a significant increase in productivity growth, *ceteris paribus*. Some remarks on the various nations will illustrate this.

Japan and Netherlands are nations with traditionally low military R & D. According to the results, a rise in military R & D does not significantly increase productivity, but such an increase cannot be ruled out either. In the case of Japan, the coefficient c_1 varies considerably with the time discount rate δ and it changes the sign within the interval $0.75 \leq \delta \leq 0.9$. Hence some productivity increase may occur when the overall level of arms production is still low and some special products are introduced.

In the case of Germany, a negative influence of an increase in military R & D on productivity can be stated. The high value of σ indicates the strong rise of real wages in the country, which could be even enhanced, according to the model, by weapon production. Stated in terms of the production model, the difference between the relative contribution of military and civil R & D to productivity is apparent, but is likely to be exaggerated and unreliable ($a_3 - a_2 \sim -3$).

The results for France do not contradict the hypotheses, but little more can be said since, in spite of the high share of military R & D, the coefficient c_1 becomes insignificant. On the other hand, for the case of USA significant estimates were obtained. Thus a 1 per cent increase in the share of military R & D reduces *ceteris paribus* the rate of productivity growth by almost 0.1 per cent. The low value for σ indicates the prominent role of arms production in the formation of wages. Although the share of military R & D is rather low in Canada, the results are within the range of those for USA; this might be attributed to the close economic relationships between the two nations.

V CONCLUSIONS

The empirical results by means of the model can be summarised briefly. The hypothesis was not contradicted, that an increasing share of military R & D reduces labour productivity growth, *ceteris paribus*. In the case of Canada, Germany and the USA, an increase in military R & D is likely to have a minor effect on productivity growth compared with an increase in civil R & D. For small nations like Japan and Netherlands and also for France with her extended weapon production such a relation is not confirmed statistically.

The interpretation in the sense of the neoclassical production function is limited for several reasons. For instance, military technological opportunities and industrial processes might not permit a sufficiently smooth substitution with the civil ones as it is required by neoclassical model building. As was mentioned in Section II, further work is needed on the response of capital and labour movements to the relative expansions of the civil and the military sector, and also on the formation of prices and wages in this context.

Finally it must be noted that technological progress is viewed in a much too narrow sense, namely in relation to technological opportunities in the arms race. For instance, civil R & D covers projects which do not stand in a direct relation to industrial processes. The empirical results suggest that some negative impacts of an increased share in military R & D on productivity might get even worse, if only those civil R & D projects are considered which are directly related to industrial processes. This leads to the question of whether the roundabout method of military R & D is at all necessary for innovation. Instead of waiting for technological diffusion, the same result could be obtained, as the example of Japan has shown, by direct application of civil R & D. In this respect, the role of government institutions in reallocating the needed resources cannot be underestimated.

APPENDIX

Figures showing (1) military R & D/total Government R & D, (2) productivity and (3) real wages over time for the following countries: Canada, France, W. Germany (FRG), Japan, Netherlands, USA

DATA SOURCES

R & D expenditures for civil and military purposes: 1955–1970: SIPRI, Stockholm; 1970–79: OECD, Paris. All other data: OECD.

In the case of Canada, a break occurred for R & D data in 1970. Although OECD data were used in collecting the SIPRI data, there is likely to be a break which calls for additional caution in all cases. In order to remove the break, a dummy variable was introduced for estimation (compare Table 14.2).

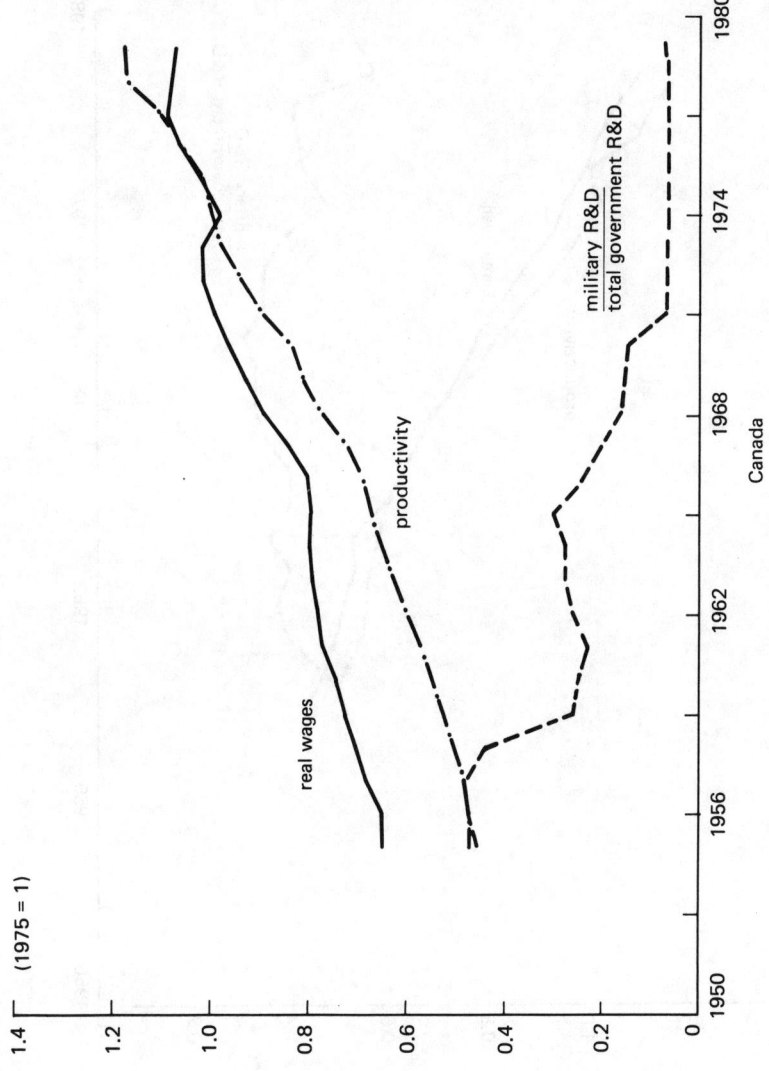

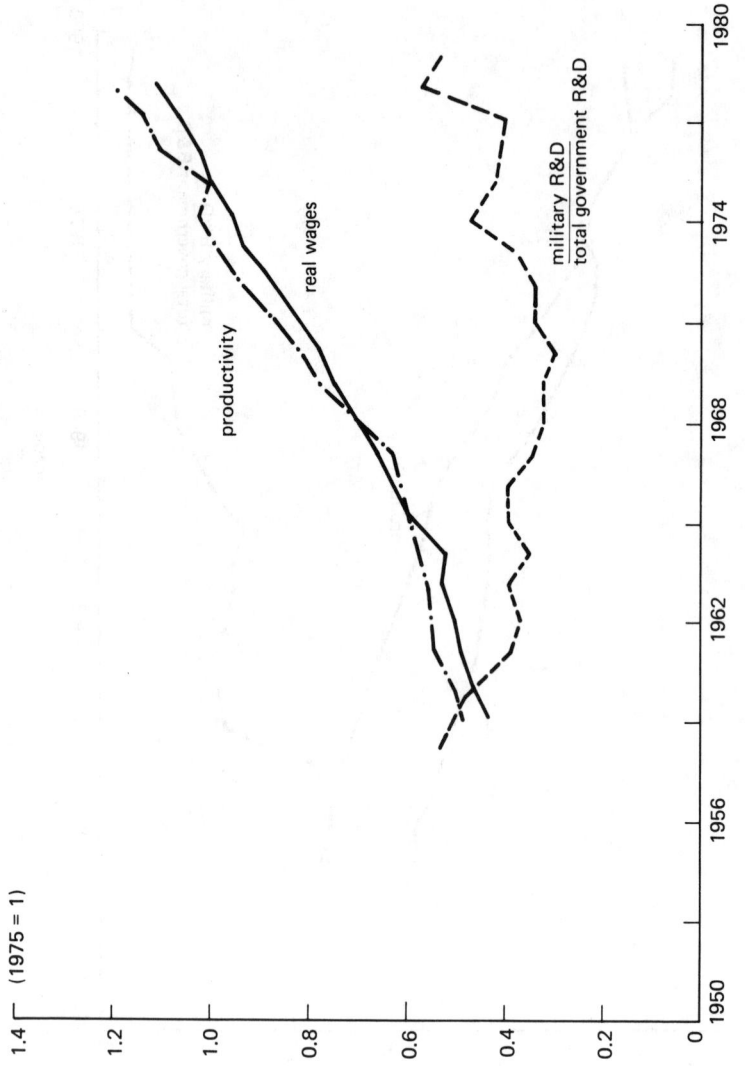

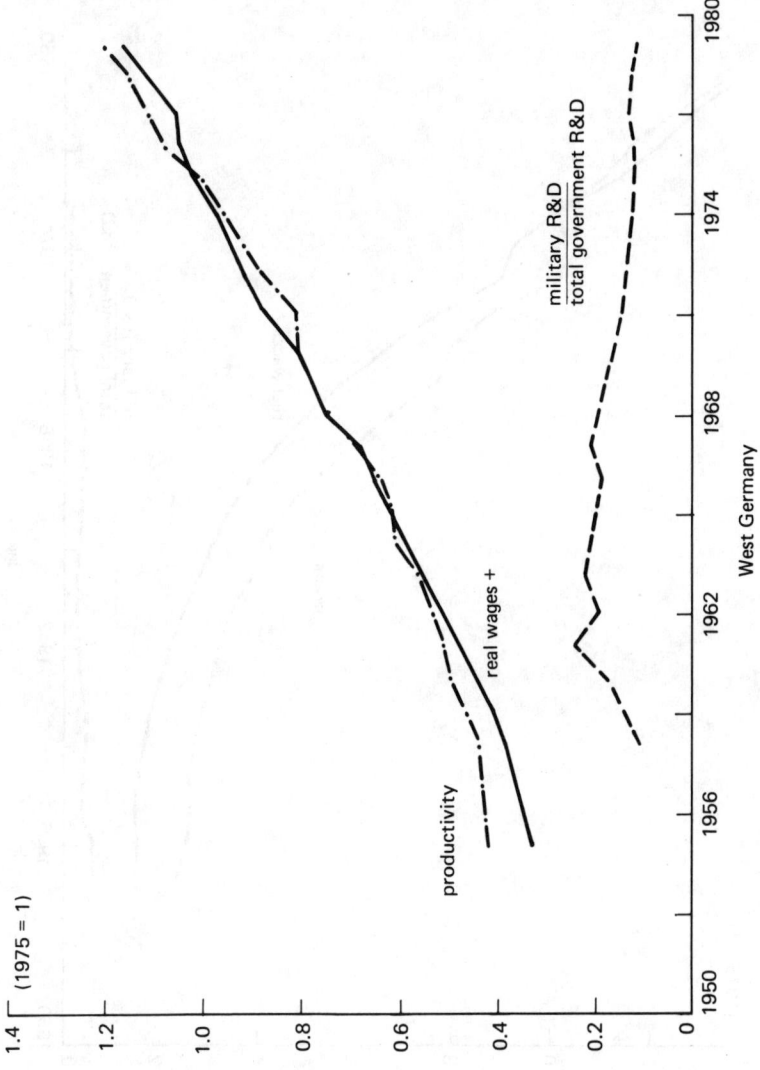

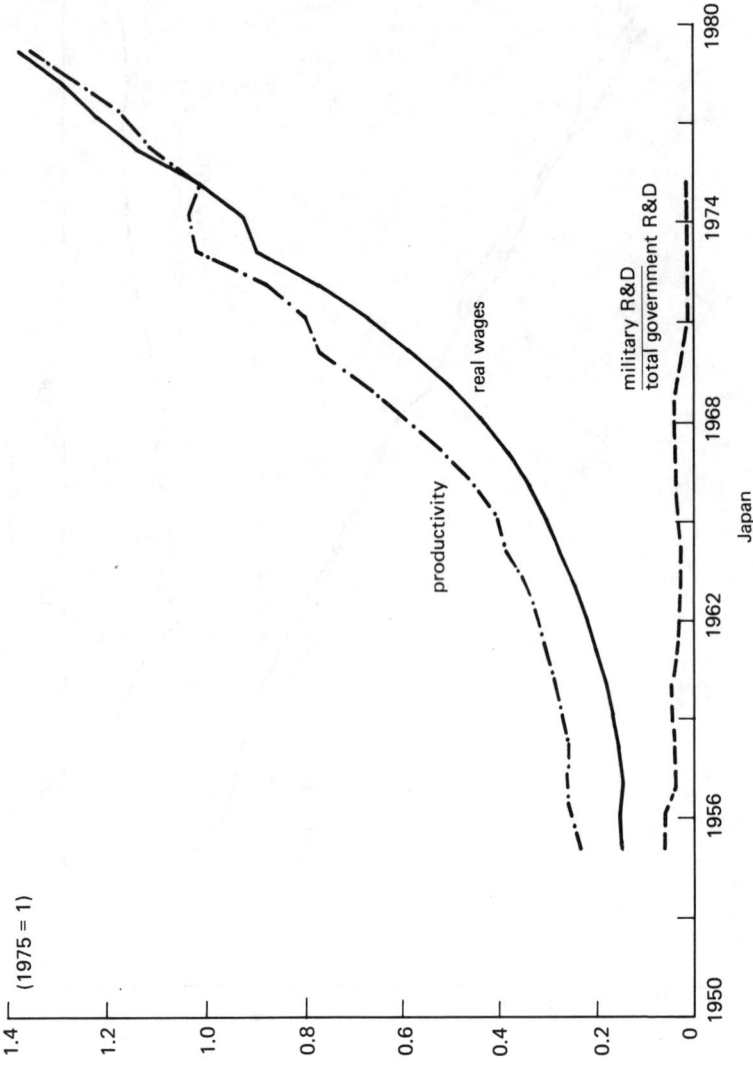

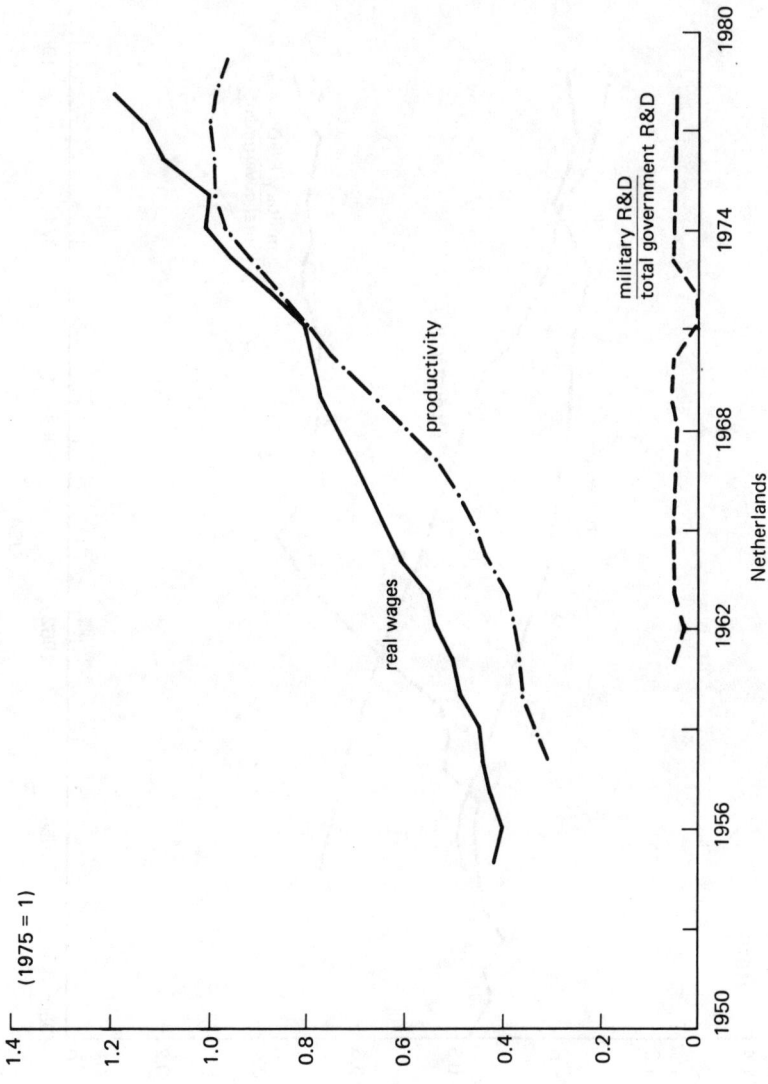

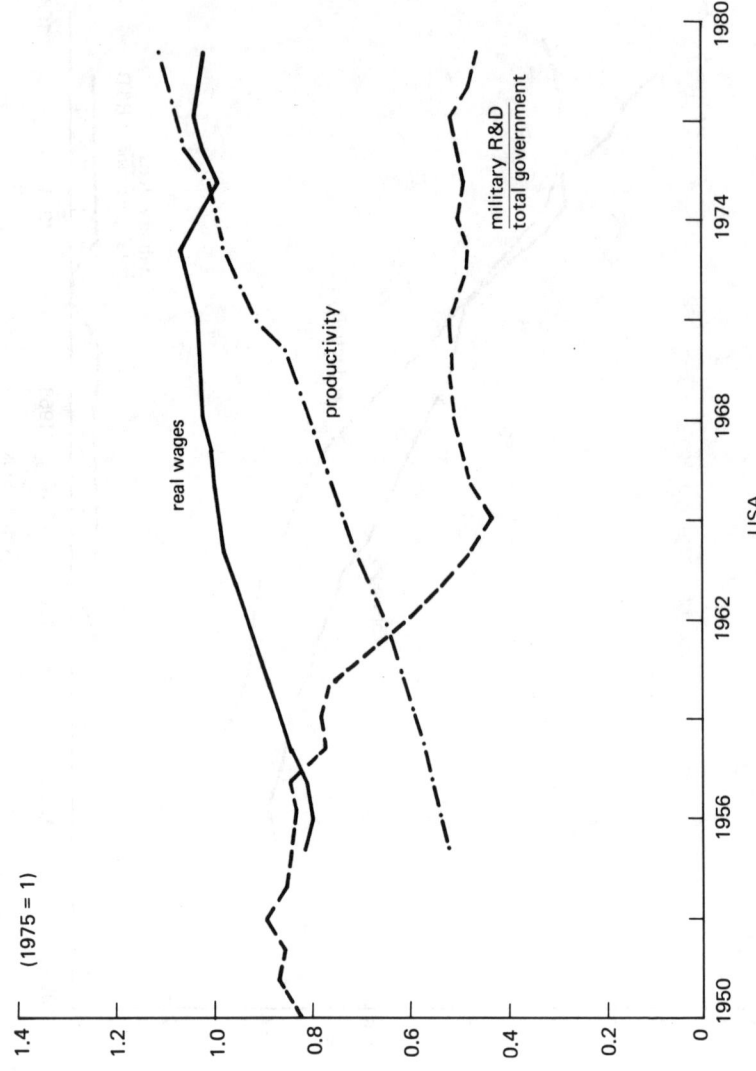

NOTES AND REFERENCES

1. Among the defence related industries, machine, electrical equipment, aircraft and car industries, supply was more than 80 per cent of military goods.
2. SIPRI, *The Arms Race and Arms Control* (London: Taylor & Francis, 1982).
3. See the figures in the appendix.
4. In practice, on an aggregated level, it is virtually impossible to discriminate between military and civil industrial processes. For instance, the assembly of a tank or of an aircraft fighter is only the last link in a complex industrial network. The quantitative analysis based on a military and a civil sector is therefore limited.
5. See data sources, appendix.
6. It must be added that Schumpeter was concerned, in his *Theory of Economic Development*, with private entrepreneurs.
7. Kamien, M. and Schwartz, N., 'Market Structure and Innovation: A Survey', *Journal of Economic Literature*, (March 1977) pp. 1–37.
8. Kaldor, M., *The Baroque Arsenal*, American Century Series, (New York: Hill and Wang, 1980).
9. Leonard, W., 'Research and Development in Industrial Growth', *Journal of Political Economy*, vol. 79/2 (March/April 1971) pp. 232–56.
10. Melman, S., *The Permanent War Economy* (New York: Simon & Schuster, 1974).
11. Classen, W., *Rüstungsausgaben und Wirtschaftsentwicklung* (Military Expenditures and Economic Development) Unpublished Thesis, University of Tübingen, 1971.
12. OECD, *Technical Change and Economic Policy* (Paris: 1981).
13. Melman, The Permanent War Economy.
14. Arrow, K., Chenery, H. B., Minhas, B. and Solow, R. M., 'Capital-Labour Substitution and Economic Efficiency', *Review of Economics and Statistics*, vol. 43/3 (August 1961) pp. 225–51.
15. Griliches, Z., 'R & D and the Productivity Slowdown', *American Economic Review*, vol. 70/2 (May 1981) pp. 343–8. Nadiri, I., 'Sectoral Productivity Slowdown', *American Economic Review*, vol. 70/2 (May 1981) pp. 349–52.
16. Ibid.
17. Ibid.

BIBLIOGRAPHY

Arrow, K. *et al.*, 'Capital-Labor Substitution and Economic Efficiency' *Review of Economics and Statistics*, vol. 43/3 (August 1961) pp. 225–51.
Minhas, B. and R. Solow, *The Review of Economies and Statistics*, vol. 43/3, (August 1961) pp. 225–51.
Classen, W., *Rüstungsausgaben und Wirtschaftsentwicklung* (Military Expenditures and Economic Development), Unpublished Thesis University of Tübingen, 1971.

Griliches, Z., 'R & D and the Productivity Slowdown', *American Economic Review*, vol. 70/2 (May 1981) pp. 343–8.

Kaldor, M., *The Baroque Arsenal*, American Century Series (New York: Hill and Wang, 1980).

Kamien, M. and N. Schwartz, 'Market Structure and Innovation: A Survey', *Journal of Economic Literature* (March 1977) pp. 1–37.

Leonard, W., 'Research and Development in Industrial Growth', *Journal of Political Economy*, vol. 79/2 (March/April 1971) pp. 232–56.

Melman, S., *The Permanent War Economy* (New York: Simon & Schuster, 1974).

Nadiri, I., 'Sectoral Productivity Slowdown', *American Economic Review*, vol. 70/2 (May 1981) pp. 349–52.

OECD, *Technical Change and Economic Policy* (Paris: 1981).

SIPRI, *The Arms Race and Arms Control* (London: Taylor & Francis, 1982).

15 Arms Production in Third World Countries, Effects on Industrialisation

Herbert Wulf
INSTITUTE OF PEACE RESEARCH AND SECURITY POLICY, UNIVERSITY OF HAMBURG

I INTRODUCTION

The domestic production of arms in developing countries is – with remarkably few exceptions – a fairly recent phenomenon.[1] The creation of arms production programmes in developing countries has been associated with a variety of conflicting motives and expectations. The first group of these are military and political in nature: it is hoped to increase independence through self-sufficiency in arms production; arms production can also be precipitated by actual or potential threats from neighbouring countries; it might be a matter of prestige to provide one's armed forces with indigenously produced arms and, occasionally, it is claimed that the arms industry can promote regional dominance. The second set of arguments in favour of domestic Third World arms production are economic in nature: it is hoped to reduce the cost of arms procurement, to contribute indirectly to the development of the economy by improving the skills of the manpower engaged in arms production, and to keep abreast of modern technology in general by making use of technological spin-offs of sophisticated arms production technology.

Whether these economic expectations can be fulfilled will be discussed in this paper.

II ARMS PRODUCTION IN DEVELOPING COUNTRIES AT A GLANCE

In Table 15.1 32 developing countries are listed[2] that are engaged in arms production or planning the manufacture of arms. In addition, there are several countries not included in this list, where only ammunition is reportedly produced (Algeria, Congo, Ghana, Guinea, Morocco, Nepal and Zaire) or where in the past a small number of simple ship hulls have been produced locally (Bangladesh, Gabon, Ivory Coast, Malagasy Republic and Sri Lanka).[3] This list of arms producing countries includes four countries in Europe, eight in Latin America, four in Africa, five in the Near/Middle East and eleven in Asia. The level of domestic arms production attained so far in the respective countries differs substantially. Many industrial undertakings are restricted to the production of small arms and ammunition in relatively small quantities (30 countries) and the construction of small naval craft only (22 countries).

Several countries, however, have attained a high level of arms production and a relatively high degree of diversification. Modern fighter aircraft are built in eight countries, generally under licence (three additional countries are planning such programmes), while light aircraft, trainers and transport aircraft are manufactured in eleven countries. Eleven aircraft manufacturers throughout the developing world produce or assemble helicopters and another twelve produce guided missiles. For military electronics or avionics the figure is ten. Major fighting ships like destroyers, frigates, corvettes or fast patrol boats are constructed in fourteen countries, but often only the hulls are produced locally while the engines, weapons and electronic equipment are imported. The production of submarines and the manufacture of tanks is limited to five countries each. Artillery and cannons are manufactured in six of the 32 countries and armoured personnel carriers and other military vehicles are built in nine countries.

III INDIGENOUS AND LICENCE PRODUCTION

Modern arms production usually requires a capacity for high technology in several branches of industry. The production process is therefore highly complex and requires inputs from a diversified industrial base. Since such a broad industrial base is atypical for developing countries and since they tend to lack adequate research and development facilities, most arms produced in developing countries are licence produced and not developed indigenously. When projects are developed indigenously, technical assistance from foreign personnel is often required; as a rule, the most sophisticated components are imported.

Table 15.2 summarises the number of major arms systems produced according to region and type of production. The majority of projects undertaken fall into two categories: aircraft and major surface ships/fast patrol boats. Of the 45 different types of aircraft produced in developing countries, more than half (23) are licence productions, with the majority located in Asia. Modern fighters are developed in three countries: India, Israel and Yugoslavia. Licence production is even more common for construction of ships: Only five out of 34 different types of major surface fighting or fast patrol boats are indigenously designed, in India, Israel, Peru and Yugoslavia. Similarly, the production of helicopters is apparently extremely difficult without the assistance of an experienced arms producer from an industrialised country. As far as is known, only one helicopter has been developed (in Argentina) for experimental purposes; fifteen other projects are all for production under licence. The fabrication of tanks has been undertaken only five times, submarines seven times. Of the five different tanks produced three were domestic developments undertaken in Israel and Brazil, while two of the seven submarine projects are known to be Yugoslavian design. Twenty-one different guided missiles, ranging from simple portable anti-tank missiles to complicated surface-to-air systems, are produced in developing countries: two-thirds are produced with licences from industrialised countries.

Tables 15.1 and 15.2 together illustrate that apart from the domestic development of light planes, trainers and transport aircraft (developed in eight countries), the development of major arms is extremely limited. Only ten countries have produced indigenously designed weapons systems of any sort. While most of them are produced, though in small production runs, it should, however, be pointed out, that some of these projects have so far not passed the stage of prototype production. To reach the phase of series production often requires heavy industrial investments and additional technology imports.

Table 15.3 shows however that three countries, Israel, India and Yugoslavia, have each developed weapons systems in five or six of eight different categories. Table 15.3 is, however, somewhat

TABLE 15.1 Arms production in developing countries

Country	(1) Fighters, jet trainers, engines	(2) Light planes, transporters	(3) Helicopters	(4) Guided missiles, rockets	(5) Major fighting ships, fast patrol boats	(6) Small fighting ships	(7) Submarines	(8) Tanks	(9) Artillery, cannons	(10) Light tanks, APC, trucks, jeeps	(11) Electronics, avionics, optronics	(12) Small arms, mortars, bombs
Europe												
1 Greece	r					d[n]		r			l	l
2 Portugal	l[a]	d			l	l	l				l	l
3 Turkey	r		l[a]			n					n	n
4 Yugoslavia	d	d	l	l	d	d	d		l		n	d
Latin America												
1 Argentina	c	l	l	d	l	d	l	l	d	l	l	d
2 Brazil	l[a]	d	l	d	l	d	l	d	l	d	l	d
3 Chile						l			l			n
4 Columbia						l[d]						l
5 Dominican Rep.						n					d	
6 Mexico						l					l	l
7 Peru					d							
8 Venezuela		l[a]	l[a]			l					n	n
Africa												
1 Nigeria	l	l	l	l		d			l	l[a]	l	l
2 South Africa				d					l	l	d	d
3 Sudan												l
4 Zimbabwe												

Near/Middle East

1 Egypt	1^n			1^a	1	1			1		1^a	1
2 Iran	(r)		1	(l)	d		d		(l)		(l)	1
3 Israel	d	1	d	d		1	d	d	d	1	d	1
4 Libya	1^a											1
5 Saudi Arabia	1^a			1^n								1

Asia

1 Burma	1		d		1	1	l		1			1
2 India	d	1	d	1	d	1	d	d^n	d	1	d	1	d
3 Indonesia	1		1		d	1	d					1
4 Korea (North)	1		1		1	1	1		1		1	1
5 Korea (South)	1		1	1	1		d	r 1^a	1		1	1
6 Malaysia				1								1
7 Pakistan	1		1	1		1			1			1
8 Philippines	1	d	1	n	1		1		1		1	1
9 Singapore	r				1				1		1	1
10 Taiwan	1	d^a	1	1	n	1			1		1	1
11 Thailand	1		d	1		1	d		1			1

Notes:
c = components only
r = repair, maintenance
l = licence know-how transfer, assembly
d = indigenously developed, produced
n = not known whether l or d
a = planned
( ) = status uncertain

SOURCE IFSH Study Group (1980) appendix updated.

TABLE 15.2 Number of major arms produced: indigenous and licence

	Aircraft	Helicopters	Tanks	Major surface ships, fast patrol boats	Submarines	Guided missiles
Europe						
Indigenous	4			1	2	1
Licences		2		5	1	1
Not known	1	1		1		
Latin America						
Indigenous	6	1	1	1		2
Licences	6	3	1	8	1	4
Not known	1			1		
Africa						
Indigenous			2			1
Licences	4	2		1		1
Not known						
Near/Middle East						
Indigenous	3		2	1		3
Licences				2		1
Not known				1		
Asia						
Indigenous	7			2		
Licences	13	8	1	10	3	7
Not known						
Total						
Indigenous	20	1	3	5	2	6
Licences	23	15	2	26	5	14
Not known	2	1		3		1

Note: Only those projects with at least prototype production, in production, or with production completed have been included
SOURCE IFSH Study Group (1980), appendix.

TABLE 15.3 *Production of indigenously designed major weapons*

Country	Submarines	Helicopters	Tanks	Fighters	Artillery	Major surface ships, fast patrol boats	Guided missiles	Other aircraft
Israel			x	x	x	x	x	x
India	x			x	x	x	x	x
Yugoslavia				x	x	x		
Brazil			x				x	x
Argentina		x					x	x
South Africa							x	
Taiwan								x
Indonesia								x
Philippines								x
Peru						x		
	1	1	2	3	3	4	5	8

SOURCE IFSH Study Group (1980) appendix.

misleading regarding South Africa's arms production. South Africa has, especially during the 1960s, started a number of licence production schemes, mainly with Italian and French cooperation. Owing to the UN arms embargo, the South African arms industry has received top priority and has thus been able to increase the domestic content of arms production. For this reason, some of the projects started with licences from abroad are now classified by some analysts as 'indigenous' projects.

Since arms production in developing countries depends heavily on licences, a large share of these projects rely on technology imports from producer nations. More than two-thirds of all licences listed in this study originated in only four countries: the United States, France, Great Britain and the Federal Republic of Germany (see Table 15.4).

Apart from considerations of industrial self-sufficiency questions of political independence and possibilities for reducing dependence on arms imports immediately arise in regard to licence production.

It is interesting to note how restrictively Soviet licences are granted. Of those licences recorded in Table 15.4, several date back many years and are related to Soviet–Yugoslav cooperation in the production of arms. More recently, India and North Korea have received licences for the production of fighters, guided missiles, and transport planes while the assembly of Soviet helicopters in Peru was reported in the past, recent information on the possible existence of the project is not available.

IV THE POTENTIAL ARMS PRODUCTION BASE

Sophisticated modern weapons systems are usually manufactured from hundreds of different kinds of industrial metals and materials; standardised components and parts demand a rigid uniformity in materials specifications and manufacturing tolerance. Literally thousands of different components have to be produced. As a consequence arms production is dependent on supplies from a variety of industries: iron and steel, electronics, foundry, metallurgy, transportation equipment, and machine tools, to name only the most obvious. To establish an enclave-type of arms industry therefore seems to be an unrealistic approach. The production of some types of major weapons systems appears to create greater difficulties than others. In an early study on the transfer of arms to developing countries it was stated:

TABLE 15.4 Origins of licences

Country	(1) Fighters, jet trainers, engines	(2) Light planes, transporters	(3) Helicopters	(4) Guided missiles, rockets	(5) Major fighting ships, fast patrol boats	(6) Small fighting ships	(7) Submarines	(8) Tanks	(9) Artillery, cannons	(10) Light tanks, APC trucks, jeeps	(11) Electronics, avionics, optronics	(12) Small arms, mortars, bombs
USA	2	7	7	3	4			1	1	2	8	8
France	2		7	7	1	1				5		2
UK	2	2	1	1	8	3		2			2	1
FRG	1		3	5	7	3	3	1		8	1	13
Italy		4	1	1	3	2			1	1		2
Belgium						1				1		5
Sweden		1					1		3			1
USSR	2	1		1	3		1		1	1		2
Others		2		2		2		1		5	1	5
Total	9	17	19	20	26	12	5	4	6	23	12	39

Note: Totals in some categories do not add up to same totals as in Table 15.3 since in Table 15.4 (1) licence agreements for production of subsystems have been included, (2) licence agreements with origins in two countries have been counted twice, (3) agreements already cancelled (as in Iran) are included.

SOURCE IFSH Study Group (1980) appendix

At first glance it may seem that the construction of tanks would be relatively simpler than that of modern aircraft. However, tank construction involves not only very heavy industrial equipment but skills which are less likely to be found in the developing areas and are more difficult to bring into being than a capacity for aircraft *assembly*. Most of the aircraft produced under licence have demanded only the development of light industry to fabricate parts and produce assemblies; the engine and more difficult electronic components were usually available from the original manufacturers or another major industrial power. (emphasis added)[4]

Large size foundry pieces used for tanks are particularly difficult to produce and this is probably the reason for the small number of tank production programmes in developing countries. The above-cited article also draws attention to the remaining import dependency in aircraft production, something that is confirmed by the large number of licence agreements mentioned above. Similarly the production of large fighting ships and artillery depends on the existence of an efficient heavy industry, assuming that most electronic systems have to be imported. But even the production of small arms requires considerable technological know-how as Kennedy has pointed out:

Small arms production requires machine-shop skills such as are found in tool-makers, machinists, fitters, drillers, borers, lathe-operators, forgers, reamers, press-workers, heat treatment specialists and so on. The workers would need to work to fine tolerance and, for operational effectiveness, the parts would need to be interchangable.[5]

A weak industrial infrastructure, typical of developing countries, imposes technological limitations on arms production. A low degree of industrial diversification and a shortage of qualified manpower, production equipment, and special raw material inhibits plans for indigenous arms production. A production base of reasonable proportions is a precondition for the initiation of arms production. The smaller the industrial base and the manpower potential the less likely the production of arms. If arms are to be produced in a particular country despite serious limitations in the industrial base and lack of skilled personnel, the greater the need for import licences, parts and other technology.

The increase in domestic arms production in developing countries can probably be explained in part by the growing manufacturing sector. Conversely, the desire to produce arms might also have enhanced the propensity to give priority to industrialisation in general and to certain industries in particular. To get an idea of the size of the capacity for arms production in developing countries we have attempted to identify what may be called the *potential arms production base*. To arrive at a rank order of countries according to this potential production base, that can in turn be compared with the actual rank order of arms producers, two basic indicators have been chosen: *the industrial base* and *the manpower base* (Table 15.5).

Since the United Nations system of International Standard Industrial Classification (ISIC) does not include a category 'arms industry' an attempt has been made here to try to identify those sub-categories which are most relevant for arms production. These are:

ISIC No. 371 iron and steel
        372 non-ferrous metal
        381 metal products
        382 machinery (not electrical)
        383 electrical machinery
        384 transportation equipment

The six key industries, which we call the '*relevant industries*' for arms production are some of the most advanced industries in terms of their ability to incorporate new technologies and to apply research and development. Their output has been taken as one indicator[6] and their manpower base has been chosen as an additional one. The second indicator, 'manpower base', consists of two sets of data: the employees or persons engaged in the 'relevant industries' and the scientists, engineers and technicians involved in research and development in the entire country.

From these two indicators a combined rank order of countries has been constructed. Since no comprehensive data are available for all the countries of interests, some estimates have had to be made to arrive at this rank order.

Only those countries up to around rank order number 15 (plus or minus the one or two previous or subsequent ones) would be in a position to initiate arms production programmes beyond the assembly of parts and simple manufacture.

If the *rank order of the actual arms production* is compared with the rank order of the *potential arms production* base a strong correlation is evident (Table 15.6).[7] All but one of the top fifteen major arms producing countries (North Korea where no information is available)

TABLE 15.5. Potential arms production base

		Industrial base			Manpower potential	
Country	Manufacturing as per cent of GDP	Relevant industries as per cent of manufacturing	Output of relevant industries in million US$	Scientists, engineers, technicians, in research & development (thousands)	Employees/persons engaged in the relevant industries (thousands)
(1) (2)	(3)	(4)	(5)	(6)	(7)
1 India	16	32	5025	97^{xy}	1688
2 Brazil	25	36	17025	8	1194
3 Yugoslavia	31	40	4800	32	578
4 South Africa	23	38^y	3925	—	396^y
5 Mexico	28	—	—	6^{xw}	167
6 Argentina	37	—	—	19	112
7 Taiwan	37	38	3375	—	263
8 Korea (South)	25	21	2500	19	322
9 Turkey	20	21	2050	9^{xy}	218
10 Greece	19	23	1375	4	114
11 Iran	13	35	3500	6^y	90
12 Israel	30	33	1300	3^x	97
13 Portugal	36	20	1275	41	130
14 Egypt	24	20^y	875	11^{xy}	98^y
15 Hong Kong	26	21^y	650	—	151^y
16 Chile	20	45	1325	6^y	76
17 Venezuela	15	22	1300	4^y	79
18 Philippines	25	15	900	—	80
19 Columbia	19	17	625	1^x	88
20 Thailand	20	21^y	900	6^x	—

21	Algeria	11	28[y]	625	—
22	Singapore	25	32	600	0.3[x]
					1
					91
23	Indonesia	9	12	525	19
					61
24	Pakistan	16	12[y]	325	9
					78[y]
25	Peru	19	25	425	—
					49[y]
26	Malaysia	18	15[y]	425	—
					72[y]
27	Nigeria	9	17	465	3[y]
					23
28	Saudi Arabia	5	—	—	—
29	Zimbabwe	21	30	225	—
					47
30	Morocco	12	14	200	—
					18[y]
31	Iraq	7	12	150	2
					16
32	Kenya	12	11	75	1[y]
					27
33	Sri Lanka	15	14	50	—
					21
34	Syria	11	11	75	—
					14

Notes:
x = only Scientists and Engineers
y = no recent data after 1974 available

SOURCES
Col. (3) World Bank, *World Development Report*, 1979.
Col. (4) United Nations, *Yearbook of Industrial Statistics*, Vol. 1, several editions.
Col. (5) Col. 3 and 4, GDP according to International Monetary Fund, *International Financial Statistics*, Nov. 1979.
Col. (6) United Nations, *Statistical Yearbook 1978*.
Col. (7) as Col. (4)
occasionally national government statistics were used in addition.

TABLE 15.6 *Relationship of arms production and production potential*

Country	Rank order of arms production (1)	Rank order of potential arms production (2)
Israel	1	12
India	2	1
Brazil	3	2
Yugoslavia	4	3
South Africa	5	4
Argentina	6	6
Taiwan	7	7
Korea (South)	8	8
Philippines	9	18
Turkey	10	9
Indonesia	11	23
Egypt	12	14
Korea (North)	13	–
Pakistan	14	24
Singapore	15	22
Iran	16	11
Columbia	17	19
Portugal	18	13
Greece	19	10
Peru	20	25
Thailand	21	20
Venezuela	22	17
Domin. Republic	23	–
Nigeria	24	27
Mexico	25	5
Malaysia	26	26
Burma	27	–
Chile	28	16
Saudi Arabia	29	28
Sudan	30	–
Zimbabwe	31	29
Libya	32	–

SOURCES Tables 15.1 and 15.5; IFSH Study Group (1980).

belong to those 25 countries having a substantial potential for arms production. There are, however, some deviant cases of particular interest for this study. A few countries with a substantial industrial and/or manpower base are not among the major arms producers: Mexico (ranked fifth in arms production potential), Greece (position 10), Hong Kong (position 15), Chile (position 16), and Algeria (position 21). According to their industrial and manpower base, these five countries are in a position to produce more weapons than they actually do. That they do not produce up to 'capacity' is due either to a policy decision or to certain constraints (like scarce hard currency reserves or difficulties in obtaining licences). The opposite also occurs. Certain countries have apparently overburdened their industrial and manpower bases with ambitious arms production programmes. A particular case in point is Israel, the largest arms producing country, having only position 12 on our list of potential for arms production.

The Philippines is ranked ninth in terms of actual arms production and eighteenth in terms of the potential to produce arms. Indonesia eleventh and twenty-third respectively and Pakistan fourteenth and twenty-fourth. It seems likely that these four countries will experience economic and technical difficulties since their arms production programmes are not based on an adequate industrial base.

V TWO CONCEPTS OF ARMS PRODUCTION

Size and diversity of arms production in developing countries are dependent on the structure and capability of a country's manufacturing industry. Arms production is also closely related to its industrial strategy. In simplifying the industrial concepts in developing countries two basic strategies of industrialisation can be identified: import substitution and export orientation. Similarly two models of arms production can be developed: a self-sufficiency concept based on substituting indigenous production for arms imports and internationally integrated arms production in developing countries.

Obvious parallels exist between the *import-substitution industrialisation and arms production* in several developing countries. Arms production was part of the industrialisation strategy and meshed well with political aspirations for maximum possible political independence. Consequently arms production programmes aiming at national self-sufficiency were instituted in some of those countries which emphasised import-substitution strategies. This is particularly true for arms production in Argentina under Peron and for India since the beginning of the 1960s. The major exception is Mexico, with intensive import substitution industrialisation but only limited arms production till the present time.

Structural difficulties and bottlenecks in the economy of developing countries hamstring a policy of self-sufficiency. As long as domestic arms production is based on a weak industrial structure, very large investments are required to initiate the design and production of the numerous components of modern weapons systems. Suboptimal utilisation of production capacities characterises both latecomer non-military industrialisation oriented towards the domestic market and latecomer arms production. Technological specialisation leads to investments in highly diverse and only partly integrated production capacities; the limited budget of the armed forces results in oversized factories and eventually substantial cost overruns.

An indicator for the extent of self-sufficiency in arms production is the content of indigenous production in a particular weapons system. Usually only a limited percentage can be produced locally. Reducing the import content below 30 per cent – even in production programmes marked as 'indigenous development' – is the exception rather than the rule. Self-reliance or self-sufficiency has been the overriding principle of arms production in India for more than three decades. Large capacities to produce arms domestically have been installed. The volume of production in the 31 government directed ordnance factories and nine public enterprises of the so-called 'defence production sector' has more than doubled during the last decade to more than 800 m US dollars; the labour force in this sector has constantly been increasing, reaching–according to the annual Report of the Ministry of Defence – a level of more than 190 000 in 1972 and over 240 000 employees in 1978.

Official figures on the domestic value added or the import content are only occasionally available; therefore, a definite answer cannot be given. The scant evidence available for India is compiled in Table 15.7. Statements by the government suggest that the indigenous content is constantly being increased.

The frigate programme, for example, required 92 per cent imports for the first frigate, while the last unit was down to 40 per cent of imports. Occasionally, doubt is cast on such figures. For example, an international journal pointed out in 1978, that western companies

TABLE 15.7 *Indigenous content of weapon systems produced in India*

Type of weapon	Share of Indigenous content %	Year
Production in ordnance factories	93	1978
Military vehicles	91–96	1978
Machine guns	80	1978
L-70 fire control radar	87	1978
Anti-tank missile	72	1977
Frigates (Leander class)	60	1978
MiG 21	40	1972
Aircraft production (total)	32	1975

SOURCE Government of India, Ministry of Defence, Report, several issues, *Internationale Wehrrevue*, 4/1979, p. 1979.

'have also been involved with the overall design and the main machinery for these ships',[8] nevertheless such programmes are usually hailed as indigenous. The fact that the government initiated a special 'indigenisation programme' and referred to certain programme delays can be taken as evidence for continued difficulties in reaching self-sufficiency. Probably the greatest failure of the Indian arms production efforts was the development of the indigenous supersonic fighter-bomber HF-24 Marut, started in the early 1960s with a total production of about 140 units of different models.[9] The aircraft never reached supersonic speed due to the failure to procure or develop the appropriate engine. The fact that the British fighter 'Jaguar' is being purchased in Britain (and partly licence-produced in India) and that the procurement of modern Soviet fighters was considered at the beginning of 1982, illustrates that the Indian arms industry is dependent on imports of the latest technological developments.

Another most pertinent example is the production of Argentina's counter-insurgency plane Pucara. Despite the experience of Argentina's aerospace industry it was necessary to import practically all major sophisticated components for this rather conventional aircraft, as Table 15.8 shows.

But even the figures on indigenous content or detailed lists on imports of components are not the final word on the technological dependence. Given a certain industrial base the initiation of assembly of weapons systems and the production of simple parts can be successfully managed within a short span of time. Beyond basic

TABLE 15.8 *Major imported equipment for Pucara*

Component	Supplier
Engines	Turbomeca (France)
Propellers	Ratier-Figeac (France)
Ejector seats	Martin-Baker (UK)
Cannon	Hispano-Oerlikon (Switzerland)
Machine-guns	Browning (USA)
Gunsight	General Precision (USA)
External stores rack	Standard Armament (USA)
Comm/nav. equipment – except tactical HF system	Bendix (USA) Sunair (USA)
Fuel system components	Dunlop (Australia), LSI-Romeo (USA) Zenith (France), Valcor (USA), Aeroquip (USA)
Fire protection system	Graviner (UK), L'Hotellier (France)
Oxygen system	Bendix (USA)
Armoured windshield	Triplex (UK)
Engine controls	AMA, Jaeger, St. Chamone-Granat, Faure-Herman (all France)
Hydraulic system components	Messier (France), Bendix (USA), Dowty (UK), Aeroquip (USA), Lockheed (USA), Valcor (USA)
Deicing system (optional)	Kleber (France), Air Equipment (France)
Cabin system	Dunlop (UK)
Electrical systems	SAFT, Bronzavia, SEB, FM-Labiral, Telexflex, Syneravia, Souriau (all France), Flite-Tronics, Amphenol (both USA)

SOURCE   *Interavia*, 7/1973, p. 771.

assembly and simple production the technical diseconomies for further import-substitution become very substantial. We can conclude: the higher the indigenous content the greater the need to use the services of foreign companies and specialists. The expected training effect on the domestic work-force therefore seems to be doubtful, especially since the arms producers of industrialised countries are not likely to adapt their technologies to the particular requirements of the developing countries' industry and industrial labour.

In several countries like Brazil, Israel, Taiwan, Korea and Singapore governments have promoted the creation of an arms industry with the explicit intention of sales on the world market. Many of the new suppliers remain none the less themselves heavily dependent on the import from industrialised countries.

Different degrees of integration of developing countries into *internationally organised arms production* can be discerned. Usually, the first stage of production consists of *assembly work* only and is mainly directed at import substitution. Occasionally, however, it takes the form of a market expansion strategy of producers from industrialised countries.

A second stage, usually in temporal sequence, is the *production of components*, starting with the least technologically sophisticated parts and gradually increasing the number of components and subsystems produced domestically. There are two distinct forms of this sort of cooperation: the first is production for local 'demand'; most of the projects fall into this category. The declared intention of such projects usually includes self-reliant production as the final stage. The second form is when components are produced for the licenser in an industrialised country. This type of cooperation comes close to the often practised international subcontracting of civilian industrial products. While this kind of co-operation in arms production is often carried out between producers in industrialised countries and is intended to be a compensation for the industry of the importing country, it is not so common between industrialised and developing countries. Few examples are known: Israel Aircraft Industries, for example, produces components for the US produced F-15 fighter. One can call this case a truly international division of labour under the guidance and control of a US company. Additional examples are the production of parts for the F-5 Northrop fighter in Brazil or the L-70 Swiss-made fire control radar in India.

A third stage of a different degree of export-oriented production of arms is fabrication *under the control of companies in developing countries*. It is probably most advanced in Israel and in Brazil. The Brazilian comany Engesa, for example, exports a so-called indigenously developed armoured personnel carrier 'Cascavel' to several countries (Libya, Iraq, Qatar). In reality the Cascavel incorporates major parts (like the engine, transmission, electronic-components, parts of the gun) imported from producers in industrialised countries or produced in Brazil by foreign owned companies. Similarly the Brazilian-made light fighter 'Bandeirante' consists of Brazilian-made as well as imported sub-systems. The sale of such products as 'Cascavel', 'Bandeirante', or the Israeli made 'Reshef' fast patrol boat, or

'Kfir' fighter on the world market is a rather new phenomenon of the late 1970s.

A fourth stage, *direct investment of foreign companies* in arms production in developing countries, is rather the exception than the rule. Several of the few foreign investments[10] are located in Israel, particularly in the electronics industry; it is also interesting to note that the plans for building up an arms industry in Egypt are largely based on foreign investments. The status of these companies is, however, at present uncertain and it is likely that not all of the companies mentioned will come into operation.

A fifth and a final stage of export-oriented arms production would be *fabrication in free production zones*. So far no information on such activities is available. One reason for the possible absence of arms production in free production zones is probably the necessity of legitimising the procurement of arms in a national context. A second reason might be the fact that arms are often sold below their actual costs because of government subsidies (like R & D reimbursement, inexpensive credits, pre-payments etc.) that are granted to arms producers. These benefits might be more attractive than the economic incentives in free production zones.

A comparison of these two approaches of domestic arms production reveals that self-reliant arms production is quantitatively less dependent on imports, but cannot be fully implemented without cooperation, technology supplies and licences from experienced arms producers in industrialised countries. In the second strategy, that of internationally integrated domestic production importation of technology is part of the production strategy. Transnational corporations are given an important role in the development and production process.

VI THE IMPACT ON INDUSTRIALISATION

Occasionally it has been argued by social scientists and political leaders in developing countries that a strong military posture is not an obstacle to achieving maximum economic development but that it might even be a prerequisite.

The break-down of the Shah's 'model' of Iran as a country of economic and military power[11] teaches important lessons about militarily overburdened and oppressed societies. It is important to note also that Iran is not just a deviant case with respect to the share of resources going into an arms build-up and the setting up of an arms industry. In many other countries scarce resources are absorbed in the military sector and the domestic production of arms is considered a vehicle for reducing foreign influence. It is therefore essential to ask what economic and political implications such a pattern of armaments will have. If arms production depends on inputs from other industrial sectors it might stimulate industrialisation through backward linkages. The initiation of arms production sends out stimuli in the direction of the manufacturing industries. Could the demand for domestically produced arms function via backward linkages with certain manufacturing industries as a stimulus for industrial growth and what kind of industry would develop? Backward linkage effects will, according to Hirschmann,[12] induce attempts to supply through domestic production the inputs needed in that activity. Investment in arms production could certainly bring with it the availability of new, expanding markets for its inputs. Arms producing companies are often basically systems management companies with a very limited share of value added in the final product, thus requiring a high percentage of inputs from other industries. This interdependence through purchases from other sectors, i.e. high backward linkages, could be an encouragement towards setting up or expanding other industries.

The first difficulty arises with respect to the volume of induced inputs. Arms production generally is characterised by short production runs. Even in Western European countries where the budget for arms procurement is generally higher than in developing countries and where exports are added to domestic demand, arms producers complain about the small numbers of units produced of particular weapons systems. In developing countries production runs are often rather limited. To develop special production machinery, to invest in special alloys factories, to start production of avionics or optronics etc. would be highly uneconomic due to the limited demand by the arms industry. The linkage effect would therefore probably be unlikely to exceed a certain critical value required and consequently arms producers are most likely to depend on imported inputs. Unless the govenment is willing to take over the risk of investment and to subsidise uneconomic production capacities their installation is not likely to materialise.

A second difficulty is closely related to the first one. The production of modern arms is characterised by incorporating high-technology products, reliance on precise and uniform components, standardised high quality materials etc. Such demands are atypical for practically all consumer products (certainly for those products consumed by the majority of the population in developing countries). Extreme requirements formulated by the military with regard to durability, mobility, precision, performance in different climatic and combat conditions etc. are realistically not demanded by the civilian industry. In other words, military and civil technology tends to diverge; capacities installed for meeting the demand of arms production are not likely to be utilised economically for alternative production. We can therefore conclude that the investment in arms production might not result in the expected backward linkages or if these backward linkages are established it might be a costly and uneconomic investment.

A third difficulty is related to the production process and to the factor endowment of developing countries. The development and the production of most modern arms are closely related to perceived conflict formation at the East–West level. The long-term historic trend of wars and war scenarios in industrial countries has been characterised by the mechanisation of armies, resulting in increasing destructive power through capital inputs rather than manpower.

At the same time, as a consequence of higher capital inputs into armies, the demand for trained manpower has been increasing; technical and engineering skills are especially required in highly mechanised armies. This particular emphasis on using capital and reducing the use of unskilled manpower is not an exclusive speciality of the armed forces. A similar development can be observed in industrial production in general. There is, however, a specific combination of factors typical for arms production in contrast to the production of 'civil goods'. The tendency of the military to be prepared for the worst case and the acceptance by governments has resulted in ever increasing research and development efforts to design and produce ever more complex weapon systems; as a consequence a fast rate of product innovations leads to the creation of technological obsolescence.

This specific trend in the military sector has particularly negative repercussions in developing countries. Looking at the factor endowment we can observe that the majority of developing countries have abundant unskilled labour, while at the same time highly skilled labour and capital is usually scarce. Vernon[13] formulated in his product cycle theory that products pass through a certain temporal cycle. The beginning of the production process is characterised by research intensity, experimentation and low numbers of units produced. With an expanding market products are standardised and less skilled manpower is required in the production process. When the product is matured a large number of less skilled personnel are used in production. For the optimal use of factors available in developing countries it would be economical according to the product cycle theory to produce fairly matured products. Modern weapons, however, generally do not reach the stage of standardisation, maturity and mass production. Owing to the high rate of obsolescence and the research intensity arms production is unsuitable especially for less industrialised countries.

Referring again to the above-mentioned backward linkages of the arms industry it is obvious that arms production induced demand is not necessarily beneficial for development. Generally speaking the evolution of the industrial pattern tends to be oriented towards the requirements of the arms industry whenever an ambitious programme is launched. The capital intensive, skilled manpower intensive production process imposes itself by backward linkages on previous production stages. Thus the choice of technology in certain sectors of industry is not based on the demands of the majority of the population, but is predetermined by the technological imperatives of arms production.

To what extent scarce factors in developing countries are absorbed in arms production, in servicing and maintenance of weapon systems can easily be illustrated. In a study by SIPRI[14] it is mentioned that at the beginning of the 1970s an efficient armoured unit of the armed forces required 150 trained mechanics for every 100 tanks and another 50 mechanics for every 100 armoured personnel carriers. Allowing for the fact that these figures might have increased during the last decade, since tanks are more complex today, and allowing also that these figures were given for a highly industrialised country with a developed industrial infrastructure, as well as taking into account that climatic conditions in developing countries might add additional wear in materials, we estimate the requirement for trained mechanics to be at least 50 per cent higher. Thousands of qualified technicians are needed in some countries in order to keep the inventory of tanks and armoured personnel carriers operational. Between 5000 and 10 000 trained mechanics are needed in nine different countries. A similar estimate has been made for the equipment in the air forces of developing countries. Obviously a substantial share of skilled work-force is needed in the military sector if we take these estimates as an indicator, add the labour input of the arms producers and compare these with the total number of scientific and technical manpower as it is recorded in United Nations statistics.

In some countries the minimum requirement for maintenance and repair might be even larger than the total number of trained personnel. Apparently, in many countries the military equipment is either underserviced and remains rusting and unused in stores or foreign personnel has to be hired, imposing a heavy economic burden on the government budget.

An additional economic burden to be taken into account is the absorption of import capacities (hard currencies) as a result of the importation of arms and arms production technology.[15]

VII SELF-SUFFICIENCY OR UNINTERRUPTED DEPENDENCE?

Self-sufficiency in the supply of arms is the most common *raison d'être* for arms production in developing countries. It is therefore legitimate to ask to what extent developing countries have, over time, developed the industrial base and the skills necessary to become self-reliant in arms production and large-scale military operation.

A qualitative change in the supplier–recipient relationship takes place when an importing country tries to diversify its supply sources. The direct leverage of a single supplier country is reduced if arms are purchased in other supplier countries and also if arms are produced domestically. There is virtually no major weapons system produced in developing countries that does not rely on the importation of licences, know-how or components from industrialised countries. Given the underdeveloped character of the arms production base, the general paucity of skilled manpower and low degree of industrial diversification, high technology transfers and substantial cooperation from industrialised countries may well be required for the foreseeable future.

The examples of India, Brazil, and Israel (as the most advanced producers in the developing world) illustrate that self-sufficiency has so far been reached only for some less sophisticated weapons systems. Brazil's arms industry is basically an assembly type industry, depending to a large degree in importation of components and subsystems and purchases from foreign enterprises. The task of coping with systems management problems and assembly has apparently been successfully achieved for some types of light aircraft and armoured personnel carriers.

The reliance of the Israeli aircraft industry on foreign technology was demonstrated by the much publicised export promotion of modern Kfir fighters which was vetoed by the US Government. While the Israeli aircraft industry claims this plane to be a truly Israeli 'combat-proven' product, it is actually equipped with an US jet engine and major US avionic systems. For that reason the US Government could successfully forestall sales to Ecuador and Taiwan.

India's arms industry has the most explicit and consistent self-sufficiency strategy. Nevertheless, as the list of 'indigenous' developments of the arms industry shows, even these projects are dependent on essential foreign inputs. Furthermore, the installation of three factory complexes for the production of Soviet MiG 21 fighters in the mid-1960s and a fourth factory for the production of avionics turned out to be such a large-scale investment that the demand of the Indian Air Force for a new fighter plane had to be postponed for more than half a decade until 1979. The decision of the Government of India to buy the MiG 21 in 1962 reduced India's reliance on British supplies and strengthened the government's policy of non-alignment; the arrangement was, however, so sizeable and complex that once an agreement was entered into it was then hardly possible to opt for alternatives for almost two decades.

The installation of arms production facilities is evidently a longer-term decision than imports of complete weapons systems, since higher economic stakes are involved in the domestic industry.

Other countries, less advanced than Brazil or India both in general industrialisation and in arms production are even more prone to depend on foreign collaboration. The South Korean arms industry is almost totally oriented towards US licences and high technology imports, even though the general industrial level is fairly advanced. Taiwan's efforts could be described in similar terms and the dependence of Egypt's plans to revive its arms production can best be demonstrated by pointing to the long list of foreign collaboration projects under discussion.

From the evidence collected in this paper it can be concluded that there is, for the time being, no short-term or even medium-term fulfillment of the desire of developing countries to reach a high degree of self-sufficiency in arms production. On the surface, a more equal partnership between the industrialised countries and those developing countries that have invested in arms production has emerged; in reality, basic asymmetries remain. As long as developing countries continue to formulate military scenarios akin to those prescribed for the East–West conflict, they are also bound to rely on the arms technology of industrialised countries, either imported as complete weapons or as production technology.

For developing countries the implications of the technological lead of the major industrial countries in arms production are that dependence upon one or several of the major arms producing countries cannot be avoided.

NOTES AND REFERENCES

1. This article is based on research undertaken at the IFSH Study Group on Armaments and Underdevelopment. Due to lack of space, numerous details about the size of production, turnover and employment of companies cannot be presented here. For further details see: IFSH Study Group on Armaments and Underdevelopment, *Transnational Transfer of Arms Production Technology*, IFSH Forschungsbericht 19 (Hamburg: 1980) and Wulf, H., *Rüstung als Technologietransfer* (Munich and London: Weltforumsverlag, 1980).

   There are only a few studies available. A pioneering study was: SIPRI, *The Arms Trade with the Third World* (Stockholm: Almqvist & Wiksell, 1971) ch. 22.

   Updated information on domestic arms production is given in the SIPRI Yearbooks (*World Armament and Disarmament – SIPRI Yearbook*, (London: Taylor & Francis)); see also: Väyrynen, R., *The Role of Transnational Corporations in the Military Sector of South Africa*, prepared for the United Nations Centre on Transnational Corporations (Helsinki: University of Helsinki, Dec. 1978) mimeo; Tuomi, H. and Väyrynen, R., *Transnational Corporations, Armaments and Development* (Tampere: Peace Research Institute, 1980) ch. v, pp. 144–207; Moodie, M., 'Defense Industries in the Third World: Problems and Promises', pp. 294–312, in Neuman, S. G. and Harkavy, R. E. (eds), *Arms Transfer in the Modern World*, (New York: Praeger, 1979).

   For US co-production in developing countries see: Klare, M., *Arms Technology, Dependency – US Military Co-production Abroad*, NACLA's Latin American Report (January 1977) pp. 25–32; Kennedy, G., *The Military in the Third World* (London: Duckworth, 1974) chs 15 and 16. Albrecht, U., Ernst, D., Lock, P. and Wulf, H. *Rüstung und Unterentwicklung, Iran, Indien, Griechenland/Türkei: Die Verschärfte Militarisierung* (Reinbek: Rowohlt, 1976) ch. 2. Lock, P. and Wulf, H., *Register of Arms Production in Developing Countries* (Hamburg: IFSH Study Group on Armament and Underdevelopment, 1977) mimeo. Lock, P. and Wulf, H., 'Consequences of the Transfer of Military-Oriented Technology on the Development Process', *Bulletin of Peace Proposals*, vol. no. 8, 2 (1977) pp. 127–36; and Wulf, *Rüstung als Technologietransfer*.

2. The group of countries described as 'developing' is not a homogeneous group. It is therefore not surprising that the number of countries included in this category varies. For the purpose of this paper, it has been considered appropriate to include several countries which are, according to the UN classification, subsumed in other categories. It was felt necessary to include them because their level of development, as expressed in such indicators as per capita income and the level of industrialisation, does not justify their classifications as industrialised countries. This is the case for Greece, Portugal, Turkey, Yugoslavia, Israel and South Africa. In addition, North Korea has been included but the Peoples' Republic of China has been excluded.
3. These are such isolated efforts that they are not considered relevant to this examination of arms production.
4. Sutton, J. L. and Kemp, G., *Arms to Developing Countries, 1945–1965*, Adelphi Papers, no. 28 (London: Institute of Strategic Studies, Oct. 1966) p. 26.
5. Kennedy, G., *The Military in the Third World*, p. 295.
6. The output of the six industrial branches is also given in the United Nations *Yearbook of Industrial Statistics* (Vol. I), an annual publication. The precision of reporting varies to some extent, however, from country to country. To arrive at comparable data, the share of the six industries as a percentage of manufacturing output was computed. Using the share of manufacturing as a percentage of gross domestic product it was possible to arrive at a comparable output figure for more than fifty developing countries.
7. Spearman's Rho comes to a correlation of +0.48 for the twenty major producers.
8. *Navy International* (July 1978) p. 25.
9. For a discussion see SIPRI (1971), p. 748.
10. For details see IFSH Study Group (1980), Table 13, p. 58.
11. The Shah and his ambitious plans are quoted in Chubin, S., 'Implications of the Military Buildup in less Industrial States: The Case of Iran', in Ra'anan, U. *et al.* (eds), *Arms Transfers to the Third World: The Military Buildup in less Industrial Countries* (Boulder, 1978) p. 268.
12. Hirschmann, A. O., *The Strategy of Economic Development* (New Haven, 1958) ch. 6.
13. Vernon, R., 'International Investment and International Trade in the Product Cycle', *Quarterly Journal of Economics*, vol. 80 (2/1966) pp. 190–207.
14. SIPRI (1971), p. 806.
15. For a discussion see Lock, P. and Wulf, H., 'Consequences of the Transfer of Military-oriented Technology on the Development Process', *Bulletin of Peace Proposals*, vol. 8 (2/1977) pp. 127–36.

Name Index

Abelson, R.P., 169n, 171n
Agarwal, R. K., 335n
Albrecht, U. 382n
Alexander, A., 333n
Allais, M. 302, 303n
Allen, P., 173n
Allison, G. T., xxiiin, 169n, 171n, 172,
Aronson, S., 334n
Arnson, C., 122
Arrow, K., 355n
Atwater, E., 278n

Baldwin, D., 134n
Ball, N., xxiin
Barry, R. H., 196n
Beattie, K. 277n
Beaufré, A., 196n
Benoit, E., xxiin, 88, 97n, 108, 112n
Bergstrom, T. C., 237n
Blackaby, F., xviii, 3–28, 44–6, 102
Blake, D., 172n
Bloomfield, L., 240, 242, 276n
Boulding, K., xvii, xxiin, 3, 169n, 172n, 176, 178
Brines, R., 277n, 278n
Brito, D., xix, xxin, 171n, 172n, 173n, 176n, 180–96
Brzoska, M., 24n
Burns, A., 170n, 172n
Butterworth, R., 242, 276n, 277n
Butz, W. P., 333n

Cahn, A., 276n
Caiden, N., 112n
Cannizzo, C., 276n
Cars, H. C., xviii, 69–84
Carter, Pres. J., administration, 136, 245, 257–60, 305, 332
Chenery, H. B., 355n
Churchill, R. and W., 276n
Chubin, S., 383n
Cioffi–Revilla, C. A., 169n, 172n
Classen, W., 355n
Clausewitz, C. V., 113, 173n

Cohen, S., 334n
Corcoran, W., 300n
Cournot, 'behaviour', 208
Creveld, van, 269, 270–1, 279n
Crocker, C., 277n
Cruz, J. B., 171n, 174n

Dacey, R., 236, 238n
Dadant, P., 279n
David, S., 277n
Debré, M., 315
Desai, M., 172n
Deutsch, E., xix, 101, 299n, 301–3, 336–356
Dismukes, B., 279n
Dossor, D., 299n
Dror, Y., 319, 334n
Duchin, F., xxiiin, 88, 97n
Duisenberg, W. F., 90, 97n

Edwards, I., 46n
Efrat, M., 108, 112n
Ernst, D., 382n

Fei, E. T., 276n
Fontanel, J., xviii, 25–46, 68n, 88, 97n
Freedman, L., 334n
Fuller, J. R. C., 269, 279n

Galbraith, J. K., 105, 112n
Galper, H., 236n
Gansler, J. xvii, xxiiin, 313n
Gaspary, W. M., 169n, 170n
Gees-Larue, C., 276n
Gelb, L., 277n
Gillespie, J. V., 152, 170n, 171n, 172n, 174n, 178n, 196n
Giscard d'Estaing, V., 332
Goldberger, A., 236n
Goodman, R. P., 236n
Gowland, D., 299n
Graham, D. O., 17, 24n
Gramlich, E. M., 236n, 237n
Gray, C. S., 195

Name Index

Gregory, P. R., 172n
Greenwood, D., xix, 98–103
Griliches, Z., 345, 355n, 356n
Groth, M., 236n

Haan, H. D. de, xix, 87–103
Hammond, P. Y., 278n
Harkavy, R. E., xxi, 239–79, 333n, 334n
Hartley, K., xix, xxi, 283–303
Harvey, R. A., 299n
Haselkorn, A., 279n
Haugh, L. D., 170n, 173n
Herrera–Lasso, L., xx, 113–34
Heston, A., 42n, 43n
Hirschmann, A. O., 377, 383n
Hollist, W. L., 169n, 171n, 172n
Holmes, J., 278n
Holsti, O. R., 195n
Holzmann, F. D., 16, 18, 24n
Hudson, C., 279n
Hughes, M., 46n
Huntingdon, S. P., 170n, 172n, 195n

Intriligator, M. E., vii, xix, xxi, 169n, 170n, 171n, 172n, 173n, 176–9, 178n, 180–96, 236
Indyk, M., 279n
Ivanov, Y., 43n

Jefferson, P., 299n
Johnson, J. J., 112n
Jones, D., 169n, 170n, 173n

Kaldor, M., 20n, 355n, 356n
Kamien, M., 338, 355n, 356n
Kemp, G., 24n, 240, 276n, 277n, 383n
Kennedy, G., xvii, xxiin, 266, 382n, 383n
Kennessey, Z., 43n
King, J. K., 334n
Klare, M. T., 122, 382n
Klingberg, F., 278n
Kolodziej, E., xviii, xxii, xxiiin, 279n, 304–35
Kravis, I. B., 30–2, 42n, 43n, 80
Kybal, D., 196n

Lambelet, J. C., 173n, 171, 195n
Lanchester, F., 141, 168n, 173n
Lawrence, E. J., 24n, 276n
Leiss, A., 240, 242, 276n, 277n
Leittenberg, M., xxiin
Leonard, W., 339, 355n, 356n
Leontief, W., xvii, xxiiin, 88, 97n, 101

Lock, P., 382n, 383n
Louscher, D. J., 278n
Lucier, C., 173n
Luebbert, G. M., 143, 169n, 173n
Luterbacher, U., 173n
Lynk, E., 293n, 299n, 300n

McConnell, J., 279n
McGuire, M., xix, 170n, 173n, 197–238
Malinvaud, E., 146, 170n, 173n
Majeski, S., xvii, xxiin, 355n, 356n
Martin, M., 317n
Melman, S., xvii, xxiin, 355n, 356n
Mihalka, M., 333n, 334n
Milenky, E., 334n
Minhas, B., 355n
Miyazaki, I., 138
Moll, K., 143, 169n, 173n
Mollis, F., 172n
Moodie, M., 277n, 333n, 382n
Myers, D. J., 334n, 335n
Myrdal, G., 108–9, 111, 112n

Nadiri, I., 303n, 345, 356n
Neumann, S. G., 276n, 277n, 279n, 333n, 335n
Nishikawa, J., 135–7
Nixon, Pres. R. M. 257
Noren, J. 46n

Ohlson, T., xviii, 3–28
Oppenheimer, P., 101
Orstrom, C., 171n, 173

Pfalzgraff, R. L., 24n, 169n, 276n
Piekarz, R., 102
Pierce, D. A., 170n, 173n
Pierre, A., 115, 134n, 333n
Pilandon, L., xviii, xxii, 47–68n
Pruitt, D. G., 195n
Pye, L., 108, 112n

Ra'anan, U., 24n, 276n, 373n
Rapoport, A., 152, 169n, 170n, 171n, 173n, 176, 194n
Rattinger, R., 169n, 170n, 173n
Reagan, Pres. R., 136–7, 260, 332
Reich, B., 334n
Richardson, L. F., xix, 141–79, 180–1, 194n, 195n
Rivlin, P., xx, 104–12n
Rosen, S., 279n, 303n
Ross, A. L., 309, 310n, 333n
Rubinson, M., 171n, 172n, 174n, 178n, 179n

Name Index

Rubinstein, A., 278n, 279n
Rudnianski, M., xxiiin, 160n, 170n, 171n, 174n
Rummel, R., 174n
Russell, B., 194
Russet, B. M., xviiin, 88, 97n, 170n, 174n, 195n

Saaty, T. L., 174n, 195n
Sadat, Pres. A., 110, 253, 260, 265, 268
Safire, W., 278n
Salazar–Carillo, J., 43n
Salomon, 278n
Sandberg, I. W., 178n
Sandler, T., 236n
Schelling, T., 236n, 237n
Schlieffer, 269
Schmidt, C. xiii, xvii–xxiii, 68n, 141–79
Schöpp, W., xix, 101, 336–56
Schrodt, P. A., 169n, 170n, 172n, 174n, 178n
Schultz, C., 276n
Schumpeter, J. A., 338, 355n
Schwartz, N. 338, 355n, 356n
Sheffer, G., 195n
Sher, R., 236n
Sherwin, R. G., 24n, 276n
Silberberg, E., 236n
Simann, M., 171n, 174n
Singer, J. D., 174n, 195n
Sintra, P. B., 334n
Sivard, R. L., 335n
Smith, D. and R., 88, 97n, 170n, 174n
Smith, T. C., 181, 195n
Smoke, R., 174n
Smoker, P., 174n
Solow, R. M., 355n

Somoza, Pres., 252, 260, 274t
Sones, R., 276n
Spielmann, R. F., 170n, 174n
Steckler, L., 102
Subrahmanyam, R. R., 334n, 355n
Summers, R., 42n, 43n
Sutton, J. L., 383n
Sutcliffe, E., 299
Sylvan, D. J., 88, 97n
Szilard, L., 196n

Tahim, G. S., 171n, 172n, 178n
Thayer, G., 276n
Thomas, G. C., 333n, 334n, 335n
Tisdell, C., 299n
Tuomi, H., 382n

Udis, B., 299n
Urquidi, V. L., xiii–xvi

Väyrynen, R., 382n
Vernon, R., 378

Wallace, M. D., 169n, 174n, 181, 195n
Wan, H. Y., 97n
Watt, P., 300n
Welter, F., 299n
Whaley, B., 279n
Wildavsky, A., 112n
Wilson, J. M., 169n, 174n
Wohlstetter, A., 196n
Wold, H., 174n
Wright, von, 156, 171n, 174n
Wulf, H., xx, xxi, 357,–83

Zinnes, D. A., 152, 170n, 171n, 172n, 174n, 176n, 196n

Subject Index

t = table; n = note; f = figure

ACDA (USACDA) (US Arms Control and Disarmament Agency), xviii, 9–28 passim, 29–37t, 78, 104, 318, 330, 334n, 335n
aerospace industry, 283–303, 373
Afghanistan, 244, 261, 271, 272
Africa, 12t, 48–67 passim, 111, 254, 261, 265, 307–9, 330–1, 358, 362t
aid, 105–11 passim, 121, 122t; see also US assistance
aircraft, 6, 20t, 123t, 124t, 127–32 passim, 262–3, 267t, 272, 208–13 passim, 322–4, 329, 330, 358–66 passim, 373, 375, 381
Albania, 49
Algeria, 50, 252–3, 259, 275t, 315, 358, 369t, 371
Angola, 244, 254–8, 261–9, 272, 274t
Argentina, xxiii, 54, 114–33 passim, 262, 275t, 311, 322
armed forces, 4–23 passim, 45, 379
arms industry, xv, 113, 121–33, 283, 306–33 passim, Part IV 283–382 passim; see also production (of arms)
arms race, 180–2, 192–4, 337
artillery, 9, 263, 358–66 passim
Ascension Island, 272
Asia, 48–57 passim, 309, 331, 358, 362t
Australia, 48, 53, 55, 58, 65t
Austria, 135
avionics, 358–66 passim, 310t

Bangladesh, 334n, 358
Belgium, 14t, 22t, 33t, 36–7t, 38t, 115, 131t, 243–8, 274t, 265t
Bengal, E., 270
Biafra, 244, 247
Bolivia, 117t–33 passim, 289t, 291t
Brazil, xv, xvii, xxi–xxiii, 49, 114–33 passim, 246, 254, 274t, 305, 311,

322, 324t, 330–5n, 359–81 passim
building-block method, 30
Burma, 361t, 370t

Cambodia, 243
Canada, xix, 14t, 22t, 135, 291t, 340t, 346t, 347–8
Chad, 248, 254, 258–60
Chile, 114–33 passim, 254, 324t, 331, 360t, 368t, 370t, 371
China (PRC), 13–16, 49, 53, 55, 108, 342–8, 252, 257, 264, 267t, 268, 270, 284–5t, 311, 383n
CIA (US) (Central Intelligence Agency), 10, 15, 16, 24n, 78, 113n, 277n
CMEA (Council for Mutual Economic Assistance), 31, 81
Columbia, 33t, 35t, 36–7t, 38t, 117t–33 passim, 334n, 360t, 368t, 370t
conflicts, 239–73; see also war
Congo, 358
Costa Rica, 117–33 passim
Costs, 312–19 passim
Cuba, 54, 114–33 passim, 259, 266, 275t

Denmark, 22t
Diego Garcia, 252, 272
DIA (US) (Defence Intelligence Agency), 16–17
disarmament, xiv, 38, 69, 70, 72–3, 90–6 passim
Dominican Republic, 117t–33 passim, 334n, 360t, 370t
Durbin–Watson test, 41n, 48, 64

East Asia (Far East), 12t, 307, 309
economic growth, xiii, xvii, 87–97, 98–103
Ecuador, 117t–33, passim, 308, 331

388

Name Index

EEC (European Economic Community), 31, 81, 289t, 291t, 297
Egypt, 106–11, 199t–201t, 218t, 232–3t, 244–76t *passim*, 324t, 333–4n, 261t, 368t, 370t, 376, 381
electronics, 123t, 307–8, 358–66 *passim*, 330, 338, 376
Eritrea, 249
Ethiopia, 242–8 *passim*, 253–69 *passim*, 274t
exchange rates, 29–39 *passim*, 44, 78–80
expenditure on arms, *throughout passim*, *notably* 11–22, 47–67, 114–21, 307–8
exports (of arms), xv, 10, 12t, 114–15, 121–33 *passim*, 315, 325; *see also* transfers

Falkland Islands, 114
Fiji, 334n
foreign trade per head, 56–9, 65t, 66–7
France, xiii, xix, xxii, 8, 12t, 14t, 19t, 21, 22t, 33t, 35t, 36, 37t, 38t, 48–9, 91, 115, 121, 127–8t, 131t, 243–74t *passim*, 289t, 291t, 314–19, 326–34n, 340t–1, 346–8, 350f, 364–5t, 374
FRG, *see* Germany, West

Gabon, 131t, 334n, 358
Germany, West (FRG), xix, 11–22t *passim*, 33t–38t, 104, 121–8t, 181, 247, 254, 265, 267t, 289t, 291t, 329–30, 240t, 366–8, 351f, 364–5t
Ghana, 358
GDP (Gross Domestic Product), 31, 34, 35t, 41n, 45, 48–54, 61, 64, 65t, 66–8n, 115–17t, 125–6t, 151, 341, 369n
GNP (Gross National Product), xvii, 17–18, 38n, 47, 53, 80–1, 87, 99, 100, 104–5, 107, 111, 115–19t, 120t, 125–6t, 135, 151, 153, 199t, 220, 225, 232–3t, 234–5t, 307, 311, 314–17n, 326–7
Greece, xv, 14t, 22t, 247, 257, 360t, 368t, 371
Guatemala, 118–19t, 126t, 257, 330
Guinea, 246, 358

Haiti, 126t
Harrod–Domar model, 88–9

helicopters, 125, 128t, 263, 266, 271, 285, 309–10t, 358–60
Honduras, 119t, 126t, 240, 243, 247, 257, 330
Hong Kong, 368t, 371
Hungary, 33t, 35t, 36–7t, 38t

ICP (International Comparison Project), 31–2, 80–1
IISS (International Institute for Strategic Studies), 7, 14, 78, 104, 107, 112n, 120t, 134n, 267t, 268, 276n, 277n, 317n
IMF (International Monetary Fund), 29, 68n, 79, 317n, 326n, 369n
imports (of arms), 10, 12t, 15, 105–6, 121–33 *passim*, 308–9, 372, 276; *see also* transfers
indebtedness, 54–6, 65t, 66–7
India, xxi, 33t–8t, 53, 105–11, 123t, 243–75t, 305, 308, 311, 319, 324t, 332–4n, 358–81
Indonesia, 123t, 324t, 330, 333n, 334n
inflation, xiii, 61–2, 65t, 67, 73, 87
Iran, 15, 33t, 35–8t, 105, 210, 242–74 *passim*, 330, 361t, 363t, 368t, 370t, 371
Iraq, 105, 131–2t, 119–201t, 218t, 323–3t, 242–75t *passim*, 308, 311, 328, 330, 369t, 375
Israel, xxiii, 9, 105–11, 122–3t, 197–238, 242–75 *passim*, 305, 308, 311, 322, 324t, 329–30n, 358–83n *passim*
Italy, 13, 14t, 22t, 33t, 35–8t, 128t, 246–9, 275t, 289t, 291t, 315, 318, 320–1t, 330, 334n, 364–5t
Ivory Coast, 334n, 358

Kenya, 33t, 35t, 36–8t, 260, 369t
Keynesian economics, xix, 88, 91–5
Korea, North, 123t, 176, 248, 308, 324t, 333–4n, 361t, 364, 370t, 383n
Korea, South, xxiii, 33–7t, 58, 231, 257, 264, 268, 272, 308, 311, 324t, 333–4n, 361t, 368–70t, 374, 381
Kurds, 244
Kuwait, 262

Latin America, xx, 12t, 31, 48–65 *passim*, 113–37, 181, 256, 308–9, 362t
Lebanon, 244
Lend-Lease Act, 256

Libya, 48, 50, 131t, 243-75t, 324t, 328, 330, 333n, 361t, 380t, 375
licences, 127, 322-5
licensed production, 128t, 298, 309, 322-5, 358-65
Luxembourg, 14t, 22t

Malagasy, Republic of, 334n, 358
Malaysia, 33-8t, 58, 334n, 361t, 369t, 370t
Mali, 243
Mauritania, 242, 248, 258
Mexico, 116t-33 *passim*, 305, 324t, 330, 334n, 360t, 368-70t, 371-2
Middle East, 12t, 15, 48-66 *passim*, 111, 197-238, 248-72 *passim*, 307-9, 330-1, 358, 362t
missiles, xiv, 6, 7, 9, 16, 123, 124t, 133, 182-94 *passim*, 266, 308-11, 320-1t, 322-4, 358-66 *passim*, 373
Morocco, 48, 50, 246-74t *passim*, 358, 369t
Mozambique, 261, 269, 275t

NATO (North Atlantic Treaty Organisation), 13, 14t, 21-2, 25, 48-66 *passim*, 104, 244, 265, 271, 283, 285n, 297-9n
Nepal, 358
Netherlands, xix, 14t, 22t, 26, 33-8t, 91, 243-4, 291t, 340t, 346-8, 353f
New Zealand, 48, 53, 58, 65t
Nicaragua, 54, 119t, 126t, 258, 260, 274t, 330
Nigeria, 247, 324t, 333n, 360t, 369-70t
Norway, 14t, 22t
nuclear weapons, xiv, 73, 143, 154, 180, 252, 268, 311, 315, 334n

Oceania, 48-67 *passim*
OECD (Organisation for Economic Co-operation and Development), 30, 68n, 135, 328-9, 338, 339, 310, 348, 355-6n
Oman, 260, 308
OPEC (Organisation of Petroleum Exporting Countries), 15, 105-7, 245, 254
output (of arms), 44-5; *see also* production

Pakistan, 58, 105, 108, 123t, 242-57, 260-75t, 308, 311, 324t, 333-4n, 361t, 369-70t, 371

Panama, 126t, 274t
Paraguay, 118-19t, 126t, 256
Pareto effectiveness, xix, 283, 302
Peru, 114-33 *passim*, 324t, 333-4n, 357, 360t, 363-4, 369t, 370t
Philippines, 33-8t, 231, 262, 305, 324t, 333-4n, 311t, 363t, 368t, 370t-1
population (and population density), 48-51, 64, 65t, 115, 116t, 209-10
Portugal, 14t, 22t, 244, 247, 252, 262, 269, 360t, 368t, 370t, 383n
PPP (Purchasing Power Parity), 27, 30-44 *passim*, 70-1, 80-1
PRC, *see* China, People's Republic of
prices (of arms), 7-21 *passim*, 27, 30-42 *passim*, 44, 70, 77-8
procurement, 283-99, 313-5
production (of arms), 304-33, 357-82; *see also* arms industry

Qatar, 330, 375

R & D (Research and Development), xiv, xix, 18-19t, 94, 100-1, 136, 285-98 *passim*, 306, 310, 322, 336-56, 376
re-supply (of arms), 239-75
Rhodesia, 275t
Rolls-Royce (study), 286-7, 299n

Sahara, Spanish, 358-9
Salvador, El, 119t-33 *passim*, 240, 243, 247, 257, 260
Saudi Arabia, 15, 199t-210t, 218t, 232-3t, 250-69 *passim*, 308, 328, 261t, 369t, 370t
ships (includes vessels, etc.), 6, 9, 20t, 124t, 272, 308-13 *passim*, 322-4, 375
Singapore, 58, 330, 334n, 361t, 369t, 370t, 374
SIPRI (Stockholm, International Peace Research Institute), xviii, xxiii, 3, 6-12t, 22n, 24n, 25-42, 47, 68n, 79, 104-5, 107, 111-12n, 117t, 120t, 123-4t, 127, 133n-4n, 201t, 232-3t, 243, 249-50, 268, 276-7n, 308-9, 317n, 342t, 333n, 348, 355-6n, 379, 382-3
small arms, 9, 330, 360t, 365t, 366
Snedecor F test, 48-67 *passim*
Somalia, 242-3, 246, 248, 253-75t *passim*
South Africa, 123t, 244, 249, 254, 266,

Subject Index

275t, 311, 324t, 330, 333–4n, 360t, 363t–4, 368t, 380t, 383n
Soviet Union, *see* USSR
Spain, 242, 244, 251–2, 264, 275t
Sri Lanka, 334n, 358, 369t
statistical problems, xviii, 3–24, 25–8, 29
stock (of arms), 23, 28
Stone–Geary function, 223, 237n
submarines, 128t, 358–66 *passim*
Sudan, 131t, 243–4, 260–2, 306t, 370t
Sweden, xiii, 247, 365t
Switzerland, 374t, 375
Syria, 199t–201t, 218t, 323–3t, 243–74 *passim*, 308–9t

Taiwan, 58, 123t, 231, 260, 264, 268, 308, 311, 322, 324t, 330, 333–4n, 361t, 363t, 368t, 370t, 374, 381
tanks, 20t, 125, 130, 262–3, 247, 272, 308, 310t, 313, 322, 358–60
Tanzania, 275t
Thailand, 264, 333–4n, 361t, 368t, 370t
Third World, xxiii, 11–15, 23, 25, 44, 114–33 *passim*, 240, 243, 270, 304, 308–9t, 319, 330, 337, 357
trade (in arms), 4–11, 23, 239, 304; *see also* transfers, imports, exports
transfers (of arms) 305–33; *see also* trade, imports, exports
Trinidad and Tobago, 126t
Tunisia, 48, 50, 254
Turkey, 14t, 22t, 245–7, 262, 265, 360t, 368t, 370t, 383n

UK (United Kingdom), xiii, 8, 12t, 14t, 21–2t, 33–8t, 91, 101, 104, 121, 127–8t, 181, 244, 247, 252, 256, 266–7t, 275t, 284–303 *passim*, 315, 318, 320–1t, 329, 364–5t, 374t
UN (United Nations), xiii, xiv, 28, 31, 42, 68n, 75, 79–80, 84n, 252, 258, 364, 367, 369n, 380, 383n; General Assembly, 70, 71, 75
Upper Volta, 131t, 243

Uruguay, 117t–33 *passim*
USA (United States of America), xiii, xix, xxi, 7–10, 12t, 14t, 15–38t, 45–66 *passim*, 91, 102, 114, 121, 127–8t, 135–7, 176, 180, 182, 194, 197–238, 240–75 *passim*, 253–303 *passim*, 330, 340t, 346t–8, 354f, 364–5t, 374–5t, 381; US assistance (and aid), xx, 106, 108, 121, 197–238, 244–59 *passim*
USACDA (United States Arms Control and Disarmament Agency), *see* ACDA
USSR (Union of Soviet Socialist Republics) (Soviet), 9–17, 25, 30–1, 45–66 *passim*, 91, 107, 121, 135, 176, 180, 182, 194, 243–75 *passim*, 305, 364–5t; Soviet aid, 107–8, 117–8, 244–79 *passim*

vehicles, 6, 123t–4t, 263, 308–11 *passim*, 322–4, 330, 358, 373
Venezuela, 116t–33 *passim*, 274t, 344n, 360t, 368t, 370t
verification, 70, 74, 82–3, 84
vessels, *see* ships
Vietnam, 105, 111, 137, 239, 243–75t *passim*, 328
Volta, Upper, 131t, 243

war, 23, 108, 196; *see also* conflict
Warsaw Pact (countries), 15, 48–67 *passim*
Warsaw Treaty Organisation, 5f
World Bank, 68n, 116t, 119t, 126, 369n

Yemen, 243, 253, 258, 260, 264
Yugoslavia, 48–9, 62, 246–7, 262, 265, 275t, 358–60t, 363t–4, 368t, 370t, 383

Zaire, 254, 258, 260, 274t, 358
Zimbabwe, 244, 275t, 277, 369t–70t

LIBRARY OF DAVIDSON COLLEGE

Books on regular loan may be checked out for **two weeks**. Books must be presented at the Circulation Desk in order to be renewed.

A fine is charged after date due.

Special books are subject to special regulations at the discretion of the library staff.

JUL. 23. 1988			
JAN. 14 1989			
FEB. -2 1990			